CATO
SUPREME COURT
REVIEW

2022 — 2023

CATO SUPREME COURT REVIEW

2022—2023

JOSHUA KATZ
Associate Editor

ROBERT A. LEVY
Associate Editor

WALTER OLSON
Associate Editor

ROGER PILON
Founder

THOMAS A. BERRY
Editor in Chief

ANASTASIA P. BODEN
Associate Editor

CLARK NEILY
Associate Editor

Board of Advisors

**ROBERT A. LEVY
CENTER FOR CONSTITUTIONAL STUDIES**

CATO INSTITUTE
Washington, D.C.

THE CATO SUPREME COURT REVIEW (ISBN 978-1-952223-75-4) is published annually at the close of each Supreme Court term by the Cato Institute, 1000 Massachusetts Ave., N.W., Washington, D.C. 20001-5403.

CORRESPONDENCE. Correspondence regarding subscriptions, changes of address, procurement of back issues, advertising and marketing matters, and so forth, should be addressed to:

Publications Department
The Cato Institute
1000 Massachusetts Ave., N.W.
Washington, D.C. 20001

All other correspondence, including requests to quote or reproduce material, should be addressed to the editor.

CITATIONS: Citation to this volume of the Review should conform to the following style: 2022-2023 Cato Sup. Ct. Rev. (2023).

DISCLAIMER. The views expressed by the authors of the articles are their own and are not attributable to the editor, the editorial board, or the Cato Institute.

INTERNET ADDRESS. Articles from past editions are available to the general public, free of charge, at www.cato.org/pubs/scr.

978-1-952223-75-4 (print)
978-1-952223-76-1 (digital)

Printed in the United States of America.

Cato Institute
1000 Massachusetts Ave., N.W.
Washington, D.C. 20001
www.cato.org

Published through the generosity of George M. Yeager

Contents

FOREWORD

The Court Is All Right.

Anastasia P. Boden*

It's often said that big Supreme Court terms are followed by quiet ones. Not this year. Big government led to big overreach, which led to big cases and yet another year of big decisions. Because the Court can't please everyone, that inevitably led to big criticism. As a result, the Court is now mired in accusations of "overreach," "activism," and "partisanship."

Dissent is to be expected, indeed welcomed in this country—particularly when it comes to judicial decisions. Our adversarial court system and the American tradition of free debate is built on the notion that strong argumentation on both sides leads to the discovery of truth. But lately, popular dissent has shifted from "the Court is wrong" to the Court is—in the words of President Joe Biden—"not normal."[1] Those who can't win at the Supreme Court are trying to discredit it.

Does a look at the past Term bear these accusations out? Not really. Yes, there were a few big decisions, but the polarized state of our nation means that all nuance about how the Court actually operates has been lost. There were far more narrow rulings than

---

* I'm thrilled to be writing my first Foreword as Director of the Robert A. Levy Center for Constitutional Studies. If you would've told me a decade ago, as I pored over italicized commas and dangling gerunds as a Cato intern, that in 12 short years I'd be writing the opening piece of this journal, I'd have fallen over in libertarian-constitutional-nerd glee. This is the Center's 22nd volume of the *Cato Supreme Court Review*, an annual critique of the Court's most important decisions and a peek at the coming term. It is the first journal of its kind to be released and the only to take a classical liberal, Madisonian perspective, grounded in the principles of liberty through constitutionally limited government. We release it every year in celebration of Constitution Day, September 17.

[1] Kelly Garrity, *'This is Not a Normal Court': Biden Blasts Affirmative Action Ruling*, POLITICO (June 29, 2023), https://tinyurl.com/3kk3yhys.

broad ones, and most cases were statutory, not constitutional. To the extent the Court appears to be overly involved in our lives, blame the dysfunctional legislative branch, which is all too eager to violate individual rights or to allow unelected bureaucrats to do their dirty work for them. The more of our lives the government sweeps into its "impetuous vortex,"[2] the more the Court will be required to pass judgment on the constitutionality of the government's actions. That's the judiciary's job.

An "activist" Court?

Critics of the Court like to say that it's too involved in our lives. "In no other democracy," wrote one, "do nine unelected officials have so much power."[3]

Judges don't make policy. They're merely a check; the "least dangerous branch," as Alexander Hamilton called them in *Federalist 78*, since they have only the power of "judgment." There are, however, a swarm of unelected officials who improperly exercise executive, legislative, and judicial power: the thousands of federal employees who make up the alphabet soup of administrative agencies. These unaccountable bureaucrats regulate everything from gas stoves to Greek yogurt,[4] yet they often can't be fired by the President (or his appointees). They enjoy deference in federal court when interpreting the scope of their own authority, and they often play judge, jury, and executioner by instituting enforcement proceedings before their own in-house judges. To the extent any branch is labeled "activist" or too powerful, it should be the so-called fourth branch.

Take *Sackett v. EPA*. There, bureaucrats in the Environmental Protection Agency insisted that the Agency could require a couple to secure an expensive Clean Water Act permit before they were allowed to build. The reason, according to the EPA, was merely that their property contained wetlands, which sat across a paved road from other wetlands, which connected to a man-made ditch, which led

---

[2] THE FEDERALIST No. 48 (James Madison).

[3] Michael Waldman, *A Regressive Supreme Court Turns Activist: A Conservative Majority Ushers in a Radical New Era*, BRENNAN CTR. FOR JUST. (May 22, 2023), https://tinyurl.com/38jxvwk7.

[4] For more, check out the first-rate podcast *Dissed*, and in particular, the episode "Lady Justice Isn't Blind," available at https://tinyurl.com/3cxr7zhd.

to a creek, which fed into a lake that itself could be regulated by the Agency. All nine Justices agreed that the Agency had no such power.

Or take *Axon Enterprise v. FTC*, wherein the Federal Trade Commission and Securities and Exchange Commission sought to keep constitutional challenges to their authority out of court and within their own in-house proceedings. In another 9–0 opinion, the Court held that the plaintiffs had a right to go to federal court.

Or consider *Biden v. Nebraska*, wherein the Secretary of Education attempted to discharge billions of dollars in debt under a statute that authorized him to "waive or modify" certain provisions of the Higher Education Act, even after Congress affirmatively decided not to pass student-debt relief. These are far more dangerous assertions of power than the Court's mere power to interpret the meaning of the Constitution and federal statutes.

For all the claims that the Court is inserting itself into our lives, the Court is taking fewer cases than ever. In recent years, it's taken about 80 cases per term, nearly half of what it took in the 1980s.[5] The "big" cases make up a small portion of this shrinking docket. Far outnumbering controversial cases like *Biden v. Nebraska* or *303 Creative v. Elenis* are cases like *Coinbase v. Bielski* (asking whether a district court must stay its proceedings while an interlocutory appeal taken pursuant to 9 U.S.C. § 16(a) on the question of arbitrability is ongoing) or *Wilkins v. U.S.* (asking whether the Quiet Title Act's 12-year statute of limitations is jurisdictional or a claims-processing rule). The Court has wide discretion over which and how many cases it takes, and it's using that discretion to take fewer of them. That fact is hard to square with the public's perception of a purportedly imperial Court.

Even the biggest decisions of the Term were modest. Chief Justice John Roberts's opinion in *Students for Fair Admissions v. UNC* was self-consciously narrow. He framed the question in the case not as whether racial preferences can *ever* be used in the admissions process, but instead as "whether the admissions systems *used by Harvard College and UNC* are lawful." (emphasis added). His opinion likely put an end to racial preferences for the purposes of generating "the educational benefits that flow from a racially diverse student body,"

---

[5] Jonathan Adler, *The Restrained Roberts Court*, NAT'L REV. (July 31, 2023), https://tinyurl.com/3xfvjnm3.

also known as the diversity rationale. But that rationale was always dubious. It's based on the pernicious assumption that a person's skin color necessarily makes them different, and not even the dissenters defended it. The Chief's opinion does not foreclose the use of race altogether, such as using narrowly tailored programs to remedy concrete instances of state-sponsored discrimination.

Or take *303 Creative*. That case did not go so far as to protect freedom of association generally. Instead, it protected people who engage in so-called "speaking professions" from being compelled to convey messages with which they disagree. Importantly, that holding protects all viewpoints. It protects not just Lorie Smith, the web designer who sued in *303 Creative*, but also a Jewish web designer who doesn't want to publish antisemitic speech. And it protects platforms like Twitter or Facebook if they don't want to host hateful or violent speech.

Many cases this term that were set to become blockbusters turned out to be nothingburgers. Despite granting certiorari and hearing arguments in *Haaland v. Brackeen*, the Court largely punted. It refused to truly reconsider the constitutionality of the Indian Child Welfare Act under the Indian Commerce Clause because, according to Justice Amy Coney Barrett, the issue wasn't briefed thoroughly enough. And it declined to address the equal protection arguments due to purported standing problems. As a result, several weighty constitutional issues that have been hinted at in previous terms went unaddressed, and ICWA was left intact.

In *Gonzalez v. Google*, the Court carefully sidestepped the hot-button issue of the scope of Section 230, which immunizes online platforms from liability for user-generated content. This is all par for the course. The Court has a long list of judge-made doctrines (standing, ripeness, mootness, abstention, deference, immunity, etc.) that it regularly invokes to avoid deciding worthy constitutional claims.

For all the talk of activism, overreach, corruption, or partisanship, several decisions were 9–0, just as they are every term. In *Tyler v. Hennepin County*, a Minnesota county seized a 98-year-old woman's home after she fell behind on her taxes. The county sold her property and kept not just what it was owed but tens of thousands of dollars in additional equity. That earned the local government the ire of pretty much everyone—including all nine Justices. Over half the cases this Term were unanimous or near-unanimous. In addition to

Tyler, Sackett, and *Axon,* all nine Justices agreed about the scope of the Lanham Act, requirements related to employers and religious exemptions under Title VII, exhaustion requirements before challenging removal orders in federal court, the ability to retry a defendant if first tried in an improper venue, certain patent validity requirements, exceptions to a statutory bar on concurrent sentences, and whether the government has to provide notice to account holders before issuing summonses to banks to collect delinquent taxes.

As in every term, there were all sorts of interesting alignments— cases that found Justice Neil Gorsuch joining Justice Sonia Sotomayor's concurrence (*Counterman v. Colorado*), Chief Justice Roberts joining Justice Elena Kagan in dissent (*Andy Warhol Foundation for Visual Arts v. Goldsmith*), and Justice Ketanji Brown Jackson joining Justice Brett Kavanaugh, Justice Samuel Alito, and the Chief Justice (*National Pork Producers v. Ross*). More than nine out of 10 cases had at least one of the so-called "liberal" Justices in the majority.[6]

And lest critics forget, the Court has recently handed several losses to political conservatives, and to the Trump administration in particular. Most notable are cases involving Obamacare's individual mandate, anti-discrimination protections for trans individuals, marriage equality, the rights of criminal defendants, the *Gingles* standard under the Voting Rights Act, Republicans' independent state legislature theory, and Trump's attempts to withhold his tax records, to block release of records related to January 6, and to challenge the 2020 election. The Court might have a majority of judicial conservatives, but it's important to distinguish that philosophy from political conservativism.

Three cheers for judicial supremacy.

In my view, the Court is indeed activist. But that's because it invokes judge-made doctrines to get out of tough cases, and it continues to ignore inconvenient portions of the Constitution that would require it to strike down *even more* "democratically passed" laws. In other words, it's the Court's modesty, not its usurpation of power, that's activist. The Court's abdication subverts civil rights law to this day, with the Privileges or Immunities Clause (the centerpiece of

---

[6] Devin Dwyer, *Supreme Court Shows Surprising Restraint in Chaotic Year of Crises: Analysis,* ABC News (July 5, 2023), https://tinyurl.com/54xvhmh.

the Fourteenth Amendment's substantive protections) having been effectively written out of the Constitution altogether.[7]

Historically the Court has been at its worst when it has deferred to the other branches under the guise of modesty.[8] And the Court has been at its best when it has engaged with the Constitution and protected political minorities of all kinds from the tyranny of the majority.[9] As far as I'm concerned, huzzah for judicial supremacy. The smallest minority is the individual.[10] Protection of liberty against majoritarianism protects us all.

In other words, though there were a few big cases this Term, it was a Term like most others—full of incrementalism, strange bedfellows, and restraint. The Supreme Court is all right.

---

[7] Brief for Petitioner, Newell-Davis v. Phillips, No. 22-1208 (petition for cert. filed Feb. 10, 2023), https://tinyurl.com/2p9tbp2a.

[8] *See, e.g.,* U.S. v. Cruikshank, 92 U.S. 542 (1876) (reversing convictions of those involved in the Colfax massacre); Korematsu v. United States, 323 U.S. 214 (1944) (upholding Japanese internment); Kelo v. City of New London, 545 U.S. 469 (2005) (allowing eminent domain of Suzette Kelo's little pink house).

[9] *See, e.g.,* Yick Wo v. Hopkins, 118 U.S. 356 (1886) (invalidating discriminatory enforcement of laundry law against Chinese business owners); Adkins v. Children's Hospital, 261 U.S. 525 (1923) (recognizing the right of women to work on the terms of their choice); Meyer v. Nebraska, 262 U.S. 390 (1923) (invalidating state's attempt to subvert parents' right to direct their children's upbringing); Brown v. Board of Education, 347 U.S. 483 (1954) (invalidating state-sponsored segregation in public schools), Wooley v. Maynard, 430 U.S. 705 (1977) (invalidating prosecution of Jehovah's Witness for covering up portion of state motto on license plate that violated his religious beliefs); City of Cleburne v. Cleburne Living Center, 473 U.S. 432 (1985) (invalidating zoning law used to disadvantage homes for people with intellectual disabilities); Lawrence v. Texas, 539 U.S. 558 (2003) (respecting the right of adults to engage in private, consensual conduct).

[10] Ayn Rand, Capitalism: The Unknown Ideal 61 (1966).

Introduction

*Thomas A. Berry**

This is the 22nd volume of the *Cato Supreme Court Review*, the nation's first in-depth critique of the Supreme Court Term just ended, plus a look at the Term ahead. This is also my first year as editor in chief of the *Review*. It's an honor to take the reins of a publication I've long admired, and I feel a responsibility to keep the *Review* at the same high level of quality our readers expect. My aim is to follow the examples set by all of my predecessors as editors of the *Review*: James Swanson, Mark Moller, Ilya Shapiro, and Trevor Burrus.

While the personnel behind the *Review* may change, its core purpose and unique speed remain the same. We release the *Review* every year in conjunction with our annual Constitution Day symposium, less than three months after the previous Term ends and two weeks before the next Term begins. It would be almost impossible to publish a journal any faster, and credit for that goes first and foremost to our authors, who year after year meet our unreasonable but necessary demands and deadlines.

This isn't a typical law review. We want you to read this, even if you're not a lawyer. We don't want to scare you off with lots of weird Latin phrases, page-long footnotes, or legalistic jargon. And we don't want to publish articles that are on niche topics, of interest only to the three other academics who write on the same topic. Instead, we publish digestible articles that help Americans understand the decisions of their highest court and why they matter, in plain English.

And as my predecessors were wont to note in the introductions to previous volumes, we freely confess our biases. We start from the first principles: We have a federal government of limited powers, those powers are divided among the several branches, and individuals have rights that act as shields against those powers. We take

---

* Research fellow, Robert A. Levy Center for Constitutional Studies, Cato Institute, and editor in chief, *Cato Supreme Court Review*.

seriously those liberty-protective parts of the Constitution that have been too often neglected, including the affirmation of unenumerated rights in the Ninth Amendment and the reservation of legislative power to only the *legislature* (not the President) in Article I.

We also reject the tired dichotomy of judicial "restraint" vs. "activism." We urge judges to engage with and follow the law, which includes most importantly the Constitution. If that means invalidating a statute or regulation, it is the judiciary's duty to do so, without putting a "deferential" thumb on the scale in favor of the elected branches. At the same time, judges should not be outcome oriented. Some decisions may lead to a bad *policy* outcome, but that's not an argument that the decision was *legally* wrong. Indeed, any honest legal philosophy must sometimes lead to policy outcomes a judge doesn't prefer, or else it is not really a *legal* methodology.

And there is another core value of the *Review*: We acknowledge that many cases are hard and that people of good faith can disagree on both outcomes and reasoning. We don't want the *Review* to simply echo every Cato position on every case; if we did, we could just reprint the amicus briefs we filed throughout the year. Rather, we gather a stellar group of authors we respect and give them the freedom to write what they believe. We don't want the *Review* to be an echo chamber. For example, this edition features an article by Professor Jed Handelsman Shugerman writing on *Biden v. Nebraska*, the student-loan forgiveness case. Professor Shugerman criticizes Justice Amy Coney Barrett's concurrence in that case, which attempted to establish a textualist justification for the major questions doctrine. Unlike Professor Shugerman, I happened to find her concurrence persuasive. And I'm proud to publish an article that disagrees with my view in good faith.

We fully acknowledge the fact that lawyers applying originalism, textualism, and a presumption of liberty can reach differing conclusions on the same cases. We believe that the differing views of authors who broadly share our judicial philosophies are evidence of the strengths and nuances of these theories, not of their weakness or under-determinacy.

* * *

This Term, the Court's operations finally returned to near normalcy, with members of the general public finally allowed back inside its walls as spectators. It is vitally important that any citizen, not just members of the Supreme Court Press, have a chance to see the High Court in action. And this term was also the first for new Justice Ketanji Brown Jackson, who immediately made her mark as the most active questioner in the Court's oral arguments. Justice Jackson has sometimes used originalist-style arguments to make a case for what might be seen as traditionally progressive judicial outcomes, such as in the affirmative action decisions. Whether she was right or wrong in any particular case, it is a noteworthy moment when a new member of the Court's "liberal" wing demonstrates a willingness to engage with originalist arguments on their own terms. Every new Justice makes an entirely new Court, and Justice Jackson has not been an exception to that rule.

This Term, there were only five cases in which the Court split 6–3 along ideological lines, a drop from 14 such cases last term. But some of the biggest cases of the term were among those 6–3 splits, including cases on affirmative action, student-debt forgiveness, and public accommodations and the First Amendment. So while the ideologically split cases may get the most attention, the Court is not a legislature and the Justices don't just vote along party lines. Within these pages, you'll read about many cases with all sorts of unexpected lineups, cases that prove litigants and advocates can't take anything for granted with this Court.

* * *

Turning to this year's *Review*, we begin as always with last year's annual B. Kenneth Simon Lecture. Professor Akhil Reed Amar of Yale Law School offers 18 arguments for 18-year term limits on the Supreme Court. Amar argues that term limits would have several beneficial effects, such as making presidential appointments of Supreme Court Justices more regular and more predictable. Amar also argues that term limits would remove the incentive for Presidents to appoint Justices when they are too young and for Justices to stay on the Court until they are too old. And Amar argues that such a regulation would be constitutional. By designating Justices who serve longer than 18 years as "emeritus" Justices, Congress can effectively impose term limits pursuant to its power to shape the operations and functions of the Supreme Court.

Next, Brannon Denning of Samford University Cumberland School of Law writes on *National Pork Producers v. Ross*. Even though the

Court rejected a challenge to a California pork regulation under the "dormant Commerce Clause doctrine," Denning explains why the decision makes clear that the doctrine is here to stay. Denning recounts how the opinion cleared up several open questions surrounding the doctrine, including how courts should consider state laws that have large, but unintended, effects in other states.

Margaret Little of the New Civil Liberties Alliance then covers the consolidates cases of *Axon v. FTC* and *SEC v. Cochran*, the latter of which she had a front-row seat for as one of Cochran's counsel. In both cases, the Court held that litigants can bring constitutional challenges to administrative agencies straight into federal court, without going through an agency proceeding first. Little explains just how important the holding of these cases will be for litigants who often don't have the time or resources to spend years in administrative proceedings before they can even reach federal court. Little also previews the battles to come over the constitutionality of the two agencies at issue.

Next, Eric Franklin Amarante of the University of Tennessee College of Law writes on the term's First Amendment overbreadth case, *United States v. Hansen*. Amarante criticizes the Court's decision, which upheld the federal statute banning speech that encourages or induces violations of immigration law. Amarante argues that the majority opinion understated the harms caused by the "chilling effect" of a broadly worded law, harms that can't be measured solely by counting the number of prosecutions under the law. Amarante makes the case that the dissenting opinion has the better of the argument on both statutory interpretation and First Amendment doctrine.

Christopher Green of the University of Mississippi School of Law then writes on *303 Creative v. Elenis*. Most commentators have focused on the First Amendment aspects of this case, in which the Court held that a website designer may not be compelled by state law to design a custom site for a same-sex wedding. Green points out that there is another issue at play, however, which is the scope of the traditional power of the state to compel access to public accommodations. Looking at the history of this power, Green argues that it has always been limited to cases where rights of access were necessary for health or safety, such as transportation bottlenecks. This suggests that in a situation where ample alternative businesses are available, the state does not have the same interest in compelling access.

Continuing with the Court's speech cases, Clay Calvert of the University of Florida Levin College of Law writes on *Counterman v. Colorado*. Calvert explains the various exceptions to the First Amendment's protection of the freedom of speech, focusing on the particular exception at issue in this case: the "true threats" doctrine. The Court held that to convict someone for making a threat, the First Amendment requires that the speaker must have been at least reckless to the risk that the message would be understood as a threat. Calvert notes that this was a middle-ground position and that the Court could have required a higher mental standard or none at all—both positions that at least some on the Court espoused. Calvert concludes by noting with encouragement that no Justice joined Justice Clarence Thomas's call to reexamine the "actual malice" standard for libel of public figures.

Next, David Bernstein of the Antonin Scalia Law School writes on the Term's affirmative action cases, *Students for Fair Admissions v. Harvard/UNC*. Bernstein focuses in particular on the Court's discussion of the racial categories that were used by universities and how those particular categories came to be standardized. This history, of which Bernstein is the leading expert, shows just how arbitrary these categories are (for example, there is no separate Middle Eastern category, meaning Afghan-American applicants are put in the same category as white immigrants from England). Bernstein explores some of the implications that the Court's decision may have in areas of the law beyond college admissions, such as racial preferences in public contracting.

Timothy Sandefur of the Goldwater Institute then tackles the Court's Indian Child Welfare Act case, *Haaland v. Brackeen*. Sandefur first lays out the history of the statute and the many ways in which it distinguishes between children on the basis of race. Sandefur then explains why the Supreme Court's decision is most notable for what it did *not* decide—whether the law violates the Equal Protection Clause of the Constitution. As Sandefur notes, the constitutional concerns with ICWA will not go away and will remain a live controversy in the courts.

Next, Jed Handelsman Shugerman of Boston University School of Law writes on *Biden v. Nebraska*, the student loans case. Shugerman argues that the Court reached the right result, because the Biden administration did not explain how the relief it wished to offer was tailored to the COVID emergency specifically. Shugerman examines some of the discussions of the major questions doctrine in both the majority opinion and a concurrence by Justice Amy Coney Barrett, finding Barrett's account unpersuasive. Shugerman suggests that going forward, courts should develop a doctrine to evaluate claims of emergency power to ensure that emergencies are not used as pretexts to enact long-term policy goals.

Moving to environmental law, Damien Schiff of Pacific Legal Foundation writes on *Sackett v. EPA*, a case he argued and won at the Supreme Court. Schiff relates the long history of the Clean Water Act and its mysterious statutory definition "waters of the United States." Multiple Supreme Court cases had considered what this definition means, but *Sackett* finally resulted in a majority of the Court setting out a clear test. Schiff contrasts the majority opinion with the opinions concurring in the judgment, finding that the textual arguments in the majority opinion were much stronger because they focused on the operative language in the statute.

Next, Vikram David Amar of UC Davis School of Law tackles *Moore v. Harper*, the "independent state legislature doctrine" case. Amar argues that the Court's rejection of the doctrine was clearly right as a matter of original constitutional meaning. Amar also explains the consequences that would have resulted if the Court had ruled the other way. Amar suggests that the case is not just a victory for state judicial review but also for originalist scholars, who aided the Court's historical inquiry through the use of scholarly historical amicus briefs.

Wrapping up the articles on cases from this past Term, Gregory Dolin of the University of Baltimore School of Law covers *Andy Warhol Foundation for the Visual Arts v. Goldsmith* and *Jack Daniel's Properties v. VIP Products*. In both cases, the Court narrowed the circumstances in which artists or parodists may adapt copyrighted or trademarked material without permission. Dolin argues that both cases were decided correctly and both can be understood as treating *intellectual* property similar to physical property. Dolin argues that we need not fear the concerns raised in the *Warhol* dissent, namely that artistic expression will be seriously hindered by a stricter copyright rule.

Finally, Wen Fa of the Beacon Center of Tennessee authors our annual "Looking Ahead" article. Fa identifies several major cases to watch next term, on topics ranging from *Chevron* deference to an agency's self-funding powers to the original meaning of "income" in the Sixteenth Amendment. The Court will also consider the First Amendment implications of public officials "blocking" citizens on social media and the standing of ADA online "testers." Even though this past Term was undoubtedly a blockbuster, Fa suggests the sequel may end up being just as exciting.

* * *

As mentioned at the outset, this is my first year as editor in chief of the *Review* after two years as its managing editor. Cato has been a huge part of my professional life since I first interned here in my second year of law school eight years ago. Reading through the introductions of past volumes of the *Review* offers snapshots of some of my own professional milestones, as I win mention for helping out as an intern, then legal associate, then contributor, then managing editor. Now, as I author my own introduction as editor in chief for the first time, I'm filled with immense gratitude to both Ilya Shapiro and Trevor Burrus, who were there on my first day as an intern and who have both been invaluable mentors in getting me to this point. I'm grateful to both for showing me the ropes and teaching me best editorial practices by example. And by the transitive property of mentorship, I also owe Roger Pilon a great deal for creating Cato's Robert A. Levy Center for Constitutional Studies and for bringing Ilya and Trevor aboard so that they could in turn bring me on. And I am very grateful for the trust that my colleagues Clark Neily and Anastasia Boden have put in me as I take the reins of the *Review*.

This year, as always, I have had help from many other people. Most important, of course, are the authors themselves, without whose work there would be no *Review*. Our authors this year produced excellent, polished articles under tremendous time pressure and for that I thank them all sincerely. Thanks also go to my Cato Institute colleagues Clark Neily, Anastasia Boden, Walter Olson, and Joshua Katz for help in editing the articles and for taking on a heavier load of other Cato work in August when I was buried in editing. Legal associates Christopher Barnewolt, Nathaniel Lawson, Isaiah McKinney, and Nicholas DeBenedetto performed the difficult (believe me, I remember) and vital task of cite checking and proofreading. Legal interns Delaney Epley and Jacob Snyder also provided essential research assistance. Recent Scalia Law School graduate Christian Bush did excellent work as an article citechecker to help us ensure accuracy. And special thanks to Laura Bondank, who handled all of the nuts and bolts of publishing the *Review* (along with pitching in on edits as well). Laura learned a complex process on the fly last year, and this volume couldn't have happened without her.

We hope that you enjoy this 22nd volume of the *Cato Supreme Court Review*.

Term Limits/Time Rules for Future Justices: Eighteen Arguments for Eighteen Years

*By Akhil Reed Amar**

I. Introduction

In a bipartisan op-ed published in the *Washington Post* on August 9, 2002, Steven G. Calabresi, the co-Founder and co-Chair of the Federalist Society, and I floated the idea that each Justice should do 18 years of full and active service on the Court and should thereafter have a different portfolio of judicial responsibilities.[1] The bipartisan co-authorship of this 2002 op-ed was purposeful. The 18-year idea was then, and remains today, neither Left nor Right, neither Blue nor Red. I was then and remain today a mainstream Democrat and Steve was then and remains today a mainstream Republican. For example, in 2000 I voted for Al Gore, whereas Steve voted for George W. Bush. In 2016 I voted for Hillary Clinton, Steve for Donald Trump. When I first publicly embraced the 18-year idea, a Republican sat in the White House, Republicans controlled the House, and the Senate was almost evenly divided. Today, the partisan alignment is almost exactly the opposite—a Democrat sits in the White House, Democrats control the House, and the Senate is almost evenly divided. Yet I still consider the 18-year idea a good one.

Indeed, in the two decades since I began mulling the 18-year idea, I have become even more persuaded that the root idea is a good one. I have over time tweaked and modified various details of my envisioned reform, *but I remain convinced that some version of the 18-year idea can and should be embraced by Congress in a simple statute.*

---

* Sterling Professor Yale Law School. This Cato Simon Lecture, delivered in honor of Constitution Day, 2022, builds upon my public testimony to the Biden Presidential Commission on the Supreme Court of the United States, July 20, 2021.

[1] Akhil Reed Amar & Steven G. Calabresi, *Term Limits for the High Court*, Wash. Post (Aug. 9, 2002), https://tinyurl.com/2knj9fwn.

Ideally, this statute should itself be bipartisan, drawing support from leaders of both parties and featuring a proper phase-in that respects the settled expectations of the current Justices and avoids any appearance of a partisan grab reminiscent of the Midnight Judges Act of 1801. At the end of this lecture, I shall share with you the nuts and bolts of my proposed statute, detailing how my 18-year idea might best be implemented in a fashion that I believe would be an entirely constitutional exercise of congressional power to structure the Court pursuant to Congress's explicit power under the Article I Necessary and Proper Clause.

That clause, of course, vests Congress with authority to pass proper laws implementing powers vested by the Constitution in "the Government of the United States, or in any Department or Officer thereof."[2] Ever since the Founding, Congress has used this clause to properly prescribe the size and shape of various executive departments; the powers and duties of various executive officers; the size, shape, and responsibilities of the Supreme Court; the powers and duties of Supreme Court members, both in active service and after voluntary retirement from active service; the rules of procedure and evidence operative in the Supreme Court; the timing of Supreme Court sittings; and myriad other kindred matters. In perfect harmony with this well-settled pattern of congressional legislation, Congress should, in the near future, properly prescribe a lifetime duty roster for Supreme Court Justices.

A quick note on terminology.[3] My specific 18-year idea and its close cousins—that is, variations of this idea that have been embraced in recent years by a wide range of legal scholars across the political spectrum[4]—have often been described as proposals for "term limits"

---

[2] U.S. CONST. art. I, § 8, cl. 18.

[3] On the value of proper terminology to reduce the risk that casual observers will be "faked out" by imprecise labels, see Akhil Reed Amar, *The Five Legged Dog*, THE AMERICAN LAWYER, Sept. 1999, at 47.

[4] *See, e.g.*, James E. DiTullio & John B. Schochet, *Saving This Honorable Court: A Proposal to Replace Life Tenure on the Supreme Court With Staggered, Nonrenewable Eighteen-Year Terms*, 90 VA. L. REV. 1093 (2004); Roger G. Cramton, *Reforming the Supreme Court*, 95 CAL. L. REV. 1313, 1323 (2007) ("eighteen years followed by lifetime service in a lower federal court"); Four Proposals for a Judiciary Act of 2009, Letter from Vikram D. Amar et al. to Joseph R. Biden Jr. et al. (Feb. 16, 2009), https://tinyurl.com/7xyfsby3, (open letter endorsed by dozens of eminent scholars including Vikram Amar, Barbara Babcock, Jack Balkin, Paul Carrington, Roger Cramton, Dan Meador, Frank Michelman, Paul Mishkin, Robert Nagel, L.A. Scot Powe Jr., Jefferson Powell, Judith Resnik, Chris Schroeder, David Shapiro, and Peter Strauss).

for Justices. Indeed, I myself have frequently used this phraseology and may well lapse into this locution in informal future conversations. Nevertheless, my proposal is, strictly speaking, not a limit on the official *term* of any given Justice. Each Justice is entitled under the Constitution to serve a life term in the federal judiciary—to serve "during good behavior," to use a more technical formulation—and I do not propose otherwise.[5] Each Justice is entitled to be paid for life/good behavior and I do not propose otherwise. Each Justice is allowed to claim the official title of "Supreme Court Justice" for life/good behavior and I do not propose otherwise. I simply propose that we modify the *manner* in which each Justice serves on the Court for life/good behavior. Put differently, my proposal merely modifies, and in a purely prospective way, the *duty roster* accompanying the official office of Supreme Court Justice.

Indeed, given that the gist of my plan is purely prospective, it is in effect merely a mechanism by which future Justices bindingly announce their retirements long in advance—not, say, 18 weeks in advance à la Stephen Breyer, but 18 years in advance, in the very process of joining the Court.

Under my proposed federal statute, each Justice in the process of being commissioned would agree that he or she will be a Justice in active service—a member of the Court's "front bench," so to speak, with the same basic responsibilities as a typical Justice in the system today— for 18 years. Thereafter, each Justice would serve in a relaxed-service capacity, with a different set of daily Supreme Court responsibilities, including but not limited to the responsibilities of current retired Justices under 28 U.S.C. § 294. A relaxed-service Justice—whom we might also call an "emeritus Justice"—would not routinely sit with active-service Justices en banc; but would be available to do so in cases when the Court is short staffed. An emeritus Justice would sit when (because of death or illness or resignation or recusal or the like) nine active-service Justices are not available for service. Emeritus Justices would devote most of their daily attention to Court-related administrative, ceremonial, educational, public-relations, circuit-riding,[6] and docket-management

---

[5] *See* U.S. Const. art. III, § 1.

[6] Note that if circuit-riding were deemed problematic, it need not be included in the bipartisan reform statute. A sensible statute could work just fine without this element—or indeed, without any particular element or combination of elements in my envisioned portfolio for emeritus Justices. Note, however, that circuit-riding is a basic feature of current federal law for retired Justices. *See* 28 U.S.C. § 294.

functions, following a more detailed set of rules to be promulgated and from time to time revised by the active-service Justices.

Strictly speaking, perhaps we should call my idea not "term limits," but "time rules." In its ultimate constitutional logic, my proposal is broadly analogous to a hypothetical statute providing that no Justice should speak for more than, say, five minutes in any hour-long oral argument. (This hypothetical oral-argument law is also best understood not as a term limit but as a time rule.)

II. Eighteen Arguments

In the April 28, 2021, episode of my weekly podcast with Dr. Andrew Lipka, *Amarica's Constitution*, I listed 18 distinct reasons supporting my particular version of the idea of 18 years of active Court service, followed by a lifetime of relaxed Court service.[7]

Here, in brief, were my "18 arguments for 18 years":

1. The status quo of lifetime active service, when combined with a partisan arms race, encourages each of our two major political parties to appoint unduly young and unseasoned jurists to the Court, in the hopes of entrenching the party vision on the Court for as many years as possible.

2. At the other end of the life cycle, the status quo allows full service of Justices who are too old, whose arteries have literally hardened and who are not at their prime. (Historically, most Justices have not done their best work in their superannuated years.)

3. The current system creates the possibility of too long a lag time between initial appointment and current judgment. The most senior active Justices may be wildly out of touch with the nation's evolving mood, because these Justices were appointed long ago (even if they are still relatively young and spry and their arteries have not hardened). This lag time is particularly problematic for younger Americans who were not even voters when many current Justices were selected. Many of America's younger generation lack a close emotional connection to the Court, in part perhaps because

---

[7] Amarica's Constitution, *Episode 18: Tinker to Amar to Strossen – Special Guest Nadine Strossen* (May 12, 2021), https://tinyurl.com/2bcvuy74.

of the long lag time. The reform statute caps this lag time at 18 years for the Court's most important function—decision-making in en banc cases.

4. The current system enables Justices to strategically and politically time their resignations. This is a less attractive model of judicial independence. Currently, some Justices act *politically* when they time their exits.

5. Eighteen is a "magic number" enabling regular and steady replacement, à la the Senate. The Senate's staggered replenishment system adds a new third every two years. The 18-year-active-service plan adds a new ninth every two years.

6. Eighteen is a "magic number" in a second and distinct way: Appointment power is regularized and smoothed out across presidencies and across quadrennial presidential elections; each President can count on two appointments, and this smoothing makes replenishment less arbitrary, random, and capricious.

7. Relatedly, regular replenishment of the front bench makes it easier for voters to think about the Court's future every presidential election without awkward and indeed ghoulish speculation about the life expectancies and health prognoses of individual sitting Justices.

8. Shortened terms of active service will reduce the stakes—and the temperature—of currently overheated Court confirmation battles.

9. Shortened terms of active service will increase judicial humility.

10. Replenishment every odd year regularizes appointments *within* each presidential term, with half the active Justices chosen pre-midterm and half post-midterm. The opening up of vacancies in odd years further reduces the political temperature of Court confirmation battles by staging these battles in nonelection years.

11. An 18-year cap on active service brings the U.S. Supreme Court model into closer alignment with the most admirable state supreme court systems, almost none of which features active service for life. The federal government can and should learn from the lessons of states, the proverbial laboratories of American democratic experimentation.

12. Ditto on the comparative international front: Almost no other modern democracy in the world has a lifetime model of active service for its apex court. America as a whole can learn from the experiences of the world's other notable democracies.

13. Unlike current reform proposals to "pack the Court," the 18-year proposal is not partisan and is unlikely to spiral out of control when party control shifts in Washington, D.C. at some point in the future.[8]

14. The 18-year proposal not only eliminates the occasional or regular *reality* of politically timed retirements; it eliminates the *public perception* of politics in judicial retirements. That perception may *wrongly* exist when a particular Justice in fact retires nowadays for entirely personal reasons, and that perception adds to current public cynicism about the Court.

15. Under the 18-year plan, every active Justice is slated to serve as Chief Justice in his or her last two years of active service. This, too, evens out power across Presidents and eliminates the current lumpiness giving some Presidents, for purely accidental reasons, more power than others to pick the Court's chief.

16. Rotation of the chief justiceship equalizes power *within* the Court. Relatedly, Associate Justices will not have incentives to pander to the President in the hopes of one day being nominated (by a President, of course) to become Chief Justice. Even if Associate Justices never in fact pander, the mere public perception that some Justices might well be auditioning to be Chief is undesirable.

17. Chief Justices will be those who clearly understand the Court, having typically served on the active bench for the previous 16 years, and having received, one would expect, special training by their predecessor Chief Justice.

18. Circuit duty of emeritus Justices could help reconnect the Supreme Court with lawyers and judges in the hinterlands—a nice echo of the original vision of the Court as implemented by the Judiciary Act of 1789.

---

[8] On reflection, this podcast point was a bit of a cheat: It did not identify an improvement on the status quo, but merely an advantage over another widely discussed approach to Court reform. But here is a true improvement, which the podcast did not count as a separate virtue: The 18-year proposal minimizes the likelihood of a short-staffed, evenly divided Court. Whenever one of the nine active Justices is unavailable, a reduced-service emeritus Justice can easily pinch hit.

III. But Is It Constitutional?

At the end of this lecture, I will set forth a more detailed description of my proposed reform package. The details will doubtless prompt specific questions that merit further conversation. For now, let me briefly explain why this proposal is, in my view, easily and obviously constitutional, able to be effectuated by a simple congressional statute and not requiring a constitutional amendment of any sort.

As mentioned earlier, the Constitution expressly and purposively vests Congress with broad power to legislate rules structuring the executive and judicial departments. This power is of course not unlimited. Congressional legislation must be "proper." It must comport with the Constitution's letter and spirit—including the specific letter and spirit of Articles II and III.

Consider for example two hypothetical congressional laws that in my view would be constitutionally improper.

First, imagine a congressional statute purporting to dictate to the Court how to construe a particular constitutional provision or how to construe the Constitution in general. Such a law would violate the Court's power to "say what the law is," to quote *Marbury v. Madison*— the power, that is, of the Court to determine for itself, in its own independent judgment, what the Constitution in fact means.

True, Congress has broad power to dictate to the Court how to construe a particular federal statute and how to construe federal statutes generally. But this power is largely derivative of the power to enact federal laws themselves. If a law can be written broadly, how is this different from a law written in rather more ambiguous language but featuring a clause telling the Court to "construe this law broadly"? Still, the power of Congress to dictate to the Court rules of statutory construction, whether local or global, is not infinite. The Court may at times read the Constitution itself to require that certain things must be said very clearly and expressly by Congress, via a super-clear statement. If the Court believes that the Constitution itself requires or invites such a clear-statement rule, Congress does not have carte blanche to direct the Court to ignore its own constitutional beliefs in deciding the cases that come before it.

More generally, Congress lacks carte blanche to tell the Court how to construe the *Constitution*, either locally or globally. Congress itself did not create the Constitution, cannot change the Constitution at will by ordinary legislation, and is not the sole master of

15

constitutional meaning. The Congress is of course free and indeed obliged to construe the Constitution for itself in many situations; and Congress is also free to express its understanding of constitutional meaning. The Court may well choose to give weight to Congress's good-faith judgment of constitutional meaning. But Congress cannot by law require the Court to follow Congress's interpretation of constitutional meaning.

This basic principle, deducible from the Constitution's structure, has been reinforced by important rulings of the Court itself, most notably in the 1871 case of *United States v. Klein*.[9] In that case, the Justices correctly held that Congress lacked power to dictate to the Court the meaning and scope of the President's pardon powers under Article II.

Second, imagine a congressional statute purporting to restructure the Court's decision-making by forbidding the Court to strike down federal legislation unless the Court vote is at least 6–3. Any statute that gave a jurist brandishing a mere congressional law a weightier vote than a dueling jurist wielding the Constitution would improperly invert the clear prioritization of legal norms established by the Article VI Supremacy Clause, which of course privileges the Constitution over a mere congressional statute. Put differently, thanks to the letter and spirit of the Supremacy Clause, Congress may pass no law giving any judge who sides *against* a constitutional claim more weight than a judge who sides *with* a constitutional claim.

And if a law may permissibly require six out of nine Supreme Court votes to disregard a congressional statute as unconstitutional, why not seven or eight or even nine out of nine? Given broad congressional power to resize the Court, why couldn't Congress require that every congressional law be strictly followed, no matter how constitutionally outrageous, unless 99 out of 99 Justices on a packed Court unanimously agreed that a given congressional law was flagrantly unconstitutional? At that point—indeed, well before that point—judicial review itself would have effectively been eliminated, in open defiance of Articles III and VI, the *Federalist* No. 78, *Marbury v. Madison*, and centuries of constitutional law built on this constitutional bedrock.

---

[9] 80 U.S. 128 (1871).

But my proposed 18-year time rule is entirely different from improper laws of the sort I have just described. The proposal is deeply respectful of the constitutional principle of judicial independence. Indeed, because this proposal would discourage mature Justices from timing their resignations in political or partisan ways, it would instantiate a *superior* version of independence compared to the status quo. Unlike the law in *Klein*, which interfered with powers directly and explicitly vested by the Constitution itself in the office of the President, my proposal does no violence to the office of Supreme Court Justice as outlined in the Constitution. The Constitution vests no particular power in any *individual* judge or Justice to hear this case or that one, apart from the power of the Chief Justice to preside at presidential impeachments. My proposal in no way intrudes upon that power (even though it does revise the process by which a given jurist becomes the nation's Chief Justice).[10] My proposal does not retroactively deprive any current member of the Court of any vested privilege; and its structure provides the same rules for Presidents of both parties, going forward: Under my proposal, every President henceforth will nominate a new Justice in year one and in year three of every presidential term. In addition, the law could provide, in veil-of-ignorance fashion, that the new system will not go into effect until after the next presidential election—an election that is at present a toss-up in the opinion of our best political prognosticators. Indeed, the law could provide that the new system will not go into effect until 2030, or any other future specified date.

In essence, the 18-year time limit would simply be a proper and prospective law structuring and shaping the Supreme Court and the office of Supreme Court Justice—constitutionally indistinguishable from a vast number of earlier and current laws shaping and structuring the Supreme Court, lower federal courts, executive departments, and various Article II and Article III offices.

---

[10] My proposal that the senior-most Associate Justice should automatically become Chief—typically in his or her last two years of active service prior to becoming an emeritus Justice—broadly tracks the statutory rules for circuit courts today and the practice of many foreign Supreme Courts. On the former, see 28 U.S.C. § 45(a)(1) ("The chief judge of the circuit shall be the circuit judge in regular active service who is senior in commission of those judges who are sixty-four years of age or under; have served for one year or more as a circuit judge; and have not served previously as chief judge.").

For example:

Beginning in 1789, in legislation signed by George Washington himself, Congress has prescribed—and over the ensuing years has from time to time modified—the number of Justices, the Court's overall jurisdiction, and the duty rosters of various executive and judicial officials. *How is the envisioned duty roster at the heart of my 18-year proposal any different as a matter of constitutional principle?*

Notably, the First Congress prescribed when, where, and how the Justices should sit en banc, including a rule prescribing that any four of the Court's initial six members would compose a proper quorum for the Court's en banc decisions.[11] *How is it any different if today's Congress says that the Court's proper en banc composition, as a rule, involves its pre-emeritus Justices as distinct from its emeritus Justices?*

Congress likewise, in its earliest statute on the judiciary—the landmark Judiciary Act of 1789—prescribed that the proper duty of a Supreme Court Justice was to ride circuit at certain times. Although some modern scholars have raised technical questions about the constitutional propriety of circuit riding, this was *an enormous and defining feature* of the celebrated Judiciary Act of 1789, which was enacted by the First Congress, including many leading Framers and ratifiers of the Constitution, and was signed into law by none other than George Washington. Every early Justice in fact rode circuit; none openly resisted circuit-riding on the grounds that this element of the job was unconstitutional. Circuit riding built squarely on earlier practices and traditions in various states and colonies, and in Britain—traditions of assize courts and *nisi prius*, in which the jurists of a legal regime's highest court sat individually or in smaller groups in courts across the countryside, bringing justice to every man's door. If this system combining local sittings and centralized en bancs was good enough for George Washington, James Madison, John Marshall, and Joseph Story, it should surely be good enough for us. Modern scholars who are squeamish on this point should yield to the great weight of early liquidation and utterly settled practice. *If the First Congress could say that a given Justice must sit en banc in month X and ride circuit in month Y, why cannot today's Congress say that a given Justice must sit en banc in years 1–18 and ride circuit thereafter?*[12]

---

[11] Judiciary Act of 1789, 1 Stat. 73, § 1.

[12] In any event, if circuit-riding were thought problematic for emeritus Justices, this particular part of the reform package can simply be eliminated.

In laws stretching back to the Washington presidency, Congress has likewise prescribed various rules of evidence and procedure to be followed by the Supreme Court and other federal courts. Surely the 18-year time rule can be understood as structuring the *procedure* of the Court—that is, its basic manner of *proceeding and conducting itself* as distinct from its substantive pronouncements of the legal rights and duties of proper litigants who come before the Court. *If all these other procedural statutes are constitutionally kosher, how is our envisioned term-limits/time-rule statute decisively different?*

There is virtually no doubt that Congress could legislate proper rules for Supreme Court ethics, including rules specifying situations requiring recusal. *How is a rule prescribing en banc recusal in general for any jurist who has already heard her fair share of en banc cases any different from all sorts of other recusal rules that Congress might properly adopt? Why cannot a rule limiting pre-emeritus front-bench service to a fixed number of years be justified as a simple judicial-ethics regulation discouraging politically timed and partisanship-tinged retirements?*

My plan also closely aligns with recent and current practice for sitting and retired Justices. In the mid-1990s, William Rehnquist sat by designation while also serving as Chief. Since 1937, at least 11 retired Justices have sat by designation and in effect have ridden circuit per 28 U.S.C. § 294—to wit, Justices De Vanter, Reed, Burton, Clark, Stewart, Powell, Brennan, Marshall, White, O'Connor, and Souter. *If modern Justices can ride circuit after voluntarily retiring, why is it any different if the announcement of their voluntary retirement occurs much earlier in the process—namely in the course of joining the Court and simultaneously promising to step off 18 years hence?*

A final point worth reiterating from my April 28, 2021, podcast is that the 18-year reform proposal would bring the U.S. Supreme Court into closer alignment with some of America's most distinguished state-court judiciaries featuring long fixed terms of active service. State constitutions of course differ from the federal Constitution in important ways. Still, the wide popularity of state judicial time limits for service is one reassuring factor in support of the basic propriety and common sense of the 18-year proposal. In its deep design (and unlike several other high-profile reform proposals currently in the air), the 18-year proposal is entirely and self-consciously in keeping with the American Way.

Appendix: The Nuts and Bolts of the Plan

Congress should enact language along the following lines:

The Supreme Court shall henceforth consist of four classes of Justices: Legacy Justices, Regularized Justices, Replacement Justices, and Emeritus Justices. All Legacy, Regularized, and Replacement Justices shall be considered Justices in *active service*.

All Justices in active service on the date of this law's enactment are hereby designated Legacy Justices. Their service, tenure, rights, and responsibilities on the Court shall remain unchanged, provided that at any time, a Legacy Justice may elect to take Emeritus status by becoming an Emeritus Justice.

Regularized Justices shall be eligible to receive good-behavior commissions that commence no sooner than July 1, 2023, and every two years thereafter, one regularized commission per every odd year. No president may nominate a Regularized Justice prior to March 1 of the commissioning year. Regularized Justices shall in all respects be equivalent to Legacy Justices except as follows: Each Regularized Justice who wishes to remain on the Court must take Emeritus status no later than eighteen years after his or her commission-eligible July 1 date.

If any Justice in active service shall take Emeritus status or leave the Court at a time when the total number of remaining active-service Justices shall be nine or more, no Court vacancy shall thereby be created. If, however, any Justice in active service shall take Emeritus status or leave the Court at a time when the total number of remaining active-service Justices shall be less than nine, the vacancy may be filled, upon presidential nomination and Senate confirmation and presidential issuance of a good-behavior commission, by a Replacement Justice. This Replacement Justice may continue in active service until displaced by the commissioning of a Regularized Justice in due course whose addition to the Court brings the total number of remaining active-service Justices back to nine; provided that in no event may any Replacement Justice continue in active service for more than eighteen years. If at any time there shall be more than one Replacement Justice, the most junior Replacement Justice shall be the first to be displaced, the next-most junior shall be the next to be displaced, and so on. At the end of his or her active service, a Replacement Justice may elect to remain on the Court by taking Emeritus status.

Whenever the Chief Justice shall take Emeritus status or leave the Court, the position of Chief Justice shall devolve upon the senior-most Legacy Justice or Regularized Justice.

Upon the death, resignation, or retirement from the Court of the Chief Justice, the senior-most Legacy Justice, or Regularized Justice, or Replacement Justice shall serve as Chief for no more than two years, after which the next most senior shall serve for no more than two years, and so on.

Except as otherwise provided for herein, all Justices in active service shall perform the same functions as do the Legacy Justices on the date of this law's enactment. Emeritus Justices shall be eligible to participate in case decisions only when the Court is short-staffed—to wit, only when in any given case the number of active-service Justices shall fall below nine as a result of vacancy, disability, or recusal. Emeritus Justices shall also be eligible to perform ancillary administrative, ceremonial, educational, circuit-riding, and docket-management functions as shall be outlined in rules to be promulgated and from time to time revised by the active-service Justices.

National Pork Producers Council v. Ross: Extraterritoriality Is Dead, Long Live the Dormant Commerce Clause

*Brannon P. Denning**

Introduction

In a 2021 decision, Ninth Circuit Judge Sandra Ikuta wrote that "[w]hile the dormant Commerce Clause is not yet a dead letter, it is moving in that direction."[1] Until quite recently, there appeared to be considerable truth in that remark.[2] The case Judge Ikuta was writing about, *National Pork Producers Council v. Ross*, ended up at the Supreme Court. And a cursory glance at the Supreme Court's subsequent opinion might not inspire confidence that the dormant Commerce Clause doctrine (DCCD) is in good health. The tangle of majority and plurality opinions on the issues before the Court, expressed through partial concurrences and dissents, might seem to suggest that the DCCD is on its last legs.

Happily, reports of the doctrine's having one foot in the grave turn out to be exaggerated. Despite a superficial messiness caused by that skein of separate opinions, *National Pork Producers* is the latest in a series of cases decided within the last decade that cement the DCCD firmly in our constitutional canon. Moreover, it performs an overdue bit of doctrinal pruning by unanimously abjuring what was once a branch of the DCCD: extraterritoriality. Finally, it provides some clarification of so-called *Pike* balancing, in which facially neutral statutes are subjected to a test that compares the local benefits of the

---

* Starnes Professor of Law, Cumberland School of Law, Samford University.

[1] Nat'l Pork Producers Council v. Ross, 6 F.4th 1021, 1033 (9th Cir. 2021), *aff'd*, 143 S. Ct. 1142, 1165 (2023).

[2] *See infra* Part III.

law with the burdens the law places on interstate commerce.[3] That test had long been subject to criticism from members of the Court, most notably the late Justice Antonin Scalia, as being beyond the judicial ken.[4] Parsing the various opinions in *National Pork Producers*, it appears that *Pike* balancing (as traditionally understood) retains the support of a solid majority of the Justices.

I summarize the facts that led up to the opinion itself in Part I. In Part II, I discuss both the Court's rejection of the claim that the challenged law operated with impermissible extraterritorial effect and the Court's rejection of extraterritoriality itself as a DCCD doctrine. Part III then looks at the Court's treatment of the *Pike* balancing claim and the clarifying statements from the Justices themselves about *Pike*'s correct application. A brief conclusion follows.

I. *National Pork Producers Council*: A Summary[5]

In 2018, 61 percent of California voters approved Proposition 12, which "revised the State's existing standards for the in-state sale of eggs and announced new standards for the in-state sale of pork and veal products."[6] Specifically, the revised law defined as "cruel" the confinement of pigs in cages that prevented them from lying down, standing up fully, or turning around.[7] Proponents argued that more humane confinement conditions could result in more sanitary conditions that, in turn, might reduce incidents of food poisoning. Opponents argued to the contrary that more restrictive confinement could better protect animals ("by preventing pig-on-pig aggression") and better protect public health ("by avoiding contamination").[8] Opponents "also warned voters that Proposition 12 would require

---

[3] *See infra* notes 67–98 and accompanying text.

[4] *See, e.g.*, Bendix Autolite Corp. v. Midwesco Enters., Inc., 486 U.S. 888, 897 (1988) (Scalia, J., concurring in judgment) (complaining that because the benefits and burdens are incommensurable, *Pike* balancing asks a court to "judg[e] whether a particular line is longer than a particular rock is heavy").

[5] This description of the case draws heavily from BRANNON P. DENNING, BITTKER ON THE REGULATION OF INTERSTATE AND FOREIGN COMMERCE § 6.07[I](1) (2nd ed. 2013) (2024-1 Supp.).

[6] Nat'l Pork Producers Council v. Ross, 143 S. Ct. 1142, 1150 (2023).

[7] *Id.* at 1150–51.

[8] *Id.* at 1151.

some farmers and processors to incur new costs . . . . that 'might be "passed through" to California consumers.'"[9]

Two groups, including the National Pork Producers Council, filed a lawsuit challenging the law under the DCCD. In broad terms, the DCCD holds that states violate the Constitution's Commerce Clause "when they seek to 'build up . . . domestic commerce' through 'burdens upon the industry and business of other States.'"[10] In their challenge, the groups conceded that California's law was facially neutral because it did not distinguish between pork produced outside California and pork produced within California. But they alleged that Proposition 12 violated the DCCD in two ways: (1) by its impermissible extraterritorial effects; and (2) by its inability to clear the bar set by *Pike v. Bruce Church, Inc.*[11] The petitioners noted that although a substantial percentage of farmers nationwide had "already converted to some form of group housing for pregnant pigs," "even some farmers who already raise group-housed pigs will have to modify their practices if they wish to comply with Proposition 12."[12] In addition, because of the vertically integrated nature of the pork industry, "[r]evising this system to segregate and trace Proposition 12-compliant pork . . . will require certain processing firms to make substantial new capital investments" of more than nine percent.[13] "These compliance costs," the petitioners argued, "will fall on California and out-of-state producers alike. . . . But because California imports almost all the pork it consumes . . . 'the majority' of Proposition 12's compliance costs will be initially borne by out-of-state firms."[14]

In the end, the Supreme Court rejected both claims. In the pages that follow, I will highlight what are, to me, the two remarkable aspects of *National Pork Producers*. First—as I speculated in an article published a decade ago[15] and as *National Pork Producers* has now made explicit—extraterritoriality is no longer a branch of the DCCD.

---

[9] *Id.*

[10] *Id.* at 1152.

[11] 397 U.S. 137 (1970).

[12] *National Pork Producers*, 143 S. Ct. at 1151.

[13] *Id.*

[14] *Id.* at 1151–52.

[15] Brannon P. Denning, *Extraterritoriality and the Dormant Commerce Clause: A Doctrinal Post-Mortem*, 73 LA. L. REV. 979 (2013).

Second, *National Pork Producers* is one of a recent string of opinions that firmly cement the position of the DCCD as a legitimate—indeed, necessary—body of constitutional doctrine. A decade ago, the DCCD's future status—especially its *Pike* balancing prong—was decidedly less certain.

II. Extraterritoriality is Dead . . . [16]

In *Baldwin v. G.A.F. Seelig*, a 1935 opinion written by Justice Benjamin Cardozo, the Court invalidated a New York law that prohibited the in-state sale of milk purchased out-of-state if the milk had been purchased below the minimum price prescribed by New York.[17] Justice Cardozo wrote that the DCCD prohibited New York from "project[ing] its legislation into Vermont by regulating the price to be paid in that state for milk acquired there."[18] In the 1980s, the Court built on Cardozo's conclusion that such projection constituted the sort of direct regulation of interstate commerce that the DCCD denies to the states. Extending Cardozo's logic, the Court decided a series of cases that grafted extraterritoriality onto the DCCD.[19]

In 1989, Justice Harry Blackmun summarized DCCD extraterritoriality in the following sweeping terms:

> The principles guiding this assessment, principles made clear in *Brown–Forman* and in the cases upon which it relied, reflect the Constitution's special concern both with the maintenance of a national economic union unfettered by state-imposed limitations on interstate commerce and with the autonomy of the individual States within their respective spheres. Taken together, our cases concerning the extraterritorial effects of state economic regulation stand at a minimum for the following propositions: First, the "Commerce Clause . . . precludes the application of a state statute to commerce that takes place wholly outside of the State's borders, whether or not the commerce has effects within the State," . . . and, specifically, a State may not adopt legislation that has the practical effect of establishing "a scale of prices for use in other states[.]" Second, a statute that directly controls commerce occurring wholly outside the boundaries of a

---

[16] Portions of this Part draw from DENNING, *supra* note 5, at § 6.08[E] (2024-1 Supp.).

[17] 294 U.S. 511 (1935).

[18] *Id.* at 521.

[19] Healy v. Beer Inst., Inc., 491 U.S. 324 (1989); Brown-Forman Distillers Corp. v. N.Y. State Liquor Auth., 476 U.S. 573 (1986); Edgar v. MITE Corp., 457 U.S. 624 (1982).

State exceeds the inherent limits of the enacting State's authority and is invalid regardless of whether the statute's extraterritorial reach was intended by the legislature. The critical inquiry is whether the practical effect of the regulation is to control conduct beyond the boundaries of the State. Third, the practical effect of the statute must be evaluated not only by considering the consequences of the statute itself, but also by considering how the challenged statute may interact with the legitimate regulatory regimes of other States and what effect would arise if not one, but many or every, State adopted similar legislation. Generally speaking, the Commerce Clause protects against inconsistent legislation arising from the projection of one state regulatory regime into the jurisdiction of another State. . . . And, specifically, the Commerce Clause dictates that no State may force an out-of-state merchant to seek regulatory approval in one State before undertaking a transaction in another.[20]

This broad and sweeping[21] articulation of DCCD extraterritoriality had the potential to disrupt state regulatory efforts in a variety of areas.[22] Seven years later in *BMW v. Gore*,[23] the Court seemed to reinforce *Healy's* sweeping conception of extraterritoriality. *Gore* struck down a jury verdict in a fraud case involving a damaged car falsely sold as new. The jury's method of calculating damages was to multiply the damage to the plaintiff's car by the total number of sales of similarly damaged BMW cars in other jurisdictions. The Court held that this verdict violated the Constitution's Due Process Clause because in some cases the out-of-state conduct was not considered fraud under those states' laws. In the opinion, the Court cited several of its DCCD extraterritoriality cases to underscore the principle that states may not export their policies into other states.

With the advent of the internet, scholars and judges alike began to appreciate the implications of a broad extraterritoriality branch

---

[20] *Healy*, 491 U.S. at 335–37 (citations and footnotes omitted).

[21] 1 Laurence H. Tribe, American Constitutional Law § 6-8, at 1077, 1078 n.21 (3d ed. 2000).

[22] *See, e.g.*, Allen Rostron, *The Supreme Court, the Gun Industry, and the Misguided Revival of Strict Territorial Limits*, 2003 Mich. St. DCL L. Rev. 115, 151–56.

[23] 517 U.S. 559 (1996).

of the DCCD.[24] One New York district court struck down a state law prohibiting the dissemination of obscene material to minors over the internet, largely on extraterritoriality grounds.[25] I myself questioned the constitutionality of municipal suits against firearm manufacturers on the same extraterritoriality grounds, arguing that the changes that cities were demanding of manufacturers were essentially attempts to regulate activities that occurred within the boundaries of other states.[26]

Other scholars argued during this period that either DCCD extraterritoriality was not as broad as was claimed or, if it was, that it should be revisited by the Court.[27] In 2003, the Court itself seemed to walk back a great deal of *Healy's* more expansive language in *Pharmaceutical Research and Manufacturers of America v. Walsh*.[28] In that case, the Court upheld Maine's prescription drug subsidy program. Under the program, prescription drug manufacturers would rebate money from drug sales to the state's Medicaid program in order to avoid a prolonged preauthorization process. That money in turn

---

[24] Am. Libraries Ass'n v. Pataki, 969 F. Supp. 160, 177 (S.D.N.Y. 1997); Dan L. Burk, *Federalism in Cyberspace*, 28 CONN. L. REV. 1095, 1127–32 (1996); Glenn Harlan Reynolds, *Virtual Reality and "Virtual Welters": A Note on the Commerce Clause Implications of Regulating Cyberporn*, 82 VA. L. REV. 535, 537–40 (1996); Kenneth D. Bassinger, Note, *Dormant Commerce Clause Limits on State Regulation of the Internet: The Transportation Analogy*, 32 GA. L. REV. 889 (1998).

[25] *Am. Libraries Ass'n*, 969 F. Supp. at 173–77.

[26] Brannon P. Denning, *Gun Litigation and the Constitution, in* SUING THE GUN INDUSTRY: A BATTLE AT THE CROSSROADS OF GUN CONTROL & MASS TORTS (Timothy D. Lytton, ed., paperback ed. 2006).

[27] *See e.g.*, Jack L. Goldsmith & Alan O. Sykes, *The Internet and the Dormant Commerce Clause*, 110 YALE L.J. 785, 786–87 (2001) ("[T]he reasoning of *American Libraries Ass'n* extends far beyond the regulation at issue in that case. In fact, the dormant Commerce Clause argument, if accepted, threatens to invalidate nearly every state regulation of Internet communications. For under the logic of *American Libraries Ass'n*, nearly every state regulation of Internet communications will have the extraterritorial consequences the court bemoaned."); Allen Rostron, *The Supreme Court, the Gun Industry, and the Misguided Revival of Strict Territorial Limits on the Reach of State Law*, 2003 L. REV. MICH. ST.-DETROIT COLL. L. 115, 176 ("At its first opportunity, the Supreme Court should go further and disavow altogether its suggestions of a renewal of strict territorial limits on the reach of state law. While the Constitution imposes limits on a state's prescriptive and adjudicatory jurisdiction, it does not demand that state law stop dead in its tracks at the state's borders.").

[28] 538 U.S. 644 (2003).

would subsidize drug sales to Maine residents under a new program.[29] The petitioners argued that the program had impermissible extraterritorial effects, but the Court rejected that argument:

> [U]nlike price control or price affirmation statutes, "the Maine Act does not regulate the price of any out-of-state transaction, either by its express terms or by its inevitable effect. Maine does not insist that manufacturers sell their drugs to a wholesaler for a certain price. Similarly, Maine is not tying the price of its in-state products to out-of-state prices." The rule that was applied in *Baldwin* and *Healy* accordingly is not applicable to this case.[30]

In a 2013 article, I concluded that extraterritoriality was moribund,[31] based in part on *Walsh* and in part on the Court's subsequent rooting of its punitive damage decisions in the Due Process Clause rather than the DCCD.[32] The doctrine continued to be cited in the lower courts,[33] however, leading some to argue that "[t]he demise of the dormant Commerce Clause's extraterritoriality doctrine has been greatly exaggerated."[34] But if there *was* still some life left in extraterritoriality, *National Pork Producers* delivered a unanimous *coup de grace*.

Justice Neil Gorsuch began the majority's analysis by stressing that the DCCD's antidiscrimination principle was not in play here, which meant that "petitioners begin in a tough spot."[35] Nevertheless, he explained, "[t]hey contend that our dormant Commerce Clause cases suggest an . . . 'almost *per se*' rule forbidding enforcement of state laws that have 'the practical effect of controlling commerce outside the state,' even when those laws do not purposely discriminate against out-of-state economic interests."[36] The law here, they argued, "offends this 'almost *per se*' rule because the law will impose

---

[29] *Id.* at 649–50.

[30] *Id.* at 669.

[31] Denning, *supra* note 15.

[32] Philip Morris, USA v. Williams, 549 U.S. 346 (2007); State Farm Mut. Auto. Ins. Co. v. Campbell, 538 U.S. 408 (2003).

[33] Denning, *supra* note 15, at 992–94 & nn.80–86.

[34] Susan Lorde Martin, *The Extraterritoriality Doctrine of the Dormant Commerce Clause is Not Dead*, 100 MARQUETTE L. REV. 497, 526 (2016).

[35] *National Pork Producers*, 143 S. Ct. at 1153.

[36] *Id.* at 1154.

substantial new costs on out-of-state pork producers who wish to sell their products in California."[37]

But Justice Gorsuch concluded that no such per se rule existed in the DCCD. Any such limits on states' abilities to legislate beyond their borders lay elsewhere—in the "original and historical understandings of the Constitution's structure and the principles of 'sovereignty and comity' it embraces," or in the Due Process and Full Faith and Credit Clauses, for example.[38] Gorsuch described the petitioners' argument as "falter[ing] out of the gate" because each of the canonical extraterritoriality cases they cited—*Baldwin, Healy,* and *Brown-Forman*—"typifies the familiar concern with preventing purposeful discrimination against out-of-state economic interests."[39] The New York price-fixing statute in *Baldwin* "'plainly discriminate[d]' against out-of-staters by 'erecting an economic barrier protecting a major local industry against competition from without the State.'"[40] Likewise, "*Brown-Forman* and *Healy* differed from *Baldwin* only in that they involved price-affirmation, rather than price-fixing, statutes."[41] The latter "amounted to 'simple economic protectionism'" by "requiring out-of-state distillers to 'surrender' whatever cost advantages they enjoyed against their in-state rivals."[42]

The petitioners had argued that the defendants' narrow reading of those cases "misses the forest for the trees."[43] But Justice Gorsuch responded that it was actually the petitioners who "read too much into too little."[44] Cautioning that judicial opinions should not be read as if they were statutes, the majority opinion noted that *Walsh* had cabined those three earlier opinions such that they stood only for the limited proposition that states cannot tie the "price of . . . in-state products to out-of-state prices."[45] To adopt the more expansive

---

[37] *Id.*

[38] *Id.* at 1156.

[39] *Id.* at 1154.

[40] *Id.* (quoting Dean Milk Co. v. Madison, 340 U.S. 349, 354 (1951)).

[41] *Id.*

[42] *Id.* (quoting Brown-Forman Distillers Corp. v. N.Y. State Liquor Auth., 476 U.S. 573, 576 (1986)).

[43] *Id.* at 1155.

[44] *Id.*

[45] *Id.* (quoting *Walsh*, 538 U.S. at 669).

reading of those cases would ignore the fact that "[i]n our interconnected national market place, many (maybe most) state laws have the 'practical effect of controlling' extraterritorial behavior."[46] If any state law that had the "practical effect" of controlling out-of-state commerce were suspect, that application of the DCCD "would cast a shadow over laws long understood to represent vital exercises of States' constitutionally reserved powers."[47]

Justice Gorsuch did not doubt that there were limits to a state's ability to project its legislative jurisdiction into other states. But he argued that those limits lay elsewhere.[48] He concluded: "The antidiscrimination principle found in our dormant Commerce Clause cases may well represent one more effort to mediate competing claims of sovereign authority under our horizontal separation of powers. But none of this means . . . that *any* question about the ability of a State to project its power extraterritorially must yield to an 'almost *per se*' rule under the dormant Commerce Clause."[49]

In a partial dissent, Chief Justice John Roberts, joined by Justices Samuel Alito, Brett Kavanaugh, and Ketanji Brown Jackson, likewise rejected extraterritoriality as a branch of the dormant Commerce Clause. That made this portion of the decision effectively unanimous. "I . . . agree," Roberts wrote, "with the Court's conclusion that our precedent does not support a *per se* rule against state laws with 'extraterritorial' effects."[50]

Professor Donald Regan once wrote that "extraterritoriality is not a dormant commerce clause problem."[51] Thirty-six years later, the Court appears to have come around to his view, recharacterizing the canonical "extraterritoriality" cases discussed above as anti-discrimination cases and leaving to other parts of the Constitution the role of limiting states' legislative jurisdiction vis-à-vis one another.

---

46 *Id.*

47 *Id.* at 1156.

48 *Id.*

49 *Id.* at 1156–57.

50 *Id.* at 1167 (Roberts, C.J., concurring in part and dissenting in part).

51 Donald H. Regan, *Siamese Essays: (I) CTS Corp. v. Dynamics Corp. of America and Dormant Commerce Clause Doctrine; (II) Extraterritorial State Legislation,* 85 MICH. L. REV. 1865, 1873 (1987).

III. . . . Long Live the Dormant Commerce Clause

In a previous article, I speculated that one of the drivers of the Court's abandonment of a strong DCCD extraterritoriality principle was its overall ambivalence towards the DCCD as a constitutional doctrine.[52] "In 2003, when *Walsh* was decided," I noted, "Justice [Clarence] Thomas announced his intention never again to vote to invalidate a state law challenged under the DCCD."[53] Norman Williams and I regarded the Court's grant of certiorari in *Comptroller v. Wynne*[54] as "ominous"[55]—possibly heralding dramatic restrictions on (or even abandonment of) the DCCD.[56] From 2000 until 2015, the Court had invalidated only one non-tax state law under the DCCD: Michigan's in-state winery exception to its ban on direct shipment of wine to consumers.[57] During that time, the Court also created a heretofore unknown exception to the DCCD's anti-discrimination principle: a law may grant a monopoly to a local public entity performing a traditional governmental service, as long as the law prohibits competition from *both* in-state and out-of-state private providers of that service.[58] Only Justices John Paul Stevens, Anthony Kennedy,

---

[52] Denning, *supra* note 15, at 1004–06.

[53] *Id.* at 1004. Justice Scalia's disdain for the doctrine was long a matter of record. *See, e.g.*, Mark V. Tushnet, *Scalia and the Dormant Commerce Clause: A Foolish Formalism?* 12 CARDOZO L. REV. 1717 (1991) (surveying and analyzing the various grounds on which Justice Scalia objected to the DCCD).

[54] Md. State Comptroller of the Treasury v. Wynne, 64 A.3d 453 (Md. 2013), *cert. granted* 572 U.S. 1134 (2014), *aff'd* 575 U.S. 542 (2015).

[55] Brannon P. Denning & Norman R. Williams, Wynne: *Lose or Draw?* 67 VAND. L. REV. EN BANC 245, 268 (2014).

[56] *Id.* at 264–67.

[57] Granholm v. Heald, 544 U.S. 460 (2005). In *MeadWestvaco Corp. v. Ill. Dep't of Revenue*, 553 U.S. 16 (2008), the Court did hold that Illinois had unconstitutionally attempted to tax a portion of income from a transaction that was not part of MeadWestvaco's unitary business.

[58] United Haulers Ass'n, Inc. v. Oenida-Herkimer Solid Waste Mgmt. Auth., 550 U.S. 330 (2007); *see also* Dep't of Rev. of Ky. v. Davis, 553 U.S. 328 (2008) (applying the public-entities exception to uphold a state tax exemption for income from bonds issued by the state or its subdivisions, where the state taxed income derived from similar out-of-state bonds). For an analysis and critique of this exception, see Norman R. Williams & Brannon Denning, *The New Protectionism and the American Common Market*, 85 NOTRE DAME L. REV. 247 (2009).

and Alito expressed support for a robust DCCD.[59] It appeared that the DCCD might have been on its last legs.

But starting with the *Wynne* decision in 2015, it began to look like the DCCD was getting its second wind. The Court began to embrace the DCCD with escalating levels of enthusiasm. In *Wynne*, the Court held that Maryland could not deny its residents a tax credit for county taxes paid on out-of-state income. The Court held that this denial violated the DCCD's "internal consistency" requirement, which ensures that state residents are not taxed twice on interstate income.[60] Three years later, in *South Dakota v. Wayfair*, the Court formally abandoned its previous holding that states may not tax the income of businesses that lack a physical presence in the state—a requirement that had become increasingly untenable in light of the growth of internet commerce.[61] While *Wayfair* broadened the ability of states to tax interstate commerce, Justice Kennedy's opinion was interesting in its treatment of the DCCD as a body of doctrine. Kennedy's opinion was unlike Justice Alito's *Wynne* opinion, which was rather minimalist insofar as it stressed that *Wynne*'s outcome was largely determined by the Court's prior cases.[62] Justice Kennedy, by contrast, undertook a broad survey of the doctrine and its application in tax cases, highlighting the doctrine's lengthy pedigree. He concluded that "[m]odern precedents rest upon two primary principles that mark the boundaries of a State's authority to regulate interstate commerce. First, state regulations may not discriminate against interstate commerce; and second, States may not impose undue burdens on interstate commerce."[63]

The next term in *Tennessee Wine & Spirits Retailers Association v. Thomas*, the Court struck down, on DCCD grounds, a state residency

---

[59] *See Davis*, 553 U.S. at 362 (Kennedy, J., dissenting); *United Haulers Ass'n*, 550 U.S. at 355 (Alito, J. dissenting).

[60] *Wynne*, 575 U.S. at 564–65. *See generally* Brannon P. Denning, *The Dormant Commerce Clause ~~Wynnes Won~~ Wins One: Five Takes on* Wynne *and* Direct Marketing Association, 100 MINN. L. REV. HEADNOTES 103 (2016).

[61] South Dakota v. Wayfair, Inc., 138 S. Ct. 2080, 2097, 2099 (2018), *overruling* Quill Corp. v. North Dakota, 504 U.S. 298 (1992).

[62] *See* Denning, *supra* note 60, at 109 (speculating about the "peculiar structure of the opinion").

[63] *Wayfair*, 138 S. Ct. at 2090–91.

requirement for persons applying for a retail liquor store license.[64] Writing for the Court's majority, Justice Alito authored his own survey of the DCCD that was no less extensive than Justice Kennedy's in *Wayfair* and even more emphatic about the importance of the DCCD to our constitutional system. While acknowledging the DCCD's critics, Justice Alito forthrightly wrote, "the proposition that the Commerce Clause by its own force restricts state protectionism is deeply rooted in our case law."[65] Moreover, he added, "without the dormant Commerce Clause, we would be left with a constitutional scheme that those who framed and ratified the Constitution would surely find surprising."[66]

Alito noted that the Constitution was, in part, a response to the states' interference with interstate commerce during the Articles of Confederation Era.[67] "In light of this background," he continued, "it would be strange if the Constitution contained no provision curbing state protectionism, and at this point in the Court's history, no provision other than the Commerce Clause could easily do the job."[68] Alito noted that the Import-Export and the Privileges and Immunities Clauses have both been interpreted in ways limiting their reach.[69] "In light of this history and our established case law," he concluded, "we reiterate that the Commerce Clause by its own force restricts state protectionism."[70]

---

[64] 139 S. Ct. 2449, 2476 (2019).

[65] *Id.* at 2460.

[66] *Id.*

[67] *Id.* For an account of this Confederation-Era period, see Brannon P. Denning, *Confederation-Era Discrimination Against Interstate Commerce and the Legitimacy of the Dormant Commerce Clause*, 94 Ky. L.J. 37 (2005).

[68] *Tenn. Wine & Spirits*, 139 S. Ct. at 2460.

[69] *Id. See, e.g.*, W. & S. Life Ins. Co. v. State Bd. of Equaliz. of Cal., 451 U.S. 648, 656 (1981) (Privileges and Immunities Clause does not apply to corporations); Woodruff v. Parham, 75 U.S. (8 Wall.) 123, 136–37 (1869) (Import-Export Clause applies only to foreign commerce). For a critique of the latter case, see Brannon P. Denning, *Justice Thomas, the Import-Export Clause, and* Camps Newfound/Owatonna v. Harrison, 70 COLO. L. REV. 155 (1999) [hereinafter Denning, Camps Newfound/Owatonna]. Justice Alito also observed that the Privileges and Immunities Clause's substantive protections may be limited in relation to the DCCD. *Tenn. Wine & Spirits*, 139 S. Ct. at 2461 (citing Brannon P. Denning, *Why the Privileges and Immunities Clause of Article IV Cannot Replace the Dormant Commerce Clause Doctrine*, 88 MINN. L. REV. 384, 393–97 (2003)).

[70] *Tenn. Wine & Spirits*, 139 S. Ct. at 2461.

What is striking about *Tennessee Wine & Spirts* is that none of the seven Justices who joined the majority seemed to disagree with Justice Alito's forthright endorsement of the DCCD and his emphatic declaration of its legitimacy. If his colleagues had had any qualms, one might have expected a brief concurring opinion or two. But none wrote separately. And Justices Gorsuch and Thomas dissented not because they disagreed with the majority's description of the DCCD, but rather because they thought the Twenty-first Amendment—which delegated control over alcohol to the states—effectively overrode the DCCD when it came to those products.[71]

Which brings us to the *National Pork Producers* case.[72] In Part II of Justice Gorsuch's opinion, which commanded a majority,[73] Gorsuch described the "antidiscrimination principle" as "the 'very core' of our dormant Commerce Clause jurisprudence."[74] Chief Justice Roberts agreed, along with Justices Alito, Kavanaugh, and Jackson.[75] What's remarkable about this unanimity is that it included Justice Thomas, who had regularly and vehemently denounced the DCCD in toto.[76] He offered no explanation for joining this part of the opinion; perhaps he felt no need to write separately because the Court upheld California's statute, because his views are well-known and oft-stated, or because of some combination of the two. His apparent acquiescence in the Court's support for the anti-discrimination prong of the DCCD, though, did lend a dog-that-didn't-bark air to the decision.

[71] *Id.* at 2484 (Gorsuch, J., dissenting). As it happens, I think the dissenters were right. *See* Brannon P. Denning, *Smokey and the Bandit in Cyberspace: The Dormant Commerce Clause, the Twenty-first Amendment, and State Regulation of Internet Alcohol Sales,* 19 Const. Comment. 297 (2002).

[72] The following paragraphs draw on Denning, *supra* note 5, at § 6.05 (2024-1 Supp.).

[73] 143 S. Ct. at 1149. Justice Gorsuch was joined by Justices Thomas, Sonia Sotomayor, Elena Kagan, and Amy Coney Barrett.

[74] *Id.* at 1153.

[75] *Id.* at 1167 (Roberts, C.J., concurring in part and dissenting in part) ("I agree with the Court's view in its thoughtful opinion that many of the leading cases invoking the dormant Commerce Clause are properly read as invalidating statutes that promoted economic protectionism.").

[76] *See, e.g.,* McBurney v. Young, 133 S. Ct. 1709, 1721 (2013) (Thomas, J., concurring) ("I continue to adhere to my view that the negative Commerce Clause has no basis in the text of the Constitution, makes little sense, and has proved virtually unworkable in application, and, consequently, cannot serve as a basis for striking down a state statute.") (cleaned up); *see also* Camps Newfound/Owantonna, Inc. v. Town of Harrison, 520 U.S. 564, 610–12 (1997) (Thomas, J., dissenting).

The other notable feature about *National Pork Producers* is that while the Court splintered on the application of *Pike* balancing, a close tally of the votes suggests that *Pike*, too, is secure for the near future.

Echoing skeptics of balancing like Justices Scalia and David Souter, Justice Gorsuch (along with Justices Thomas and Barrett, in part) argued that the true purpose of *Pike* was to serve as an "anti-evasion"[77] mechanism. On this view, *Pike* allowed the Court to smoke out protectionist purposes or effects hiding in facially neutral statutes.[78] It did *not* empower the Court to conduct a freewheeling balancing of costs and benefits anytime a state law has implications for interstate commerce.[79]

"How is a court," Gorsuch asked, "supposed to compare or weigh economic costs (to some) against noneconomic benefits (to others)? No neutral legal rule guides the way. The competing goods before us are insusceptible to resolution by reference to any juridical principle."[80] Although the petitioners had argued that the putative benefits ought to be "heavily discount[ed]," they had conceded that states could ban "the in-state sale of products they deem unethical or immoral without regard to where those products are made . . . ."[81] Thus,

> we remain left with a task no court is equipped to undertake. On the one hand, some out-of-state producers who choose to comply with Proposition 12 may incur new costs. On the other hand, the law serves moral and health interests of some

---

[77] *Cf.* Michael B. Kent, Jr. & Brannon P. Denning, *Anti-Evasion Doctrines in Constitutional Law*, 2012 UTAH L. REV. 1773 (2012).

[78] *National Pork Producers*, 143 S. Ct. at 1156 (plurality op.) ("[I]f some of our cases focus on whether a state law discriminates on its face, the *Pike* line serves as an important reminder that a law's practical effects may also disclose the presence of a discriminatory purpose."). Gorsuch did concede that "this Court left the 'courtroom door open' to challenges premised on 'even nondiscriminatory burdens' . . . and while 'a small number of our cases have invalidated state laws . . . that appear to have been genuinely nondiscriminatory . . . petitioners' claims fall well outside *Pike*'s heartland. . . .'" *Id.* at 1158–59. Gorsuch's characterization of *Pike* seemed to command a majority of the Court (himself along with Justices Thomas, Sotomayor, Kagan, and Barrett).

[79] *Id.* at 1159.

[80] *Id.* at 1159–60 (quoting Justice Scalia's "whether a particular line is longer than a particular rock is heavy" line from *Bendix Autolite Corp.*, 486 U.S. at 897 (Scalia, J., concurring in judgment)).

[81] *National Pork Producers*, 143 S. Ct. at 1160 (plurality op.).

(disputable) magnitude for in-state residents. Some might reasonably find one set of concerns more compelling. Others might fairly disagree. How should we settle that dispute? The competing goods are incommensurable. Your guess is as good as ours. More accurately, your guess is *better* than ours.[82]

Given this incommensurability, democratic decisionmaking should prevail. And Justice Gorsuch concluded that if the economic disruption turns out to be as massive as petitioners alleged, then Congress should step in to preempt the disruptive state laws. That is Congress's prerogative "[u]nder the *wakeful* Commerce Clause."[83]

Gorsuch concluded that even *were* the Court to apply balancing in this case, the pleadings showed that "[a] substantial harm to interstate commerce remains nothing more than a speculative possibility."[84] In this conclusion, he and Justice Thomas were joined by Justices Sotomayor and Kagan. Gorsuch noted that "[p]etitioners must plead facts 'plausibly' suggesting a substantial harm to interstate commerce; facts that render that outcome a 'speculative' possibility are not enough."[85] The alleged harms to interstate commerce were speculative, because it was possible that Proposition 12 could *benefit* some out-of-state pork producers. The fact that *some* out-of-state producers "may face difficulty complying (or may choose not to comply) with Proposition 12" meant that "*other* out-of-state competitors seeking to enhance their own profits may choose to modify their existing operations or create new ones to fill the void."[86] Equally speculative was the allegation that these costs would be passed along to California consumers who, after all, voted for the law. In any event, raising costs for in-state consumers is not a cognizable harm under the DCCD.

Justice Barrett declined to join this part of Justice Gorsuch's opinion, however. She acknowledged that "Proposition 12's costs are pervasive, burdensome, and will be felt primarily (but not exclusively) outside California."[87] But, she argued, "California's interest in eliminating

---

[82] *Id.* (emphasis in original).

[83] *Id.* at 1160.

[84] *Id.* at 1163.

[85] *Id.* at 1162 (quoting Bell Atl. Corp. v. Twombly, 550 U.S. 554, 555, 557 (2007)).

[86] *Id.* (footnote omitted).

[87] *Id.* at 1167 (Barrett, J., concurring in part).

allegedly inhumane products from its markets cannot be weighed on a scale opposite dollars and cents—at least not without second-guessing the moral judgments of California voters or making the kind of policy decisions reserved for politicians."[88] Thus, "the benefits and burdens of Proposition 12 are incommensurable." In contrast to Justice Gorsuch, she thought the benefits and burdens on interstate commerce *could* be weighed against each other in cases where the burdens and benefits could be measured according to some common metric.

Justice Sotomayor (joined by Justice Kagan) concurred with Justice Gorsuch's conclusion that the petitioners had failed to plead sufficient facts to succeed on their *Pike* claim, but she wrote separately to disclaim any "fundamental reworking" of *Pike* balancing.[89] She made clear that although "*Pike* claims that do not allege discrimination or a burden on an artery of commerce are further from *Pike's* core" of smoking out discriminatory purposes or effects, nevertheless "courts generally are able to weigh disparate burdens and benefits against each other, and . . . they are called on to do so in other areas of the law."[90] She denied that the incommensurability issue that Justice Gorsuch stressed meant *Pike* balancing was a fool's errand, but she did argue that proof of a substantial burden was "a threshold requirement" that must be established before "courts need even engage in *Pike's* balancing and tailoring analyses."[91]

Chief Justice Roberts wrote what Justice Gorsuch characterized as the "lead dissent," but it's only a partial dissent. Writing for himself and Justices Alito, Kavanaugh, and Jackson, Chief Justice Roberts agreed that the point of the DCCD was to guard against economic protectionism. The four likewise agreed that "our precedent does not support a *per se* rule against state laws with 'extraterritorial' effects."[92] The four disagreed, however, with the plurality's *Pike* analysis. Roberts and company "would find that petitioners[] have plausibly alleged a substantial burden against interstate commerce, and would therefore vacate the judgment and remand the case for

---

[88] *Id.*

[89] *Id.* at 1165 (Sotomayor, J., concurring in part).

[90] *Id.* at 1166.

[91] *Id.*

[92] *Id.* at 1167 (Roberts, C.J., concurring in part and dissenting in part).

the court below to decide whether petitioners have stated a claim under *Pike*."[93]

Chief Justice Roberts defended *Pike* as more than simply a tool for detecting latent protectionism and stressed that *Pike* balancing retained the endorsement of a solid majority:

> Although *Pike* is susceptible to misapplication as a free-wheeling judicial weighing of benefits and burdens, it also reflects the basic concern of our Commerce Clause jurisprudence that there be "free private trade in the national marketplace."[94] Nor is *Pike* confined to cases "involving discriminatory state laws and those implicating the 'instrumentalities of interstate transportation.' . . . [W]e have since applied *Pike* to invalidate nondiscriminatory state laws that do not concern transportation."[95]

Contrary to what Justice Gorsuch claimed, the petitioners' complaint "alleges more than simply an increase in 'compliance costs,' unless such costs are defined to include all the fallout from a challenged regulatory regime."[96] "Petitioners," he continued, "identify broader, market-wide *consequences* of compliance—economic harms that our precedents have recognized can amount to a burden on interstate commerce."[97] The immediate costs to producers to become California-compliant were estimated to be between $290 and $348 million, or $13 per pig.[98] "Separate and apart from those costs," he continued,

> petitioners assert harms to the interstate market itself. The complaint alleges that the interstate pork market is so interconnected that producers will be "forced to comply" with Proposition 12, "even though some or even most of the cuts from a hog are sold in other States." Proposition 12 may not expressly regulate farmers operating out of State. But due to the nature of the national pork market, California has enacted rules that carry implications for producers as far flung as Indiana

[93] *Id.*

[94] *Id.* at 1167–68.

[95] *Id.* at 1168 (citations omitted).

[96] *Id.* at 1169.

[97] *Id.*

[98] *Id.* at 1170.

and North Carolina, whether or not they sell in California.
The panel below acknowledged petitioners' allegation that,
"[a]s a practical matter, given the interconnected nature of
the nationwide pork industry, all or most hog farmers will be
forced to comply with California requirements."[99]

Such extraterritorial effects, he noted, "even if not considered as
a *per se* invalidation, [are] pertinent in applying *Pike*."[100] Moreover,
"petitioners here allege that Proposition 12 will force compliance on
farmers who do not wish to sell into the California market, exacerbate health issues in the national pig population, and undercut established operational practices."[101]

Responding to Justice Gorsuch's claim that this approach can't
be distinguished from a *per se* ban on extraterritorial regulations,
Roberts replied that the difference is "between mere cross-border
effects and broad impact requiring . . . compliance even by producers who do not wish to sell in the regulated market."[102] Even then,
he noted, the burdens must be "clearly excessive" in light of the benefits.[103] For the Chief Justice, the "broader, market-wide *consequences*
of compliance" with Proposition 12 were enormous—large enough
that he would have remanded the case to the Ninth Circuit for the
application of *Pike* balancing.[104]

For those keeping score, it appears that there is still a solid majority of the Court that regards *Pike* balancing as an independent
branch of the DCCD—a doctrine for reviewing facially neutral yet
burdensome laws that impact interstate commerce, as opposed to
simply a tool for detecting hidden discrimination. The Chief Justice,
along with Justices Alito, Sotomayor, Kagan, Kavanaugh, and Jackson, endorsed that view. And Justice Barrett did as well, so long as
the benefits and burdens are commensurable. Only Justices Gorsuch
and Thomas—along with Justice Barrett if the benefits and burdens
are incommensurable—would seem prepared to abjure balancing
entirely and restrict *Pike* to an anti-evasion role in detecting protectionism. *Pike* thus lives to fight another day.

[99] *Id.*

[100] *Id.*

[101] *Id.* at 1171.

[102] *Id.*

[103] *Id.*

[104] *Id.* at 1169.

Conclusion

National Pork Producers performs a useful mopping up function for a doctrine long derided as a "conceptual disaster area"[105]—to crib Charles Black's characterization of the state action doctrine—by its critics.[106] The opinion locates the core of the DCCD in the elimination of protectionism, whether "sophisticated [or] simple-minded,"[107] and generally acknowledges the doctrine's longstanding pedigree. It clears up the status of DCCD extraterritoriality, confirming Donald Regan's conclusion from nearly four decades ago that wherever the constitutional limits to a state's ability to project its authority beyond its borders were to be found, they weren't in the DCCD. It also gives *Pike* balancing a new lease on life, with the Justices recognizing *Pike* not only as a useful anti-evasion doctrine to backstop the anti-discrimination principle, but also as valuable in its own right in certain cases.[108]

Extraterritoriality is dead! Long live the DCCD!

---

[105] Charles L. Black, Jr., *The Supreme Court, 1966 Term—Foreword: "State Action," Equal Protection, and California's Proposition 14*, 81 Harv. L. Rev. 69, 95 (1967).

[106] For a summary of contemporary critiques, see Denning, Camps Newfound/Owatonna, *supra* note 69, at 156 nn.2–4.

[107] Lane v. Wilson, 307 U.S. 268, 275 (1939).

[108] I once argued that the Court should drop balancing in favor of developing its facially-neutral-but-discriminatory-effects-or-purpose criteria. Brannon P. Denning, *Reconstructing the Dormant Commerce Clause Doctrine*, 50 Wm. & Mary L. Rev. 417, 493–94 (2008). At the time, I didn't appreciate *Pike* balancing's utility as an anti-evasion doctrine. In any event, given *Wayfair's* suggestion that *Pike* balancing may have a heretofore unknown role in tax cases, *Pike* appears poised to take on an expanded role in DCCD cases. *Wayfair*, 138 S. Ct. at 2098–99 (responding to arguments that the compliance costs would be unduly burdensome for small businesses to pay state taxes in states where they lack a physical presence by suggesting that "other aspects of the Court's Commerce Clause doctrine can protect against any undue burden on interstate commerce" and mentioning *Pike* balancing as an example). *But see* Bradley W. Joondeph, *State Taxes and "Pike Balancing,"* 99 Ind. L. J. __ (forthcoming), available at https://tinyurl.com/y3xnff5f (arguing that *Pike* balancing has at best a small role to play in assessing tax compliance burdens, but none in the assessment of the amount of tax liabilities).

The SEC Puts Itself on Moot—Answering Justice Robert Jackson's Eight-Decade-Old Query—Has the SEC Become a Law Unto Itself?

*Margaret A. Little**

The Supreme Court's opinion in *Axon Enterprise Inc. v. FTC* (*Axon/Cochran*)[1] is full of surprises, from its inception—launched despite a seemingly impenetrable barrier of five adverse circuit precedents (hereinafter the *SEC ALJ Cases*)[2]—to conclusion in a unanimous victory that overruled all those cases. Its significance is still playing out in the courts—and will continue to do so in litigation across all administrative agencies. Its abrupt denouement, with the SEC dismissing all 42 open cases that could be affected by the decision including Michelle Cochran's, conjures up a kind of agency seppuku—or perhaps kabuki. It's hard to know.

The object of this paper is to bring to the surface what all too often gets buried or omitted altogether in necessarily selective academic commentary and judicial opinions. Paul Clement, who argued the appeal for Axon, has called the case "a sleeper" that will have surprising and far-ranging repercussions. As counsel for Michelle Cochran, I agree.

---

* Senior Litigation Counsel, New Civil Liberties Alliance. I am indebted to my colleagues Russ Ryan, Kara Rollins, and Sheng Li for their contributions to this article. Many thanks to Randy Quarles and Jessica Moeller for research and editorial support. Any errors are mine alone.

[1] 143 S. Ct. 890 (2023).

[2] Jarkesy v. SEC, 803 F.3d 9 (D.C. Cir. 2015); Bebo v. SEC, 799 F.3d 765 (7th Cir. 2015); Tilton v. SEC, 824 F.3d 276 (2d Cir. 2016); Bennett v. SEC, 844 F.3d 174 (4th Cir. 2016); Hill v. SEC, 825 F.3d 1236 (11th Cir. 2016). Dear Westlaw and Lexis: Your Shepardizing and Case Analysis functions correctly show that *Axon/Cochran* reversed the Ninth Circuit *Axon* decision. However, you both still show the five *SEC ALJ Cases* as good law. They are not.

I. The Problem

For many decades, critics of SEC and FTC administrative adjudication have expressed grave concerns with the utter lack of due process, structural biases, lack of jury trial, and baked-in prejudgment inherent in agency adjudication. For both agencies, the Commission first votes to charge you, then its enforcement staff prosecutes you before a "judge" who is employed by your prosecutor, then your first right of appeal goes back to the agency that charged you in the first place—with no jury of your peers to curb prosecutorial excesses. These defects also include tenure protections that put administrative law judges (ALJs) beyond executive control or accountability, sharply curtailed discovery with parsimonious rights to call and cross-examine witnesses, a dearth of any of the procedural protections provided by the Federal Rules of Evidence and Procedure that are available in real courts, and asymmetrical rules and extensions that make no pretense about always favoring the agency. When you finally make it to an Article III court, you are at a federal court of appeals that has to defer to the administrative record shaped by the very gang that prosecuted you. This is what Justice Clarence Thomas dubs in his *Axon/Cochran* concurrence the "appellate review model." Notice how it extinguishes any possibility of a trial judge or jury mediating the exercise of administrative power—including *judicial* power—by structurally unaccountable bureaucrats.

With the procedural and substantive deck thus stacked against targets, is it any wonder that the SEC, which only wins 61 percent of the time in real courts, has an over 90 percent win rate before its own in-house judges? Targets of FTC enforcement reportedly have it worse—they lose 90–100 percent of the time in its in-house proceedings. Even if you prevail before the FTC's ALJ, the Commission often reverses that win.[3]

Other structural defects include:

- "Unlike Article III judges, executive officials are not, nor are they supposed to be, 'wholly impartial.' They have their own interests, their own constituencies, and their own policy goals—and when interpreting a regulation, they may

---

[3] *See Axon/Cochran*, 143 S. Ct. at 917–918.

choose to 'press the case for the side [they] represen[t]' instead of adopting the fairest and best reading."[4]

- Agency administrative law procedures generally provide significantly fewer protections for respondents than corresponding district-court rules; administrative proceedings lack early dispositive motions, admit hearsay, reportedly shift the burden to the accused, and curtail witness testimony and rights of cross-examination.[5]

- The most prominent procedural disadvantage is that targets are hurried into a three-track system that gives them as little as four months (and no more than 10 months) to prepare a defense against an agency that has been investigating them for years.[6]

- Once the foreshortened hearing takes place, agency proceedings take far longer than trials before real judges. "[D]ata suggest that after factoring in delays associated with Commission review, 'the overall period for completion of an administrative proceeding is likely *slower* than the time required to complete a trial in district court.'"[7]

Agency enforcement respondents thus have the worst of both worlds. They are rushed to summary proceedings with far less time to prepare than in federal district court, and then they are forced to remain in limbo for years longer than those privileged to be in a real court.

---

[4] Kisor v. Wilkie, 139 S. Ct. 2400, 2439 (2019) (Gorsuch, J., concurring in judgment) (quoting Archibald Cox, *Judge Learned Hand and the Interpretation of Statutes*, 60 Harv. L. Rev. 370, 390–91 & n.58 (1947)).

[5] *See generally* Douglas J. Davison, *Litigating with the SEC* at 709, SEC Compliance and Enforcement AB 2015 (2015), https://tinyurl.com/y29xkbxz.

[6] 17 C.F.R. § 201.360(a)(2)(ii). "The SEC administrative courts' unrealistic time constraints relating to decision issuances are perhaps the forum's most prominent procedural disadvantage." Ryan Jones, *Comment: The Fight Over Home Court: An Analysis of SEC's Increased Use of Administrative Proceedings*, 68 SMU L. Rev. 507, 524 (2015) (citing Peter J. Henning, *The S.E.C.'s Use of the 'Rocket Docket' is Challenged*, N.Y. Times Dealbook (Aug. 25, 2014), https://tinyurl.com/529kjbtt).

[7] Joseph A. Grundfest, *Fair or Foul?: SEC Administrative Proceedings and the Prospects for Reform Through Removal Legislation*, 85 Fordham L. Rev. 1143, 1164 (2016) (quoting Ctr. For Capital Mkts. Competitiveness, U.S. Chamber Of Commerce, Examining U.S. Securities And Exchange Commission Enforcement: Recommendations On Current Processes And Practices 16 (2015)).

And at the end of all this, until *Axon/Cochran*, you could only have the constitutionality of this scheme reviewed by a real court in a court of appeals after the unconstitutional protracted agency adjudication takes place and the agency issues a final order! That's right. You have to undergo the very unconstitutional proceeding and appeals to which you object before you can go to a court and argue that the whole costly, depleting, reputation-destroying shebang is unconstitutional. And if you win? Congratulations, you face a renewed years-long agency prosecution!

When I first ventured into challenging these "quasi-judicial" aspects of administrative power, I was warned that the word "Kafkaesque" would frequently come to mind—an oracle that would prove to be an understatement. Welcome to the world of Axon Enterprise and Michelle Cochran.

Lucia *Sheds Light*

The first hint of how lawless these schemes are and have always been came in 2018 when the SEC was caught with its pants down trying to conceal that *none of its ALJs had ever been constitutionally appointed.*[8] This is like having five federal judges preside over thousands of cases for decades without ever having been properly nominated, confirmed, and sworn in. Once this embarrassing omission slipped out of SEC's grasp of attempted concealment, the agency hurriedly "ratified" its ALJs *on the day after the Supreme Court granted certiorari* in *Lucia v. SEC,*[9] the landmark case that would hold a few months later that this lack of appointment meant that SEC ALJ decisions in open cases had to be vacated. For the Supreme Court, the SEC's "shotgun" appointment ratification would not legitimize the baby—and so about a hundred cases were sent back to be retried before different ALJs who had since been lawfully appointed by the Commission. To this day, even though *Lucia* meant all federal agencies had

---

[8] The fact that *all* of the SEC ALJs lacked a constitutionally required appointment came to light in a case involving Timbervest LLC. *See* Timbervest, LLC v. SEC, 2015 U.S. Dist. LEXIS 132082, *35. The SEC responded to an erupting scandal by refusing to say whether the appointments were constitutional and instead filing cryptic affidavits and unsworn notices regarding both the ALJ hiring process and the agency's non-conformity with the Office of Personnel Management hiring process. *See* Affidavit of Jayne L. Seidman, https://tinyurl.com/5a6d6epv. *See also* SEC Notice, http://bit.ly/2CprDyj.

[9] 138 S. Ct. 2044, 2055 n.6 (2018).

to properly appoint their ALJs, agencies simply have not bothered to do so.

The Supreme Court had nothing to say about the thousands of SEC targets who had been haled before and judged by these lawless ALJs for many decades. The *Lucia* case was crucial because it cracked the door of freedom from the administrative maze in which Americans had been trapped for nearly 90 years.

II. Nine Surprising Aspects of *Axon/Cochran*

A. *"This is what a win looks like under* Thunder Basin*"*

The first surprise of the SCOTUS opinion in *Axon/Cochran* is that one Justice, Neil Gorsuch, made an unusual decision to set forth for "consider[ation] some of the facts of Ms. Cochran's case that do not find their way into the Court's opinion." These facts tell the story of the costs of this "appellate review model":

> A single mother of two and a certified public accountant, Ms. Cochran began looking for part-time work in 2007. Eventually, she found a position at a small company called The Hall Group. Soon, however, she discovered that the owner, David Hall, was not just abrasive but dishonest. At one point, he even added Ms. Cochran's name to the firm's business license without her permission, all to facilitate his idea of rebranding his company as "The Hall Group CPAs." When Ms. Cochran protested, Mr. Hall offered her a choice: become a nonequity partner with no increase in pay so that he could use the new name or leave the firm. Ms. Cochran chose to quit and put the whole ordeal behind her.
>
> Or so she thought. Years later, in 2016, Ms. Cochran learned that the SEC had initiated an enforcement proceeding against Mr. Hall, another of his former employees, and herself. . . . In English, the SEC alleged that Ms. Cochran had failed to complete auditing checklists, leaving certain sections of certain forms "blank." The agency brought these charges even though there was "no evidence" that the incomplete paperwork had resulted in any "monetary harm to clients or investors."[10]

---

[10] *Axon/Cochran*, 143 S. Ct. at 916 (Gorsuch, J. concurring in judgment) (citing *In re Hall*, SEC Release No. 3-17229, p. 1, 12–13, 28 (2017)).

Now in the administrative maze, Cochran learns firsthand how bad it can get:

> The SEC elected to proceed against Ms. Cochran before its own internal tribunal rather than (as it could have) a court of law. The agency assigned the case to [an ALJ] . . . Reportedly, that ALJ made a practice of warning defendants during settlement discussions that he had "never ruled against the agency's enforcement division."[11] It seems, though, Ms. Cochran didn't take the hint. She refused to settle and sought to represent herself in the hearing that followed. It did not go well. Just as her hearing was about to start, her former boss settled his own case and then turned about to testify against Ms. Cochran. In the end, the ALJ fined Ms. Cochran $22,500 and banned her from practicing before the SEC as an accountant for at least five years.[12]

> Ms. Cochran responded by asking the full Commission to review the ALJ's decision. Around the same time, this Court held in an unrelated case [*Lucia*] that the ALJ who presided over Ms. Cochran's case had been unconstitutionally appointed. . . . Ms. Cochran might have thought that would bring her own case to a close. But the SEC chose instead to take a mulligan. In 2018, the agency vacated the initial decision against Ms. Cochran and assigned a different, properly appointed ALJ to retry the case. So two years after her administrative proceedings began, they began again.[13]

Cochran immediately sued to vindicate her constitutional rights, because if she acceded to the new in-house prosecution and won years later on her constitutional challenges in the appellate courts, that "win" would mean she was subject to a *third* prosecution to begin over a decade after the uncompleted paperwork at issue. To end this

---

[11] *Id.* (citing Jean Eaglesham, *SEC Judges' Fairness Is in Spotlight*, WALL ST. J., Nov. 23, 2015, p. C6).

[12] This shout-out confers the dubious distinction on former SEC ALJ Cameron Elliot of being named, disqualified, and negatively quoted in two Supreme Court decisions. *See Lucia*, 138 S. Ct. at 2055. Elliot was also name-checked by two SEC Commissioners in Ray Lucia's appeal to the Commission, who noted in dissent that ALJ Elliot had made up the grounds for liability out of "whole cloth." Statement, Daniel M. Gallagher & Michael S. Piwowar, Comm'rs, SEC, Opinion of Commissioner Gallagher and Commissioner Piwowar, Dissenting from the Opinion of the Commission (Oct. 2, 2015), https://perma.cc/8WDQ-SJ3X.

[13] *Axon/Cochran*, 143 S. Ct. at 916–17.

cruel and unending process of serial, to-be-repeated prosecutions by the SEC, Cochran had to sue in district court—to stop the madness.

Because the five *SEC ALJ Cases* had already denied jurisdiction for just such claims, Cochran's district court judge, John McBryde, reluctantly dismissed her constitutional challenge, noting the injustice of the existing weight of authority:

> The court is deeply concerned with the fact that plaintiff already has been subjected to extensive proceedings before an ALJ who was not constitutionally appointed and contends that the one she must now face for further, undoubtedly extended, proceedings likewise is unconstitutionally appointed. She should not have been put to the stress of the first proceedings, and, if she is correct in her contentions, she again will be put to further proceedings, undoubtedly at considerable expense and stress, before another unconstitutionally appointed administrative law judge.[14]

By contrast, Cochran's panel majority opinion derided McBryde's concerns:

> This appeal is not about whether Cochran will have the opportunity to press her separation-of-powers claim. She will. It instead asks: Where and when? . . . To be sure, requiring the adjudication to run its course before we consider her constitutional claim could impose unnecessary costs on Cochran. But . . . Cochran may raise her removal-power claim before the ALJ and, if she loses before the agency, in a court of appeals. She may even be able to get her claim all the way to the Supreme Court as Lucia did.[15]

The concurring opinion in the Fifth Circuit *en banc* did not share this sanguine view of respondents having to go all the way to the Supreme Court—for Lucia it would have been *two* trips—to secure a constitutional adjudication:

> [A]llowing Cochran to raise her removal-power challenge at the beginning of her enforcement proceeding may prove *more* efficient than requiring her to first wade through the potentially unconstitutional review process. To see why,

---

[14] Cochran v. SEC, No. 4:19-CV-066-A, 2019 WL 1359252, at *2 (N.D. Tex. Mar. 25, 2019) (McBryde, J.).

[15] Cochran v. SEC, 969 F.3d 507, 511, 516, 518 (5th Cir. 2020).

> consider the case of Raymond Lucia—a case the dissent cites for the proposition that Cochran could get meaningful post-enforcement review of her constitutional claim. . . . Lucia, using § 78y, prevailed in the Supreme Court after years of SEC enforcement proceedings and appellate review. . . . So, the Court said, Lucia was entitled to a new hearing before a new, properly appointed ALJ. . . . [B]ecause the Supreme Court chose not to address his removal-power challenge, . . . Lucia was still proceeding before an ALJ he contended was constitutionally illegitimate.[16]

Like Cochran, Lucia sued in district court, to stop the madness. The district court tossed his claims, saying he must await *another* SEC final order before pursuing the removal constitutional claim. Lucia appealed, but unlike in *Cochran*, the Ninth Circuit refused to stay his case pending appeal.[17] Lucia, then age 70, threw in the towel and settled.

> At that point, Lucia had had enough; like many others in this situation, he settled after eight years of administrative proceedings and federal court litigation—thus sacrificing the constitutional claim that Cochran now must press instead. So much for efficiency.[18]

Justice Gorsuch likewise lays bare the illogic and years of financial and human costs of forcing respondents through serial administrative adjudications:

> A year and a half later, a panel of the Fifth Circuit . . . affirmed. 969 F.3d 507 (2020). A year and a half after that, the en banc Fifth Circuit took another look and largely reversed. 20 F.4th 194 (2021). Now, more than four years after Ms. Cochran filed her complaint, this Court balances the *Thunder Basin* factors anew and holds that her case *belonged in district court all along.*[19]

---

[16] Cochran v. SEC, 20 F.4th 194, 235 (5th Cir. 2021) (en banc) (Oldham, J. concurring) (cleaned up).

[17] The stay pending appeal that Cochran was able to secure from a Fifth Circuit motions panel (Jones, Higginson, and Oldham, JJ.) was crucial. The panel generously allowed argument on the stay, which was granted just hours after argument, so that Cochran did not have to litigate these matters on parallel judicial and administrative tracks—another way agencies strong-arm respondents into submission.

[18] Cochran v. SEC, 20 F.4th 194, 235 (5th Cir. 2021) (en banc) (Oldham, J., concurring) (cleaned up).

[19] *Axon/Cochran*, 143 S. Ct. at 917 (Gorsuch, J., concurring in judgment) (emphasis added).

This is what they mean when they say the process is the punishment.

One cannot overstate the importance of Cochran's trial and en banc judges, now joined by Justice Gorsuch, setting out in detail *exactly* the enormous imposition of human and economic costs and life disruption of this constitutionally and procedurally flawed scheme. That is because, by the SEC's own reckoning, 98 percent of respondents settle their cases because they lack the resources to mount a real defense.

Justice Thomas asked at oral argument in *Cochran*, "How many years has this been going on?"[20] The answer given was that it has been going on at least since Dodd-Frank expanded administrative jurisdiction. But at a higher level of generality, this has been going on since Congress set up James Landis's experiment in rule by expert, combining lawmaking, enforcement, adjudication, and appeals in "efficient" expert agencies.[21] As powerfully argued by the Fifth Circuit in the en banc concurring opinion in *Cochran*, Landis's plan for agency assumption of all powers of government has allowed "administrative agencies to operate in a separate, anti-constitutional, and anti-democratic space—free from pesky things like law and an increasingly diverse electorate."[22]

Why do neither the courts (including the Supreme Court) nor the public know about what my colleague Russ Ryan calls "the SEC's version of the Hotel California—The accused can check out, but they can never leave"?[23] The answer is simple and comes in two parts. Shockingly, for 50 years a *non-negotiable* condition of settlement with

---

[20] Transcript of Oral Argument at 6:15-16 (Thomas, J.), SEC v. Cochran, 143 S. Ct. 890 (2023) (No. 21-1239).

[21] *Cochran*, 20 F.4th at 213–237 (concurrency by Oldham, Smith, Willett, Duncan, Engelhardt, Wilson, JJs.) (considering "the 80-plus year history of the SEC," the purported policy "benefit[s] of agency expertise," and the supposed "efficiency" purpose of § 78y's appellate review model).

[22] *Id.* at 214.

[23] Russell Ryan, Opinion, *The Dangers of the SEC's 'Hotel California' Docket*, LAW360 (Nov. 28, 2022) (emphasis added), https://perma.cc/WXN8-ZR78. Ryan observes: "For decades, the SEC and other agencies have assured courts and litigants that the notoriously paltry due process protection they offer in their captive, home-court administrative tribunals is worth the deprivations because administrative adjudication is so much more streamlined and efficient, thereby producing prompt decisions. The SEC's Hotel California docket demonstrates exactly the opposite reality."

the SEC has been a *lifetime gag order*,[24] which has cruelly silenced thousands of Americans subjected to this Kafkaesque regime. People can't publicly air these injustices under threat of reprosecution! Judges Edith Jones and Kyle Duncan of the Fifth Circuit acknowledge that this is an unlawful prior restraint, the worst and most serious of First Amendment violations: "If you want to settle, SEC's policy says, 'Hold your tongue, and don't say anything truthful—ever'— or get bankrupted by having to continue litigating with the SEC. A more effective prior restraint is hard to imagine."[25] District Judges Jed Rakoff and Ronnie Abrams of the Southern District of New York have also called out the gag's unconstitutionality.[26]

The second reason no one knows about Hotel California is that no one is watching the regulators. Courts are under a regular duty to report to the Administrative Conference about the time to resolution of all cases on their docket. Had the SEC prosecuted Michelle Cochran for her uncompleted paperwork in district court in Texas, the time to resolution through a full trial would have averaged 20.4 months, with early resolution on motion or settlement averaging 7.1 months.[27] As it stands, Cochran has been in administrative limbo for seven years.

Not one of the *SEC ALJ Cases* paid any mind whatsoever to these wrenching human and financial costs and disruption. The Second Circuit's cavalier dismissal in *Tilton* was particularly brazen, but characteristic of the *SEC ALJ Cases*: "The litigant's financial and emotional costs in litigating the initial proceeding are simply the price of participating in the American legal system . . . [and] endur[ing]

---

[24] 17 C.F.R. § 202.5(e). A petition to review and revoke this SEC policy, which was unlawfully promulgated without notice and comment, was filed nearly five years ago. New Civil Liberties Alliance, Petition to Amend (Oct. 30, 2018), available at https://bit.ly/3qQGbBJ.

[25] SEC v. Novinger, 40 F.4th 297, 308 (5th Cir. 2022).

[26] SEC v. Citigroup Glob. Markets Inc., 827 F. Supp. 2d 328, 333 n.5 (S.D.N.Y. 2011), *vacated and remanded on other grounds*, 752 F.3d 285 (2d Cir. 2014) ("On its face, the SEC's no-denial policy raises a potential First Amendment problem."); SEC v. Moraes, No. 22-cv-8343, 2022 WL 15774011, at *4 (S.D.N.Y. Oct. 28, 2022) ("[T]he Constitution prevents courts from enforcing the waiver of First Amendment rights as a condition of settlements.").

[27] Median time for civil cases from filing to disposition in the Northern District of Texas was 7.1 months, and from filing to trial it was 20.4 months, for the year ending March 21, 2017. That data holds steady for the surrounding years. *See* U.S. Dist. Ct., Nat'l Jud. Caseload Profile, available at https://tinyurl.com/28k2jah3 (last accessed August 1, 2023).

'substantial' expense and disruption before the administrative proceeding concluded . . . [is just a] . . . hardship . . . [that is] 'part of the
social burden of living under government.'"[28] And because 98 percent of the victims of this scheme can never talk about this insane
and unjust system or otherwise question the prosecution against
them, the constitutional infirmities of agency adjudication have lan-
guished unvindicated for over eight decades.

Axon's Shocking Treatment by FTC

This madness was and is not confined to the SEC. Justice Gorsuch recognized that Axon, an Arizona maker of police body cameras, "endured
a similarly tortuous path."[29] Indeed, Axon's treatment by the FTC was
beyond lawless. The FTC sought to block Axon's acquisition of a small
competitor without any showing of anticompetitive effect. Axon was
willing to divest the company but balked when the FTC demanded that
Axon also surrender its intellectual property to the now-competitor—
or else be haled before an FTC ALJ. The FTC lacks any power to force
companies to surrender their intellectual property in this manner. So,
rather than submit to a years-long administrative trial where FTC wins
100 percent of the time, Axon sued in district court so that its case might
be heard before a constitutional adjudicator. Axon, like Cochran, was
denied relief and also lost on appeal over a powerful dissent—where
even the majority recognized the constitutional problems.[30]

---

[28] Tilton v. SEC, 824 F.3d 276, 285–286 (2d Cir. 2016) (quoting in part FTC v. Standard
Oil of California, 449 U.S. 232, 244–45 (1980)). And just in case this heartless and unjust
message wasn't clear, the Second Circuit poured salt into the wound: "Cf. Learned
Hand, *The Deficiencies of Trials To Reach the Heart of the Matter*, 3 Association of the Bar
of the City of New York, Lectures on Legal Topics 89, 105 (1926) (musing that becoming a party to a lawsuit should be 'dread[ed] . . . beyond almost anything else short of
sickness and death')." *Id.* n.5.

[29] *Axon/Cochran*, 143 S. Ct. at 917 (Gorsuch, J., concurring in the judgment).

[30] "Axon's argument makes sense from a policy perspective: it seems odd to
force a party to raise constitutional challenges before an agency that cannot decide
them. . . . As the Supreme Court cautioned in *Free Enterprise*, the 'growth of the Executive Branch, which now wields vast power and touches almost every aspect of
daily life, heightens the concern that it may slip from the Executive's control, and
thus from that of the people.' . . . Further, Axon raises legitimate questions about
whether the FTC has stacked the deck in its favor in its administrative proceedings. Axon claims—and FTC does not appear to dispute—that FTC has not lost a
single case in the past quarter-century. Even the 1972 Miami Dolphins would envy
that type of record." Axon Enter. v. FTC, 986 F.3d 1173, 1187 (9th Cir. 2021).

Fortunately, Cochran was finally able to persuade a majority of the judges of the Fifth Circuit Court of Appeals, sitting en banc, that this process makes no sense. Her en banc victory broke through a now six-circuit roadblock (including Axon's 2–1 loss in the Ninth) to create the circuit split that launched both *Cochran* and *Axon* to the Supreme Court.

B. *That* Axon/Cochran *Was Necessary at All*

In *Free Enterprise Fund v. PCAOB* (*FEF*), the Supreme Court already unanimously decided that nothing in the text or structure of 15 U.S.C. § 78y ousts federal court jurisdiction to hear constitutional questions:

> The Government reads § 78y as an exclusive route to review. But the text does not expressly limit the jurisdiction that other statutes confer on district courts. See, *e.g.,* 28 U.S.C. §§ 1331, 2201. *Nor does it do so implicitly.* . . . We do not see how petitioners could meaningfully pursue their constitutional claims under the Government's theory [of exclusive jurisdiction]. . . . Petitioners' constitutional claims are also outside the Commission's *competence* and expertise. . . . We therefore conclude that § 78y did not strip the District Court of jurisdiction over these claims[.][31]

That binding and unanimous holding from 2010 predated *all* of the *SEC ALJ Cases.* It is an enduring, and ultimately inexplicable mystery why this litigation was necessary at all—at least for Cochran where the statutory review scheme was identical to that in *FEF.*[32] Ray Lucia, Michelle Cochran—and uncounted others—spent over a decade in litigation purgatory over an issue the Court had already decided—on both jurisdiction and the merits![33] Justice Elena Kagan's opinion for the Court unambiguously agreed: "The answer appears from 30,000 feet not very hard. . . . The claims here are of the same ilk as the one in *Free Enterprise Fund.*"

> They are instead challenges, again as in *Free Enterprise Fund,* to the structure or very existence of an agency: They charge

---

[31] Free Enterprise Fund v. PCAOB, 561 U.S. 477, 489–91 (2010) (emphases added).

[32] Further, *FEF* also held that more than one level of insulation from removal of executive officers was unconstitutional.

[33] "What's curious about [the SEC's] argument [in Lucia's district court challenge] is that the Supreme Court has already rejected it." Joel Nolette, *Post-Lucia, It's Déjà Vu with the SEC,* LAW360 (Apr. 22, 2019), https://perma.cc/S9Z8-N6ST.

that an agency is wielding authority unconstitutionally in all or a broad swath of its work. Given that equivalence, it would be surprising to treat the claims here differently from the one in *Free Enterprise Fund*—which we held belonged in district court.[34]

Or, as Justice Kagan pithily told the government at argument: "I thought Free Enterprise Fund pretty clearly put the kibosh on your cause of action argument."[35]

C. THUNDER BASIN *AND ITS DISCONTENTS*

How do we explain the decade of darkness? One culprit is certainly the judge-made, atextual *Thunder Basin* multi-part test that the circuit courts felt compelled to apply. At oral argument, the Justices displayed confusion over and open discomfort—if not disdain—for *Thunder Basin*. Appendix A to this piece sets forth excerpts from the oral argument about *Thunder Basin* that argue more eloquently than I can in favor of abandoning the doctrine.[36]

The *Thunder Basin* factors, named after the case in which the test was first announced, are generally understood to consider (1) whether the issue for which district court jurisdiction is sought is wholly collateral to the specific merits of the case; (2) whether the agency has the competence and expertise to decide the question; and (3) whether the delayed circuit court review of the appellate review model provides "meaningful judicial review."[37]

Thunder Basin's multi-part test spawned much confusion and inconsistent, if not incoherent, holdings over seven circuits. District and circuit courts differed on whether there are stages or tiers in which the factors are applied (compare *Jarkesy* with *Axon/Cochran*). "[T]he D.C. Circuit in [*Jarkesy*] reversed the burden of proof, stating that the *plaintiff* must demonstrate 'a strong countervailing rationale' against implied preclusion. Besides misanalysing the issue, the appellate courts have labored to resolve the litigation in the SEC's favor. At times, their

---

[34] *Axon/Cochran*, 143 S. Ct. at 902.

[35] Transcript, *supra* note 20, at 59:21.

[36] Available on the Cato Institute's website at https://tinyurl.com/bdekatwr.

[37] Thunder Basin Coal Co. v. Reich, 510 U.S. 200, 207, 212–13 (1994).

reasoning has been almost nonsensical."[38] No one could ever figure out whether all of the factors mattered, whether some mattered more than others, and what weight to give them when the factors pointed in opposite directions. The systematic misapplication of those factors put thousands of Americans in involuntary, protracted thrall to ALJ adjudications and called into question the use of such atextual, judge-made, multi-part tests. A test this vague and indeterminate flunks its own multiple-choice exam.

This ten-year jaunt in the wilderness of incoherent doctrine was enormously costly to the few litigants who could fight against this misdirection—to say nothing of those who had to surrender and settle without ever vindicating their constitutional rights (and, because of the gag order, give up even constitutional rights). As Professor Jellum has observed, "Losing before the SEC would effectively end their careers because the appellate court does not automatically grant a stay of the SEC's orders . . . during appeals to federal court. And the SEC typically denies stay requests" and "has no expertise interpreting the U.S. Constitution." She argues that "the SEC should not have the power to decide its own constitutionality. . . . [nor should plaintiffs] be dragged through years of litigation at the SEC before an Article III court can resolve their constitutional claims."[39]

By the time this doctrine reached the Northern District of Arizona in *Axon*,[40] *Thunder Basin* had ascended into a "trilogy" of cases along with *Elgin v. Department of Treasury*,[41] and *FEF*. Once a trilogy, *Thunder Basin* and *Elgin* served to knock the wits out of *Free Enterprise Fund*—the only relevant precedent.[42] Thus do we consecrate and expand error. Thankfully, the Supreme Court

---

[38] Linda D. Jellum, *Why the SEC is Wrong About Implied Preclusion*, THE REGULATORY REVIEW, (Aug. 22, 2022) https://bit.ly/3PbZ7Dl. *See also* Linda D. Jellum, Opinion, *Why the SEC Is Wrong About Implied Preclusion*, REGUL. REV. (Aug. 22, 2022), https://perma.cc/RB9U-SHGZ.

[39] *Id. See generally* Linda D. Jellum, *The SEC's Fight to Stop District Courts from Declaring Its Hearings Unconstitutional*, 101 TEXAS L. REV. 339 (2022) [hereinafter Jellum, *The SEC's Fight*], for a masterful, detailed analysis of how illogical and incorrectly reasoned appellate opinions have enabled the SEC to hold respondents captive in its unconstitutional in-house courts.

[40] Axon Enter., Inc. v. FTC, 452 F. Supp. 3d 882 (D. Ariz. 2020), *aff'd*, 986 F.3d 1173 (9th Cir. 2021), *rev'd*, 143 S. Ct. 890 (2023).

[41] 567 U.S. 1 (2012)

[42] *See also* Jellum, *Why the SEC Is Wrong, supra* note 38.

correctly applied the *Thunder Basin* factors in *Axon*, affirming *Cochran* and overruling six circuit courts of appeals' misapplication of those factors.

The most insightful explanation I have heard about *Thunder Basin* was from retired Second Circuit Judge Christopher Droney, the first circuit judge to dissent from the calamitous circuit chorus of conformity and correctly apply the *Thunder Basin* factors as *Axon/Cochran* ultimately would.[43] At a panel discussion on this issue, Judge Droney said, "I just don't think there's real, faithful application of the three factors."[44] And perhaps one may be forgiven for wondering if long habits of judicial deference to agencies—especially under a test that raised agency expertise and "eventual" judicial review—was all too reflexively familiar to courts.

D. THAT IT WAS UNANIMOUS AND THAT THE MAJORITY OPINION FAILED TO EVEN MENTION A SINGLE ADVERSE CIRCUIT DECISION THAT HAD REACHED A DIAMETRICALLY OPPOSED CONCLUSION

Logic lies at the heart of Justice Kagan's opinion applying the "meaningful review" prong of *Thunder Basin*. After cycling through the other factors, which many courts conceded argued in favor of district-court jurisdiction, Kagan noted that "a problem remains, stemming from the . . . timing of review." That problem is what the Supreme Court in *Seila Law* recognized as a "here-and-now" injury:[45]

> The claim . . . is about subjection to an illegitimate proceeding, led by an illegitimate decisionmaker. And as to that grievance, the court of appeals can do nothing: A proceeding that has already happened cannot be undone. Judicial review of Axon's (and Cochran's) structural constitutional claims would come too late to be meaningful.[46]

True, but obvious, and compelled since 2010's *FEF* holding.

---

[43] *See Tilton*, 824 F.3d at 292–99 (Droney, J., dissenting) (applying all three *Thunder Basin* factors to argue in favor of district-court jurisdiction of structural constitutional claims).

[44] *When Your Judge's Boss Is Also Your Prosecutor*, at 41:28, NCLA (Oct. 1, 2020), https://tinyurl.com/murs73v3.

[45] Seila Law LLC v. Consumer Financial Protection Bureau, 140 S. Ct. 2183, 2196 (2020).

[46] *Axon/Cochran*, 143 S. Ct. at 903–04.

The Court's reasoning on what far too many circuit courts persisted in calling *Thunder Basin*'s "agency expertise" factor also merits a reminder that *FEF* held that agencies lack relevant *"competence* and expertise"[47] on constitutional questions. The fact that agency ALJs lack competence to decide constitutional questions is decisive. The *Axon/Cochran* decision correctly quotes both aspects of the test but fails to completely deliver when it falls into sloppy verbiage, noting that "[t]he Commission knows a good deal about competition policy, but nothing special about the separation of powers. For that reason, . . . 'agency adjudications are generally ill suited to address structural constitutional challenges.'"[48] The problem is not that they are "ill-suited"—they lack *competence.* It was just this kind of verbal slippage on the expertise prong that allowed six circuits to be so wrong for so long.[49]

The majority decision never once mentions any one of the *SEC ALJ Cases,* presumably because their flaws in reasoning and decade-long defiance of the ruling compelled by *FEF* made such discussion uncomfortable. It would be nice if an admonishment about precision in language and logic was the only fallout. Sadly, scores of litigants were held captive in the administrative maw enduring serial to-be-vacated proceedings while a decade of persistent misreadings of clearly written precedents gained momentum, checked only by the Fifth Circuit, and even then requiring an en banc court to make the correction.

---

[47] *See id.* at 902, 905 (emphasis added).

[48] *Id.* at 905.

[49] The circuits also bandied about a "mootness" argument in applying *Thunder Basin* that the *Axon/Cochran* majority neatly demolishes: "On this last factor, even the Government mostly gives up the ghost. Its argument goes: 'Even when an agency lacks expertise in interpreting the Constitution, it can still "apply its expertise by deciding other issues"—whether "statutory, regulatory, or factual"—"that 'may obviate the need to address the constitutional challenge.'"' . . . The first clause of that sentence concedes the expertise point—and the rest cannot reclaim it. . . . But the Government here does not pretend that Axon's and Cochran's constitutional claims are similarly intertwined with or embedded in matters on which the Commissions are expert. (It is precisely because those claims are not so entangled that the Government must try to redefine what it means for claims to be 'collateral' to an agency action. . . . [R]uling for Axon and Cochran on expertise-laden grounds would not 'obviate the need' to address their constitutional claims—which, again, allege injury not from this or that ruling but from subjection to all agency authority. Those claims of here-and-now harm would remain no matter how much expertise could be 'brought to bear' on the other issues these cases involve." 143 S. Ct. at 905–6 (cleaned up). Again, these points are obvious. The unanimous Court's dissection of such poor reasoning may explain why none of the errant circuit court cases get even a mention in the majority opinion.

E. THAT AXON/COCHRAN FAILS TO MENTION THAT THE COURT COULD HAVE DECIDED THAT SEC ALJ'S WERE UNCONSTITUTIONALLY INSULATED FROM REMOVAL FIVE YEARS AGO

Which brings us to Ray Lucia, whose 2018 case was a tragic missed opportunity to address not only SEC ALJs' lack of appointment, but also their unconstitutional multi-layer removal protections. In *Lucia*, the Solicitor General—on behalf of the government—had confessed error not only on appointments but removal, asking the Supreme Court to also find that SEC ALJs enjoyed unconstitutional multi-layer removal protection under *FEF's* directly-on-point decision allowing pre-enforcement challenges.[50]

Justice Kagan's *Lucia* decision declined to hear the removal protections challenge so that the Court could await lower courts' consideration of this point.[51] The majority opinion ordered that to cure the constitutional error, the SEC had to retry Lucia before a "properly appointed" ALJ "or the Commission itself." But percolation on this issue was not needed! The Supreme Court had already decided in 2010 that any more than one level of tenure protection violated the law—and had unanimously held that federal courts had jurisdiction to hear such claims—even in a pre-enforcement posture under the very same SEC statute, 15 U.S.C. § 78y.

To put this starkly: the government admitted it put Ray Lucia through six years of lawless, soon-to-be-vacated proceedings, and the Court allowed the SEC to require him *to do it all over again* on what Justice Stephen Breyer's dissent made clear was a logically related "embedded" constitutional question. In this context, awaiting percolation amounted to judicial abdication.

Justice Gorsuch's separate opinion directly discusses the human cost associated with flawed doctrine:

> Maybe even worse is what *Thunder Basin* means for others. Not many possess the perseverance of Ms. Cochran and Axon. The cost, time, and uncertainty associated with litigating a raft of opaque jurisdictional factors will deter many people from even trying to reach the court of law to which they are entitled.

---

[50] *See Lucia*, 138 S. Ct. at 2050 n.1 (outlining the Solicitor General's request); *id.* at 2057–58 (Breyer, J., concurring in the judgment in part and dissenting in part) (outlining the *Free Enterprise* framework).

[51] *Id.* at 2050 n.1 (majority opinion).

> Nor is the loss of a day in court in favor of one before an agency a small thing. . . . The numbers reveal just how tilted this game is. From 2010 to 2015, the SEC won 90% of its contested in-house proceedings compared to 69% of the cases it brought in federal court.[52]

F. THAT AXON/COCHRAN GENERATED TWO ALTERNATE PATHS TO THE SAME END

Justice Thomas, characteristically visionary, wrote separately even though he joined the majority opinion's application of *Thunder Basin*. He called into serious question any use of administrative adjudication to decide private rights. Justice Gorsuch declined to descend into *Thunder Basin*'s morass, instead arguing that a plain reading of the statute as conferring jurisdiction on federal courts to enforce the constitution was all that was needed. Relying on the jurisdictional statute is also in harmony with, if not compelled by, *FEF*:

> [E]quitable relief "has long been recognized as the proper means for preventing entities from acting unconstitutionally[.]" "[I]t is established practice for this Court to sustain the jurisdiction of federal courts to issue injunctions to protect rights safeguarded by the Constitution[.]" . . . If the Government's point is that an Appointments Clause or separation-of-powers claim should be treated differently than every other constitutional claim, it offers no reason and cites no authority why that might be so.[53]

Justice Gorsuch ended his opinion with a call to discard the *Thunder Basin* experiment. It might be a good time for the Court to reconsider *Elgin* as well. *Elgin*'s dissent (Justices Samuel Alito, Ruth Bader Ginsburg, and Kagan) is far better reasoned than the majority opinion, and considering the composition of the Court, it is an open question whether the case would be decided the same way if first presented today.

---

[52] *Axon/Cochran*, 143 S. Ct. at 917 (Gorsuch, J., concurring in the judgment).

[53] *FEF*, 561 U.S. at 491 n.2 (cleaned up). A federal court "properly appealed to in a case over which it has by law jurisdiction" is duty-bound to take such jurisdiction. New Orleans Pub. Serv., Inc. v. Council of New Orleans, 491 U.S. 350, 358–59 (1989). "The right of a party plaintiff to choose a Federal court where there is a choice cannot be properly denied." *Id.* at 359.

Justice Ketanji Brown Jackson's questioning at oral argument displayed considerable discomfort with Gorsuch's statutory approach, so it is a fair assumption that the price of *Axon/Cochran's* unanimity was to hitch the wagon to *Thunder Basin*. If that is correct, one cannot tell which, if any, of the other Justices would join in a later adoption of either the Thomas concurrence regarding private rights or Justice Gorsuch's separate opinion urging adherence to 28 U.S.C. § 1331's conferral of jurisdiction on district courts to decide constitutional questions. No colloquy between opinions enlightens that question.

G. THE "CONTROL DEFICIENCY" THAT DARE NOT EXPLAIN ITS NAME

Just as Cochran's case was headed to the Supreme Court, damning evidence confirming the worst fears of respondents was disclosed by the SEC. On April 5, 2022, the SEC filed an alarming Notice with the Supreme Court and district court in *Cochran*[54] and also with the Fifth Circuit in the landmark *Jarkesy*[55] case:

> The Commission has identified a control deficiency related to the separation of its enforcement and adjudicatory functions within its system for administrative adjudications . . .

> The Commission has determined that, for a period of time, certain databases maintained by the Commission's Office of the Secretary were not configured to restrict access by Enforcement personnel to memoranda drafted by Adjudication staff. As a result, in a number of adjudicatory matters, administrative support personnel from Enforcement, who were responsible for maintaining Enforcement's case files, accessed Adjudication memoranda via the Office of the Secretary's databases. Those individuals then emailed Adjudication memoranda to other administrative staff who in many cases uploaded the files into Enforcement databases.

As the *Wall Street Journal* put it

> It's the equivalent of a party in litigation having access to a judge's briefs from her law clerks . . . This breach reinforces

---

[54] SEC v. Cochran, 143 S. Ct. 890 (2023), Notice at 21-1293, Dkt. 3; Cochran v. SEC, 2019 WL 1359252, Notice at 4:19cv66, Dkt. 45.

[55] Jarkesy v. SEC, 34 F.4th 446 (5th Cir. 2022) (Jarkesy II), Notice at 20-61007, Dkt. 00516268389.

the problem with the SEC's administrative process in which the commission has total discretion to deprive parties of their ability to have matters litigated in federal court.[56]

Instapundit declared: "The SEC needs a Special Counsel Investigation," stressing,

> Understand: The "prosecutors" at the SEC illegally accessed files belonging to the "judges." This raises serious questions about the trustworthiness of the SEC, and demands an outside investigation with subpoena power.[57]

What really happened here? We don't know. The SEC will not tell us.

On July 19, 2022, Congress called SEC Chairman Gary Gensler for questioning, but Gensler sent SEC Director of Enforcement Gurbir Grewal in his stead. Asked if SEC's Inspector General (IG) was investigating, Grewal claimed ignorance, telling Rep. William Huizenga: "I would direct you to the office of [the] Inspector General."[58] Avoiding the IG process allows the agency to avoid mandatory criminal referrals to the Department of Justice and detailed reports to Congress.

Instead, SEC hired the Berkeley Research Group (BRG) to conduct an internal investigation. Public records show that BRG regularly provides expert witness and other services to the SEC in its enforcement actions under contracts totaling millions of dollars.

The notices filed with the *Cochran* and *Jarkesy* courts represented that BRG found "nothing to see here," while adding that the investigation was not complete and the breach had also occurred in other, unnamed cases.

Promptly filed Freedom of Information Act (FOIA) requests of the SEC turned up nothing other than a redacted copy of the BRG contract, blacking out the cost and hourly rates for this

---

[56] Dave Michaels, *SEC Says Employees Improperly Accessed Privileged Legal Records*, WALL ST. J. (April 6, 2022), https://tinyurl.com/42cz9mbm.

[57] Glenn Reynolds, *The SEC Needs a Special Counsel Investigation*, INSTAPUNDIT.COM (April 14, 2022, 10:14 AM) https://tinyurl.com/2xm5px6b.

[58] U.S. House Committee on Financial Services-Oversight of the SEC's Division of Enforcement [hereinafter House Hearing] (July 19, 2022), https://tinyurl.com/3evp9kr6, at 26:00–28:00.

internal investigation.[59] FOIA litigation against SEC is pending in *Cochran* and in the Southern District of Texas for *Jarkesy*. The SEC produced no documents, emails, or witness interviews relating to the breach.

Grewal represented to Congress that the control deficiency was publicly reported when it happened.[60] Later in the hearing, Rep. Huizenga presented him with information from the *Wall Street Journal* that the breach dated back to 2017 and the SEC discovered it in the fall of 2021, but only disclosed it in April of 2022.[61]

H. CASE DISMISSED! OH WAIT, 42 CASES DISMISSED!

The next-to-final and most intriguing aspect of *Axon/Cochran* is what happened afterwards. Guests at The Hotel California sought release. Marian Young, who had been trapped in the administrative maze for years, had a fully briefed mandamus petition before the Fifth Circuit that was ripe for decision. Just days after *Axon/Cochran*, Christopher Gibson filed a complaint in a Georgia district court. And Michelle Cochran was ready to file a fresh complaint in the Northern District of Texas.

So . . . rather than allow Michelle Cochran—or Gibson or Young— to challenge the constitutionality of their SEC administrative enforcement proceedings, on June 2, 2023, the SEC dismissed all 42 open proceedings that could have brought these questions to an Article III Court. Forty-five industry bar orders were also lifted. A 10-year quest by at least 12 intrepid plaintiffs for judicial review of these unconstitutional proceedings was wiped out in the blink of an eye. Untold years of enforcement resources over 10 years and millions of taxpayer dollars were tossed to the wind.

---

[59] If there is one thing that is clearly not covered by any FOIA exception, it would be the cost incurred by SEC privatizing an investigation to a vendor with a conflict of interest, when a taxpayer-supported IG office is salaried and charged with the duty of conducting such internal investigations. For what the SEC does to private individuals who engage in internal coverups, see *SEC v. Engler*, 2022 WL 4596745 (E.D.N.Y. 2022).

[60] House Hearing, *supra* note 58, at 26:24-28:00.

[61] *Id.* at 1:28:00. The *Wall Street Journal* article states that the breach was discovered in the fall of 2021. Rep. Huizenga likely erred in saying the fall of 2020. In any event, there was at least a six-month delay in notifying only two—Cochran and Jarkesy—of the many affected respondents, and that notification came only in a public filing. The other 40 respondents were not informed for over a year and a half. SEC claims that it owes no disclosure in affected cases that are closed or settled.

What reason did the SEC give for its unprecedented, sweeping attempt to insulate its administrative processes from judicial review?

The "control deficiency."

The same one SEC said was a nothingburger. Where SEC says no one's rights to a fair adjudication were compromised, while fighting any disclosure whatsoever in the Freedom of Information proceedings and in the FOIA federal suit.

These unprecedented dismissal orders and lifts of industry bars in nearly 90 matters were accompanied by a report apparently prepared by BRG. It's a sorry piece of work, long on conclusory exculpatory statements and devoid of primary documents, interviews, or any other material that Cochran, Gibson, and others could have readily obtained in litigation to test those *ipse dixit* claims that there is "nothing to see here." The SEC has taken the position in the FOIA litigation that this is all the public will get. The SEC's view is that enforcement targets in closed or settled cases tainted by the "control deficiency" should get no relief at all, even though they may be the ones most damaged by a corrupted prosecution.

The sole exception to the dismissal orders? George Jarkesy, whose case produced a blockbuster ruling by a Fifth Circuit panel holding that those administrative proceedings were unconstitutional because:

> (1) the SEC's in-house adjudication of [Jarkesy's and his fund's] case violated their Seventh Amendment right to a jury trial; (2) Congress unconstitutionally delegated legislative power to the SEC by failing to provide an intelligible principle by which the SEC would exercise the delegated power, in violation of Article I's vesting of "all" legislative power in Congress; and (3) statutory removal restrictions on SEC ALJs violate the Take Care Clause of Article II.[62]

Jarkesy is now the lone standard bearer. SEC likely felt that having just petitioned for certiorari, it could not include the case in the June 2 dismissal orders. Certiorari was granted in *Jarkesy* on June 30, 2023.

The fallout from this unprecedented mass dismissal seriously impacts the rule of law. People in settled cases are silenced. Enforcement respondents in closed cases are forever denied relief. And in

---

[62] *Jarkesy II*, 34 F.4th at 449.

the 42 just-dismissed cases, the SEC seeks massive nullification of their constitutional rights—and *forever denies them exoneration on the merits or any relief for the SEC's misconduct.* SEC's undeniable goal is obviously to bury the record of what went on using the "control deficiency" as a cynical ploy to control the federal dockets by dismissing any case that could bring the "fundamental, even existential" claims that SEC, "as currently structured, [is] unconstitutional in much of [its] work."[63]

I. A RECORD OF DECEPTION AND DEFIANCE ACROSS AGENCIES

This article opened with a bill of particulars about the defects of agency adjudication, the most glaring and dangerous of which is "the combination of prosecutorial and adjudication functions." When your judge's boss is also your prosecutor, this constitutes not only a structural constitutional violation but an obvious due process violation. Throw in regulation by enforcement, where agency ALJs make up rules out of whole cloth that they apply retroactively, and an enforcement division that uses prior ALJ rulings, settlements, and guidance as sources of law,[64] and it becomes clear that Americans' civil liberties are at the mercy of agencies that have become governments unto themselves. When agencies exercise law making, enforcement and adjudication powers in one "efficient" and wildly unconstitutional agency, "it is the very definition of tyranny."[65]

---

[63] *Axon/Cochran*, 143 S. Ct. 890, 897.

[64] *See* Commissioner Hester Peirce, SEC, The Why Behind the No: Remarks at the 50th Annual Rocky Mountain Securities Conference (May 11, 2018), https://bit.ly/44swzuw ("[A] settlement negotiated by someone desperate to end an investigation that is disrupting or destroying her life should not form the basis on which the law applicable to others is based."; "Enforcement is a faster and more convenient approach to establishing obligations than rulemaking given how cumbersome and time-consuming the rulemaking process is under the Administrative Procedure Act ('APA'). However, the APA's obstacles to rulemaking are intentional; before imposing a new regulatory burden, an agency must take a set of steps designed to ensure that there is a problem that needs fixing and that the agency's solution is appropriate.").

[65] "The accumulation of all powers, legislative, executive, and judiciary, in the same hands, whether of one, a few, or many, and whether hereditary, self-appointed, or elective, may justly be pronounced the very definition of tyranny." FEDERALIST No. 47 (Madison).

The SEC is far from the only administrative agency that thinks it is a law unto itself. Despite the *Lucia* case's requirement that all federal agencies properly appoint their ALJs, the Department of Transportation (DOT) has yet to do so. DOT has not only conceded that it ignored *Lucia*, allowing an unappointed officer to preside over its in-house adjudications for the last four years; it disclosed this in order to avoid answering for that official's unconstitutional removal protections.[66] Just days after the removal challenge was deemed mooted by this disclosure, that same unappointed, tenure-protected ALJ issued penalties in another enforcement action.[67] In other words, DOT strategically revealed predicate ALJ unconstitutionality to dodge the removal bullet, but it was happy to continue in its merrily multiplied unconstitutional ways.[68] In what world does this make any sense?

III. Conclusion

Axon/Cochran is a cross-agency ruling with legs that will travel well beyond the SEC and FTC. Challenges to the FDIC, DOT, and other agencies are already being litigated in the federal courts.[69] This means that however hard the SEC tries to avoid judicial oversight of the constitutionality of its adjudications—including tossing unlawful cases like a speakeasy before a raid—these challenges will continue in the courts with respect to any agency that deprives Americans of their constitutional liberties.

This discussion has not only sought to explore the many formal constitutional and due process deficits of administrative adjudication. It has also delved into the dark underbelly of agency

---

[66] Polyweave Packaging v. DOT, 2023 WL 1112247 (6th Cir. 2023), Motion at 21-4202, Dkt. 29.

[67] Metal Conversion Tech. v. DOT, 2023 WL 4789084 (11th Cir. 2023), Petition at 22-14140, Dkt. 1-2.

[68] I am indebted to my colleague Sheng Li for this example of agency defiance of the Supreme Court's administrative law rulings.

[69] *See e.g.*, Burgess v. FDIC, No. 7:22-cv-00100-O, 2022 WL 17173893 (N.D. Tex. Nov. 6, 2022); Alpine Securities Corp. v. FINRA, No. 23-5129, 2023 WL 4703307 (D.D.C. Jul. 5, 2023); John Doe v. PCAOB, No. 3:23-cv-00149-S, 2023 WL 2988259 (N.D. Tex Jan. 26, 2023); Polyweave Packaging Inc. v. DOT, 51 F.4th 675 (6th Cir. 2023); gh PACKAGE PRODUCT TESTING AND CONSULTING, INC., v. Buttigieg, 1:23-cv-00403-MRB (S.D. Ohio 2023); Colt & Joe Trucking v. DOT, 23-9564 (10th Cir 2023); POSTMEDS, INC. v. DEA, No. 1:23-cv-00648 (E.D. Va. 2023); Illumina, Inc.v. FTC, No. 23-60167 (5th Cir. 2023).

misconduct, particularly, but not solely, at the SEC. From the SEC's attempt to suppress the truth about its ALJ's lack of appointments in *Timbervest*, to Judge Elliot's myriad abuses of power,[70] to the DOT's assumption of immunity from law, to the FTC's delusion that it has the power to order Axon to surrender its intellectual property to a competitor, to the SEC's illegally promulgated gag rule;[71] to the SEC's lockup of respondents for years in a Hotel California; to the "control deficiency" showing years-long illegal file sharing in scores of cases, and the SEC's current disdain for and refusal to disclose to Congress, FOIA and the courts any records regarding that breach—all lead to the conclusion that our agencies are out of control.

Justice Gorsuch showed his concern about such lawlessness when he noted that agencies can "outlast or outspend" their targets and use this power "as leverage to extract settlement terms they could not lawfully obtain any other way."[72] This applies to gags, Axon's IP, settlement conditions on use of insurance or tax deductions, and even penalties that follow a regulated person from one company to another and purport to bind a new company that was not a party to the proceeding.[73]

Justice Robert Jackson famously stated in *Chenery II*, "Surely an administrative agency is not a law unto itself."[74] Sadly, in the modern government it is! The Founders understood all too well that men are not angels. The control deficiency that tainted the *Cochran* and *Jarkesy* adjudications and the FTC's lawless demand that Axon surrender its

---

[70] Peggy Little, *Ray Lucia's Mythic Lift*, NCLA (Jun. 19, 2020), https://tinyurl.com/6axtvr24.

[71] Petition to Amend SEC Gag Rule, October 30, 2018, https://tinyurl.com/bdhff7dh; Petition to Amend CFTC Gag Rule, July 18, 2019, https://tinyurl.com/bdzb5xrs.

[72] *Axon/Cochran*, 143 S. Ct. at 918. *See also id.* at 907 n.4: *See* P. HAMBURGER, PURCHASING SUBMISSION: CONDITIONS, POWER, AND FREEDOM 223 (2021) (describing this as "regulatory extortion"); Douglas H. Ginsburg & Joshua D. Wright, *Antitrust Settlement: The Culture of Consent, in* 1 WILLIAM E. KOVACIC: AN ANTITRUST TRIBUTE 177 (N. Charbit et al. eds. 2013) ("Consent decrees create potential for an enforcement agency to extract from parties under investigation commitments well beyond what the agency could obtain in litigation").

[73] In the Matter of Drizly, LLC, No. C-4780, Decision & Order, 10 (F.T.C. Jan. 9, 2023). https://tinyurl.com/4hnrtwnr, the consent order provision is at PDF page 21 (consent order page 10).

[74] *SEC v. Chenery Corp.* (II), 332 U.S. 194, 215 (1947) (Jackson J., dissenting).

patents shows, like nothing else can, how wise the Framers were to insist that the powers of government be separated.

The Fifth Circuit's en banc concurrence in *Cochran* found the Supreme Court's prescient warnings in *Jones v. SEC* to be an oracle about the dangers of runaway administrative power:

> The action of the commission finds no support in right principle or in law. It is wholly unreasonable and arbitrary. It violates the cardinal precept upon which the constitutional safeguards of personal liberty ultimately rest—that this shall be a government of laws—because to the precise extent that the mere will of an official or an official body is permitted to take the place of allowable official discretion or to supplant the standing law as a rule of human conduct, the government ceases to be one of laws and becomes an autocracy. Against the threat of such a contingency the courts have always been vigilant, and, if they are to perform their constitutional duties in the future, must never cease to be vigilant, to detect and turn aside the danger at its beginning. . . . If [administrative agencies] . . . are permitted gradually to extend their powers by encroachments—even petty encroachments—upon the fundamental rights, privileges and immunities of the people, we shall in the end, while avoiding the fatal consequences of a supreme autocracy, become submerged by a multitude of minor invasions of personal rights, less destructive but no less violative of constitutional guaranties.[75]

The SEC's disturbing evasions of law and defiant shrugging off of judicial review should serve as a catalyst for all Americans to take the agencies to court when they infringe upon personal liberties—to keep the administrative state within constitutional bounds, its regulatory guardrails, and the law.

---

[75] *Jones v. SEC*, 298 U.S. 1, 23–25 (1936).

The Absurdity of Criminalizing Encouraging Words

*Eric Franklin Amarante**

Introduction

No one jaywalks in Seattle.[1] It's the damnedest thing. If you've never been to Seattle, you'll have to trust me—it's truly astonishing to see grown adults wait patiently for a "WALK" sign with nary a car in sight.

Although I lived in Seattle for a time, I grew up in Texas and knew how to cross a street. So back in 2010, when I crossed Third Avenue as the red "DON'T WALK" light stopped blinking, Sullivan, my Seattlelite friend, stayed behind. We spent a few dumb seconds standing on opposite curbs, staring at the empty street between us, and waiting for the light to change. I finally got impatient and said, "Dude, come on!" After a slight hesitation, he jogged across the street. Moments later, a cop on a bike rolled up and gave him a $70 ticket.

Do I bear any fault here? A decent argument could be made. If not for my encouragement, Sullivan would've followed the law, waited for the light to change, and been $70 richer. Had I inadvertently aided and abetted a minor traffic violation?

Now let's consider a different scenario. Imagine that you hired someone to clean your home. This person happens to be undocumented and lives in the United States in violation of immigration laws. One day, she tells you that she plans to go to her home country for a family obligation. You know that it might not only be very difficult for her to return, but also that crossing the border would

---

* Eric Franklin Amarante is an Associate Professor at the University of Tennessee College of Law.

[1] *See* Deborah Wang & Adwoa Gyimah-Brempong, *Why Don't Longtime Seattleites Jaywalk?*, NPR (July 4, 2019), https://tinyurl.com/mr36r54h.

constitute a separate, additional offense. So, you implore her not to leave the country, telling her, "Don't leave the country, you won't be able to get back in."[2]

Remaining in the United States without proper documentation is a civil violation, punishable by a $500 fine.[3] If your housekeeper takes your advice and stays in the United States, do you bear any fault? Similar to my aiding and abetting Sullivan's jaywalking, it feels like you might have aided and abetted a civil violation of our country's immigration laws.

However intuitive this logic may be, thanks to the First Amendment's protection of speech, most speech cannot be prohibited by the government. There are, of course, exceptions, but this simple understanding of our freedom of speech rights is a good place to start. And it suggests that neither "don't leave the country, you won't be able to get back in," nor "dude, cross the street," should be punishable. After all, these are only words, and the First Amendment prohibits the government from making my words illegal.

But we've decided that some words are so harmful that they ought to be punishable. For example, words that incite illegal acts, words that defame, words that defraud, "fighting words," and obscene speech are not protected by the First Amendment.[4] Of particular interest to this article is the "speech integral to criminal conduct" exception. This exception allows the government to criminalize speech that is tantamount to the prohibited conduct. In other words, this exception reaches speech that serves as "a mechanism or instrumentality in the commission of a separate unlawful act."[5] This is why the government can criminalize, for example, conspiracy to commit a crime and requests for illegal material, even if there is no act other than speaking.

So would I bear liability for hollering "dude, come on!" to Sullivan? Thankfully, no. Even though the jaywalking would not likely have occurred without my speech, my speech was not "integral" to

---

[2] These facts closely track *United States v. Henderson*, 857 F. Supp. 2d 191 (D. Mass. 2012).

[3] 8 U.S.C. § 1324d(a)(2).

[4] *See, e.g.,* Chaplinsky v. New Hampshire, 315 U.S. 568, 571–72 (1942); Brandenburg v. Ohio 395 U.S. 444, 447 (1969); Miller v. California 413 U.S. 15, 18–19, 21 (1973).

[5] People v. Relerford, 104 N.E.3d 341, 352 (Ill. 2017).

Sullivan's act. At worst, I was merely advocating for illegal conduct, something that the First Amendment protects. For similar reasons, one might assume that uttering "don't leave the country, you won't be able to get back in" is merely advocacy of illegal activity, and not speech that is "integral" to criminal conduct.

But now imagine that a court concludes that my words ("dude, come on") were deemed to be not only integral to jaywalking, but also a felony. Because jaywalking is a civil violation, Sullivan would only owe $70 for failing to respect a traffic light, but I would get up to ten years in jail for encouraging his illegality.

With only slightly less absurdity, this is the effect of a little-used subsection of the Immigration Reform and Control Act ("IRCA"). Although it is only a civil violation for a noncitizen to stay in the United States without proper documentation,[6] IRCA makes it a felony for anyone to "encourage[] or induce[]" a noncitizen to, among other things, "reside in the United States" (I will call this the "Encouragement Provision").[7] Thus, under the Encouragement Provision, the person who commits the prohibited act (i.e., staying in the United States without documentation) is subject to a civil penalty, while the person who encourages the act is a felon.

There are two major problems here. The first is that the Encouragement Provision, on its face, covers an unduly large amount of speech. It doesn't take a great imagination to conjure scenarios in which speech would be impermissibly restricted by a law that criminalizes mere encouragement. And indeed, litigants and critics have argued that the plain language of the Encouragement Provision prohibits large swaths of constitutionally protected speech, including legal advice, political advocacy, and intimate discussions among family members.[8] As such, these critics argue that the Encouragement Provision is facially invalid because of

---

[6] *See* Arizona v. United States, 567 U.S. 387, 407 (2012) ("As a general rule, it is not a crime for a removable alien to remain present in the United States.").

[7] 8 U.S.C. § 1324(a)(1)(A)(iv).

[8] *See* United States v. Sineneng-Smith, 910 F.3d 461, 483–84 (2018) (noting that the statute's prohibition reaches "a loving grandmother who urges her grandson to over stay his visa, by telling him 'I encourage you to stay'" and a speaker at a rally who says, "I encourage all you folks out there without legal status to stay in the U.S.!"), *rev'd*, 140 S. Ct. 1575 (2020).

overbreadth.[9] The second problem is that if the Encouragement Provision makes it a felony to encourage someone to commit a civil violation (i.e., staying in the United States without documentation), it would be an outlier in the "speech integral to criminal conduct" exception's jurisprudence. Since *Giboney v. Empire Storage & Ice Co.*,[10] the leading case on the "speech integral to criminal conduct" exception, the Supreme Court has never punished the solicitation of a civilly punishable act as a crime.[11] If the Encouragement Provision were to be upheld, it would be the first time.

In *United States v. Hansen*, the Supreme Court had a chance to assess the constitutionality of the Encouragement Provision and mostly blew it.[12] In *Hansen*, the Court ultimately dismissed the overbreadth challenge with a tortured and strained statutory interpretation, and the expansion of the "speech integral to criminal conduct" exception was mostly ignored.[13] Along the way, the court left the Encouragement Provision intact, established a difficult precedent for future overbreadth challenges, and for the first time, blessed a criminal punishment for speech integral to a civil violation.

This article proceeds in four parts. Part I discusses the facts of *Hansen*, briefly describing the scam that precipitated Mr. Hansen's conviction under the Encouragement Provision. Part II examines the Supreme Court's holding in *Hansen*, highlighting the unorthodox statutory interpretation that led the court to dismiss the overbreadth challenge. Part III discusses an issue that the Supreme Court left largely unaddressed: the expansion of the "speech integral to criminal conduct" exception to permit legislatures to apply *criminal* penalties to speech that is integral to *civil* violations. Part III also briefly considers the future of overbreadth challenges after *Hansen*, and part IV is a conclusion.

---

[9] Eric Franklin Amarante, *Criminalizing Immigrant Entrepreneurs (and Their Lawyers)*, 61 B.C. L. Rev. 1323, 1341 (2020).

[10] 336 U.S. 490 (1949).

[11] For a fulsome discussion of the "speech integral to criminal conduct" exception, see Eugene Volokh, *The "Speech Integral to Criminal Conduct" Exception*, 101 CORNELL L. REV. 981 (2016).

[12] 143 S. Ct. 1932 (2023).

[13] *See id.* at 1946–48.

I. Helaman Hansen: A Would-be Free Speech Anti-Hero

We have crafted the contours of our freedom of speech rights largely by defending a gaggle of assholes.[14] Helaman Hansen, the defendant in *Hansen*, would fit right in. Hansen was arrested for scamming millions of dollars out of hundreds of undocumented people with a fraudulent promise of U.S. citizenship. In a depressingly common scheme, Hansen offered a path to citizenship through adult adoption—something that doesn't exist unless you were adopted as a child[15]—and urged his clients to overstay visas and remain in the United States. In the process, he amassed almost $2 million from over 450 noncitizens. In addition to fraud, Hansen was convicted of unlawfully encouraging or inducing illegal immigration under the Encouragement Provision. Hansen challenged this part of the conviction, arguing that the Encouragement Provision was an unconstitutionally overbroad restriction of speech.[16]

Hansen's timing was impeccable. Around the same time, the Ninth Circuit heard the case of *United States v. Sineneng-Smith*.[17] In that case, Evelyn Sineneng-Smith promised legal permanent residence to noncitizens through a long-defunct labor certification program. In other words, like Hansen, Sineneng-Smith conned numerous families out of large sums of money with the false promise of citizenship. Unlike Hansen, Sineneng-Smith did not challenge the constitutionality of the Encouragement Provision. Undaunted, the Ninth Circuit struck down the Encouragement Provision as unconstitutionally overbroad, despite Sineneng-Smith's failure to raise this claim. More specifically, the Ninth Circuit held that the Encouragement Provision criminalized not only conduct, but also speech; that it could not be saved by established exceptions to the First Amendment (holding that the speech criminalized by the Encouragement Provision was neither incitement nor aiding and abetting); and that there was a real danger that the Encouragement Provision would capture protected speech.[18]

---

[14] *See, e.g.*, Hustler Mag. v. Falwell, 485 U.S. 46 (1988); Nat'l Socialist Party of Am. v. Vill. of Skokie, 432 U.S. 43 (1977).

[15] *See Adult Adoptees and U.S. Citizenship*, U.S. Citizenship and Immigr. Servs., https://tinyurl.com/5bb9shrc (last visited Aug. 30, 2023).

[16] *See Hansen*, 143 S. Ct. at 1938.

[17] 910 F.3d 461 (2018), *rev'd*, 140 S. Ct. 1575 (2020).

[18] *See id.* at 482, 485.

Good news for Hansen? Well, not so fast. This proved to be a short-lived victory, as the Supreme Court quickly vacated *Sineneng-Smith*, chiding the Ninth Circuit for raising the overbreadth issue in the absence of presentation by the parties.[19] Turns out, courts are not supposed to raise constitutional issues willy-nilly. Or in the words of Justice Ruth Bader Ginsburg, courts "do not, or should not, sally forth each day looking for wrongs to right. [They] wait for cases to come to [them], and when [cases arise, courts] normally decide only questions presented by the parties."[20] Thus, *Sineneng-Smith* was vacated. But recall that Hansen's case was waiting to be heard and his appeal raised the overbreadth issue. Thus, with no sallying required, the Ninth Circuit had another chance to assess the constitutionality of the Encouragement Provision. This is how the Ninth Circuit, for the second time, struck down the Encouragement Provision as facially overbroad.[21]

So this time, really good news for Hansen? Again, not so fast. The Supreme Court ultimately disagreed with the Ninth Circuit again, upheld the Encouragement Provision, and robbed Hansen of his well-earned spot in the infamous canon of First Amendment ne'er-do-wells. Along the way, the Court made future overbreadth challenges very difficult and rather thoughtlessly expanded the First Amendment's "speech integral to criminal conduct" exception.

II. Strong Medicine, Weak Statutory Interpretation

A. The Overbreadth Doctrine, Generally

The overbreadth doctrine is used to invalidate statutes that restrict a substantial amount of constitutionally protected speech. Needless to say, invalidating a statute passed by a democratically elected legislature is a big deal, and it should make courts uncomfortable.[22] For this reason, the Supreme Court has called the overbreadth doctrine

---

[19] United States v. Sineneng-Smith, 140 S. Ct. 1575, 1578 (2020).

[20] *Id.* at 1579 (quoting United States v. Samuels, 808 F. 2d 1298, 1301 (8th Cir. 1987) (Arnold, J., concurring)).

[21] United States v. Hansen, 25 F. 4th 1103, 1106 (9th Cir. 2022), *rev'd*, 143 S. Ct. 1932 (2023).

[22] *See* William Baude & Stephen E. Sachs, *The Law of Interpretation*, 130 HARV. L. REV. 1079, 1097 (2017) (noting that interpreting statutes "might seem to invade the legislature's authority, denying it the power to express its will as it pleases").

"strong medicine" that should not be "casually employed."[23] But of course, sometimes strong medicine is appropriate. After all, chemotherapy sucks, but it is preferable to cancer.[24] If the overbreadth doctrine is chemotherapy, the cancer is an impermissibly broad statute's tendency to chill speech. "Chilling" speech, or deterring people from engaging in constitutionally protected speech from fear of prosecution, is the evil targeted by the overbreadth doctrine. As noted by Justice Antonin Scalia, "the threat of enforcement of an overbroad law deters people from engaging in constitutionally protected speech, inhibiting the free exchange of ideas."[25]

In other words, we have two potential harms here that must be balanced. On the one hand, we value speech and do not want poorly drafted statutes to limit what we can say. On the other hand, criminal laws aim to prohibit some sort of harmful activity, and striking down a law for overbreadth effectively overrules the actions of a democratically elected legislature. Therein lies the tension; we do not want to chill speech, but we also do not want the judiciary to invalidate laws for fear of unlikely—or even limited—chilling. The overbreadth analysis attempts to strike an appropriate balance between these two competing desires.

There are two prongs to an overbreadth analysis: First, a court determines what the statute says; second, the court weighs whether the statute, properly construed, "prohibits a substantial amount of protected speech relative to its plainly legitimate sweep."[26] The first step involves basic statutory interpretation. Once the court has determined what the statute says (or more precisely, what type of speech is prohibited), the second step requires the court to weigh the amount of protected speech prohibited by the challenged statute against the amount of speech properly restricted. If the amount of protected speech is substantial, "not only in an absolute sense, but

---

[23] L.A. Police Dep't v. United Reporting Publ'g Corp., 528 U.S. 32, 39 (1999) (quoting *New York v. Ferber*, 458 U.S. 747, 769 (1982)).

[24] *See* Friends of Georges, Inc. v. Mulroy, 2023 U.S. Dist. LEXIS 96766, at 97–98 ("The Court understands that the overbreadth doctrine is strong medicine. But a debilitated patient should not forgo medicine on account of its strength.").

[25] United States v. Williams, 553 U.S. 285, 292 (2008).

[26] *Hansen*, 143 S. Ct. at 1939 (citing Williams, 553 U.S. at 292) (internal quotation marks omitted).

also relative to the statute's plainly legitimate sweep," then the statute should be held invalid.[27]

B. The Hansen Court's Interpretative Odyssey

As noted above, the first step in the overbreadth analysis is for the court to interpret the statute to determine what speech the statute prohibits. Here, the Encouragement Provision makes it a crime to "encourage" and "induce" undocumented people to stay in the United States. Statutory interpretation normally—and intuitively, I might add—starts by reading the text. One would expect a court to begin its analysis by determining the meaning of the words used in the statute, but the Hansen court took a different approach. Rather than determining what "encourage" or "induce" might mean, the Court launched its analysis with an exploration of the meaning of "solicitation and facilitation."[28]

This is a curious approach, as neither "solicitation" nor "facilitation" appears in the Encouragement Provision. Undaunted, the seven-Justice majority (with Justice Amy Coney Barrett writing for the Court) launched into a discussion of the meaning of these words—words that, again, are not in the statute at issue. The majority pointed out that "encourage" and "induce" are often used to define "solicit" and "facilitate," which leads the majority to conclude that the definitions are interchangeable.[29] Needless to say, as Justice Ketanji Brown Jackson noted in dissent (with some well-earned snark), this is not "how dictionary definitions tend to work" and "the fact that a word is used to help define another word does not necessarily mean that the former is synonymous with the latter or incorporates all of its connotations."[30] To illustrate, Jackson pointed out that "the word 'furniture' might be used in the definition of a 'chair,' but not all pieces of furniture are chairs, nor do all pieces of furniture have four legs or other common chair-like characteristics."[31]

To justify this novel interpretive approach, the majority traced the history of the various antecedents of the Encouragement Provision,

[27] Williams, 553 U.S. at 292.
[28] Hansen, 143 S. Ct. at 1940.
[29] Id. at 1940–41.
[30] Id. at 1955 (Jackson, J., dissenting).
[31] Id.

going as far back as 1885 and following the thread to analyze amendments enacted in 1903, 1907, 1917, and 1952. In early iterations of the Encouragement Provision, the statute used the words "assist" and "solicit."[32] This might have justified the majority's decision to explore the meanings of the words "solicitation" and "facilitation," if not for the fact that "assist" and "solicit" were deleted by Congress in 1952.[33] It is such an obvious point that it seems absurd to state, but statutory interpretation normally assumes deletions are intentional. As such, courts are admonished to "presume differences in language . . . convey differences in meaning."[34] But instead of giving these deletions any meaning—i.e., instead of assuming that the legislature intentionally deleted "assist" and "solicit"—the majority concluded that the deletions were not meant to change the statute's meaning. Without any evidence, the majority concluded that the deletions were a product of congressional attempts to streamline the statute.[35]

Justice Jackson questioned this historical analysis. First, she noted that the history of the statute strongly evinces a trend of expanding, rather than narrowing, the statute's reach. As support, Jackson pointed out that in 1952, Congress "*deleted* the statute's references to solicitation and assistance—leaving 'encourages' and 'induces' to stand alone."[36] Jackson noted that in 1986, Congress "removed the *mens rea* requirement relating to the encouragement or inducement element;" and "made it a crime to encourage or induce an unauthorized noncitizen not merely to *enter* the United States, but also to encourage or induce such a person to 'reside' here unlawfully."[37] Jackson argued that taken in total, these changes strongly indicate a desire to expand the reach of the Encouragement Provision.[38] This history flies in the face of the majority's adoption of a narrowing interpretation.[39]

---

[32] *Id.* at 1943–44 (majority op.).

[33] *See id.* at 1943–44.

[34] *Id.* at 1958 (Jackson, J., dissenting) (citing BNSF R. Co. v. Loos, 139 S. Ct. 893, 902 (2019))

[35] *See id.* at 1944 (majority op.).

[36] *Id.* at 1956 (Jackson, J., dissenting) (emphasis in original).

[37] *Id.* at 1956–57 (emphasis in original).

[38] *See id.* at 1956 (noting that "[t]he history of the encouragement provision is a tale of expansion.").

[39] *See id.* at 1957–58 ("Tracing the history over time clearly establishes that Congress deleted the very narrowing terms that the majority now reads back into the statute.").

Not only does the history of the statute suggest a different interpretation, but also the subsection following the Encouragement Provision is perhaps more damning to the majority's interpretation. This subsection imposes criminal penalties on anyone who "aids or abets the commission" of certain acts.[40] But by interpreting "encourage" and "induce" to have the same legal effect as "facilitate" and "solicit" (the words often used in criminal statutes to capture aiding and abetting), the majority effectively added an aiding and abetting component to the Encouragement Provision. The only problem is that such a provision already existed in another section of the statute, casting doubt upon the majority's interpretation. In other words, "Congress knows how to create an aiding and abetting prohibition when it wants to" and "it did not do so in" the Encouragement Provision.[41]

Now, to be clear, I'm not suggesting the majority had forgotten how to interpret a statute. Indeed, the majority's interpretation, however unorthodox, was inspired by good intentions. Ultimately, the majority's interpretation was driven by the principle of constitutional avoidance.[42] Under this doctrine, if the Supreme Court has two interpretations of a statute—one unconstitutional and one constitutional—it ought to adopt the constitutional interpretation to avoid a conflict.[43] Following this logic, the majority reimagined the meaning of the Encouragement Provision in order to avoid its invalidation, thereby respecting the legislature's role in writing and enacting laws. But counterintuitively, by relying upon constitutional avoidance to reinterpret the Encouragement Provision, the majority's interpretive odyssey unceremoniously stepped all over Congress's role in drafting legislation. The majority's interpretation changed the plain meaning of the statute to such a degree that it usurped Congress's drafting role by effectively rewriting the Encouragement Provision. Although recognizing that the Court should "seek harmony" and not "manufacture conflict," Jackson emphasized that

---

[40] 8 U.S.C. § 1324(a)(1)(A)(v)(II).

[41] *Hansen*, 143 S. Ct. at 1956 (Jackson, J., dissenting).

[42] *See id.* 1946 (majority op.) ("When legislation and the Constitution brush up against each other, our task is to seek harmony, not to manufacture conflict.").

[43] Panama R.R. Co. v. Johnson, 264 U.S. 375, 390 (1924).

"this Court also has a duty to refrain from taking the legislative reins and revising the text of a statute."[44]

Thus, we have yet another tension between two competing dictates: constitutional avoidance and judicial usurpation of the legislature. Jackson argued that the majority gave the doctrine of constitutional avoidance too much weight and in the process mangled the ordinary principles of statutory interpretation. I agree with Jackson. After all, as Justice Samuel Alito has warned, constitutional avoidance "comes into play only when, after the application of *ordinary textual analysis*, the statute is found to be susceptible of more than one construction," and it should not be used to "rewrite a statute."[45] Here, the majority engaged in *extra*ordinary textual analysis and effectively rewrote the Encouragement Provision.

To be sure, it is appropriate for the Court to adopt a reasonable construction of a statute if that construction would render the statute constitutional.[46] But an unduly strained interpretation of a statute trespasses upon the legislative realm just as egregiously as the overbreadth doctrine's invalidation of a statute. Such an interpretation amounts to modification, which is "neither [the Supreme Court's] job nor [its] prerogative."[47] To make her point, Jackson highlighted the majority's argument that "solicitation and facilitation . . . require 'an *intent* to bring about a particular unlawful act.'"[48] Jackson explained that neither the text of the Encouragement Provision nor the ordinary meanings of "encourages or induces" (as opposed to "facilitate" and "solicit") require intent. One can encourage or induce someone to do something without intending to do so, something that I think everyone can sympathize with.[49] I spent years telling my sisters-in-law how great Knoxville was, but I was still surprised that they ended up becoming my neighbors.[50] But I digress. The important

---

[44] *Hansen*, 143 S. Ct. at 1954 (Jackson, J., dissenting).

[45] Jennings v. Rodriguez, 138 S. Ct. 830, 842, 843 (2018) (emphasis added).

[46] *See Williams*, 553 U.S. at 307 (Stevens, J., concurring).

[47] *Hansen*, 143 S. Ct. at 1952 (Jackson, J., dissenting).

[48] *Id.* at 1955 (quoting *id.* at 1940 (majority op.)). (emphasis in original).

[49] *See id.* at 1955–56 ("By describing the attractions of my hometown, for instance, I might end up inducing a listener to move there, even if that was not my intent.").

[50] Jackie and Day, I'm kidding! I love that you live here.

point is that the majority's interpretation inserted a *mens rea* element into the Encouragement Provision.

In this manner, the majority decided that the ghosts of "assist" and "solicit" should inform its interpretation of "encourage" and "induce." These long-deleted words allowed the majority to suggest that the definitions of "encourage" and "induce" have "solicitation and facilitation" overtones because they "substantially overlap in meaning" with "assist" and "solicit."[51] These overtones helped the majority settle upon a narrow construction of the Encouragement Provision, one that "reaches no further than the purposeful solicitation and facilitation of specific acts known to violate federal law."[52] In the process, the majority effectively rewrote the Encouragement Provision to apply only to a narrow category of speech.

C. The balancing act of the overbreadth analysis.

Once the statute's meaning has been determined, the second prong of overbreadth analysis charges the court with weighing the statute's unconstitutional applications against its lawful applications. If a statute negatively affects only an insignificant amount of constitutionally protected speech while simultaneously covering many unprotected activities, then the statute is properly drafted and an overbreadth challenge will fail. Ultimately, the question is whether the constitutional harm is minor when compared to the statute's constitutionally appropriate reach.

The majority approached this balancing test by first identifying the valid scope of the Encouragement Provision. To do so, the majority recited a list of prosecutions under the Encouragement Provision of nonexpressive conduct (i.e., conduct not protected by the First Amendment).[53] These included prosecutions for smuggling undocumented people into the United States, procuring counterfeit identification documents, and selling fake Social Security numbers.[54]

---

[51] *Hansen,* 143 S. Ct. at 1944.

[52] *Id.* at 1946.

[53] *Id.* at 1946

[54] *Id.* (citing United States v. Okatan, 728 F.3d 111, 113–14 (2nd Cir. 2013); United States v. Yoshida, 303 F.3d 1145, 1148–51 (9th Cir. 2002); Edwards v. Prime, Inc. 602 F.3d 1276, 1295–97 (11th Cir. 2010); United States v. Tracy, 456 F. App'x 267, 269–70 (4th Cir. 2011); and United States v. Castillo-Felix, 539 F.2d 9, 11 (9th Cir. 1976)).

Because these prosecutions targeted unexpressive acts and not speech, the First Amendment was not implicated.

The majority placed these examples on one end of the second prong's hypothetical scales before turning to identifying the protected expression prohibited by the Encouragement Provision. Although the majority was able to identify a number of permissible prosecutions, it chastised Hansen for failing "to identify a single prosecution for ostensibly protected expression in the 70 years since Congress enacted" the Encouragement Provision.[55]

Hansen failed because the majority was only willing to credit actual prosecutions, rather than assessing the potential chilling effect of the Encouragement Provision.[56] Recall that the core goal of overbreadth analysis is to identify statutes that might chill speech. In other words, we're not focused solely on speech for which a speaker was actually prosecuted, we're worried about speech that was never uttered out of fear of an unconstitutionally broad statute. If the majority had credited potential prosecutions (i.e., speech chilling), rather than just successful prosecutions, the balance would certainly have turned out differently. After all, Hansen and amici marshaled a number of examples of constitutionally protected speech that would be captured by the Encouragement Provision. This should not be a surprise since, according to the plain language of the statute, simply saying "I encourage you to stay in the United States" to an undocumented person would violate the statute. It is therefore not a stretch to imagine that the Encouragement Provision might prohibit an uncomfortably large amount of socially productive and constitutionally protected speech. Indeed, Hansen argued that the text of the Encouragement Provision would prohibit, among other acts, the following:

- A priest telling a noncitizen congregant who has overstayed her visa that the church will provide charitable assistance, which might have the effect of encouraging her to remain;
- A U.S. citizen telling her undocumented spouse that he is needed in the country to provide financial support for the family;

---

[55] *Hansen*, 143 S. Ct. at 1946–47.

[56] *See infra* notes 87–96 for a more traditional overbreadth analysis.

- A public safety official advising undocumented members of the community to shelter in place during a natural disaster;
- A coach advising an undocumented student athlete that if she travels with her team for an international competition she will likely not be able to return to the United States;
- A college counselor advising an undocumented student that they can obtain a private scholarship to pay for dormitory fees and other expenses to fund their life as a college student in the United States;
- A doctor providing medical advice to a noncitizen with a visa that will shortly expire that a particular medical treatment is more readily available in the United States than elsewhere, leading that noncitizen to overstay the visa to wait for treatment; [and]
- A lawyer providing advice to a client that overstaying his visa is not a bar to adjusting his status to that of a lawful permanent resident if he marries a U.S. citizen.[57]

The majority admitted that "[i]f the statute reaches the many examples that Hansen posits, its applications to protected speech might swamp its lawful applications, rendering it vulnerable to an overbreadth challenge."[58] However, the majority was able to reject assertions that the statute reaches an impermissible amount of constitutionally protected speech by narrowly defining the words "encourage" and "induce" to only include meanings consonant with how these words are commonly used in criminal law statutes (i.e., as criminal solicitation and facilitation). The majority concluded its overbreadth analysis by averring that "[t]o the extent [the Encouragement Provision] reaches *any* speech, it stretches no further than speech integral to unlawful conduct."[59]

III. Hansen's Potential Legacy

The majority's opinion, at a mercifully slim 20 pages, has the potential to have outsized influence on First Amendment jurisprudence. This is because the Court, for the first time, upheld criminal penalties for people who encourage others to commit a civil violation. This

---

[57] Brief for Respondent at 16–17, United States v. Hansen, 143 S. Ct 1932 (2023) (No. 22-179) [hereinafter Brief for ACLU].

[58] *Hansen*, 143 S. Ct. at 1942.

[59] *Id.* at 1947.

represents an unprecedented expansion of the "speech integral to criminal conduct" exception, an exception that desperately needed limiting. Additionally, this case has the potential to significantly curtail the ability of overbreadth challenges to address the problem of chilling free speech. The balance of this section discusses each of these potential legacies.

A. Criminal Speech Integral to Uncivil Conduct

Curiously, the majority failed to address one of Hansen's more novel arguments—the fact that the Encouragement Provision makes it a *crime* to encourage someone to commit a *civil* violation. Calling this argument the "mismatch" theory, the majority summed up Hansen's argument in the following manner:

> Congress can impose criminal penalties on speech that solicits or facilitates a criminal violation and civil penalties on speech that solicits or facilitates a civil violation—but it cannot impose criminal penalties on speech that solicits or facilitates a civil violation.[60]

The majority dismissed this theory by saying "[w]e need not address this novel theory, because even if Hansen is right, his overbreadth challenge fails."[61] This suggests that the failure of Hansen's overbreadth challenge renders the "mismatch" argument moot. However, the majority was a bit too quick to dismiss this argument. As ably argued by Professor Eugene Volokh, this is not merely a question of overbreadth, but it is rather a question of the proper application of the "speech integral to criminal conduct" exception to the First Amendment.[62]

The "speech integral to criminal conduct" exception is "long familiar to the bar," and represents "well-defined and narrowly limited classes of speech, the prevention and punishment of which have never been thought to raise any Constitutional problem."[63] This is, perhaps, an overstatement,[64] but we certainly have a substantial body

---

[60] *Id.* at 1948 (citing Brief of Amicus Curiae Professor Eugene Volokh in Support of Respondent at 5–7, United States v. Hansen, 143 S. Ct 1932 (2023) (No. 22-179) [hereinafter Volokh Brief]).

[61] *Id.*

[62] *See generally* Volokh Brief.

[63] United States v. Stevens, 559 U.S. 460, 468–69 (2010) (quoting *Chaplinsky*, 315 U.S. 568).

[64] *See* Volokh, *supra* note 11.

of caselaw to help us understand the exception. Perhaps the most common example of the "speech integral to criminal conduct" exception is the fact that the government is permitted to criminalize speech that solicits crimes. In *Giboney*, the Court noted that "[i]t rarely has been suggested that the constitutional freedom for speech . . . extends . . . to speech or writing used as an integral part of conduct in violation of a valid criminal statute."[65]

Under this exception, it is constitutionally permissible for a law to criminalize an offer to sell heroin, but a law that criminalizes nonspecific encouragement to do the same (e.g., "You should really get into selling heroin, it's a grand old time!") would be unconstitutional. Similarly, a statute that criminalizes the pandering of child pornography is constitutional because it does not prohibit "abstract advocacy" of child pornography (which would be unconstitutional), but instead only criminalizes "the recommendation of a particular piece of purported child pornography with the intent of initiating a transfer."[66] For this reason, the government cannot prohibit someone from saying, "I encourage you to obtain child pornography," because such a statement, however horrific, is mere advocacy; the speech is not, in other words, integral to a crime.[67]

This is how the "speech integral to criminal conduct" exception permits restrictions on someone using words or speech to cause illegal activity.[68] As summarized by Volokh, the exception stands for the following proposition:

> When speech tends to cause, attempts to cause, or makes a threat to cause some illegal conduct (illegal conduct other than the prohibited speech itself)—such as murder, fights, restraints of trade, child sexual abuse, discriminatory refusal to hire, and the like—this opens the door to possible restrictions on such speech.[69]

Thus, if you speak in a manner that causes a criminal act, you may be held criminally liable. Similarly, if you speak in a manner

---

[65] *Giboney*, 336 U.S. at 498.

[66] *Williams*, 553 U.S. at 300.

[67] *See id.*

[68] Volokh, *supra* note 11, at 1015 ("[T]he legal system may prohibit you from causing illegal conduct, even causing it through speech.").

[69] *Id.* at 986–87.

that results in a civil violation, you may be liable for civil penalties.[70] However, what this exception has never done, until *Hansen*, is make it a *crime* to speak in a way that gives rise to a *civil* violation.

As Jackson noted, the 1986 revision to the Encouragement Provision "made it a crime to encourage or induce a noncitizen not just to 'come to' or 'enter' the United States, but also to 'reside' in this country."[71] The problem is that it is not a crime for an undocumented person to reside in the United States; it is a civil violation.[72] But under the majority's interpretation of the Encouragement Provision, a person who encourages someone to commit a civil violation may earn a felony. In more concrete terms, the person whose actions violated the statute (i.e., the undocumented person remaining in the U.S.) may receive a $500 fine, while the person who encouraged the violation may be imprisoned up to ten years.[73] Absurdly, the punishment for encouraging someone to commit a prohibited activity is punished far more severely than the punishment for actually doing the prohibited activity. As Volokh argues, the justification for the "speech integral to criminal conduct" exception is that in order to punish speech, the "speech should be legally tantamount to the crime to which is it integral."[74] To do otherwise would be to "unmoor the exception from its rationale," with the absurd result of criminalizing speech integral to noncriminal conduct.[75] This is precisely what the *Hansen* court held.

Although the Court claimed not to address the issue, its silence on the matter rings loudly. By failing to credit Hansen's so-called mismatch theory, it upheld a statute that imposes criminal liability upon someone who encourages another to engage in activity that amounts to a civil violation. It is difficult to argue that this is anything other than an unprecedented expansion of the "speech integral to criminal conduct" exception. Before *Hansen*, we could point to no precedent

---

[70] *See* Int'l Brotherhood of Elec. Workers v. NLRB, 341 U.S. 694 (1951).

[71] *Hansen*, 143 S. Ct. at 1959 (Jackson, J., dissenting).

[72] *See id.* at 1947–48 (majority op.) ("[R]esiding in the United States without lawful status is subject to the hefty penalty of removal, but it generally does not carry a criminal sentence.").

[73] 8 U.S.C. §§ 1324(a)(1)(B); (a)(2).

[74] Volokh Brief at 1–2.

[75] *Id.* at 8.

that upheld criminal sanctions for the encouragement of a civil violation. That is no longer the case.

The consequences of this expansion could be quite profound. As Prof. Volokh argues, we are now left with "an exception with no discernable boundaries."[76] An expansive "speech integral to criminal conduct" exception would not be limited to violent conduct or even serious criminal conduct. Instead, it would provide the government with the freedom to bar any speech that it views as merely harmful. This could "potentially open the door to the government punishing any behavior that seems in some way connected to some behavior that is criminal, or civilly actionable, or just dangerous."[77] Prior to *Hansen*, the Supreme Court had upheld the "speech integral to criminal conduct" exception because it reached "well-defined and narrowly limited classes of speech, the prevention and punishment of which have never been thought to raise any Constitutional problem."[78] After Hansen, the court can no longer make this claim. Under *Hansen*, the "speech integral to criminal conduct" exception may now impose criminal punishments on those who encourage, but do not commit, a civil violation. Such a result is not only facially absurd, but is also a dangerous incursion into our First Amendment rights.

B. The End of Overbreadth Challenges

In addition to expanding the "speech integral to criminal conduct" exception, the majority's opinion will render future overbreadth challenges very difficult. The majority dismissively ended its opinion by saying that "as-applied challenges can take it from here."[79] This blithe aside completely misses the point of the overbreadth doctrine, which is "to keep overly broad statutes off the books in order to avoid chilling constitutionally protected speech."[80] The goal of the overbreadth doctrine is to avoid the tendency of poorly drafted

---

[76] *Id.*

[77] *Id.* at 11.

[78] *Stevens*, 559 U.S. at 468–69 (quoting *Chaplinsky*, 315 U.S. at 571–72).

[79] *Hansen*, 143 S. Ct. at 1948.

[80] *Id.* at 1953 (Jackson, J., dissenting) ("[T]he majority undermines the goal of the overbreadth doctrine, which aims to keep overly broad statutes off the books in order to avoid chilling constitutionally protected speech.").

laws to chill speech, something a case-by-case approach can never do. As Jackson noted, the whole point of the overbreadth doctrine is to avoid the need to rely upon "those hardy enough to risk criminal prosecution to determine the proper scope of regulation."[81] Tallying up the number of impermissible successful prosecutions is nonsensical if one is concerned about "whether speech is being chilled by a facially overbroad statute" because "[t]he number of people who have not exercised their right to speak out of fear of prosecution is, quite frankly, unknowable."[82] The overbreadth doctrine doesn't force us to make "vindication of freedom of expression await the outcome of protracted litigation"[83] and it permits someone "to challenge a statute not because their own rights of free expression are violated, but because of a judicial prediction or assumption that the statute's very existence may cause others not before the court to refrain from constitutionally protected speech or expression."[84]

Here, the majority dismissed hypothetical applications of the Encouragement Provision as "fanciful." The problem is that such hypotheticals are often the bread and butter of overbreadth analysis, serving as the means of determining the second prong of the overbreadth doctrine—i.e., whether "a 'substantial number' of its applications are unconstitutional, 'judged in relation to the statute's plainly legitimate sweep.'"[85] As the Sixth Circuit has noted, "[a]lthough '[l]itigation by hypothetical' generally is frowned upon, if not barred . . . , it is sometimes *required* in free-speech cases."[86] How else can one assess the *potential* sweep of a statute—with an eye toward its *potential* to chill speech—without considering hypothetical applications?

Two Supreme Court cases, *United States v. Stevens* and *United States v. Williams*, illustrate the Court's willingness to consider hypothetical applications in overbreadth analyses. In *Stevens*, the Court considered the potential reach of a statute criminalizing "the commercial creation, sale, or possession of certain depictions of animal

---

[81] *Id.* at 1961 (quoting Dombrowski v. Pfister, 380 U.S. 479, 487 (1965)).

[82] *Id.* at 1963.

[83] *Dombrowski*, 380 U.S. at 487.

[84] Broadrick v. Oklahoma, 413 U.S. 601, 612 (1973).

[85] Wash. State Grange v. Wash. State Republican Party, 552 U.S. 442, 449 n. 6 (2008) (quoting *Ferber*, 458 U.S. at 770).

[86] Connection Distrib. Co. v. Holder, 557 F. 3d 321, 335 (6th Cir. 2009).

cruelty."[87] In an attempt to determine whether "a substantial number of its applications are unconstitutional," the majority considered a number of hypothetical prosecutions in which otherwise legal activities might be captured by the statute's definition of "animal cruelty," including whether the statute would reach hunting, slaughtering livestock, amputating cow tails, and cockfighting. All such activities, to varying degrees, involve harm to animals and were legal in some or all states at the time of the *Stevens* decision.[88] Notably, the *Stevens* Court did not shy away from considering such hypotheticals, however fanciful, despite the fact that the government had not attempted to prosecute such activities under the challenged statute.

In *Williams*, the Court considered a statute that criminalized the possession and distribution of material pandered as child pornography. In its overbreadth analysis, the *Williams* Court engaged in a similar examination of hypothetical applications, albeit with some palpable annoyance.[89] Writing for the *Williams* majority, Justice Scalia bemoaned "the tendency of our overbreadth doctrine to summon forth an endless stream of fanciful hypotheticals."[90] But he nonetheless considered whether the statute would capture a person offering nonpornographic photographs of minors, mainstream movies depicting underage intercourse, a good Samaritan turning offending material over to authorities, and a documentary film about war crimes depicting the rape of children.[91] Despite his clear distaste at having to wrestle with such hypotheticals, Scalia considered and dismissed each example as either inapplicable, implausible, or in the case of the documentary, a minor unconstitutional application.[92] In other words, the *Williams* court held its nose and considered the hypothetical reach of the statute in question. The *Hansen* majority, on the other hand, dismissed the proffered hypotheticals because none of the hypotheticals had been prosecuted.

The majority's argument—which relied on the fact that a protected activity has not yet been prosecuted—is both incorrect and

---

[87] *Stevens*, 559 U.S. at 464.

[88] *See id.* at 475–77.

[89] *Williams*, 553 U.S. at 301.

[90] *Id.*

[91] *Id.* at 301–02.

[92] *Id.*

irrelevant. It is incorrect because there has been at least one prosecution of the Encouragement Provision. In *United States v. Henderson*, an employer of an undocumented house cleaner was prosecuted for repeatedly encouraging the noncitizen to remain in the United States, saying "if you leave, they won't let you back" and "you can't leave, don't leave."[93] The Massachusetts district court, with great reluctance, agreed that such facts supported a conviction under the Encouragement Provision.[94]

Perhaps more importantly, the majority's argument that the Encouragement Provision has not been used to prosecute "ostensibly protected expression" is completely irrelevant. When weighing the constitutionality of a statute under the overbreadth doctrine, we should not be forced to wait for the government to act in an unconstitutional manner. This is because "the First Amendment . . . does not leave us at the mercy of *noblesse oblige*." [95] A track record of inoffensive use does nothing to stem the chilling effect of a statute that, on its face, prohibits significant amounts of protected speech.[96]

To be sure, we should jealously protect the separation of powers, and whenever one branch of the government takes an action to invalidate the actions of another branch, we should raise our guard. It is therefore appropriate to refer to the overbreadth doctrine as "strong medicine" and to use it sparingly. But that does not mean that the doctrine should be cast aside. As the *Stevens* Court noted, "The First Amendment itself reflects a judgment by the American people that the benefits of its restrictions on the Government outweigh the costs."[97] To determine this, we need to know the costs—not just the prosecutions, but the tendency of a statute to chill speech. On the other hand, some restrictions on speech are clearly important. For this reason, we have determined that certain restrictions on speech are justified, and one way for us to determine if a speech restriction strikes the appropriate balance is the overbreadth doctrine, which

[93] United States v. Henderson, 857 F. Supp. 2d 191, 196 (D. Mass. 2012).

[94] *See id.* at 193–94 (noting that the court was "puzzled" by the "stern, solemn, and implacable sanctimony of the government" in maintaining a prosecution of such "pedestrian" conduct).

[95] *Stevens*, 559 U.S. at 480.

[96] *See id.* ("We would not uphold an unconstitutional statute merely because the Government promised to use it responsibly.").

[97] *Id.* at 470.

"seeks to balance the 'harmful effects' of 'invalidating a law that in some of its applications is perfectly constitutional' against the possibility that 'the threat of enforcement of an overbroad law [will] dete[r] people from engaging in constitutionally protected speech.'"[98] The doctrine does not, in fact, encourage parties to conjure up "fanciful hypotheticals," but it does require an examination of "real-world conduct" that would be captured by the statute at issue.[99]

Rather than striking down the law and requiring Congress to write a provision that would not offend the constitution, the majority left the Encouragement Provision intact. Thus, anyone seeking guidance from the statute "will see only its broad, speech-chilling language."[100] One wonders if the court will require future overbreadth challenges to provide examples of actual prosecutions, rather than potential prosecutions. If so, it will be very difficult for future overbreadth challenges to succeed.

IV. Conclusion

The *Hansen* opinion has two potentially troubling consequences: the expansion of the "speech integral to criminal conduct" exception to the First Amendment and leaving the Encouragement Provision's facially broad language intact. With respect to the first consequence, the majority dramatically expanded the potential reach of the "speech integral to criminal conduct" exception to the First Amendment by allowing speech that results in a civil violation to be punished as a crime. Regardless of the wisdom of this expansion, the failure for the majority to address the issue in any detail is deeply troubling. Those critics who have called for the Supreme Court to properly cabin the exception in a thoughtful manner are no doubt sorely disappointed in the majority's willingness to completely ignore the problem.[101] Only time will tell if legislatures take advantage of this newfound flexibility to criminalize speech that incites civil violations. I don't think I'm alone in hoping that legislatures do not take this opportunity to criminalize large swaths of speech.

---

[98] *Id.* at 484–85. (quoting *Williams*, 553 U.S. at 292).

[99] *Id.* at 485.

[100] *Hansen*, 143 S. Ct. at 1961 (Jackson, J., dissenting).

[101] *See generally* Volokh, *supra* note 11.

In terms of the second consequence, with a near absurdist approach to statutory interpretation, the majority successfully saved the Encouragement Provision from invalidation. Despite my misgivings, the instinct to protect congressional acts from judicial invalidation is certainly a good one. However, the Court struck the wrong balance between respecting the realm of congressional action, on the one hand, and protecting our freedom of speech, on the other. By upholding a narrow interpretation of the Encouragement Provision, the majority has left a statute on the books that, on its face, reaches a significant amount of protected speech. We will never know the amount of speech that will never be uttered for fear of criminal prosecution.[102] Further, the Court's approach disincentivizes Congress to draft laws that do not, on their face, tread upon constitutional rights. As Jackson noted in closing her dissent, "at the end of the day, [the fears of amici] reflect a determination to view enacted statutes as serious business, and essentially, to take Congress at its word. The Court should have done the same."[103] I couldn't have said it better.

* * *

---

[102] *See Hansen*, 143 S. Ct. at 1962 (Jackson, J., dissenting) (noting that even if one were to consult the majority's decision, there are a number of "known unknowns of the majority's course [that] portend further chill").

[103] *Id.* at 1964.

Speech, Complicity, Scarcity, and Public Accommodation

Christopher R. Green*

303 Creative LLC v. Elenis[1] is the Supreme Court's second, but almost certainly not its last, case on the extent of state power to require wedding-related professionals to participate in same-sex wedding ceremonies or their accoutrements. Five years ago, *Masterpiece Cakeshop, Ltd. v. Colorado Civil Rights Commission* held, in one of Justice Anthony Kennedy's last opinions for the Court, that Colorado had been improperly hostile to baker Jack Phillips's religious views in requiring him to design a cake for a same-sex wedding.[2] This time, after limiting the question presented to free speech,[3] the Court held that requiring Lorie Smith to prepare websites for same-sex weddings if she prepared them for traditional weddings would unconstitutionally compel her to speak, akin to requiring a group to salute the flag[4] or to add discordant

* Jamie L. Whitten Chair in Law and Government, University of Mississippi School of Law. Thanks to Will Berry, Steve Crampton, Richard Epstein, Adam Grainger, David Upham, and Randall Wenger for conversation.

[1] 143 S. Ct. 2298 (2023).

[2] Masterpiece Cakeshop, Ltd. v. Colorado Civil Rights Comm'n, 138 S. Ct. 1719, 1723–24 (2018).

[3] The petition for certiorari included a full gamut of free-exercise as well as free-speech issues: "The questions presented are: 1. Whether applying a public-accommodation law to compel an artist to speak or stay silent, contrary to the artist's sincerely held religious beliefs, violates the Free Speech or Free Exercise Clauses of the First Amendment. 2. Whether a public-accommodations law that authorizes secular but not religious exemptions is generally applicable under *Smith*, and if so, whether this Court should overrule Smith." Petition for Writ of Certiorari at i, 303 Creative LLC v. Elenis, 143 S. Ct. 2298 (2023) (No. 21-476). The Court granted review limited to the free-speech question: "Whether applying a public-accommodation law to compel an artist to speak or stay silent violates the Free Speech Clause of the First Amendment." 303 Creative LLC v. Elenis, 142 S. Ct. 1106 (2022). This is the same as the petitioner's first question presented, only deleting "contrary to the artist's sincerely held religious beliefs" and the reference to the Free Exercise Clause.

[4] West Virginia Bd. of Ed. v. Barnette, 319 U.S. 624 (1943).

elements to its parade[5] or its membership.[6] Justice Neil Gorsuch, who like Justice Kennedy had written in support of the rights of those in same-sex relationships in other contexts,[7] wrote for the Court's six-Justice majority.[8]

Justiciability and ripeness consumed a surprising amount of the initial media coverage of the case. Unlike many other similar controversies, which have featured a particular couple denied wedding-related services, Smith filed a pre-enforcement suit against Colorado officials based on the "credible threat" that they would treat her as they had treated Jack Phillips.[9] The Court mentioned that she was "worrie[d]" that Colorado would enforce its public-accommodation laws against her if she added wedding-related services to her business, but this, of course, was just a description of her motivation, not a new standard for ripeness. Shortly after the decision, however, District Judge Carlton Reeves joked about the "worries" language: "In certain civil rights claims, we have just learned, a plaintiff can establish subject matter jurisdiction merely by expressing 'worries' about the defendant's future course of conduct."[10] But Smith met the long-established "credible threat" requirement not merely by being worried, but by pointing

---

[5] Hurley v. Irish-American Gay, Lesbian and Bisexual Grp. of Bos., Inc., 515 U.S. 557 (1995).

[6] Boy Scouts of Am. v. Dale, 530 U.S. 640 (2000).

[7] Three years before *303 Creative*, Justice Gorsuch had written for the Court in interpreting Title VII to include discrimination based on homosexual or transgender status in *Bostock v. Clayton County*, 140 S. Ct. 1731 (2020). Three years before *Masterpiece*, Justice Kennedy had written for the Court in requiring states to recognize same-sex marriage in *Obergefell v. Hodges*, 576 U.S. 644 (2015).

[8] While *Masterpiece* was 7–2, with Justices Stephen Breyer and Elena Kagan joining the majority and only Justices Ruth Bader Ginsburg and Sonia Sotomayor dissenting, *303 Creative* was 6–3, with Justices Sotomayor, Kagan, and Ketanji Brown Jackson all dissenting.

[9] See *303 Creative*, 143 S. Ct. at 2308–09.

[10] Bullock v. Revell Enterprises, LLC, 2023 WL 4355036, at *1 (S.D. Miss. July 5, 2023) (citing *303 Creative*). Judge Reeves had dealt with ripeness issues at length in an earlier opinion, creatively finding a range of injuries from Mississippi's House Bill 1523, a bill passed in the wake of *Obergefell* to accommodate individual public employees with objections to same-sex marriage. The Fifth Circuit found no justiciable injury and the Supreme Court denied review. See Barber v. Bryant, 193 F. Supp. 3d 677, 697–703 (S.D. Miss. 2016), *rev'd*, 860 F.3d 345 (5th Cir. 2017), *rehearing and rehearing en banc denied*, 872 F.3d 671, *cert. denied*, 138 S. Ct. 652 (2018), *cert. denied sub. nom.* Campaign for Southern Equality v. Bryant, 138 S. Ct. 671 (2018).

to Colorado's history with the likes of Jack Phillips. *The New Republic* further added to the drama over whether Smith's claims were ripe by reporting breathlessly that some of the information submitted to the district court on the ripeness issue—but not relied on by the Tenth Circuit or the Supreme Court—was possibly fake.[11] The controversy between Smith and Colorado, though, was all too real.

The Court's opinion gave little attention to the sorts of doctrinal "tiers of scrutiny" details that have sometimes filled other cases. A lessening of enthusiasm for the tiers may thus be a trend. Last year's gun case, for instance, anchored limits in Second Amendment law in particular exemplars of traditionally accepted gun regulations, rather than the means-end scrutiny that lower courts had been using.[12] *303 Creative* similarly rooted its analysis in particular instances of compelled speech rather than doctrinal labels and categories. The Court mentioned "strict scrutiny" only in recapitulating the lower court,[13] mentioned "compelling interest" only in describing an earlier holding,[14] and did not mention tailoring at all. The Court instead resolved the case by directly comparing Lorie Smith's situation to the particular fact patterns in its precedents—the Jehovah's Witnesses resisting the flag salute,[15] the Boston St. Patrick's Day parade resisting inclusion of a gay-rights group,[16] and the Boy Scouts resisting membership for a gay scoutmaster.[17] The Court similarly resisted counterarguments with a few fact patterns, not doctrinal labels: a Muslim filmmaker required to make a Zionist film, an atheist required to paint an evangelical mural, or someone in a same-sex marriage required to design websites for anti-same-sex-marriage advocates.[18] Future cases will surely test what sorts of work related to same-sex weddings might count as the vendor's "speech." Are florists speaking in their own voice? Photographers? Calligraphers? Bakers? Musicians? DJs? The "guy who provides

---

[11] *See* Melissa Gira Grant, *The Mysterious Case of the Fake Gay Marriage Website, the Real Straight Man, and the Supreme Court*, THE NEW REPUBLIC (June 29, 2023), https://tinyurl.com/4b384rdf.

[12] N.Y. Rifle & Pistol Ass'n, Inc. v. Bruen, 142 S. Ct. 2111, 2126–27 (2022).

[13] *303 Creative*, 143 S. Ct. at 2310.

[14] *Id.* at 2314 (quoting Roberts v. U.S. Jaycees, 468 U.S. 609, 628 (1984)).

[15] *Barnette*, 319 U.S. at 624.

[16] *Hurley*, 515 U.S. 557.

[17] *Boy Scouts of America*, 530 U.S. 640.

[18] *303 Creative*, 143 S. Ct. at 2314.

the chairs"?[19] Because Colorado had stipulated that the proposed wedding websites would in fact be speech,[20] none of these follow-on questions were posed directly. To decide in Lorie Smith's favor, the Court only had to take the small additional step beyond the stipulation of concluding that the websites would be partly *her* speech, and not just her customers'.[21]

Colorado's concession on the expressive nature of Smith's proposed websites also meant the Court could avoid considering the broader issue of complicity. Even if *services* themselves are non-expressive— as in the "guy who provides the chairs" example—might compelled commercial interaction itself sometimes be deemed to be expressive? This was the big issue involved in the parade and membership cases, *Hurley* and *Boy Scouts*, as well as cases in which freedom-of-association claims failed, like *Runyon v. McCrary* (no exemption to ban on racially discriminatory school admissions), *Roberts v. U.S. Jaycees* (another membership case), and *Rumsfeld v. FAIR* (requiring law schools to allow the military to recruit). Did inclusion of another group in a parade change the parade's message? Would the inclusion of a gay scoutmaster amount to compelled "expressive association"? The Court in *Hurley* and *Boy Scouts* said yes. In *Runyon*, though, the Court relied on a lower court assessment that "there is no showing that discontinuance of (the) discriminatory admission practices would inhibit in any way the teaching in these schools of any ideas or dogma."[22] In *Roberts*, the Court similarly held, "The Act requires no change in the Jaycees' creed of promoting the interests of young men, and it imposes no restrictions on the organization's ability to exclude individuals with ideologies or philosophies different from those of its existing members."[23] In *FAIR*, the Court said that merely arranging meetings was not expressive: "The only expressive activity required of the law schools, the Court found, involved the posting of logistical notices along these lines: 'The U. S. Army recruiter will meet interested students in Room 123 at 11 a.m.'"[24]

[19] *See* Transcript of Oral Argument at 40, 303 Creative LLC v. Elenis, 143 S. Ct. 2298 (2023) (No. 21-476) (question of Justice Kagan).

[20] *303 Creative*, 143 S. Ct. at 2309.

[21] *Id.* at 2313.

[22] 427 U.S. 160, 176 (1976).

[23] 468 U.S. 609, 627 (1984).

[24] *303 Creative*, 143 S. Ct. at 2317 (quoting Rumsfeld v. FAIR, 547 U.S. 47, 61–62 (2006)).

Controversies over when marketplace interactions express complicity with another's actions are very difficult. Unsurprisingly, they have ancient roots, and they were difficult for the ancients to resolve too. Paul's letters to the Corinthians, for instance, discussed whether and when purchasing or eating meat that had been sacrificed to an idol would improperly send a message of approval of idol worship. Meat is not in itself expressive, but depending on the context, eating it can send a message. Paul offered four hypotheticals, two of which he thought were cases of improper encouragement of idol worship and two of which he did not. The easy case of complicity was eating in a temple itself: "[I]f anyone sees you who have knowledge eating in an idol's temple, will he not be encouraged, if his conscience is weak, to eat food offered to idols?"[25] At the other end of the spectrum, Paul told the Corinthians that when shopping in a marketplace, they should feel free to buy meat that may well have been sacrificed to an idol, but was not labeled as such. "Eat whatever is sold in the meat market without raising any question on the ground of conscience."[26] In the middle were two cases of eating in another's house. As long as nothing is said about sacrifice, there was no illicit complicity: "If one of the unbelievers invites you to dinner and you are disposed to go, eat whatever is set before you without raising any question on the ground of conscience."[27] However, when food is explicitly presented as having been offered to an idol, Paul told the Corinthians not to eat it. "But if someone says to you, 'This has been offered in sacrifice,' then do not eat it, for the sake of the one who informed you, and for the sake of conscience—I do not mean your conscience, but his."[28] Note that Paul did not tell the Corinthians to refuse to condone idol worship because he wanted them to express hostility to idol worshippers as people, but because he wanted them to serve unbelievers' own best interests—"for the sake of the one who informed you." The most charitable interpretation of objections to participation in same-sex weddings is similar: not as expressing bigoted hostility to others' well-being, but expressing a different view about what would in fact promote those interests.

[25] 1 Cor. 8:10.
[26] 1 Cor. 10:25.
[27] 1 Cor. 10:27.
[28] 1 Cor. 10:28-29.

For all its attention to the word "speech" in the First Amendment, the Court yet again[29] ignored the first word of the First Amendment— "Congress"—and did not mention the Fourteenth Amendment even in passing. The First Amendment was, of course, written to limit the activities not of states, but of a federal government with a much more limited menu of responsibilities. As the first Justice Jackson explained in his dissent in *Beauharnais v. Illinois,* and as the second Justice Harlan reiterated many times without ever receiving a compelling reply from his fellow Justices, the federal and state governments' different responsibilities make different collections of rights sensible with respect to the two governments.[30] Entrepreneurial rights and the right to engage in professions, for instance, are critically important for citizens against states, and the "right . . . to make contracts" was the very first right listed in the Civil Rights Act of 1866, which the Fourteenth Amendment proposed to constitutionalize. But the federal government lacks any general regulatory power over labor conditions; even the most severe abuse of the right to work—slavery in the states—lay beyond the commerce power at the Founding,[31] and the Thirteenth Amendment did not change the commerce itself. The Bill of Rights of 1791 was thus not designed as a guide for establishing an inclusive republic for all citizens in the context of a general governmental power over

---

[29] *See, e.g.,* Counterman v. Colorado, 143 S. Ct. 2106 (2023) (the Court, in a decision issued three days before *303 Creative,* deciding a First Amendment case involving a state, but not even mentioning the Fourteenth Amendment).

[30] 343 U.S. 250, 287–95 (1952) (Jackson, J., dissenting); *see also* Roth v. United States, 354 U.S. 476, 503-07 (1957) (Harlan, J., dissenting); Zelman v. Simmons-Harris, 536 U.S. 639, 679 (2002) (Thomas, J., concurring); Gitlow v. New York, 268 U.S. 652, 672 (1925) (Holmes, J., dissenting); *but see* First National Bank of Bos. v. Bellotti, 435 U.S. 765, 780 n.16 (1978) (noting Court's rejection of the view that Jackson and Harlan "advanced forcefully," but not answering their arguments); McDonald v. Chicago, 561 U.S. 742, 784 (2010) (noting that Harlan argued "repeatedly and eloquently" and that he "fought a determined rearguard action," but that he failed to persuade the Court, and again, failing to answer Jackson and Harlan's argument about the difference between state and federal responsibilities).

[31] Besides the historical "federal consensus" behind this proposition, the lack of federal power over slavery in the states is made perfectly plain by Article I section 9 clause 1's careful limitation in time and space of congressional power to control the slave trade. For states not "now existing"—i.e., territories—Congress had power to do what it did in the Northwest Ordinance: exclude slavery altogether. But for existing states, Congress only had the power to limit the slave *trade,* and only beginning in 1808. That would make no sense if its commerce power extended to the power to prohibit slavery itself in existing states.

citizens' professional lives. Like the federal government itself, it had a much more limited aim. If instead of the 1791 meaning of "speech," the Court had focused on the 1868 meaning of "privileges or immunities of citizens of the United States," it could have struck a much more significant and historically grounded blow in favor of liberty and equality. The Fourteenth Amendment guarantees equality in civil rights for all similarly-situated citizens of each state, whatever their religious or political creed,[32] and thus secures the equal right of all citizens to enter *all* professions, even those not oriented around speech. Because this entrepreneurial liberty is "subject nevertheless to such restraints as the government may justly prescribe for the general good of the whole,"[33] however, detailed knowledge of traditional uses of the police power is essential. In the future, as the Court tests the limits of what counts as "speech" under *303 Creative*, arguments from equal citizenship will remain important if those speech claims fall short. When that happens, clarity about the historical scope of states' police power will be essential.

Because of the Court's lack of doctrinal emphasis on the details of the state's interests, it had no need to characterize the interests served by public-accommodation law with much precision. The Court noted only that historically, public-accommodation laws were important in situations of local scarcity:

> Statutes like Colorado's grow from nondiscrimination rules the common law sometimes imposed on common carriers and places of traditional public accommodation like hotels and restaurants. Often, these enterprises exercised something like monopoly power or hosted or transported others or their belongings much like bailees. Over time, some States, Colorado included, have expanded the reach of these nondiscrimination rules to cover virtually every place of business engaged in any sales to the public.[34]

32 *See, e.g.*, Civil Rights Act of 1875, 18 Stat. 335 (1875) ("equal and exact justice to all, of whatever nativity, race, color, or persuasion, religious or political").

33 Corfield v. Coryell, 6 Fed. Cas. 546, 552 (E.D. Pa. 1825); *cf.* Dobbs v. Jackson Women's Health Org., 142 S. Ct. 2228, 2248 at n.22 (2022) (recognizing the importance of *Corfield* to interpreting the Privileges or Immunities Clause).

34 *303 Creative*, 143 S. Ct. at 2314 (citations omitted); *cf. id.* at 2326 (Sotomayor, J., dissenting) (reading Court to "suggest that public accommodations or common carriers historically assumed duties to serve all comers because they enjoyed monopolies or otherwise had market power").

In saying only this, the Court thus did not accept the invitation of some amici, including this author, to tie the legitimate goals of public-accommodation law directly to local scarcity, in line with the Court's limited historic permission for special regulation of businesses "clothed with a public interest."[35] But neither did the Court reject such a theory, as the dissenters did at length.[36] The Court's failure to agree with the dissenters on this point leaves a scarcity-based approach to Fourteenth Amendment entrepreneurial liberty clearly viable. The weakness of the dissent's response on this score, moreover, should give advocates of a scarcity-based limit considerable optimism for its future success. The bulk of the rest of this essay will explain what the majority might have said in response to the dissent had it followed such a path, or should it follow it in the future.

The idea that not all businesses that offer to serve the public are "clothed with a public interest" traces back to Lord Chief Justice Matthew Hale's seventeenth-century treatise, *De Portibus Maris.* Hale discussed special duties placed on wharves because of their unique place in the economy: "because they are the wharfs only licensed by the queen . . . or because there is no other wharf in that port."[37] In the 1877 case of *Munn v. Illinois* and its companion cases, the Supreme Court took Hale's scarcity-based analysis of public-accommodation duties as its framework for assessing the constitutionality of the use of the police power to regulate grain elevators and railroads.[38] The Court's most pointed explanation of the *Munn* doctrine, and its most pointed rejection of the *303 Creative* dissent's view of public-accommodation law, came a hundred years ago, in 1923's unanimous *Charles Wolff Packing* case: "[O]ne does not devote one's property or business to the public use or clothe it with a public interest merely

---

[35] Brief of Law and Economics Scholars as Amici Curiae Supporting Petitioners at 14–17, 303 Creative LLC v. Elenis, 143 S. Ct. 2298 (2023) (No. 21-476), 2022 WL 2048478; Brief of Professor Christopher R. Green as Amicus Curiae Supporting Petitioners at 22–32, 303 Creative LLC v. Elenis, 143 S. Ct. 2298 (2023) (No. 21-476), 2022 WL 2047742.

[36] *303 Creative*, 143 S. Ct. at 2323–29 (Sotomayor, J., dissenting).

[37] MATTHEW HALE, DE PORTIBUS MARIS, *in* FRANCIS HARGRAVE, A COLLECTION OF TRACTS RELATIVE TO THE LAW OF ENGLAND 77 (Professional Books Ltd., 1982) (1787).

[38] Munn v. Illinois, 94 U.S. 113, 126–30 (1877); Chicago, Burlington, & Quincy Railroad Co. v. Iowa, 94 U.S. 155, 161 (1877); Peik v. Chicago & North-Western Railway Co., 94 U.S. 164, 176 (1877).

because one makes commodities for, and sells to, the public . . ."[39] Scarcity was very clearly the key for the Court: "the indispensable nature of the service and the exorbitant charges and arbitrary control to which the public might be subjected without regulation."[40] Besides cases like *Charles Wolff Packing*, early-twentieth-century thinkers like Harvard law professor Bruce Wyman explained a scarcity-based rationale for public-accommodation duties at great length.[41] Alfred Avins later identified two dozen "representative cases about the monopoly characteristics of common carriers and their franchises and licenses."[42] None of this material, alas, is mentioned by the *303 Creative* dissent. The clothed-with-a-public-interest doctrine has, moreover, been important for equality, not just liberty. *Munn* was the basis for the first Justice Harlan's dissent in the *Civil Rights Cases* of 1883[43] as well as Senator Warren Magnuson's February 1964 report for the Senate Commerce Committee in support of what became Title II of the Civil Rights Act of 1964.[44]

The *303 Creative* dissenters painted a very different picture of the common law; they thought the issue was important enough that they began here, rather than with the compelled-speech issue presented

---

[39] Charles Wolff Packing Co. v. Ct. of Indus. Rels., 262 U.S. 522, 537 (1923). While the Court took a very relaxed approach to the *Munn* issue in *Nebbia v. New York*, 291 U.S. 502 (1934), it did not overrule *Charles Wolff Packing*, and in fact relied on it. *See id.* at 536.

[40] *Id.* at 538.

[41] BRUCE WYMAN, THE SPECIAL LAW GOVERNING PUBLIC SERVICE CORPORATIONS (1911). Wyman had given a much slimmer version of the account in earlier articles, *The Law of the Public Callings as a Solution of the Trust Problem*, 17 HARV. L. REV. 156 (1904), and *The Inherent Limitation of the Public Service Duty to Particular Classes*, 23 HARV. L. REV. 339 (1910), and in a treatise co-authored with Joseph Henry Beale, THE LAW OF RAILROAD RATE REGULATION (1907).

[42] Alfred Avins, *The Civil Rights Act of 1875: Some Reflected Light on the Fourteenth Amendment and Public Accommodations*, 66 COLUM. L. REV. 873, 888 n.80 (1966).

[43] 109 U.S. 3, 41–42 (1883) (Harlan, J., dissenting).

[44] S. REP. No. 88-872, at 9 (1964) (also noting reliance of *Munn* on Lord Chief Justice Hale). *See also* 110 CONG. REC. 7403 (1964) (Senator Magnuson again relying on Hale and *Munn*); *id.* at 14185 (same). The House report similarly focused on tangible needs of commercial access: "If we consider the matter solely in commercial and economic terms, we can also substantiate the need for Title II. . . . The strain of traveling long distances without respite, the nagging uncertainty of locating a decent place to eat or sleep, or the fear of finding oneself on a lonely road at night with car trouble and no place to turn for assistance has forced innumerable families and individuals to stay at home." H. REP. No. 88-914, pt. 2, at 9 (1963).

by the Court. The dissenters recapitulated at considerable length the account of public-accommodation law by another Harvard professor, Joseph Singer.[45] Justice Sonia Sotomayor, writing for the dissenters, presented public-accommodation law as serving two independent purposes: equal access to goods and equal dignity.[46] The independence of these purposes was critical to the dissenters' view. They contended that requiring those in the market to express respect for other citizens' views about human flourishing, *even if those other citizens already have full access to all relevant goods and services*, is still an important governmental rationale. But the very sources the dissent relied on at this point show that these two goals are not independent. Justice Sotomayor quoted *Heart of Atlanta Motel*'s reference to Senator Magnuson's concern with "the deprivation of personal dignity *that surely accompanies* denials of equal access to public establishments."[47] Freestanding dignity, *unaccompanied* by the denial of equal access to the market, was obviously not at issue. And as noted earlier, Magnuson took his cue on the nature of the common law from Lord Chief Justice Hale and *Munn*. Sotomayor then used two examples here that do not make her point at all: the Brooklyn Dodgers being required to split up the overnight accommodations for its team because of discrimination against players like Jackie Robinson,[48] and a same-sex couple in Mississippi being required to go 70 miles down the road for funeral-home services.[49] Both of these hypotheticals feature access to the market that is clearly different in

---

[45] *303 Creative*, 143 S. Ct. at 2323–29 (Sotomayor, J., dissenting) (citing and recapitulating Joseph W. Singer, *No Right To Exclude: Public Accommodations and Private Property*, 90 Nw. U. L. Rev. 1283 (1996)). Singer and two other law professors filed an amicus brief in the case. *See* Brief of Public Accommodations Law Scholars as Amici Curiae in Support of Respondents, 303 Creative LLC v. Elenis, 143 S. Ct. 2298 (2023) (No. 21-476), 2022 WL 3648218. The same three professors and two others had written a similar brief in *Masterpiece*. Brief of Amici Curiae Public Accommodation Law Scholars in Support of Respondents, Masterpiece Cakeshop, Ltd. v. Colorado Civil Rights Comm'n, 138 S. Ct. 1719 (2018) (No. 16-111), 2017 WL 5127312.

[46] *303 Creative*, 143 S. Ct. at 2323–24 (Sotomayor, J., dissenting).

[47] *Id.* at 2324 (quoting Heart of Atlanta Motel, Inc., v. United States, 379 U.S. 241, 250 (1964), in turn quoting S. Rep. No. 88-872, at 22) (emphasis added). Sotomayor would return to this page of the Senate report later in her dissent. *See id.* at 2328.

[48] *Id.* at 2324 (citing J. Oleske, *The Evolution of Accommodation*, 50 Harv. Civ. Rights-Civ. Lib. L. Rev. 99, 138 (2015)).

[49] *Id.*

tangible ways because of the local scarcity of a good or service, not the mere unadorned expression of "otherness."[50]

Sotomayor next argued that imposing a duty on all businesses open to the public was narrowly tailored to achieve the goals of public-accommodation law.[51] However, the case that she cited at this point, *Roberts v. U.S. Jaycees*, described the compelling importance not of merely avoiding dignitary harm, but of women obtaining equal access to "leadership skills," "business contacts," and "employment promotions."[52] *Roberts* said nothing about the tailoring of an any-business-serving-the-public criterion to the avoidance of purely dignitary harm severed from any market-access limits. Indeed, it is hard to see how the use of public-accommodation law in this context could ever be narrowly tailored to promote dignity by avoiding unpleasant messages in the marketplace. Equivalently upsetting messages are often publicly expressed by those who are *not* in the market. Using public-accommodation law to promote dignity unaccompanied by tangible impact on market access will thus always be woefully underinclusive. Imagine a prospective plaintiff, in the market for wedding-related goods and services, walking along a city street. Behind door number 1 is someone like Jack Phillips or Lorie Smith, who is willing to sell goods and services for some weddings but not for weddings like the plaintiff's, and who makes this view painfully obvious by posting a sign at the door. The plaintiff is offended and thinks of suing. But then the plaintiff looks next door and finds, behind door number 2, another vendor perfectly willing to scoop up the profits abandoned by the vendor behind door number 1. After obtaining the goods and services, the plaintiff happily heads out the door. But this happiness is short-lived as the plaintiff walks past door number 3, the former shop of someone like Barronelle Stutzman, who no longer sells goods or services to anyone,[53] but who still includes a sign at her

---

[50] *Id.* at 2324–25 (citing K. Williams, *Ostracism*, 58 ANN. REV. PSYCHOLOGY 425, 432–435 (2007)).

[51] *Id.* at 2325.

[52] Roberts v. U.S. Jaycees, 468 U.S. 609, 626 (1984).

[53] *See* State v. Arlene's Flowers, Inc., 389 P.3d 543 (Wash. 2017), *cert. granted, judgment vacated*, Arlene's Flowers v. Washington, 138 S. Ct. 2671 (2018), *on remand*, State v. Arlene's Flowers, 441 P.3d 1203 (Wash. 2019), *cert. denied*, 141 S. Ct. 2884 (2021), *rehearing petition dismissed*, 142 S. Ct. 521. For Stutzman's statement on settling her case, see Letter from Barronelle Stutzman (Nov. 17, 2021), https://tinyurl.com/rex9mftc.

door expressing support for the vendor behind door number 1. The plaintiff is again offended, in the same way and for the same reason as before, but of course cannot sue a vendor who has already left the market. Living in a nation with a First Amendment—and analogous principles governing states!—means sometimes encountering the expression of views about human flourishing that one may find distasteful. Shorn of any actual impairment of market access, there is no reason to allow a suit against the door 1 vendor that would not also apply against the equally offensive sign displayed by the door 3 former vendor. Because the dignity-promoting goal of public-accommodation law requires far more than any such law could ever achieve, such a purpose is inevitably poorly tailored to its coverage.

After presenting this picture of the dual, independent purposes of public-accommodation law, Sotomayor explained its supposed roots in the common law, citing five cases, four treatises, and an article. A careful examination of all nine of these sources undermines the dissent's claim. Following Singer, the dissent began[54] with Lord Chief Justice Holt's explanation of common-carrier law in 1701 in *Lane v. Cotton*, which said that common-carrier duties attach "where-ever any subject takes upon himself a public trust for the benefit of the rest of his fellow-subjects."[55] Singer and the dissent read Holt's "take upon himself a public trust" to refer to any offer to the public, in any sort of business at all. They similarly read the reference in the very short 1710 case *Gisbourn v. Hurst* to "any man undertaking for hire to carry the goods of all persons indifferently."[56] But in the light of another of Holt's cases called *Coggs v. Bernard* from 1703, which went unmentioned by the dissent, this interpretation of *Lane* is not plausible. Only in certain contexts would a universal offer subject sellers to special public-accommodation duties. It is a mistake to confuse the criterion used in particular fields that feature local scarcity as if it were a general rationale that applied everywhere. *Coggs* explained that the special regulation of common carriers was "contrived by the policy of the law, for the safety of all persons, the *necessity of whose affairs* oblige them to trust these sorts

---

[54] *303 Creative*, 143 S. Ct. at 2325–26 (Sotomayor, J., dissenting).

[55] 88 Eng. Rep. 1458, 1465 (K.B. 1701).

[56] 91 Eng. Rep. 220, 220 (K.B. 1710).

of persons."⁵⁷ The idea is that by inviting the public to rely on a general offer—for instance, by leaving home in the belief that certain services are regularly available without subjecting the vulnerable to price gouging—common carriers help *induce* local scarcity of certain goods and services. Sotomayor quoted Singer's statement that *Lane* was "cited over and over again in the nineteenth century in the United States."⁵⁸ However, *Coggs* was cited repeatedly as well,⁵⁹ and so was Lord Chief Justice Hale, most prominently in *Munn*, but in many other cases too.⁶⁰

Like Sotomayor's erroneous assumption that the dignitary and market-access goals of common-carrier law are independent, Singer's key mistake in his account of the common law is his assumption that local scarcity of goods and services, on the one hand, and a vendor's general offer to the public, on the other, represent two *different* rationales, rather than two aspects of *one* rationale. Singer simply ignores thinkers like Lord Chief Justice Hale and the way that *Munn* heavily relies on him. The best account is to harmonize these two emphases: local scarcity, *induced by reliance on a general offer to the public*, is why common carriers and others at critical marketplace junctures or bottlenecks are subject to special duties to serve everyone. Preventing common carriers from backing out of their general offers prevents the bait-and-switch exploitation of the vulnerable. It is thus a mistake to put two possible justifications for common-carrier law—the fact that travelers have nowhere else to turn, and the fact that common carriers have held themselves out to the public to be trusted—in competition.

---

⁵⁷ 92 Eng. Rep. 107, 112 (K.B. 1703).

⁵⁸ *303 Creative*, 143 S. Ct. at 2325–26 (Sotomayor, J., dissenting) (quoting Singer, *supra* note 45, at 1304).

⁵⁹ *See, e.g.*, one of the articles on which Sotomayor herself relied, Edward A. Adler, *Business Jurisprudence*, 28 Harv. L. Rev. 135, 156 (1914) (calling *Coggs* as well as *Lane* "frequently cited cases").

⁶⁰ *See, e.g.*, Young v. Harrison, 6 Ga. 130, 142 (1849) ("I will say, what is well known to jurists, that in England, this work, from which the above principle is extracted, is considered as conclusive upon any question relating to the rights of Sovereign or subject, either in the sea, arms of the sea, or public or private streams of water; and that its authority has been repeatedly recognized in this country."); Enfield Bridge v. Hartford Railroad, 17 Conn. 40, 63–65 (1845) (referring to Hale's treatise merely by citing "Harg. L.T.," i.e., Hargrave's Law Tracts); and a case that *Munn* cites repeatedly, Lord Chief Justice Ellenborough's opinion in Allnutt v. Inglis, 104 Eng. Rep. 206 (K.B. 1810).

To support Singer's claim that *any* business dealing with the public had public-accommodation duties, and indeed that this view was "firmly established in early American case law," Sotomayor cited a string of two treatises and three more cases.[61] James Kent's *Commentaries*, Sotomayor's first source, is a nice explanation of the two emphases of common-carrier law set side by side. It is true that Kent defines common carriers, in the course of describing their bailment duties, as "those persons who undertake to carry goods generally, and for all people indifferently."[62] But *why* were such businesses subject to special duties? The immediately preceding sentence explains, with a footnote to Holt's opinion in *Coggs*, that "the rule is founded on the same broad principles of policy and convenience which govern the case of innkeepers."[63] What principles were those? Five pages earlier, Kent explains in detail why innkeepers were subject to special bailment duties: because there was no other game in town.

> It is not necessary to prove negligence in the innkeeper, for it is his duty to provide honest servants, according to the confidence reposed in him by the public, and he ought to answer civilly for their acts, even if they should rob the guests who sleep under his roof. Rigorous as this law may seem, and hard as it may actually be in some instances, it is, as Sir William Jones observes, founded on the principle of public utility, to which all private considerations ought to yield. Travellers, who must be numerous in a rich and commercial country, *are obliged to rely almost implicitly on the good faith of innkeepers* . . .[64]

Sotomayor's other treatise, by Justice Story, likewise defined common carriers as those who "undertake to carry goods for persons generally."[65] But three pages earlier, Story quoted Holt's rationale for

---

[61] *303 Creative*, 143 S. Ct. at 2326 (Sotomayor, J., dissenting).

[62] 2 James Kent, Commentaries on American Law 464 (New York, O. Halsted 1827).

[63] *Id.*

[64] *Id.* at 459–60 (emphasis added); *cf.* William Jones, An Essay on the Law of Bailments 96 (Garland Publishing 1978) (1781).

[65] Joseph Story, Commentaries on the Law of Bailments § 495, at 322 (Cambridge, Hilliard & Brown 1832); *cf. id.* § 591 at 374–75 (common-carrier obligation "results from their setting themselves up, like innkeepers, farriers, and other carriers, for common public employment.").

common-carrier law from *Coggs,* which explained that it is "contrived by the policy of the law for the safety of all persons, *the necessity of whose affairs* obliges them to trust these sorts of persons."[66] Elsewhere Story referred to common-carrier law as "the public policy of subjecting particular classes of persons to extraordinary responsibility, in *cases where an extraordinary confidence is necessarily reposed* in them."[67] Story went back to Roman-law explanations: "[T]he reason assigned by Ulpian for this edict is, that *it is necessary to place confidence* in such persons . . ."[68] Story quoted the same source on which Kent relied, Sir William Jones, who said that "travellers . . . are obliged to rely almost implicitly on the good faith of innholders."[69]

None of the three early cases cited by the dissenters helps their case:

- *Markham v. Brown* involved an argument, made in reliance on Story's treatise on bailments, that "none but travellers have right in a common inn."[70] This would fit, of course, with the limited solicitude in *Coggs* for those the "necessity of whose affairs oblige them to trust these sorts of persons." The plaintiff in *Markham* was not himself a traveler, but a coach driver who sought to enter an inn to solicit passengers. The court did not reject the inn's argument, saying "perhaps there may be cases in which he may have a right to exclude all but travellers and those who have been sent for by them," but held that it was not necessary to answer the question, because the coach driver's connection to travelers was close enough.

- Justice Story in *Jencks v. Coleman* faced no question about the common-carrier status, beginning his charge to the jury, "There is no doubt, that this steamboat is a common-carrier of passengers for hire."[71] His opinion contained nothing suggesting any difference from his *Coggs*-following views in his bailment treatise.

---

[66] *Id.* § 490 at 319 (emphasis added).

[67] *Id.* § 464 at 303 (emphasis added).

[68] *Id.* (emphasis added).

[69] *Id.* § 471 at 308 (quoting JONES, *supra* note 64).

[70] 8 N.H. 523, 528 (1837).

[71] 13 Fed. Cas. 442, 443 (C.C.D.R.I. 1835).

- *Dwight v. Brewster* briefly mentioned the issue of whether a common carrier of passengers is also a common carrier of their packages, but without explaining the rationale of the area of law at all.[72] A footnote later added by the reporter on the common-carrier issue cites Kent's Commentaries, which as noted above give an obliged-to-rely-almost-implicitly-on-the-good-faith-of-innkeepers rationale for common-carrier law.[73]

Next, Sotomayor quoted Edward Adler's provocative statement in 1914 that "Nowhere is monopoly suggested as the distinguishing characteristic."[74] Sotomayor glossed this as "nowhere in the relevant case law."[75] However, in context, this referred only to the very old "carrier cases" that Adler had been discussing at that point in his article. Earlier in the article, Adler claimed that "[n]o distinction based upon monopoly between a private and a common carrier *prior to the year 1600* has been set forth."[76] At the point at which Adler makes the "[n]owhere is monopoly suggested" comment, he had been discussing cases prior to the eighteenth century; he had not even yet mentioned *Lane* and *Coggs*.[77] The next page, Adler noted that "a great change took place in business conditions toward the close of the eighteenth century."[78] According to Adler, the railroad was the big driver for changes in the conceptual apparatus applied to common carriers: "In the course of time, with the introduction of railroads, other special and peculiar features, such as the enjoyment of peculiar privileges, franchises, and rights of way, became characteristic of carriage, and the relative importance of the carrier's calling was greatly accentuated."[79] While Adler disagreed with

---

[72] 18 Mass. 50, 53–54 (1822).

[73] *Id.* at 54 n.1 (footnote citing Kent's Commentaries, not published until five years after the opinion was released in 1822).

[74] *303 Creative*, 143 S. Ct. at 2326 (Sotomayor, J., dissenting) (quoting Adler, *supra* note 59, at 156).

[75] *Id.*

[76] Adler, *supra* note 59, at 148 (emphasis added).

[77] *Id.* at 156; *see also id.* at 156–57 n.77 (quoting the early-eighteenth-century cases).

[78] *Id.* at 157.

[79] *Id.* at 158. Adler quoted Justices Field and Strong's dissent in *Munn*, which would have actually struck down the grain-elevator (and railroad) regulations, at length. *See id.* at 159.

Wyman's local-scarcity-based rationalization of the older common law,[80] Adler knew well that there were many, many nineteenth-century cases agreeing with Wyman. Adler called Wyman's explanation of the distinction between private and public callings the "doctrine uniformly accepted by our courts as well as by students of the common law today."[81] Adler explicitly said he wanted to return to a view of the common law that was "remote . . . from our modern thinking," and the modern thinking of which he spoke was exemplified in cases like *Munn*.[82] Adler's article does not suggest in the slightest that cases like *Charles Wolff Packing* had misread *Munn* itself.

A footnote in the dissent then cited two more treatises (in addition to citing Story's treatise and *Lane* again).[83] William Blackstone included a few sorts of common carriers in his list of those subject to implied contractual duties. "[I]f an inn-keeper, or other victualler, hangs out a sign and opens his house for travellers, it is an implied engagement to entertain all persons who travel that way; and upon this universal *assumpsit* an action on the case will lie against him for damages, if he without good reason refuses to admit a traveller."[84] Note the limit to travelers—i.e., those not in a position to find alternatives—and the reference to damages, the ordinary sort of which would not exist unless local scarcity were involved.

Finally, Sotomayor cited Theophilus Parsons's treatise on contracts. Parsons used the same general definition as Kent and Story, and also like them, Parsons relied on Holt's view in *Coggs* repeatedly. In *Coggs*, Parsons said, Holt "laid the foundation of this system

---

[80] *See id.* at 148, disagreeing with Wyman's treatise co-authored with Joseph Beale. For some representative samples for how Wyman explains early cases in terms of a local-scarcity rationale, see WYMAN, *supra* note 41, at 7 (fewer doctors at the time) and 8 (fewer tailors). For Wyman's general take on the evolution of the common law, see *id.* at 17: "The common law persists from age to age, and though the instance of its rules may be seen to change as old conditions pass away and new conditions arise, its fundamental principles remain. The early cases which were just under discussion are illustrations of this course of events. Barber, surgeon, smith and tailor are no longer in common calling because the situation in the modern times does not require it; but innkeeper, carrier, ferryman and wharfinger are still in that classification, since even in modern business the conditions require them to be so treated."

[81] Adler, *supra* note 59, at 141.

[82] *Id.* at 159.

[83] *303 Creative*, 143 S. Ct. at 2326 n.6 (Sotomayor, J., dissenting).

[84] 3 WILLIAM BLACKSTONE, COMMENTARIES ON THE LAW OF ENGLAND 164 (Oxford, Clarendon Press 1768).

109

of law."[85] Parsons referred to "the case of *Coggs v. Bernard*, so often cited."[86] Further, Parsons recapitulated many other scarcity-based explanations of the reason for common-carrier duties put forward by various courts. He quoted Pennsylvania Chief Justice John Gibson on the rationale for imposing common-carrier duties even on merely-occasional wagoners, explaining that America's much lower population density relative to England meant that greater common-carrier duties were appropriate: "[T]he policy of holding him answerable as an insurer was more obviously dictated by the solitary and mountainous regions through which his course for the most part lay, than it is by the frequented thoroughfares of England."[87] Finally, Parsons quoted Connecticut Justice Ellsworth on the inability of passengers to protect themselves: "The driver must, of course, be attentive and watchful. He has, for the time being, committed to his trust, the safety and lives of people, old and young, women and children, locked up as it were in the coach or rail-car, ignorant, helpless, and having no eyes, or ears, or power to guard against dangers, and who look to him for safety in their transportation."[88] Parsons added that the rule stated in the case "has been repeatedly declared to be the law in this country."[89] In short, Parsons, like Lord Chief Justice Holt and the other sources that rely on him, plainly saw common-carrier regulation as a response for preventing owners from taking advantage of particular market bottlenecks, not as a mechanism for requiring everyone in the market to think the same way about human flourishing.

* * *

Sometimes generals and Supreme Court Justices seem to be fighting the last war, rather than the conflict directly requiring their attention.[90] At other times, however, they seem to be fighting the *next*

---

[85] 1 Theophilus Parsons, The Law of Contracts 569–70 (Boston, Little Brown & Co. 1853).

[86] *Id.* at 590.

[87] *Id.* at 640 note r (quoting Gordon v. Hutchinson, 1 Watts & Serg. 285, 287 (Pa. 1841)).

[88] *Id.* at 691 note m (quoting Derwort v. Loomer, 21 Conn. 245, 253–54 (1851)).

[89] *Id.*

[90] *See, e.g.*, Lawrence v. Texas, 539 U.S. 558, 586–92 (2003) (Scalia, J., dissenting) (devoting the first part of his dissent to an extended criticism of Planned Parenthood v. Casey, 505 U.S. 833 (1992)).

war as well as the one they are in. Given the majority's failure to use a scarcity-based view of public-accommodation law to give relief to Lorie Smith, it is hard to see why the dissenters would devote such space and prominence to rebutting that view, unless they expect to see it make headway in the future. Ideas that are really dead do not deserve this much bother. There is, accordingly, some reason to think that someday soon the Court may give entrepreneurial liberty the sort of attention it received from the Fourteenth Amendment's adopters and from the Court in cases like *Munn* and *Charles Wolff Packing*. When that happens, the precise scope of the Anglo-American traditions of market intervention to promote the general good of all citizens in an inclusive republic will once again be important. This intellectual terrain will be fought over again.

Counterman v. Colorado: Defining True Threats of Violence under the First Amendment

Clay Calvert*

Introduction

Despite the First Amendment's absolutist command that "no law" shall be made abridging free speech, the U.S. Supreme Court has identified several varieties of expression that generally can be regulated without raising constitutional concerns.[1] In brief, "no law" doesn't really mean what it says; laws banning some types of speech are okay. These categorical carveouts from First Amendment protection typically evolve over decades. Such is the case for the "true threats" exception, which the Court addressed in the 2023 online-stalking case of *Counterman v. Colorado*.[2] Grasping this reality, encapsulated below, helps in better understanding the evolution of the true threats doctrine.

A. How Unprotected Categories of Speech Develop over Time

Consider the obscenity carveout. In 1942, the Court suggested in *Chaplinsky v. New Hampshire* that regulating obscenity "[has] never been thought to raise any Constitutional problem."[3] Fifteen years later, the Court definitively declared that "obscenity is not within the area of constitutionally protected speech or press."[4]

---

* Professor Emeritus, University of Florida.

[1] *See* Ashcroft v. Free Speech Coal., 535 U.S. 234, 245–46 (2002) ("The freedom of speech has its limits; it does not embrace certain categories of speech, including defamation, incitement, obscenity, and pornography produced with real children.").

[2] 143 S. Ct. 2106 (2023).

[3] 315 U.S. 568, 572 (1942).

[4] Roth v. United States, 354 U.S. 476, 485 (1957).

Less clear then, however, was the Court's eventual definition of obscenity. That definition developed across multiple cases, including the Court's 1964 *Jacobellis v. Ohio* decision best remembered for Justice Potter Stewart's definitional lament about obscenity: "I know it when I see it."[5] It wasn't until 1973 in *Miller v. California* that the Court adopted its current obscenity test.[6]

Or think about another type of unprotected expression: incitement to unlawful conduct. Incitement doctrine evolved from the clear-and-present danger standard fashioned more than a century ago in *Schenck v. United States*,[7] the case that spawned the oft-misquoted maxim about "falsely shouting fire in a theatre."[8] It developed into the more demanding, free-speech friendly test articulated in 1969 in *Brandenburg v. Ohio*.[9] It holds that the First Amendment protects "advocacy of the use of force or of law violation except where such advocacy is directed to inciting or producing imminent lawless action and is likely to incite or produce such action."[10]

The illicit category called "fighting words" has similarly morphed since its initial articulation in *Chaplinsky* as words "which by their very utterance inflict injury or tend to incite an immediate breach of the peace."[11] Later cases closely cabined the fighting words exception.[12] Today, fighting words narrowly include only personally

[5] 378 U.S. 184, 197 (1964) (Stewart, J., concurring). Other key cases in the series of decisions in which the Court refined the requirements for convicting a person for obscenity include *Smith v. California*, 361 U.S. 147 (1959), and *A Book Named "John Cleland's Memoirs of a Woman of Pleasure" v. Att'y Gen. of Mass.*, 383 U.S. 413 (1966).

[6] 413 U.S. 15 (1973). The *Miller* test for obscenity focuses on whether content: (1) appeals to a prurient interest in sex, when considered as a whole and from the perspective of an average adult applying contemporary community standards; (2) depicts in a patently offensive manner the display of sexual conduct, as defined by state law; and (3) lacks serious literary, artistic, political, or scientific value. *See id.* at 24.

[7] 249 U.S. 47, 52 (1919) ("The question in every case is whether the words used are used in such circumstances and are of such a nature as to create a clear and present danger that they will bring about the substantive evils that Congress has a right to prevent.").

[8] *Id.* People often omit "falsely" from this statement. *See, e.g.*, Carlton F.W. Larson, *"Shouting 'Fire' in a Theater": The Life and Times of Constitutional Law's Most Enduring Analogy*, 24 WM. & MARY BILL OF RTS. J. 181 (2015).

[9] 395 U.S. 444 (1969).

[10] *Id.* at 447.

[11] *Chaplinsky*, 315 U.S. at 572.

[12] *See* Cohen v. California, 403 U.S. 15 (1971); Hess v. Indiana, 414 U.S. 105 (1973).

abusive epithets, directed in person at specific individuals, that are inherently likely to make their targets swing back and hit the speaker (hence the moniker "fighting words"). That likelihood is determined based on the context of the words' utterance and the characteristics of their targets.[13]

This all renders unsurprising the comparably protracted development of true threats, a newer category of unprotected speech at issue in *Counterman v. Colorado*. As described later in this article, *Counterman* is a criminal stalking case centering on hundreds of unsolicited direct messages sent via Facebook by a stranger, Billy Raymond Counterman, to Colorado singer-songwriter Coles Whalen. Counterman was convicted of stalking Whalen, but he claimed that the First Amendment protected his messages because they weren't true threats. The U.S. Supreme Court took the case to decide exactly when threats fall beyond First Amendment protection.

Before delving deeper, it's useful to clarify in non-legalese the fundamental differences among three already-noted types of unprotected expression—incitement, fighting words, and true threats. Here's a broad-brushstrokes encapsulation:

- **Incitement:** I say something to you to get you to commit violence or an unlawful act against someone else. For instance: Did Donald Trump unlawfully incite violence at the Capitol when he spoke to supporters, shortly before it erupted, at a nearby rally on January 6, 2021?
- **Fighting Words:** I say something to you that's very likely to make you hit me. For instance: A white person angrily and repeatedly calling a Black person the N-word in a face-to-face encounter is "a classic case" of fighting words, according to North Carolina's Supreme Court.[14]

---

[13] *See* Clay Calvert, *Taking the Fight Out of Fighting Words on the Doctrine's Eightieth Anniversary: What "N" Word Litigation Today Reveals About Assumptions, Flaws and Goals of a First Amendment Principle in Disarray*, 87 Mo. L. Rev. 493 (2022) (addressing the evolution of the fighting words doctrine and the factors that courts consider in determining whether speech constitutes fighting words).

[14] *In re* Spivey, 480 S.E.2d 693, 699 (N.C. 1997). The Court added that "[n]o fact is more generally known than that a white man who calls a black man [an N-word] within his hearing will hurt and anger the black man and often provoke him to confront the white man and retaliate." *Id.*

- **True Threats:** I say something to you that, given the context in which I say it, puts you in fear of imminent violence or death. For instance: Several menacing posters mailed to a person's residence—one depicting "a man in a skull mask holding a Molotov cocktail in front of a burning house" and reading "your actions have consequences our patience has its limits," and another including swastikas and stating "we are watching . . . we know where you live do not fuck with us"—were recently dubbed true threats by a federal appellate court.[15] A brief origin story of the true threats doctrine that led to that outcome and paved the path to *Counterman* follows.

B. The Evolving True Threats Doctrine

In the 1969 case of *Watts v. United States,* the Supreme Court held for the first time that true threats of violence are not shielded by the First Amendment.[16] The Court concluded that 18-year-old Robert Watts did not make an illegal threat during a 1966 anti-war rally near the Washington Monument. Responding to being drafted and reporting for a physical exam, Watts told the crowd of teens and others in their early twenties, "I am not going. If they ever make me carry a rifle the first man I want to get in my sights is L. B. J."[17] Watts and his audience then laughed.[18]

The Supreme Court, in a short unsigned opinion, deemed Watts's words protected "political hyperbole," thereby reversing his conviction for threatening President Lyndon Baines Johnson.[19] But the Court didn't define true threats. It reasoned only that the "context" of Watts's speech (a political rally), the "expressly conditional nature of the statement" (his use of "if"), and the audience's reaction (laughter) all suggested that it was merely a crude form of political opposition.[20]

In the 1992 cross-burning case of *R.A.V. v. City of St. Paul,* the Court explained why the First Amendment does not safeguard true

---

[15] United States v. Cole, 2023 U.S. App. LEXIS 8757, at *2 (9th Cir. Apr. 12, 2023).

[16] 394 U.S. 705, 707 (1969) ("What is a threat must be distinguished from what is constitutionally protected speech.").

[17] *Id.* at 706.

[18] *See id.* at 707.

[19] *Id.* at 708.

[20] *Id.*

threats.[21] Justice Antonin Scalia wrote that "threats of violence are outside the First Amendment" due to concerns about "protecting individuals from the fear of violence, from the disruption that fear engenders, and from the possibility that the threatened violence will occur."[22] In short, the acute harms that threats cause justify jettisoning threats from constitutional protection.

In 2003, the Court reinforced the principle that the First Amendment does not safeguard true threats in another cross-burning case, *Virginia v. Black*.[23] The Court there elaborated a bit more definitionally, noting that true threats include "statements where the speaker means to communicate a serious expression of an intent to commit an act of unlawful violence to a particular individual or group of individuals."[24] This definition may seem clear, but as the next section reveals, it raised complicated questions that the Supreme Court ultimately resolved in *Counterman*.

C. Does a Speaker's Subjective Mental State about or Awareness of a Statement's Threatening Nature Matter?

What exactly does "intent" refer to in the quotation from *Black* immediately above? Does it simply mean an intent to communicate a statement? Or does it mean something more—an intent by the speaker for the statement to be understood as a serious expression of a threat of violence?

In other words, the Court in *Black* didn't clarify what the government must prove regarding a defendant-speaker's state of mind or understanding about a message's threatening character for it to be unprotected by the First Amendment.[25] Must the government prove

---

[21] 505 U.S. 377 (1992).

[22] *Id.* at 388.

[23] 538 U.S. 343 (2003). Citing the Court's decision in *Watts* for support, Justice Sandra Day O'Connor wrote that "the First Amendment . . . permits a State to ban a 'true threat.'" *Id.* at 359.

[24] *Id.*

[25] *See* Lyrissa Barnett Lidsky & Linda Riedemann Norbut, *#I♥U: Considering the Context of Online Threats*, 106 Calif. L. Rev. 1886, 1889–90 (2018) ("The Court has failed . . . to answer fundamental questions regarding the 'true threats exception' to First Amendment protection, including whether courts should view threats from the vantage of the speaker, a reasonable recipient, a reasonable disinterested reader, or all of the above; and what mens rea the First Amendment requires in threats cases.") (footnote omitted).

something about a speaker's subjective mental state—a speaker's mens rea, in legal parlance[26]—regarding whether a message might be understood as a threat? Is that subjective mental state relevant under a First Amendment–based true threats inquiry?

The questions, however, don't stop there. If a speaker's mental state about a threatening meaning *is* relevant, then another issue arises: What *level* of mens rea on a speaker's part must the government prove for a threat to fall beyond First Amendment shelter? Must the government prove: (1) that the speaker acted *purposely* to put the target in fear (the highest level of mens rea); or (2) that the speaker *knew* the target would be fearful (a slightly lower level); or (3) merely that the speaker acted *recklessly* as to whether the target would experience fear (a still lower level of mens rea, requiring a speaker's awareness of a substantial risk of conveying a threatening meaning and ignoring it)? Spoiler alert: A five-Justice majority in *Counterman* concluded that a speaker's state of mind *is* relevant in the true threats calculus and, more specifically, that the government must prove that a speaker recklessly conveyed a threat.

But, stepping back, why do these differences even matter? Because the higher the level of mens rea that applies, the more difficult it is for prosecutors to demonstrate that statements are unprotected by the First Amendment. Put differently, requiring prosecutors to prove that a defendant *purposely* conveyed a threatening meaning is a more free-speech-friendly standard than requiring them only to prove that a defendant *recklessly* conveyed a threatening meaning.

Conversely, if a speaker's subjective mental state about a threatening meaning were totally irrelevant, then prosecutors would only need to prove that an objectively reasonable person in the target's position would find the message threatening. An objective, reasonable person standard is known as a negligence test.[27]

---

[26] *See* Andrew Ingram, *Out of Sight and Out of Mind: Criminal Law's Disguised Moral Culpability Requirement*, 56 U. RICH. L. REV. 491, 499 (2022) ("The mens rea inquiry asks what the defendant believed, intended, or knew at the time that he acted. It is shorthand for the mental state element of a crime."); Erik Luna, *Mezzanine Law: The Case of a Mens Rea Presumption*, 53 ARIZ. ST. L.J. 565, 565 (2021) (calling mens rea "the mental state element of crime").

[27] *See* Elonis v. United States, 575 U.S. 723, 738–39 (2015).

As Justice Sonia Sotomayor explained during oral argument in *Counterman*, "a pure negligence standard . . . doesn't take into account any of the intentions of the speaker when we prosecute for speech."[28]

If courts completely ignore a speaker-defendant's subjective understanding of a message's threatening meaning, there is a danger (from a free-speech perspective) that the meaning either intended or understood by a speaker and the meaning understood by the message's target will be different. In short, intended meanings might get lost in translation, and speakers might be convicted for conveying threatening meanings they neither understood nor intended.

Furthermore, risk-averse speakers who fear being convicted for misunderstood messages may self-censor, stifling their expression of statements that would actually be safeguarded by the First Amendment. In other words, fear of liability might produce a chilling effect on protected expression. Justice Elena Kagan explained for the *Counterman* majority how self-censorship and a chilling effect may arise whenever speech is banned:

> Prohibitions on speech have the potential to chill, or deter, speech outside their boundaries. A speaker may be unsure about the side of a line on which his speech falls. Or he may worry that the legal system will err, and count speech that is permissible as instead not. . . . Or he may simply be concerned about the expense of becoming entangled in the legal system. The result is "self-censorship" of speech that could not be proscribed—a "cautious and restrictive exercise" of First Amendment freedoms.[29]

In short, requiring a prosecutor to prove that a defendant-speaker had *some* level of mental awareness (some degree "of a culpable mental state,"[30] as Justice Kagan wrote) about a statement's threatening nature provides a buffer against self-censorship.

---

[28] Transcript of Oral Argument at 20, Counterman v. Colorado, 143 S. Ct. 2106 (2023) (No. 22-138), https://tinyurl.com/3xcz2mv3.

[29] *Counterman*, 143 S. Ct. at 2114–15.

[30] *Id.* at 2115.

D. Counterman Resolves the Speaker's State of Mind Issues: A Synopsis of the Opinions

The issues described above sparked the question that the Supreme Court agreed to answer in January 2023, when it granted review in *Counterman v. Colorado*:

> Whether, to establish that a statement is a "true threat" unprotected by the First Amendment, the government must show that the speaker subjectively knew or intended the threatening nature of the statement, or whether it is enough to show that an objective "reasonable person" would regard the statement as a threat of violence.[31]

On June 27, 2023, the Court issued its ruling, which included a five-Justice majority opinion, a two-Justice concurrence, and two dissents. Here's a synopsis of those opinions.

1. Justice Kagan's Opinion for the Court

The Court concluded that the First Amendment guarantee of free speech demands proving *more* than just that an objectively reasonable person would understand a message's threatening nature. Specifically, it requires proving that a speaker recklessly conveyed a threatening meaning.[32]

Penning the Court's opinion, Justice Kagan explained that prosecutors must prove a "defendant consciously disregarded a substantial risk that his communications would be viewed as threatening violence."[33] She elaborated that "reckless defendants have done more than make a bad mistake. They have consciously accepted a substantial risk of inflicting serious harm."[34] In short, a defendant's mental state about a message's threatening meaning *does* determine if a threat is unprotected by the First Amendment.

As noted earlier, recklessness is a less demanding mental-state standard than proving that speakers either *purposely* placed people in fear or *knew* they were placing people in fear. The majority, however,

---

[31] Question Presented, Counterman v. Colorado, 143 S. Ct. 2106 (2023) (No. 22-138), https://tinyurl.com/mry8fc6j.

[32] *See Counterman,* 143 S. Ct. at 2111.

[33] *Id.* at 2112.

[34] *Id.* at 2118.

believed that recklessness "is enough"[35] to balance two competing interests. There is, on the one hand, a First Amendment interest in preventing self-censorship of, and a chilling effect on, fully protected, non-threatening expression (dangers described earlier). But there are also "the profound harms, to both individuals and society, that attend true threats of violence."[36] Imposing a higher mens rea standard—purpose or knowledge—would make it too difficult to convict "morally culpable defendants."[37] Recklessness, instead, provides a constitutionally sufficient guardrail against chilling protected expression. Justice Kagan's opinion was joined by Chief Justice John Roberts and Justices Samuel Alito, Brett Kavanaugh, and Ketanji Brown Jackson.

If you're keeping tabs, that's five Justices nominated by four Presidents from two parties: George W. Bush (Roberts and Alito), Barack Obama (Kagan), Donald Trump (Kavanaugh), and Joe Biden (Jackson). Free-speech cases thus sometimes unite Justices despite perceived ideological differences. That wasn't the situation, however, in the same-sex wedding website case of *303 Creative v. Elenis*, which was decided within days of *Counterman* (*303 Creative* is also analyzed in this edition of the *Cato Supreme Court Review*).

2. Justice Sotomayor's Concurrence

Justice Sotomayor wrote a concurrence joined in several parts by Justice Neil Gorsuch.[38] She agreed with the Court's judgment that a recklessness mens rea standard was appropriate in the *Counterman* case specifically because, as she saw it, *Counterman* was a case about *stalking* that just happened to involve *threats*. But Justice Sotomayor contended that a mens rea level *higher* than recklessness is likely warranted under the First Amendment "to prosecute true threats *generally*."[39]

She suggested that in typical threats (not stalking) cases, the government must prove "that an individual desires to threaten or is substantially certain that her statements will be understood as

---

35 *Id.* at 2113.

36 *Id.* at 2117.

37 *Id.* at 2118.

38 *Id.* at 2119 (Sotomayor, J., concurring in part and concurring in the judgment).

39 *Id.* at 2132 (emphasis added).

threatening."[40] In short, an "intent to threaten" element should be included in a true threats analysis. This renders Justice Sotomayor's stance more free-speech friendly than Justice Kagan's in safeguarding unintentional threats.[41]

Justice Sotomayor reasoned that this higher mental-state standard was necessary partly because "in a climate of intense polarization, it is dangerous to allow criminal prosecutions for heated words based solely on an amorphous recklessness standard."[42] Additionally, Sotomayor cited rap music as a concrete example of how "[m]embers of certain groups, including religious and cultural minorities, can . . . use language that is more susceptible to being misinterpreted by outsiders. And unfortunately yet predictably, racial and cultural stereotypes can also influence whether speech is perceived as dangerous."[43] In short, Sotomayor was concerned about "overcriminalizing upsetting or frightening speech."[44] This included speech on the internet, which "lack[s] many normal contextual clues, such as who is speaking, tone of voice, and expression."[45]

3. The Dissents of Justices Barrett and Thomas

Justice Amy Coney Barrett authored a dissent joined in full by Justice Clarence Thomas.[46] They believed that *no* subjective mens rea standard of any level is required. The First Amendment is satisfied by a purely objective test—one requiring the government to "show that a reasonable person would regard the statement as a threat of violence."[47]

Justice Barrett reasoned that because an objective analysis already "captures (among other things) the speaker's tone, the audience, the medium for the communication, and the broader exchange in which the statement occurs," it sufficiently "weed[s] out protected speech from true threats."[48] Reflecting both Justice Thomas's and her own

[40] *Id.* at 2120.
[41] *Id.* at 2129.
[42] *Id.* at 2132
[43] *Id.* at 2123.
[44] *Id.* at 2122.
[45] *Id.*
[46] *Id.* at 2133 (Barrett, J., dissenting).
[47] *Id.*
[48] *Id.* at 2137.

embrace of historicism, Barrett added that Billy Raymond Counterman was "plainly not asking the Court to enforce a historically sanctioned rule, but rather to fashion a new one."[49] In other words, the Court shouldn't function as a legislative body and adopt interest-balancing rules untethered from history and tradition.

Justice Thomas issued a brief solo dissent lambasting the Court's landmark 1964 defamation decision of *New York Times Co. v. Sullivan*[50] for adopting the "actual malice" fault standard.[51] How is *Sullivan* even remotely related to a true threats case? Because the definition of actual malice embraced in *Sullivan* requires considering a defamation defendant's subjective *recklessness* about publishing reputation-harming falsities.[52] In short, Justice Thomas objects to recklessness (as part of the actual malice standard) in defamation law because it's a judicially created rule, *not* a historically grounded one. And he equally opposes extending recklessness to the true threats realm on the same grounds.

With this understanding of true threats, as well as the issues and outcome in *Counterman* in mind, this article now digs deeper into both the doctrine and *Counterman's* facts. The next part briefly reviews two cases decided prior to *Counterman*—*Elonis v. United States*[53] in 2015 and *Perez v. Florida*[54] in 2017—where the Supreme Court passed on resolving the speaker's state-of-mind question. Understanding the facts of these cases is important because they illustrate why *Counterman's* incorporation of a recklessness mental-state element into the test for true threats is beneficial. The recklessness element will support free-speech interests in situations involving ambiguous messages and lost-in-translation meanings.

The article then reviews *Counterman's* facts in more detail and the Colorado appellate court's ruling that preceded the Supreme Court's decision. It also addresses oral argument before the nation's highest court, including concerns raised by the Justices and key points made by the attorneys who addressed them: (1) John Elwood, arguing for

[49] *Id.* at 2139.

[50] 376 U.S. 254 (1964).

[51] *Counterman*, 143 S. Ct. at 2132 (Thomas, J., dissenting).

[52] *See Sullivan*, 376 U.S. at 280 (defining actual malice as publishing a statement "with knowledge that it was false or with *reckless disregard* of whether it was false or not") (emphasis added).

[53] 575 U.S. 723 (2015).

[54] 580 U.S. 1187 (2017).

Billy Raymond Counterman, the defendant in the underlying criminal case; (2) Philip Weiser, the Colorado Attorney General, on behalf of the prosecution in *Counterman*; and (3) Eric Feigin, a U.S. Deputy Solicitor General who argued as a friend-of-the-court on Colorado's behalf.

Finally, the article recaps the outcome in *Counterman* and explores a bone of contention between Justice Kagan's majority opinion and the dissenters. That dispute centers on whether the Supreme Court's ruling in the defamation case noted earlier, *New York Times Co. v. Sullivan*, provides relevant support for the adoption of a recklessness requirement in true threats cases.

I. The Road to *Counterman*: When Alleged Rap Lyrics and Drunken Jokes Might Be Misunderstood as True Threats of Violence

The Supreme Court punted twice on answering the speaker's state-of-mind question shortly before resolving it in *Counterman*. The facts in these cases reveal how incorporating *Counterman*'s now-mandated recklessness mental-state requirement into the true threats doctrine may sometimes safeguard speakers against threats convictions.

A. Elonis v. United States

In the early 2010s, Anthony Elonis was convicted under a federal threats statute for several violent-themed Facebook posts, including ones about his estranged wife and an FBI agent. Elonis claimed that his posts were merely fictitious rap lyrics inspired by Eminem.[55] Posting them under his rap alias, "Tone Dougie," Elonis contended his words were therapeutic, helping him cope with his collapsing marriage.[56] In short, Elonis said he didn't intend the posts to be taken as threats.

Elonis was convicted under a statute that criminalizes transmitting "any threat to injure the person of another" in interstate commerce.[57] Elonis requested a jury instruction that the government had to prove that he subjectively intended to threaten violence, but the trial court judge denied that request. The only intent on Elonis's part that the jury considered was simply whether he intended to communicate a statement.

---

[55] *Elonis*, 575 U.S. at 731.

[56] *Id.* at 727.

[57] 18 U.S.C. § 875(c).

In brief, whether Elonis intended to threaten was irrelevant. What mattered, per the instructions, was whether "a reasonable person would foresee that the statement[s] would be interpreted by those to whom the maker communicates the statement[s] as a serious expression of an intention to inflict bodily injury or take the life of an individual."[58] This is an objective test; it focuses only on how an objectively reasonable—albeit hypothetical—person would understand a message.

A federal appellate court affirmed Elonis's conviction.[59] It reasoned that the Supreme Court's decision in *Virginia v. Black* (noted earlier) "does not say that the true threats exception requires a subjective intent to threaten."[60] This teed up the case for the Supreme Court to consider the relevance, if any, of Anthony Elonis's alleged intent not to threaten via his supposed rap lyrics.

The Supreme Court heard the case but avoided the constitutional question. The Court did not decide what the First Amendment requires the government to prove about a defendant-speaker's state of mind regarding a threatening meaning. It passed on this issue by focusing *only* on what the federal threats statute under which Elonis was convicted requires the government to prove about a defendant-speaker's state of mind. The Court thereby resolved *Elonis* on *statutory*—not *constitutional*—grounds.

Writing the majority opinion, Chief Justice Roberts reasoned that while "the statute does not specify any required mental state, [that] does not mean that none exists."[61] Indeed, the majority concluded that the statute implicitly requires the government to prove some level of mental awareness—some quantum of mens rea—on a defendant's part "to the fact that the communication contains a threat."[62] The jury, however, wasn't instructed to consider this; it only evaluated how a reasonable person would understand Elonis's Facebook posts.[63] This instructional error regarding the federal statute allowed the Court to

---

[58] *Elonis*, 575 U.S. at 731.

[59] United States v. Elonis, 730 F.3d 321 (3rd Cir. 2013), *rev'd sub nom.* Elonis v. United States, 575 U.S. 723 (2015).

[60] *Id.* at 332.

[61] *Elonis*, 575 U.S. at 734.

[62] *Id.* at 737.

[63] *Id.*

conclude that "Elonis's conviction cannot stand."[64] Chief Justice Roberts, in turn, reckoned it "not necessary to consider any First Amendment issues,"[65] thereby letting the Court punt on whether the First Amendment true threats doctrine—not just a federal statute—also requires some level of mental awareness on a speaker's part.

This limited outcome in *Elonis* comports with a doctrine called constitutional avoidance.[66] That doctrine holds that the Court should refrain from addressing constitutional questions when a case can be decided on statutory grounds.[67] In sum, *Elonis* was a narrow statutory decision, with the Court kicking the constitutional can down the road. That missed opportunity was thoroughly unsatisfying, a colleague and I observed, because "[i]f one First Amendment doctrine screams out the loudest for clarification, it may well be true threats."[68]

Elonis's claim that his posts were rap lyrics also gave the Court another opportunity it elided. It could have explored the ambiguities of meaning and the problems with deploying an objectively reasonable person standard that arise when "a complex genre"[69] like rap—which melds "art, poetry and fantasy,"[70] "sometimes is political,"[71] and "carries with it the heavy baggage of negative controversy"[72]—is in play. A key problem, as two former students (now attorneys) and I explained nearly a decade ago, is this: "What should courts and jurors expect a reasonable person to know and understand about rap music?"[73] The danger in only considering how a supposedly reasonable person would interpret rap lyrics is

---

[64] *Id.* at 740.

[65] *Id.*

[66] *See* Clay Calvert & Matthew D. Bunker, *Fissures, Fractures & Doctrinal Drifts: Paying the Price in First Amendment Jurisprudence for a Half Decade of Avoidance, Minimalism & Partisanship*, 24 WM. & MARY BILL OF RTS. J. 943, 945 (2016).

[67] *See id.*

[68] *Id.* at 957.

[69] Clay Calvert, Emma Morehart & Sarah Papadelias, *Rap Music and the True Threats Quagmire: When Does One Man's Lyric Become Another's Crime?*, 38 COLUM. J.L. & ARTS 1, 20 (2014).

[70] *Id.* at 19.

[71] *Id.* at 18.

[72] *Id.* at 17.

[73] *Id.* at 22.

that an innocent meaning intended by a rap-literate speaker will get lost in translation by a rap-illiterate jury and taken as an illicit threat. Recall here Justice Sotomayor's concern about rap music in her *Counterman* concurrence.[74]

Furthermore, problems with interpreting rap surfaced during the oral argument before the Court in *Counterman*. Justice Sotomayor— telegraphing her concurrence that would call for a mental-state level higher than recklessness in typical true threats cases—broached the topic of rap. She suggested that possible societal biases are embedded in a reasonable person standard due to jurors' beliefs about a particular community's interpretive norms, such as a community of rappers versus non-rappers.[75] John Elwood, who represented Counterman and who had also represented Anthony Elonis before the Court, responded that "fringe speech" and "fringe art[s] tend[] to be viewed as threatening . . . to people who are unfamiliar with it."[76] In short, the danger of wrongful convictions increases when courts deploy an objective, reasonable person test regarding a threatening meaning.

B. Perez v. Florida

Two years after the Court dodged the speaker's state-of-mind issue in *Elonis*, it did so again in *Perez v. Florida*.[77] The Court summarily declined to review a Florida appellate court ruling[78] affirming Robert Perez's conviction for violating a state threats statute.[79]

Although Justice Sotomayor "reluctantly concur[red]"[80] with denying Perez's petition, she wrote separately—the only Justice who penned a signed opinion—expressing dismay that "Perez is serving more than 15 years in a Florida prison for what may have been nothing more than a drunken joke."[81] That's because, as Sotomayor

---

[74] *See supra* note 43 and accompanying text.

[75] *See* Transcript, *supra* note 28, at 35–36.

[76] *Id.* at 36.

[77] 580 U.S. 1187 (2017).

[78] Perez v. State of Florida, 189 So.3d 797 (Fla. Dist. Ct. App. 2016).

[79] Fla. Stat. § 790.162 (making it a second-degree felony "to threaten to throw, project, place, or discharge any destructive device with intent to do bodily harm to any person or with intent to do damage to any property of any person").

[80] *Perez*, 580 U.S. at 1188 (Sotomayor, J., concurring).

[81] *Id.* at 1187.

explained, the instructions given in Perez's case permitted the jury "to convict Perez based on what he 'stated' alone—irrespective of whether his words represented a joke, the ramblings of an intoxicated individual, or a credible threat."[82] Thus, for Sotomayor, "the jury instruction—and Perez's conviction—raise[d] serious First Amendment concerns worthy of this Court's review."[83] But because both Perez (in his pro se petition to the Supreme Court) and the Florida courts (in addressing his case) had not focused on the First Amendment–based mens rea question (only on the statutory one), she agreed the Court should not hear the case.

So, how might a jury instruction requiring the government to prove "*some* level of intent,"[84] as Sotomayor put it, have led to a different result and Robert Perez's possible acquittal? Because, if one believes Perez's story, his only offense was making a misunderstood joke while at a Publix liquor store to buy vodka after a long day of beach drinking.[85] The joke dealt with a drink Perez called a Molotov cocktail—referenced, he pointed out, in Eagle-flying-solo Don Henley's 1980s hit song, "All She Wants to Do Is Dance."[86] According to Perez, a Molotov cocktail (the drink, that is) consists of "ruby red grapefruit juice and vodka."[87]

His joke, told to a Publix employee after Perez and others (including a different employee) had laughed about the drink's name and how it wasn't to be confused with an incendiary weapon, was that

> he had only "one Molotov cocktail" and could "blow the whole place up." . . . Perez later returned to the store and allegedly said, "'I'm going to blow up this whole [expletive] world.'" Store employees reported the incident to police the next day.[88]

---

[82] *Id.* at 1188.

[83] *Id.*

[84] *Id.* at 1189 (emphasis in original).

[85] Petitioner's Reply to Brief in Opposition at 1–2, Perez v. State of Florida, 580 U.S. 1187 (2017) (No. 16-6250), https://tinyurl.com/mu9mhvpj.

[86] *Hear* DON HENLEY, *All She Wants to Do is Dance, on* BUILDING THE PERFECT BEAST (Geffen Records 1984) (including the lyric "Molotov cocktail – the local drink").

[87] Petitioner's Reply, *supra* note 85, at 1.

[88] *Perez*, 580 U.S. at 1187 (Sotomayor, J., concurring).

For Perez, shopping at Publix was not, contrary to the supermar-ket's slogan, a pleasure.[89] More importantly, Sotomayor was dis-turbed that the jury was not instructed to consider either Perez's subjective mental state about what he said or the context in which he said it—only the statement itself. She pointed out that even "the prosecutor acknowledged that Perez may have been 'just a harmless drunk guy at the beach,' . . . and it appears that at least one witness testified that she did not find Perez threatening."[90] This raised grave First Amendment concerns for Sotomayor because she believed that the Court's decisions in *Watts* and *Black*

> make clear that to sustain a threat conviction without encroaching upon the First Amendment, States must prove more than the mere utterance of threatening words—some level of intent is required. And these two cases strongly suggest that it is not enough that a reasonable person might have understood the words as a threat—a jury must find that the speaker actually intended to convey a threat.[91]

In closing, Sotomayor urged her fellow Justices to "decide pre-cisely what level of intent suffices under the First Amendment"[92] to deem speech an unprotected true threat. As I wrote elsewhere, her concurrence strongly suggested that she wanted "her colleagues to recognize the real-life implications of repeatedly avoiding the intent question in true threats cases"[93] because "[i]ncarceration of fifteen years is a steep price to pay for what may have been a drunken joke lost in translation."[94]

Unfortunately, the Court waited another half-dozen years before heeding her advice and finally sorting out the speaker-intent quan-dary in *Counterman*. But when it did, Justice Sotomayor returned to her observations in *Perez*, crisply encapsulating them with the

---

[89] *See* Jennifer B., *How Publix's Slogan Came to Be*, THE PUBLIX CHECKOUT (Mar. 11, 2019), https://tinyurl.com/yyvddnr9 (describing the advent of Publix's "Where Shopping is a Pleasure" slogan).

[90] *Perez*, 580 U.S. at 1189–90 (Sotomayor, J., concurring).

[91] *Id.* at 1189.

[92] *Id.* at 1190.

[93] Clay Calvert, *Beyond Headlines & Holdings: Exploring Some Less Obvious Ramifications of the Supreme Court's 2017 Free-Speech Rulings*, 26 WM. & MARY BILL OF RTS. J. 899, 910 (2018).

[94] *Id.* at 907.

ominous observation that "'[a] drunken joke' in bad taste can lead to criminal prosecution."[95]

II. *Counterman*: From the Facts and Colorado State Court Rulings to Oral Argument before the U.S. Supreme Court

A. The Facts and Trial Court Ruling

The facts in *Counterman v. Colorado* are disturbing. As described in 2021 by the Colorado appellate court that affirmed Billy Raymond Counterman's conviction,[96] he sent clusters of unsolicited and unwanted direct messages via Facebook over several years to musician Coles Whalen, leaving her "fearful" and "extremely scared."[97] Some of the messages the jury considered were:

- "How can I take your interest in me seriously if you keep going back to my rejected existence?"
- "Fuck off permanently."
- "Your arrogance offends anyone in my position."
- "You're not being good for human relations. Die. Don't need you."
- "Staying in cyber life is going to kill you. Come out for coffee. You have my number."[98]

In her friend-of-the-court brief filed with the Supreme Court, Whalen—identified only as "C.W." in all of the opinions—called herself "the survivor of a terrifying years-long stalking campaign by . . . Counterman, who sent her thousands of disturbing, alarming, and threatening messages. The messages were life threatening and life altering."[99] While they began in 2014, Whalen explained that "things came to a head in spring 2016, after Counterman told [her] to '[d]ie, don't need you,' to '[f]uck off permanently,' and that '[s]taying in cyber life is going to kill you.' . . . He also made clear that

---

[95] *Counterman*, 143 S. Ct. at 2122 (Sotomayor, J., concurring in part and concurring in the judgment) (quoting *Perez*, 580 U.S. at 1187 (Sotomayor, J., concurring)).

[96] People v. Counterman, 497 P.3d 1039 (Colo. App. 2021), *rev'd*, Counterman v. Colorado, 143 S. Ct. 2106 (2023).

[97] *Id.* at 1042–43.

[98] *Id.* at 1044.

[99] Brief of Coles Whalen as *Amicus Curiae* in Support of Respondent at 1, Counterman v. Colorado, 143 S. Ct. 2106 (2023) (No. 22-138), https://tinyurl.com/4wwmah4z.

he'd been watching her—describing her car and the people around her."[100] Whalen blocked Counterman on Facebook at least four times, but he "created new profiles to resume messaging her and turned to other platforms, like the contact function on her website."[101] Terrified that Counterman would appear at her shows[102] and "paralyzed by anxiety and fear,"[103] Whalen cancelled some performances and declined new ones.[104]

She ultimately got a protective order against Counterman, who was arrested in May 2016.[105] A jury convicted him under a Colorado statute for stalking causing serious emotional distress.[106] The statute criminalizes repeatedly contacting or communicating with another person "in a manner that would cause a reasonable person to suffer serious emotional distress and does cause that person . . . to suffer serious emotional distress."[107]

So, how did the constitutional true threats issue arise if *Counterman* was a stalking case, not a threats case? Counterman contended that his messages were protected by the First Amendment because they did not reach the level of true threats.[108] He thus asserted that prosecuting him under Colorado's stalking statute violated his First Amendment right of free expression.[109] The trial court judge rejected that argument, but Counterman raised it again on appeal.[110]

B. The Colorado Appellate Court Ruling

The Colorado appellate court analyzed whether Counterman's messages were true threats unprotected by the First Amendment.[111] In doing so, it considered several Supreme Court rulings described

---

[100] *Id.* at 3.

[101] *Id.* at 10.

[102] *See id.* at 10–13.

[103] *Id.* at 13.

[104] *See id.*

[105] *See Counterman*, 497 P.3d at 1043.

[106] *See id.* at 1044.

[107] Colo. Rev. Stat. § 18-3-602(c).

[108] *See Counterman*, 497 P.3d at 1044–45.

[109] *See id.*

[110] *See id.*

[111] *See id.* at 1045–50.

earlier, including *Watts, Black, R.A.V.,* and *Elonis.*[112] It also relied on a recent Colorado Supreme Court decision, *People in the Interest of R.D.*[113] The Centennial State's highest court there defined a true threat as "a statement that, considered in context and under the totality of the circumstances, an intended or foreseeable recipient would reasonably perceive as a serious expression of intent to commit an act of unlawful violence."[114]

That definition, which both the Colorado appellate court and the parties in *Counterman* deemed controlling on the true threats issue, is purely objective. It concentrates on how a person ("an intended or foreseeable recipient") would reasonably interpret a message (would the person "perceive [it] as a serious expression of intent to commit an act of unlawful violence"?). The definition ignores a speaker's state of mind and intent regarding the meaning his statements convey. Whether Counterman intended, knew, or recklessly disregarded the risk that his Facebook messages would be understood as threats of violence was irrelevant.

The Colorado appellate court applied this objective test to determine whether a person in Whalen's position would reasonably understand Counterman's messages as serious expressions of an intent to violently harm her. The court focused on both the "plain language" of the messages and five contextual variables. Those factors were:

1. The fact that Counterman's statements weren't part of some broader exchange of messages between himself and Whalen, but rather were uninvited missives to which Whalen never responded;
2. The medium of Facebook on which the statements were made, including how Counterman repeatedly created new accounts to send Whalen messages after she blocked him, with her blocking signaling "an unequivocal indication that she wished not to be contacted by him";
3. The manner in which Counterman made the statements, including how they were private messages directly targeting Whalen on both her public and private Facebook accounts;

---

[112] *See id.* at 1045–46.
[113] 464 P.3d 717 (Colo. 2020).
[114] *Id.* at 734.

4. The nature of the relationship between Counterman and Whalen, which the appellate court characterized as a stranger "ceaselessly pursuing a public figure" via "unanswered and increasingly disturbing messages"; and

5. Whalen's actual reaction—one of "escalating alarm and fear of Counterman" and "fear[] for her life and safety," prompting her to speak with an attorney and law enforcement, plus cancel scheduled performances.[115]

The appellate court concluded that Counterman's messages were true threats unshielded by the First Amendment from prosecution.[116] Colorado's Supreme Court declined to review the decision,[117] setting the table for Counterman's request in August 2022 for the U.S. Supreme Court to examine his case.[118]

Counterman's petition called on the Court to settle the disagreement among both state and federal appellate courts about "what constitutes a true threat under the Constitution."[119] Specifically, the lower courts disagreed about the relevance of a speaker's subjective state of mind regarding a statement's threatening meaning.

Such a split of authority enhances the odds the Supreme Court will hear a case. Counterman's petition stressed that this disagreement among the lower courts was particularly troubling where online communications are concerned because those communications "can be read anywhere, subjecting online speakers to different constitutional standards based on geographical chance."[120] Additionally, the petition pointed to Justice Sotomayor's call in *Perez* to answer the state-of-mind issue.[121] Furthermore, Counterman contended that "[t]he purely objective test [used] in Colorado and some other jurisdictions is incompatible with this Court's true threats jurisprudence."[122]

---

[115] *Counterman*, 497 P.3d at 1047–50.

[116] *See id.* at 1050.

[117] Counterman v. People, 2022 Colo. LEXIS 292 (Colo. Sup. Ct. Apr. 11, 2022).

[118] *See* Petition for a Writ of Certiorari, Counterman v. Colorado, 143 S. Ct. 2106 (2023) (No. 22–138), https://tinyurl.com/3jd9vxh9.

[119] *Id.* at 3.

[120] *Id.* at 24.

[121] *See id.* at 3–4, 21.

[122] *Id.* at 18.

In January 2023, the Supreme Court agreed to hear *Counterman v. Colorado* to resolve what, if anything, the government must prove about a speaker's mindset regarding a statement's threatening nature for it to be unprotected by the First Amendment.[123] After the Court decided to hear the case, Counterman's opening brief revealed how the trial might have been affected if the jury had considered his mindset. The brief alleged that Counterman "suffers from mental illness [and] thought that [Coles Whalen] was regularly corresponding with him through other websites and did not understand—much less intend—his messages as threatening."[124] In brief, Counterman claimed ignorance of the threatening nature of his messages.

C. Oral Argument in the Supreme Court

Oral argument occurred on April 19, 2023.[125] It involved not only the attorneys for Counterman (John Elwood) and Colorado (Philip Weiser), but also Eric Feigen, a deputy solicitor general for the U.S. Department of Justice who represented the Unites States as a friend of the court, supporting Colorado. The following are some of their key points, as well as various lines of questions by the Justices.

1. John Elwood's Argument for Counterman

In his opening remarks, Elwood stressed that unless a speaker's mental state about a message's meaning is considered, there is a danger of "criminalizing misunderstanding."[126] In other words, the meaning either intended or known by a speaker might not be the one a jury determines a reasonable person would understand. The alleged joke gone wrong in *Perez* (the "Molotov cocktail" case) was purportedly a disconnect of meaning—illustrating one possibility of criminalizing misunderstanding.

Additionally, Elwood focused heavily on the chilling effect on free expression caused by using only an objective standard to impose criminal liability—one centering on an objectively reasonable

---

[123] 143 S. Ct. 644 (2023). *See* Question Presented, *supra* note 31 (framing the issue the Court agreed to address).

[124] Brief for the Petitioner at 2, Counterman v. Colorado, 143 S. Ct. 2106 (2023) (No. 22-138), https://tinyurl.com/tm43x8kj.

[125] *See* Transcript, *supra* note 28, at unnumbered cover page.

[126] *Id.* at 5.

person's supposed understanding of a message.[127] The chilling effect concern clearly resonated with Justice Kagan and the *Counterman* majority, as noted earlier.

In a nutshell, Elwood asserted that speakers will stifle their own speech (they will self-censor) because they must "tailor their views to suit their audience" to stay out of prison.[128] Elwood elaborated that the chilling effect comes from "a speaker being told it doesn't matter what you think, you have to think about the reaction of your audience."[129] He explained that adding a subjective-intent element is "a bulwark in speech cases" because "the thing that speakers know . . . [is] their intent. They don't know . . . what a reasonable person standard means."[130] Elwood added that "[w]e could talk about it for another hour and still not know who a reasonable person is in this case or how a reasonable person would interpret that."[131]

Elwood wasn't the only person questioning the merits of the reasonable person standard, however. Several conservative-leaning Justices intimated that today's "reasonable person" may be too sensitive to provide robust protection for free speech. To wit, Justice Thomas asserted that "we're more hypersensitive about different things now, and people could feel threatened in different ways."[132] Addressing Colorado's attorney Philip Weiser, Thomas queried, "I don't know how you're monitoring for that—what if it's now that people are more sensitive, that that is now considered the reasonable person?"[133] Similarly, Justice Gorsuch contended that "[w]e live in a world in which people are sensitive . . . and maybe increasingly sensitive,"[134] noting the use of trigger warnings in classrooms. More bluntly, Justice Barrett asked Weiser, "Who is the reasonable person?"[135] She

---

[127] *See id.* at 5, 10, 28–30, 39–40.
[128] *Id.* at 5.
[129] *Id.* at 28–29.
[130] *Id.* at 110.
[131] *Id.* at 110–111.
[132] *Id.* at 72.
[133] *Id.* at 72–73.
[134] *Id.* at 65.
[135] *Id.* at 79.

suggested that "there's no protection built in"[136] to the reasonable person standard for speakers if, in accord with Thomas's assertion, "it's the case that nowadays people would be more sensitive."[137]

Ironically, as described earlier, Thomas and Barrett turned out to be the only Justices to conclude that a speaker's subjective mental state about a threatening meaning is completely irrelevant. In dissent, they embraced a purely objective reasonable person test. So much, then, for oral argument questions tipping a Justice's hand.

Elwood argued that the solution to these problems was to incorporate into the true threats doctrine "a subjective intent requirement at least at the knowledge level,"[138] specifically requiring "knowledge of the thing that makes the conduct wrongful."[139] Fleshing out this standard, Elwood explained that "[i]n most threat statutes, that's knowledge that the words you use are going to cause fear. I could see with the Colorado statute that it would be knowledge that it would cause a reasonable person to suffer emotional distress."[140] As discussed earlier, this is a lower level of mens rea than needing to prove a speaker *purposefully intended* to put a person in fear; it only requires *knowledge* on the speaker's part that a statement would make a person fearful.[141] Recall here, however, that a five-Justice majority ultimately adopted a *recklessness* mens rea standard (one lower than either purpose or knowledge) to balance free-speech interests (preventing a chilling effect and self-censorship) with the harms caused by true threats (life-disrupting fear and terror).

Elwood suggested that adding a subjective knowledge element to the true threats doctrine likely would not "make a big difference in a lot of cases" because "in most cases, what . . . words normally mean is going to be the . . . mental state of the defendant too."[142]

[136] *Id.* at 81.

[137] *Id.* at 82.

[138] *Id.* at 7.

[139] *Id.* at 14.

[140] *Id.*

[141] Elwood made this point explicit in responding to a question from Justice Sotomayor, stating "[w]e are only arguing for a knowledge standard, that they knew that the words would cause fear." *Id.* at 49. He also responded "yes" when Justice Alito asked, "So you don't think purpose is required, but knowledge is required? It has to be knowing as to that?" *Id.* at 14.

[142] *Id.* at 17.

Put differently, the floodgates that prevent people from escaping liability for alleged threats would not suddenly open by adding a subjective knowledge mandate. That's because, Elwood contended, speakers must mount "a persuasive argument [to a jury] for why [their] words meant something different to them"[143] in order to affect the outcome of a threats case.[144] Pushing back against the notion that speakers would soon get away with threats simply by claiming they were only joking, Elwood asserted that "[i]t's not enough to say it's a joke. You have to put together a persuasive reason why you didn't know it would cause fear." In other words, without such persuasive evidence, a jury will reject a speaker's claim of not knowing his words would make someone fearful.

2. Philip Weiser's Argument for Colorado

In stark contrast to Elwood, Philip Weiser argued that a speaker's subjective mental state about meaning is irrelevant.[145] Only Justices Thomas and Barrett bought that stance in their dissents. Adding such a requirement to the true threats doctrine, Weiser contended, "would thwart the goals of the First Amendment, enabling more harm and leading to less valuable discourse."[146]

How so? It would enable more harm by shielding both delusional and devious speakers from liability.[147] As Weiser explained, "requiring specific intent in cases of threatening stalkers would immunize stalkers who are untethered from reality. It would also allow devious stalkers to escape accountability by insisting that they meant nothing by their harmful statements."[148]

The harm, in turn, is borne by the terrorized stalking victims of these delusional and devious individuals whose speech "doesn't come close to contributing to the marketplace of ideas,"[149] the metaphor

---

[143] *Id.*

[144] Elwood reiterated this point later, stating "this is not going to make a difference in the run of cases because, ordinarily, the way a reasonable person would view remarks is the way that the defendant probably viewed the remarks, unless they can present some sort of persuasive reason why it meant something different to them." *Id.* at 41.

[145] *See id.* at 83.

[146] *Id.* at 51.

[147] *See id.* at 69.

[148] *Id.* at 50.

[149] *Id.* at 52.

that underlies much of today's First Amendment jurisprudence.[150] Weiser elaborated that "threats made by stalkers terrorize victims and for good reason. Ninety percent of actual or attempted domestic violence murder cases begin with stalking."[151] Weiser attempted to focus the Justices' attention on the victims and the real-world consequences they suffer, asserting that they "routinely face scores and scores, hear hundreds and hundreds of unwanted, invasive engagements from somebody, and the consequence in stalking cases is, if you don't give me what I want, I can turn violent, and that, indeed, does happen a significant amount of the time."[152] The "nature of the harm"[153] against which the true threats doctrine guards— "protecting individuals from the fear of violence, from the disruption that fear engenders, and from the possibility that the threatened violence will occur," as the Court explained in *R.A.V.*[154]—thus renders speakers' subjective beliefs irrelevant.

Weiser also illustrated how some of Counterman's statements would constitute true threats under an objective, reasonable person standard, taking into account both text (the words uttered) and context (the circumstances surrounding the words, including Counterman's ongoing stalking and Whalen's repeated efforts to block him). For instance, Chief Justice Roberts asked Weiser about the following message Counterman sent to Whalen: "Staying in cyber life is going to kill you. Come out for coffee. You have my number."[155] Roberts questioned how it could be construed as a threat, drawing some laughter when he quipped, "'Staying in cyber life is going to

---

[150] *See* Jared Schroeder, *Fixing False Truths: Rethinking Truth Assumptions and Free-Expression Rationales in the Networked Era*, 29 WM. & MARY BILL OF RTS. J. 1097, 1098 (2021) (noting that "a line of prominent Justices, beginning with Oliver Wendell Holmes, wed their understandings and justifications for free expression to the marketplace of ideas theory, which assumes truth will generally succeed and falsity will fail in a relatively unregulated exchange of ideas"); Rodney A. Smolla, *The Meaning of the "Marketplace of Ideas" in First Amendment Law*, 24 COMMC'N L. & POL'Y 437, 437 (2019) (asserting that the marketplace of ideas has "assumed the status of seminal secular scripture, becoming to First Amendment law what Genesis is to the Bible").

[151] Transcript, *supra* note 28, at 50.

[152] *Id.* at 54.

[153] *Id.* at 64.

[154] *See supra* notes 21–22 and accompanying text (addressing *R.A.V.*'s discussion of the harms caused by true threats).

[155] Transcript, *supra* note 28, at 53.

kill you.' I can't promise I haven't said that."[156] Weiser countered, explaining "[t]he threat in that is, if you don't come out and meet me, your life's in danger. And the stalking context here, like many stalking situations, has someone who believes they're entitled to the attention and the affection of a victim."[157]

Weiser additionally addressed a key question from Justice Kavanaugh: Why wouldn't adding a level of mens rea slightly *lower* than the knowledge standard Elwood had argued for—namely, the recklessness standard that the *Counterman* majority ultimately adopted—strike the proper balance between safeguarding free-speech interests and preventing the harms with which the true threats doctrine is concerned?[158] The question presciently suggested that some of the Justices believed that proving *some* level of mens rea on a speaker's part was essential, but that the level shouldn't be as high as proving that a speaker *knew* his statement would make a person fearful.

Pushing back (unsuccessfully, as it turned out) on recklessness, Weiser returned to the problem of letting delusional speakers walk free: "[R]ecklessness does require some proof of what a defendant knew. He then or she then would disregard it. But proving knowledge in a case of someone who can say, because they're untethered from reality, I didn't mean it, could still allow them to escape accountability."[159]

3. Eric Feigin's Friend-of-the-Court Argument Supporting Colorado

Eric Feigin, in accord with Weiser, asserted that "our frontline position is that there shouldn't be a recklessness standard at all."[160] Yet, he suggested that what a speaker thought when he made a statement actually might be relevant under an objective, reasonable person standard. Specifically, he suggested that a speaker's thoughts could provide contextual evidence to help a jury suss out what exactly a reasonable interpretation of a message is.[161] Justice Gorsuch responded

---

156 *Id.* at 53.
157 *Id.* at 54.
158 *See id.* at 77–79.
159 *Id.* at 78.
160 *Id.* at 84.
161 *See id.* at 89.

that Counterman "wasn't allowed to produce any evidence about his mens rea. And I think you just admitted that, even under your version of the objective standard, that's relevant contextual evidence."[162]

Also in line with Weiser's argument, Feigin emphasized the difficulties that would arise in prosecuting "delusional stalkers" and "delusional threateners" if a subjective mens rea element were required under the First Amendment true threats doctrine.[163] Furthermore, adding a mens rea component would delay prosecutors in filing charges, because they would have to develop more circumstantial evidence to prove a speaker's guilty mindset.[164] As Feigin stated, "we have to wait quite a while before the statements rise to the level where we are comfortable bringing the prosecution and sure that we're going to get a guilty verdict."[165] Given the *Counterman* majority's imposition of a recklessness mens rea standard, it will be interesting to see how Feigin's fears now play out.

III. Bones of Contention about the Majority's Reliance on a Defamation Case to Reach Its Decision about True Threats

To recap, a five-Justice majority in *Counterman* held that to convict a speaker for a threat, the government must prove that the speaker recklessly conveyed that threat. The majority concluded that this requirement appropriately balances the First Amendment interest in preventing a chilling effect on protected expression with punishing morally culpable individuals who engender fear of violence and disrupt lives. Put differently, demonstrating that defendants were aware of and consciously disregarded a substantial risk of communicating threats adequately accounts for both free-speech interests and speech-caused harms. Recklessness provides greater protection for speakers than a purely objective, reasonable person standard, under which they could be convicted for conveying threatening meanings of which they were unaware.

Counterman thus is a victory for free speech, but a relatively minor one. It is *not* as big of a win for free speech as it would have been had the Court required prosecutors to prove a level of mens rea higher

---

162 *Id.* at 90.

163 *See id.* at 99.

164 *See id.* at 100–101.

165 *Id.* at 100.

than recklessness—one demanding proof that a defendant-speaker *purposely* put a person in fear or *knew* his statements would cause fear. The majority's balancing-of-interests (rather than all-or-nothing) approach, however, united Justices from across the ideological spectrum.

Because the *Counterman* jury wasn't instructed to consider *anything* about Billy Raymond Counterman's awareness of the threatening nature of his messages, his conviction violated the First Amendment. The case now returns to Colorado, where Counterman can be retried, with the prosecution needing to prove that he consciously disregarded the substantial risk that his messages would be understood by Whalen as threats.

One final point—a contentious one regarding a long-standing First Amendment rule noted earlier—merits brief consideration. In determining that recklessness was the appropriate mental-state requirement, Justice Kagan and four other Justices relied partly on the Court's 1964 defamation decision of *New York Times Co. v. Sullivan*.[166] The Court there adopted "actual malice" as a buffer against a chilling effect on journalists who report on the official conduct of public officials. Actual malice protects journalists from civil liability for false and defamatory statements about public officials (and, today, public figures more broadly) unless the journalists either know the statements are false or recklessly disregard the possibility that they are false.[167]

Adopting this recklessness standard in *Sullivan* gave the press "breathing space"[168] to make innocent mistakes and to promote "uninhibited, robust, and wide-open"[169] debate about public officials. The *Sullivan* Court reasoned that "[a] rule compelling the critic of official conduct to guarantee the truth of all his factual assertions—and to do so on pain of libel judgments virtually unlimited in amount—leads to . . . 'self-censorship.'"[170] In short, the *Sullivan* Court's use of a recklessness standard (as part of actual malice) to thwart a chilling effect on speech supported the *Counterman* majority's deployment of a recklessness standard to similarly guard against self-censorship.

[166] 376 U.S. 254 (1964).
[167] *Id.* at 280.
[168] *Id.* at 272.
[169] *Id.* at 270.
[170] *Id.* at 279.

This didn't sit well with the dissenters. Justice Thomas decried both the *Counterman* majority's reliance on *Sullivan* and, as a precursory matter, the *Sullivan* Court's embrace of recklessness within actual malice.[171] Thomas reiterated his prior concern that actual malice is nothing more than a judicially created, policy-driven rule that conflicts with "the First Amendment as it was understood at the time of the Founding."[172] This is important because it indicates Thomas's continuing desire to roll back actual malice—a move that would strip investigative journalists of a key defense against liability for innocent errors when reporting on public officials and public figures. The good news, however, for free-speech and free-press proponents is that no one joined Justice Thomas's dissent.

Justice Barrett also criticized the majority's reliance on *Sullivan* in her dissent (joined by Thomas), which contended that no subjective mental-state standard is required under the true threats doctrine. For Justice Barrett, *Sullivan*'s defamation-law buffer against a chilling effect when reporting on public officials and their conduct supports a far different and more laudable goal than *Counterman*'s prevention of a chilling effect in the context of threats. "Because true threats are not typically proximate to debate on matters of public concern, the Court's newly erected buffer zone does not serve the end of protecting heated political commentary," she opined.[173] For Justice Barrett, *Counterman*'s embrace of recklessness needlessly raises the bar for prosecuting low-value speech (threats); *Sullivan*, in contrast, deals with safeguarding speech of "high social value" relating to "public discourse."[174] In short, Justice Barrett panned the majority's borrowing of recklessness from actual malice and defamation law, but for a very different reason than Justice Thomas. For now, then, the actual malice standard in defamation law seems safely ensconced, despite Justice Thomas's continuous carping in a solo dissent.

---

[171] *Counterman*, 143 S. Ct. at 2132 (Thomas, J., dissenting).

[172] *Id.*

[173] *Id.* at 2136 (Barrett, J., dissenting).

[174] *Id.*

Students for Fair Admissions and the End of Racial Classification as We Know It

*David E. Bernstein**

The Supreme Court's decision in *Students for Fair Admissions, Inc. v. President and Fellows of Harvard College (SFFA)*[1] likely marks the beginning of the end of the overt use of race in university admissions. The Court's decision, however, has much broader implications.

Harvard University and the University of North Carolina (UNC) classified applicants based on racial and ethnic categories adopted by the federal government in the 1970s. *SFFA* concluded that these classifications were so arbitrary as to be unconstitutional. *SFFA* therefore offers a broad new avenue of attack for litigants challenging racial preferences and other race-based policies based on these ubiquitous classifications. Any entity that is sued for engaging in discriminatory preferences or for otherwise allocating goods or services by race will need to explain why the racial classifications it relies upon don't fail the arbitrariness test.

Part I of this article briefly reviews the history of the use of racial preferences by universities starting in the 1960s. From the *Bakke* case in 1978 to the commencement of the *SFFA* litigation in 2014, universities were required, at least officially, to limit their racial preferences to those necessary to achieve "diversity" on campus. Universities divided their applicants by racial classifications concocted by the federal bureaucracy. They then gave admissions preferences to "underrepresented" groups—African Americans, Hispanics, and Native Americans—to enhance diversity. This meant, by logical necessity, disfavoring members of groups deemed to detract from diversity, namely whites and Asian Americans.

* Distinguished University Professor, Antonin Scalia Law School, George Mason University; Adjunct Fellow, Cato Institute.

[1] 143 S. Ct. 2141 (2023).

Part II of this article discusses how the *SFFA* case disrupted a cozy status quo, in which universities pretended to abide by the limitations the Court had imposed on the use of racial preferences and the Supreme Court pretended not to notice that universities were ignoring those limitations. While not officially overruling precedent, the *SFFA* Court finally applied, rather than pretended to apply, the requisite legal standard: "strict scrutiny." This standard requires that racial classifications only be used to allocate benefits when those classifications serve a compelling government interest and are narrowly tailored to serve that interest. The Court found that Harvard and UNC's way of using race in admissions failed this test on multiple grounds.

Part III of this article notes that, for the first time, a Supreme Court majority has concluded that the standard racial classifications used by universities and many other institutions are arbitrary and incoherent. This part reviews the discussion of this issue during oral argument, Chief Justice John Roberts's holding on this issue in his majority opinion, and Justice Neil Gorsuch's longer analysis in his concurring opinion regarding why the classifications in question were not narrowly tailored to achieve diversity.

The Court has now held that when the standard racial classifications are used to allocate benefits, the classifications must be narrowly tailored to achieve a lawful objective. This means that many other uses of racial classifications beyond university admissions are suddenly more vulnerable to legal challenge. That is the subject of Part IV of this article. It discusses potential challenges to the use of race-based preferences in government contracting; to the mandatory use of racial classifications in biomedical research; and to the arbitrary standards the government uses to classify people as American Indians.

I. Racial Classifications in University Admissions

American universities with selective admissions policies began using racial preferences for minority applicants in the 1960s. The primary impetus for these preferences was to increase the enrollment of African American students.[2] Some universities gave preferences

---

[2] *See* JEROME KARABEL, THE CHOSEN: THE HIDDEN HISTORY OF ADMISSION AND EXCLUSION AT HARVARD, YALE, AND PRINCETON (2005).

only to black applicants. Other universities favored a varied range of additional minorities.[3]

Over time, selective universities' policies regarding how to divide their applicant pool into racial and ethnic demographic categories converged, thanks to an obscure but very important federal regulation known as Statistical Policy Directive No. 15 (Directive 15).[4] The directive created uniform standards for virtually all federal agencies charged with collecting racial and ethnic data. The American population was broken up into four racial classifications—white, black, Asian American/Pacific Islander, and American Indian—and one ethnic classification, Hispanic.[5]

When the federal Office of Management and Budget (OMB) published Directive 15 in the *Federal Register*, the directive came with the warning that the "classifications should not be interpreted as being scientific or anthropological in nature."[6] OMB also warned that the classifications should not be "viewed as determinants of eligibility for participation in any Federal program," such as affirmative action programs.[7] Nevertheless, these classifications spread throughout American society, greatly affecting both public policy and the perception of race in the United States. For example, few Americans thought of themselves, or of other Americans, as "Hispanic" before Directive 15. Most important for purposes of this article, the Directive 15 classifications became the baseline categories for affirmative action preferences in college admissions.

When Directive 15 was enacted, the most recent (1970) census showed that the country was still overwhelmingly black and

---

[3] These included, alone or in combination, Chicanos, Mexican Americans, Filipino Americans, Asian Americans, Mexican Americans, Puerto Ricans, people with Spanish surnames, American Indians, and even Italian Americans. On Italian Americans, *see* Liana Kirillova, *The Ironies of Whiteness: Italian Americans Pursue Affirmative Action in the City University of New York, 1976–2015*, 51 ESSAYS IN HISTORY (2017).

[4] Office of Management and Budget (OMB) Directive No. 15, Race and Ethnic Standards for Federal Statistics and Administrative Reporting, 43 Fed. Reg. 19, 260 (May 4, 1978).

[5] *Id.* In 1997, the Office of Management and Budget divided the Asian American/ Pacific Islander group into two groups, Asian Americans and Native Hawaiian/ Pacific Islanders. The latter classification is sufficiently small that it has not played a significant role in the controversy over affirmative action preferences.

[6] *Id.*

[7] *Id.*

white—about 81 percent white and 13 percent black. An additional 5 percent or so of Americans were of Spanish-speaking origin, but the federal government traditionally considered this to be a "white" ethnic classification.[8]

The bureaucracy failed to anticipate that Directive 15 classifications would be widely used for affirmative action purposes. It also failed to anticipate that large-scale immigration from Asia, Latin America, and Africa, plus a vast increase in intergroup coupling, would destabilize the Directive 15 classification scheme.

Today, thanks to immigration and in stark contrast to 1978, a large majority of members of the official Directive 15 minority classifications are Hispanic or Asian American. Increased intergroup coupling, meanwhile, has led to a large increase in people who can plausibly check a "minority" box but who have only partial and sometimes distant non-white ancestry. As a result of these forces, numerous programs that were originally meant to help descendants of American slaves instead now primarily assist post-1965 "minority" immigrants and their children, or individuals with only distant minority ancestry.

Even within the Black/African American classification, the benefits of affirmative action increasingly go to relatively new American families. At Harvard, for example, almost two-thirds of the university's black undergraduates in 2004 were first- or second-generation immigrants, or to a lesser extent, children of interracial couples.[9] Other elite schools have seen similar, albeit not quite as dramatic, increases in the percentage of such students. Admitting these students may have increased official "racial diversity," but it did much less to satisfy the social justice impulses that originally led colleges to adopt affirmative action preferences.

When the Directive 15 categories went into effect, most government agencies responded by placing a two-part race/ethnicity question on demographic forms. These forms asked individuals if they were Hispanic and, separately, what race they saw themselves as belonging to (White, Black, Native American, or Asian American).

[8] *See* DAVID E. BERNSTEIN, CLASSIFIED: THE UNTOLD STORY OF RACIAL CLASSIFICATION IN AMERICA 29–57 (2022).

[9] Sara Rimer and Karen W. Arenson, *Top Colleges Take More Blacks, but Which Ones?*, N.Y. TIMES (June 24, 2004), https://tinyurl.com/2sck2day.

The Department of Education, however, demurred. Its Office of Civil Rights left it up to the schools and universities gathering statistics about their applicants and student bodies to decide whether to use a two-part question or a one-part question. The one-part question asked individuals whether they were Black, White, Hispanic, Native American, or Asian.[10]

Universities overwhelmingly chose the one-question route, and applicants were only allowed to check one box. This made Hispanic status the equivalent of a racial status—for example, one could not be both Hispanic and White on these universities' admissions forms. The Department of Education did not change its rules to require a two-question ethnicity classification until 2007, about a decade after OMB told the Department it had to do so. By then, the notion that Hispanic affirmative action preferences in university admissions amounted to a "racial" preference was entrenched, not least in the Supreme Court.[11]

No university has explained, in litigation or otherwise, why it chose to copy the Directive 15 classifications in pursuing affirmative action preferences for diversity. This is a significant oversight, given that the classifications were not created with such a purpose in mind. For example, why should a university give a preference to those of Spanish-speaking ancestry, regardless of racial background, but not to members of other groups that could add ethnic diversity and that have faced discrimination in American society, such as Arab, Armenian, or Iranian Americans?

Nevertheless, by the time the first Common Application was released in 1994, its demographic questions mimicked the Directive 15 classifications, except for having an additional Mexican American classification.[12] By the time Students for Fair Admissions sued Harvard and UNC, the classifications on the Common App mapped

---

[10] *See* David E. Bernstein, *Why Does the Supreme Court Refer to Preferences for Hispanics/ Latinos as "Racial Preferences?,"* Volokh Conspiracy (Jan. 24, 2022), https://tinyurl.com/mrxbvjvw.

[11] *Id.*

[12] Common Application, 1994–95 (on file with author). This separate category was a vestige of Mexican Americans, or at least those with discernable indigenous heritage, being singled out as a minority racial category on many civil rights forms starting in the 1950s. *See* Bernstein, Classified, *supra* note 8.

the Directive 15 classifications exactly, including by assigning "Hispanic" to a separate ethnicity category rather than a racial one.[13]

By the early 2000s, selective universities gave the greatest admissions preferences to black Americans, smaller preferences to Hispanics and Native Americans, and no preferences to whites, regardless of ethnic background. Many of these universities, meanwhile, were widely thought to be imposing soft quotas on, or otherwise discriminating against, Asian Americans, who were deemed "overrepresented."[14]

A wide range of demographic groups, then, have been affected by affirmative action. Yet since the beginning of racial preferences in higher education, both sides of the affirmative action debate have focused primarily on whether it was appropriate to give African American applicants preferences over whites:[15]

- Opponents have described racial preferences in admissions as illicit, immoral "reverse discrimination"; proponents have argued that the preferences are compensation for centuries of systemic racism in American education that put African Americans in a worse position to be admitted to elite schools.

- Opponents have contended that preferences are illegal under the Fourteenth Amendment's Equal Protection Clause and Title VI of the 1964 Civil Rights Act, each of which should be read to create an extremely strong legal presumption against

---

[13] Common Application, 2014–15 (on file with author).

[14] By 1987, the media was already reporting on perceived discrimination against Asian Americans in admissions. Eloise Salholz, *Do Colleges Set Asian Quotas?*, NEWSWEEK, Feb. 9, 1987, at 60. In the early 2000s, data began to appear that backed up this perception. Thomas J. Espenshade et al., *Admission Preferences for Minority Students, Athletes, and Legacies at Elite Universities*, 85 Soc. Sci. Q. 1422 (2004).

[15] For example, books such as RANDALL KENNEDY, FOR DISCRIMINATION: RACE, AFFIRMATIVE ACTION, AND THE LAW (2015), and MELVIN I. UROFSKY, THE AFFIRMATIVE ACTION PUZZLE: A LIVING HISTORY FROM RECONSTRUCTION TO TODAY (2020), treat Hispanic participation in affirmative action as at best an afterthought. Yet by the time the authors were writing their books, more Hispanics than African Americans were likely benefiting from affirmative action.

In *SFFA*, Justice Thomas noted the same dynamic in Justice Jackson's dissent: "While articulating her black and white world (literally), Justice Jackson ignores the experiences of other immigrant groups (like Asians, see *supra*, at 43–44) and white communities that have faced historic barriers." *SFFA*, 143 S. Ct. at 2205 (Thomas, J., concurring).

decision-making based on an individual's race; proponents have responded that the Constitution and civil rights laws should be read in light of the underlying purpose of helping African Americans overcome centuries of oppression and discrimination, and thus to provide leeway for policies that remedy the exclusion of black Americans from elite educational institutions.

- Opponents have argued, more broadly, that the underlying command of the Equal Protection Clause was to get the government out of the business of divvying up benefits based on racial class and to have a colorblind Constitution; proponents have rejoined that the underlying purpose of the Clause was to undo the racial subordination of black Americans.

In 1978, Supreme Court Justice Lewis Powell cast the deciding vote in *Regents of the University of California v. Bakke*.[16] His opinion concluded that universities could use racial preferences in admissions, but only if the preferences met the demanding legal test of strict scrutiny. This satisfied almost no one involved in the debates noted above.

Powell decided that universities had a compelling interest in the purported educational benefits of "diversity" and that achieving that goal through racial preferences satisfied strict scrutiny. Elite universities had long given admissions preferences to athletes, musicians, residents of rural areas, and other constituencies. Powell decreed that universities were allowed to similarly give a preference to applicants based on race or ethnicity without running afoul of the law. However, universities could not use quotas and were required to give applicants individualized consideration based on their entire application.

The practical result of Powell's compromise was that admissions officers at selective universities continued to do what they had been doing before *Bakke*, except without formal quotas. Admissions staff first determined a goal for the percentage of African Americans and other designated minorities they wished to admit. They then manipulated their admissions processes to achieve that goal.

---

[16] 438 U.S. 265 (1978).

University leaders surmised, correctly, that if they did not create formal quotas and couched their admissions strategies in terms of "diversity," they were unlikely to face lawsuits or punitive administrative actions. It helped that admissions practices at selective universities were almost universally opaque, and that any individual plaintiff who threatened to sue could be quietly admitted if the university believed the threat was serious.

Universities also correctly surmised that judges of a conservative temperament, themselves largely the products of elite, selective educational institutions, were going to be very reluctant to invalidate policies universally adopted by such institutions. Despite some close calls, affirmative action preferences in higher education withstood doubts about their legality for over 50 years. In *Grutter v. Bollinger*[17] and *Fisher v. University of Texas*,[18] a majority of the Court ignored strong evidence that the university defendants were essentially pursuing soft, informal racial quotas and otherwise ignoring the limits imposed by Powell in *Bakke*. The Court in both cases upheld the use of racial preferences as satisfying strict scrutiny. This brings us to *SFFA*.

II. *SFFA* Disrupts the Status Quo

The status quo was finally disrupted when Students for Fair Admissions (SFFA) filed a lawsuit against the University of North Carolina, an elite, selective public university, under the Fourteenth Amendment's Equal Protection Clause and Title VI of the 1964 Civil Rights Act. SFFA filed a separate lawsuit against Harvard University, perhaps America's most renowned private university, under Title VI. Supreme Court precedent dictated that the legal standard for illegal racial discrimination is identical under both Title VI and the Fourteenth Amendment, so the cases raised the same legal issues.

The timing of these cases was propitious. In the early years of affirmative action, some liberals vociferously opposed the use of racial preferences, while some relatively conservative figures, such as Richard Nixon, strongly favored them. Over time, however, proponents of affirmative action preferences became highly concentrated

17 539 U.S. 306 (2003).
18 579 U.S. 365 (2016).

on the political left, while conservatives overwhelming opposed them on both moral and legal grounds.[19]

In fall 2022, when the *SFFA* cases were argued before the Supreme Court, the Court had a 6–3 conservative majority for the first time in almost 100 years. Moreover, the Court's majority had already overturned *Roe v. Wade* in the previous term, proving its willingness to issue a decision that both rejected longstanding precedent and upset the American establishment.[20]

Meanwhile, over the previous decades the Supreme Court had consistently and increasingly emphatically told universities that they needed to use race in a narrowly tailored way, indeed only as a last resort.[21] Nevertheless, like other universities, Harvard and UNC had acted as if they could do whatever they wanted so long as they didn't use official quotas.

Indeed, Harvard had never even examined the viability of race-neutral alternatives before the *SFFA* litigation began.[22] Harvard ultimately acknowledged that eliminating donor and alumni preferences, certain athletic preferences, and children-of-employee preferences would increase racial diversity without relying on racial preferences. Harvard's attorneys argued, however, that it should not have to do these things, because that would interfere with its institutional prerogatives.[23]

The six-vote majority in favor of the plaintiffs in both the Harvard and the UNC cases therefore came as no surprise. Much of Chief Justice Roberts's majority opinion covered familiar territory. First, Roberts contended that racial preferences are illegal reverse discrimination. College admissions are "zero-sum" and thus a "benefit

---

[19] As of June 2023, 80 percent of conservative Republicans disapproved of using race in college admissions, while 67 percent of liberal Democrats approved. *See More Americans Disapprove Than Approve of Colleges Considering Race, Ethnicity in Admissions Decisions*, Pew Rsch. Center (June 8, 2023), https://tinyurl.com/wuuuc5dk.

[20] Dobbs v. Jackson Women's Health Org., 142 S. Ct. 2228, 2242 (2022).

[21] Fisher v. Univ. of Tex. at Austin, 570 U.S. 297, 312 (2013) ("The reviewing court must ultimately be satisfied that no workable race-neutral alternatives would produce the educational benefits of diversity."); *see also Grutter*, 539 U.S. at 339 (requiring that universities engage in "serious, good faith consideration of workable race-neutral alternatives" before resorting to racial preferences to achieve diversity).

[22] Brief for Petitioner at 18, Students for Fair Admissions, Inc. v. President and Fellows of Harvard College, 143 S. Ct. 2141 (2023) (No. 20-1199).

[23] *See id.* at 33–35.

provided to some applicants but not to others necessarily advantages the former group at the expense of the latter."[24]

Second, the Equal Protection Clause, both in its original meaning and as its interpretation has evolved in the Supreme Court, creates an extremely strong presumption against racial classification. The notion that the Clause permits the use of race to achieve a racially "balanced" university class turns the Clause "on its head."[25] Roberts noted that some critics dismiss the Court's prior pronouncement that the Constitution is colorblind as "'rhetorical flourishes,'" but these, he argued, were actually the "proud pronouncements" of the Court's cases.[26]

Justices Sonia Sotomayor and Ketanji Brown Jackson both dissented (and Justice Elena Kagan joined both of their dissents). Both Justices abandoned the diversity rationale now that it no longer attracted a swing vote to uphold preferences, as it had in past cases. Instead, the Justices argued that the Fourteenth Amendment is properly interpreted to allow the government to use racial classification to redress the exclusion of underrepresented minorities, African Americans in particular.

Forty-five years after Justice Powell's opinion in *Bakke* allowed for racial preferences in university admissions under a narrow diversity rationale, the debate in 2023 had returned to the debate among the eight other Justices in *Bakke*. The conservative Justices argued that the government may not rely on racial classification to allocate resources. The liberal Justices rejoined that while the government may not discriminate in favor of historically dominant groups, it may use race-based preferences to aid certain minority groups.

Three aspects of the *SFFA* opinions, however, are relatively novel. First, Justice Clarence Thomas, concurring, issued by far the Court's most lengthy, detailed defense of the notion that the original meaning of the Equal Protection Clause required that state policy be colorblind.[27] In turn, Justice Sotomayor issued a rebuttal.[28] This article

---

[24] *SFFA*, 143 S. Ct. at 2169.

[25] *Id.* at 2251.

[26] *Id.* at 2174.

[27] *Id.* at 2178–89 (Thomas, J., concurring).

[28] *Id.* at 2225–30 (Sotomayor, J., dissenting).

will leave commentary on the Thomas-Sotomayor debate over originalism to others.

The second *SFFA* novelty was that the plaintiffs presented detailed evidence that Asian American applicants to Harvard had the lowest chance of admission among the various designated "racial" groups. Harvard admissions staff accomplished this result by arbitrarily assigning Asian Americans artificially low personality scores. The evidence of anti-Asian discrimination that the plaintiffs acquired in discovery was backed up by a telling statistic. In 1991, 21 percent of Harvard's class was Asian American. Twenty-three years later, when the *SFFA* litigation commenced, the figure was 22 percent,[29] despite a large increase in the Asian American applicant pool.

Roberts's opinion briefly alluded to this issue.[30] Thomas's concurrence, meanwhile, hammered home the point that even though Asian Americans were historically subject to brutal discrimination,[31] Harvard's admissions policy disfavored them, just as it once disfavored Jews. Justice Sotomayor, straining credulity, retorted that Asian Americans benefit from racial preferences in higher education admissions provided to other groups.[32]

The third and most important novelty of *SFFA* has been overlooked in most of the early commentary on the cases. For the first time, a Supreme Court majority surmised that the Directive 15 racial classifications used by universities (and throughout American law and society) are so arbitrary that using them to decide who gets preferential treatment is unconstitutional. The next section of this article discusses this aspect of the Court's holding in more detail.

III. The *SFFA* Majority Questions the American System of Racial Classification

Prevailing Supreme Court doctrine before *SFFA* was that preferences given to members of certain racial classifications must meet the constitutional standard of "strict scrutiny." To be deemed

---

[29] Jeremy Ashkenas et al., *Even with Affirmative Action, Blacks and Hispanics Are More Underrepresented at Top Colleges Than 35 Years Ago*, N.Y. Times (Aug. 24, 2017), https://tinyurl.com/2ak7x7wt.

[30] *SFFA*, 143 S. Ct. at 2170–72.

[31] *Id.* at 2199–2200 (Thomas, J., concurring).

[32] *Id.* at 2258 (Sotomayor, J., dissenting).

compliant with constitutional requirements, preferences had to serve a compelling interest and be narrowly tailored to serve that interest. Using that test, the Court consistently focused, first, on whether "diversity" in higher education is a compelling government interest, and second, whether the preferences were narrowly tailored in the sense that the same objective could not have been met with race-neutral policies.

Until 2016, Supreme Court Justices did not question (outside sporadic, brief dicta[33]) whether the classifications used by universities to pursue diversity—Asian American, Black, Hispanic, Native American, Native Hawaiian/Pacific Islander, and White—raised constitutional problems. This oversight neglected a rather obvious argument: The Directive 15 classifications arbitrarily combined multiple subgroups that do not have a common heritage or culture. Therefore, the classifications were not narrowly tailored to achieve real diversity.

The first Supreme Court opinion to address this issue in a significant way was Justice Samuel Alito's dissenting opinion in *Fisher v. University of Texas*.[34] Alito argued that University of Texas's (UT) method of classifying students in the admissions process was not narrowly tailored to achieve diversity. Alito noted, for example, that students labeled "Asian American" included students of Chinese, Japanese, Korean, Vietnamese, Cambodian, Hmong, Indian, and other Asian backgrounds. "It would be ludicrous," he wrote, "to suggest that all of these students have similar backgrounds and similar ideas and experiences to share. So why has UT lumped them together and concluded that it is appropriate to discriminate against

---

[33] Justice Powell briefly raised this issue in *Bakke*, though this was in the context of the University of California Davis Medical School's quota system based on historic and current disadvantage, not diversity. "[T]he University is unable to explain its selection of only the four favored groups—Negroes, Mexican-Americans, American-Indians, and Asians—for preferential treatment. The inclusion of the last group is especially curious in light of the substantial numbers of Asians [over 10 ten percent of the students, much higher than their share of the population] admitted through the regular admissions process." *Bakke*, 438 U.S. at 309 n.45. Powell apparently believed that his opinion gave universities permission to consider *everyone's* ethnic or racial background and how it might add to diversity, but that is not how it worked out.

[34] 579 U.S. 365 (2016).

Asian-American students because they are 'overrepresented' in the UT student body? UT has no good answer."[35]

Alito added that UT failed to "provide any definition of the various racial and ethnic groups"; classified multiracial students "as falling into only a single racial or ethnic group"; and failed to address the fact that an applicant who checks a minority box may have only "one grandparent, great-grandparent, or great-great-grandparent who was a member of a favored group."[36] UT did not say whether it believed such students "reflect a distinctive perspective or set of experiences associated with that group."[37] However, UT relied "on applicants to 'classify themselves.'"[38] This necessarily gave any applicant who checked the preferred racial box favored admissions treatment for purportedly adding to classroom diversity.[39]

Alito's discussion of the classification issue came in a dissenting opinion, which meant *SFFA* marked the first time a *majority* opinion of the Supreme Court addressed the classification issue in some detail. This discussion was something of a surprise. At least until oral argument, it seemed that *SFFA* would follow the pattern of the Court largely ignoring the arbitrariness of the classifications used by universities to purportedly achieve diversity.

SFFA had not focused on this issue during the litigation, and it played no role in the lower courts' decisions upholding Harvard's and UNC's racial preferences. SFFA's brief to the Supreme Court only mentions the issue tangentially in a footnote: "SFFA uses the term 'Asian American' only because Harvard does. The term is incoherent, sweeping in 'wildly disparate national groups' with little in common."[40] SFFA's reply brief devoted a single line to the issue, noting that the boxes themselves are arbitrary—they lump totally different cultures together in categories that were never designed

[35] *Id.* at 414 (Alito, J., dissenting).

[36] *Id.* at 414–15.

[37] *Id.* at 415.

[38] *Id.*

[39] *Id.*

[40] Brief for Petitioner at 15 n.1, Students for Fair Admissions, Inc. v. President and Fellows of Harvard College, 143 S. Ct. 2141 (2023) (No. 20-1199).

to achieve educational benefits.[41] The defendants and their amici ignored the issue almost entirely.[42]

The classification issue was the focus of an amicus brief that I filed supporting the plaintiffs (which I'll call the Bernstein brief).[43] That brief, in turn, received substantial media attention, including a lengthy interview in the *Wall Street Journal*.[44] Given that over 100 amicus briefs were filed in the case, the attention given to the Bernstein brief suggested broad interest in the argument.

In any event, at oral argument the Justices showed some sustained interest in whether the classifications themselves undermined the defendant universities' diversity argument. Justice Alito asked UNC's attorney:

> I'd like your response to the argument that these racial categories are so broad that any use of them is arbitrary and, therefore, unconstitutional. So what would you say to, for example, a student whose family came from Afghanistan and doesn't get in because the student doesn't get the plus factor that the student would get if the student's family had come from someplace else?
>
> So you would say to the student: Well, we don't—we don't need you to contribute to a diversity of views at our school because we already have enough Asians. We have a lot of students whose families came from China or other Asian countries. And the student says:
>
> Well, you don't have anybody like me, I'm from Afghanistan.

---

[41] Reply Brief for Petitioner at 11, Students for Fair Admissions, Inc. v. President and Fellows of Harvard College, 143 S. Ct. 2141 (2023) (No. 20-1199).

[42] The Asian American Legal Defense Fund addressed classification with regard to Asian Americans, and in doing so made a significant error. In the process of claiming that schools like Harvard and UNC are truly interested in more granular information than the standard classifications, the brief claims that "universities utilize broad categories like 'Asian' not by choice, but by federal mandate." That is true when it comes to reporting the race of students and staff. When it comes to college admissions, however, there is no federal law requiring universities to inquire about the race of applicants at all, much less dictating how such inquiries should proceed. *See* Brief of Amici Curiae Asian American Legal Defense and Education Fund et al., in Support of Respondent, *Students for Fair Admissions*, at 9.

[43] Brief of Professor David E. Bernstein as Amicus Curiae in Support of Petitioner, *Students for Fair Admissions*.

[44] Kyle Peterson, *Affirmative Action Mocks Ethnic Diversity*, WALL ST. J. (Oct. 28, 2022), https://tinyurl.com/2s3dfrte; *see also, e.g.*, William McGurn, *Racial Discrimination and Harvard's Invidious Boxes*, WALL ST. J. (Aug. 22, 2022), https://tinyurl.com/2vf4kccw.

What—what similarity does a family background to the person from Afghanistan have with somebody whose family's background is in, let's say, Japan . . .?

[W]hat is the justification for lumping together students whose families came from China with someone—with students whose families came from Afghanistan? What do they have in common? . . . [W]hy do you have them check a box that I'm Asian? What do you learn from the mere checking of the box?[45]

Justice Brett Kavanaugh asked UNC's attorney, North Carolina Solicitor General Ryan Park, how "applicants from Middle Eastern countries" are classified, "from Jordan, Iraq, Iran, Egypt and the like? . . . [I]f they honestly check one of the boxes, which one are they supposed to check?" Park responded, "I—I don't—do not know the answer to that question."[46]

This was a remarkable colloquy. The Common App's demographic questions explicitly treat Middle Eastern as a subset of "white" (and did so in 2014, when the litigation commenced). First, the form asks applicants to

[P]lease indicate how you identify yourself. (You may select one or more)
American Indian or Alaska Native
Asian
Black or African American
Native Hawaiian or Other Pacific Islander
White[47]

If the applicant checks "White," the form then asks,

Which best describes your White background? (You may select one or more)
Europe
Middle East
Other[48]

---

[45] Transcript of Oral Argument at 94–96, Students for Fair Admissions, Inc. v. University of North Carolina, 143 S. Ct. 2141 (2023) (No. 21-707). The Common App is not clear on the matter, but federal policy dictates that Afghan Americans are considered white, not Asian. Alito's confusion about this issue inadvertently reveals the arbitrariness of the classifications.

[46] *Id.* at 107–08.

[47] Common Application, *supra* note 13.

[48] *Id.*

Justice Kavanaugh also asked SFFA's attorney a question about an issue that had not been raised previously but is likely to be litigated in the future. If the Court were to decide that universities may not use race in admissions, could they instead implement a preference for descendants of American slaves as a nonracial classification?[49]

The tenor of the oral arguments in both cases did not mislead. As was widely anticipated, the Court eventually ruled against both Harvard and UNC. In doing so, Chief Justice Roberts's opinion for the Court did not formally overrule precedent. Instead, he interpreted the relevant line of cases as holding that race-based college admissions are permissible only if they can be shown to meet a compelling interest. Meanwhile, a university may never use race as a stereotype or negative, and a university must expect its preferences to terminate within a reasonable time frame. Harvard's and UNC's admissions policies did not coherently advance a compelling interest, Roberts concluded, and they also failed the other two criteria. The preferences therefore violated the Equal Protection Clause of the Fourteenth Amendment and Title VI.

Roberts's exact language regarding why the classifications the universities used to divide applicants demographically were illicit is worth quoting in full:

> For starters, the categories are themselves imprecise in many ways. Some of them are plainly overbroad: by grouping together all Asian students, for instance, respondents are apparently uninterested in whether *South* Asian or *East* Asian students are adequately represented, so long as there is enough of one to compensate for a lack of the other. Meanwhile other racial categories, such as "Hispanic," are arbitrary or undefined. See, *e.g.*, M. Lopez, J. Krogstad, & J. Passel, Pew Research Center, Who is Hispanic? (Sept. 15, 2022) (referencing the "long history of changing labels [and] shifting categories . . . reflect[ing] evolving cultural norms about what it means to be Hispanic or Latino in the U. S. today"). And still other categories are underinclusive. When asked at oral argument "how are applicants from Middle Eastern countries classified, [such as] Jordan, Iraq, Iran,

[49] Transcript of Oral Argument at 44–45, Students for Fair Admissions, Inc. v. President and Fellows of Harvard College, 143 S. Ct. 2141 (2023) (No. 20-1199).

[and] Egypt," UNC's counsel responded, "[I] do not know the answer to that question." Tr. of Oral Arg. in No. 21–707, p. 107; cf. *post*, at 6–7 (GORSUCH, J., concurring) (detailing the "incoherent" and "irrational stereotypes" that these racial categories further).

Indeed, the use of these opaque racial categories undermines, instead of promotes, respondents' goals. By focusing on underrepresentation, respondents would apparently prefer a class with 15% of students from Mexico over a class with 10% of students from several Latin American countries, simply because the former contains more Hispanic students than the latter. Yet "[i]t is hard to understand how a plan that could allow these results can be viewed as being concerned with achieving enrollment that is 'broadly diverse.'" *Parents Involved*, 551 U. S., at 724 (quoting *Grutter*, 539 U. S., at 329). And given the mismatch between the means respondents employ and the goals they seek, it is especially hard to understand how courts are supposed to scrutinize the admissions programs that respondents use.

The universities' main response to these criticisms is, essentially, "trust us." None of the questions recited above need answering, they say, because universities are "owed deference" when using race to benefit some applicants but not others. Brief for University Respondents in No. 21–707, at 39 (internal quotation marks omitted). It is true that our cases have recognized a "tradition of giving a degree of deference to a university's academic decisions." *Grutter*, 539 U. S., at 328. But we have been unmistakably clear that any deference must exist "within constitutionally prescribed limits," *ibid.*, and that "deference does not imply abandonment or abdication of judicial review," *Miller–El v. Cockrell*, 537 U. S. 322, 340 (2003). Universities may define their missions as they see fit. The Constitution defines ours. Courts may not license separating students on the basis of race without an exceedingly persuasive justification that is measurable and concrete enough to permit judicial review. As this Court has repeatedly reaffirmed, "[r]acial classifications are simply too pernicious to permit any but the most exact connection between justification and classification." *Gratz v. Bollinger*, 539 U. S. 244, 270 (2003) (internal quotation marks omitted). The programs at issue here do not satisfy that standard.[50]

---

[50] *SFFA*, 143 S. Ct. at 2167–68.

Justice Thomas, concurring, also noted that Harvard and UNC relied on sorting students into one of "only a few reductionist racial groups"[51] that are "vastly oversimplistic."[52] Applicants therefore would get illicitly siloed "into an artificial category."[53]

Roberts and Thomas each favorably cited a section of Justice Gorsuch's concurrence in which Gorsuch criticized the classifications used by universities in greater detail. Gorsuch, relying heavily on the Bernstein brief, explained that these classifications are based on classifications that bureaucrats created via Directive 15 "without any input from anthropologists, sociologists, ethnologists, or other experts."[54] Despite explicit warnings accompanying the publication of Directive 15 in the *Federal Register* that the classifications "should not be . . . viewed as determinants of eligibility for participation in any Federal program," they were "eventually used . . . for that very purpose—to 'sor[t] out winners and losers in a process that, by the end of the century, would grant preference[s] in jobs . . . and university admissions."[55]

The classifications, Gorsuch continued, "rest on incoherent stereotypes."[56] He recounted several examples of this incoherence:

- The Asian American category "sweeps into one pile East Asians (e.g., Chinese, Korean, Japanese) and South Asians (e.g., Indian, Pakistani, Bangladeshi), even though together they constitute about 60% of the world's population."[57] The Native Hawaiian/Pacific Islander classification was separated from the Asian American classification in response to political lobbying in the 1990s, but this reform curiously left Filipino Americans in the Asian American classification, even though the Philippines are literally Pacific Islands.[58]
- The "Hispanic" category covers those whose ancestral language is Spanish, Basque, or Catalan—but it also covers

---

[51] *Id.* at 2201 (Thomas, J., concurring).

[52] *Id.* at 2200 n.10.

[53] *Id.* at 2202.

[54] *Id.* at 2210 (Gorsuch, J., concurring).

[55] *Id.* (citations omitted) (emphasis deleted).

[56] *Id.*

[57] *Id.*

[58] *Id.*

individuals of Mayan, Mixtec, or Zapotec descent who do not speak any of those languages and whose ancestry does not trace to the Iberian Peninsula but bears deep ties to the Americas.[59]

- The "White" category "sweeps in anyone from 'Europe, Asia west of India, and North Africa.'"[60] That includes "those of Welsh, Norwegian, Greek, Italian, Moroccan, Lebanese, Turkish, or Iranian descent. It embraces an Iraqi or Ukrainian refugee as much as a member of the British royal family."[61]

- The "Black or African American" classification "covers everyone from a descendant of enslaved persons who grew up poor in the rural South, to a first-generation child of wealthy Nigerian immigrants, to a Black-identifying applicant with multiracial ancestry whose family lives in a typical American suburb."[62]

Gorsuch added that "attempts to divide us all up into a handful of groups have become only more incoherent with time. American families have become increasingly multicultural, a fact that has led to unseemly disputes about whether someone is *really* a member of a certain racial or ethnic group."[63] He then cited cases discussing who counts as Hispanic. These ranged from a decision denying Hispanic status to someone of Italian Argentine descent, to one granting Hispanic status to someone of Sephardic Jewish ancestry, to one giving partial Hispanic credit to a petitioner who had one Cuban grandparent.[64]

"Given all this," Gorsuch concluded, "is it any surprise that members of certain groups sometimes try to conceal their race or ethnicity? Or that a cottage industry has sprung up to help college applicants do so?"[65] In particular, "one effect of lumping so many

[59] *Id.* at 2210–11.
[60] *Id.* at 2211.
[61] *Id.*
[62] *Id.*
[63] *Id.*
[64] *Id.*
[65] *Id.*

people of so many disparate backgrounds into the 'Asian' category is that many colleges consider 'Asians' to be 'overrepresented' in their admission pools."[66] Instead of explaining how their unique experiences and national origins add to diversity, Asian American applicants are therefore advised by admissions consultants to hide or downplay their identity.[67]

Justice Sotomayor, dissenting, attacked the majority for questioning classifications that had been developed by "experts" and had been widely used and relied upon by the government and private actors in all sorts of contexts. But in fact, the classifications were developed in an ad hoc manner, and they were specifically intended *not* to be used for affirmative action in general, much less in university admissions specifically.

It's true, as Sotomayor pointed out, that census data relying on the same classifications is widely used. But that is because the Census Bureau gathers such data, making it cheap and easily available, not because it's the best possible data to use. In any event, contrary to Sotomayor's expressed concerns, the *SFFA* opinion only addresses classifying individuals by race, not looking at census data when making broad public policy.[68]

Sotomayor did not make much of a legal, as opposed to policy, argument in this context. But translating her argument into legal terms, she essentially maintained that the "narrow tailoring" requirement should not apply to a university's choice of classifications. Rather, Sotomayor believed that the Court should have deferred to the universities in their choice to rely on the most widely used racial categories.

In any event, while the mundane collection and use of Directive 15 racial data by the Census Bureau, social scientists, and others is legally secure for now, Sotomayor was right to notice that the majority's attention to the arbitrariness issue has implications well beyond the context of university admissions. Some of those implications are addressed in the next section of this article.

66 *Id.*

67 *Id.*

68 *Id.* at 2254 (Sotomayor, J., dissenting).

IV. *SFFA's* Implications: The End of Racial Classification as We Know It?

A six-vote majority of the Supreme Court has declared that the racial and ethnic classifications used throughout government and American society are "plainly overbroad," both "underinclusive" and "overinclusive," and "arbitrary." This holding provides an opportunity for litigants to challenge the classifications used to provide racial preferences, inter alia, in government contracting, in biomedical research by government dictate, and in laws that classify people by American Indian status and that rely on factors other than tribal membership.

A. Racial Preferences in Government Contracting

New challenges to racial preferences in government contracting seem inevitable.

For over 30 years, the relevant precedents have allowed plaintiffs to challenge these preferences on the grounds that they are only permitted when they target a specific past intentional discrimination that the government itself had a hand in, with the discrimination continuing to have lingering effects.[69]

In practice, governments have found that if courts invalidated their racial preference policies, they could simply reenact them. They just had to purport to rely on a "disparity study" from a paid consultant. These studies inevitably showed the requisite history in the jurisdiction of discrimination in contracting, combined with the continuing effects of that discrimination. Government officials would even "admit" that they were still engaging in discrimination, regardless of the truth, to ensure that the disparity study came out the "right" way.

Faced with willful government officials determined to continue using racial preferences, potential plaintiffs eventually either gave up or found a way to take advantage of the preferences themselves.[70] Racial preferences in government contracting are currently more common than ever.

---

[69] City of Richmond v. J.A. Croson Co., 488 U.S. 469 (1989); Adarand Constructors, Inc. v. Peña, 515 U.S. 200 (1995).

[70] *See* MARTIN J. SWEET, MERELY JUDGMENT: IGNORING, EVADING, AND TRUMPING THE SUPREME COURT (2010).

Before *SFFA*, plaintiffs rarely raised the arbitrariness of the classifications when they challenged racial preferences in government contracting. In turn, courts had few opportunities to discuss whether courts should defer to the classifications used in minority-preference programs in government contracting, or whether strict scrutiny should apply to the classifications.[71] After *SFFA*, and assuming that willing plaintiffs are found, litigation will likely cause the end of preferences for "minority business enterprises." Directive 15 classifications are even more arbitrary in allocating government contracts than in pursuing diversity in higher education. For example, there were very few Asian Indians in the United States until the 1970s. Asian Indian Americans therefore have not experienced generations of discrimination. Moreover, on average they have much higher incomes and educational achievement than Americans in general. Nevertheless, they get preferences in government contracting as members of the "Asian American" classification. Meanwhile, anyone classified as white gets no preference. The latter classification includes Italian, Lebanese, Armenian, and other Americans whose ancestors faced significant discrimination in the pre–civil rights era and beyond.

Further, businesses owned by white Argentine and Spanish Americans get preferences via what Chief Justice Roberts called "arbitrary or undefined" Hispanic ethnic classification, but Afghan- and Iranian-American-owned businesses are deemed white-owned and get no preferences. Under federal law, a man who is 1/1024th Cherokee and is from a wealthy, well-established white family gets an automatic preference for his business so long as he is a

---

[71] *See* Builders Ass'n of Greater Chi. v. Cnty. of Cook, 256 F.3d 642, 647 (7th Cir. 2001) (concluding that preferences were overinclusive in including Spanish Americans, though not specifically applying strict scrutiny); Jana–Rock Constr., Inc. v. N.Y. State Dep't of Econ. Dev., 438 F.3d 195, 206 n.5 (2d Cir. 2006) (holding that a claim of underinclusiveness of the classifications used must lose, because allowing such claims would undermine Supreme Court precedent stating that racial preference programs should be as narrow as possible); Ritchey Produce Co. v. State of Ohio Dep't of Admin. Servs., 1997 WL 629965 at *2 (Ohio Ct. App. 1997) (holding that strict scrutiny applied and that the preferences were not narrowly tailored because they arbitrarily favored certain groups), *rev'd*, 707 N.E.2d 871, 928 (Ohio 1999). In *Vitolo v. Guzman*, 999 F.3d 353, 360–61 (6th Cir. 2021), a case involving racial preferences in the distribution of coronavirus relief funds, the court found that the classifications relied upon by the government were arbitrary and for that reason held that the preferences were not narrowly tailored and failed strict scrutiny.

tribal member. A man from an impoverished Appalachian family who grew up in a shack with an alcoholic single mother gets no such automatic preference.

The original impetus for government contracting preferences was to bring previously excluded black Americans into the economic mainstream. Yet less than one-fifth of the federal transportation dollars covered by racial preferences go to black-owned businesses, including those owned by immigrants.[72] Most of the racial preferences go to first- or second-generation immigrants from all over the world. It would seem to be virtually impossible to show that such preferences are narrowly tailored to help victims of historical patterns of discrimination that have effects bleeding into today.

B. Biomedical Research

Hopefully, *SSFA* will also doom federal "diversity" requirements imposed on biomedical researchers.[73] The Directive 15 classifications came with an explicit warning that these "classifications should not be interpreted as being scientific or anthropological in nature."[74] And indeed, the classifications have no valid scientific or anthropological basis.[75] Yet the Food and Drug Administration and the National Institutes of Health require medical researchers to classify study participants by Directive 15 categories.[76]

The problems with using these classifications in biomedical research have been discussed elsewhere. In short, scientists have been forced to use these classifications even though no valid studies suggest they should be used for the relevant purposes.[77] And the classifications mask vast genetic differences within each category.

The "compelling interest" that is served by the use of these classifications in biomedical research is, at best, unclear. There was, for

---

[72] Editorial, *Philly, Fraud and "Equity" Gone Wrong*, WALL ST. J. (April 11, 2023), https://tinyurl.com/46b6tcxu.

[73] *SFFA* will also hopefully doom nascent dangerous and ill-conceived efforts to pursue "equity" by giving individuals belonging to certain Directive 15 classifications preferential access to medical care.

[74] Directive No. 15, *supra* note 4.

[75] *See* BERNSTEIN, CLASSIFIED, *supra* note 8, at 141–67.

[76] *Id.*

[77] Janet K. Shim et al., *Race and Ancestry in the Age of Inclusion: Technique and Meaning in Post-Genomic Science*, 55 J. HEALTH & SOC. BEHAV. 504 (2014).

example, no plausible scientific reason for government bureaucrats to delay approval of Moderna's COVID-19 vaccine until the company recruited "enough" study subjects from the official minority classifications.[78]

C. American Indian Classifications

Finally, *SFFA* may have a significant influence on classifications of American Indians in American law. The Supreme Court has long held that tribal membership is not a racial classification. The government may therefore treat tribal members differently than others without being subject to strict scrutiny.[79]

Some federal laws, however, recognize individuals as American Indian based on factors other than tribal membership. These include community recognition, community affiliation, descent from indigenous Americans, "blood quantum,"[80] and even discretionary designation as Indian by the Secretary of the Interior.[81]

New challenges to at least some of these laws and regulations are likely, especially to laws that sometimes operate to the detriment of individual Indians. An example of such a law is the Major Crimes Act,[82] which often exposes people deemed "Indian" to long federal sentences for illegal acts that state courts would treat less harshly.[83]

[78] Meg Tirrell & Leanne Miller, *Moderna Slows Coronavirus Vaccine Trial Enrollment to Ensure Minority Representation, CEO Says,* CNBC (Sept. 4, 2020), https://tinyurl.com/mrx4dbpz.

Some prominent government officials have argued that if the subjects in vaccine testing studies are not "representative," the public will not trust the vaccines. But this reasoning is circular. If indeed Americans would not "trust" a vaccine unless its research subjects were sufficiently "diverse," that is largely because the government insists that vaccines should not be deemed trustworthy unless they have been tested on a diverse population—as defined by the unscientific Directive 15 categories. One doesn't see Icelanders, Ashkenazic Jews, or other groups with distinct genetic heritages expressing concern about vaccines; yet if anything, they should be more concerned than, say, "Hispanics."

[79] Morton v. Mancari, 417 U.S. 535, 548–49 (1974).

[80] The Department of the Interior even issues "Certificates of Indian Blood Quantum" to facilitate this policy. BUREAU OF INDIAN AFFAIRS, CERTIFICATE OF DEGREE OF INDIAN OR ALASKA NATIVE BLOOD INSTRUCTIONS, https://tinyurl.com/39pcz5ad (last accessed Aug. 16, 2023).

[81] *See* BERNSTEIN, CLASSIFIED, *supra* note 8, at 117–40.

[82] 18 U.S.C. § 1153 (1994).

[83] BERNSTEIN, CLASSIFIED, *supra* note 8, at 117–40.

A challenge is also undoubtedly forthcoming to the Indian Child Welfare Act (ICWA).[84] ICWA arbitrarily deems any child who is "eligible for membership in an Indian tribe and is the biological child of a member of an Indian tribe" to be exclusively an "Indian" for purposes of the Act.

The Supreme Court recently stated that the purpose of ICWA is "to keep Indian children connected to Indian families."[85] To the extent that's a valid government interest, the child should need to have some meaningful ties to his hereditary Indian tribal community for ICWA to apply. Yet under ICWA, a child could be, for example, 3/256th Cherokee on his father's side,[86] with no cultural connections to the tribe, and nonetheless be arbitrarily deemed an Indian for purposes of ICWA.

Relatedly, under ICWA, any Indian tribe can intervene on behalf of a child who is deemed to be an Indian, so long as the child's own tribe chooses not to intervene in the proceedings. In other words, the Sioux tribe can intervene to insist, for example, that a Hopi child be placed with a Sioux family rather than with a non-Indian family. This is true even though the Sioux and the Hopi have nothing in common except being "racially" Indian.

In the *Brackeen* case, the Court found that the plaintiffs had no standing to assert an equal protection claim. However, Justice Kavanaugh wrote a concurring opinion that virtually invited plaintiffs to bring such a claim in the future. Kavanaugh noted that ICWA raises troubling questions about race-based decisionmaking.[87] When such a case eventually arises, the Court will likely conclude that keeping Indian children attached to their heritage is a compelling government interest. But the Court will still have to address the arbitrary manner in which (1) ICWA deems children of mixed heritage to be Indian in a way that trumps any other identity they may have; and (2) "Indian" is treated as a singular class despite vast differences in tribal cultures, histories, religions, and so on. The Court will have to decide whether this arbitrary treatment shows that ICWA is not narrowly tailored to achieve its stated objective.

[84] 25 U.S.C. §§ 1901–1963.

[85] Haaland v. Brackeen, 143 S. Ct. 1609, 1623 (2023).

[86] *See* Adoptive Couple v. Baby Girl, 570 U.S. 637 (2013) (child who was only 3/256th Cherokee came under ICWA jurisdiction because her father was a member of the Cherokee tribe).

[87] *Brackeen*, 143 S. Ct. at 1661 (Kavanaugh, J., concurring).

Conclusion

When the U.S. government created the Directive 15 racial classifications in 1978, relevant officials thought that they were simply ensuring uniformity in data collection across government agencies. They had no inkling that these classifications would be used by institutions throughout American society to indefinitely divide Americans into demographic groups, with some receiving preferential treatment based on their classification.

In the ensuing 45 years, the United States has become more tolerant and more ethnically diverse, including a large population of people of mixed heritage. Nevertheless, the establishment—government, big business, universities, and the media, among others—has tenaciously clung to using the Directive 15 classifications for diversity and other purposes. At the grassroots level, Americans are increasingly adopting a multiethnic, multiracial American identity. At the elite level, corporate "affinity" groups, segregated orientations, graduations, and dorms, and overt racial discrimination in favor of certain Directive 15 groups have increasingly become the norm.

Until 2023, the Supreme Court watched these developments from afar, declining to intervene. Finally, in *SFFA*, the Court stepped in to condemn the Directive 15 classifications as unlawfully arbitrary, divisive, incoherent, poorly or ambiguously defined, gameable, and, most important, unsuited to serving a compelling interest in diversity in higher education.

In fact, the Directive 15 classifications are generally unsuited for almost anything, beyond creating artificial interest groups seeking to defend and expand their turf. *SFFA* marked the opening salvo in what is sure to be a much longer battle to stop government and other powerful entities from determining people's fate based on nonsensical, government-dictated racial classifications. There is reason to hope that *SFFA* marks the beginning of the end of racial classification as we know it.

Why *Haaland v. Brackeen* Is Not the End of the Story

*Timothy Sandefur**

> *The story does not end with the last word. It goes on in the silence of the mind . . . . I profess the conviction that there is only one story, but there are many stories in the one.*

—*N. Scott Momaday*[†]

Introduction

The Indian Child Welfare Act (ICWA) is a federal law which establishes a set of rules state governments must follow in "child custody proceedings" involving "Indian children."[1] Shockingly enough, these rules are less solicitous of the child's welfare than are the rules that apply to children of non-Native ancestry, and they actually put Indian children at greater risk of harm. For example, ICWA overrides the "best interests of the child" rule that is the standard guidepost in cases involving all other kids, replacing it with race-based "placement preferences" that effectively bar non-Natives from adopting Indian children. Other provisions of ICWA make it harder for states to rescue Indian children from abuse or neglect than children of other races. As a result, ICWA, although passed with good intentions, harms the very children it was meant to protect, depriving them of legal protections that children of other races enjoy.

* Vice President for Legal Affairs, Goldwater Institute. Mr. Sandefur authored several amicus briefs in the *Brackeen* litigation on behalf of the Goldwater Institute, the Cato Institute, the Texas Public Policy Foundation, and individual victims of ICWA. Thanks to Alethea Chaney for helpful edits.

[†] N. Scott Momaday, The Death of Sitting Bear: New and Selected Poems xiv (2022).

[1] 25 U.S.C. § 1903. This article uses the term "Indian" because ICWA uses that term, and does so as a term of art. Under ICWA, not all Native Americans are "Indian." This article also uses the term "tribal membership" as synonymous with "tribal citizenship" because ICWA uses the former term. No pejorative is intended.

In the process, it violates an astonishing number of constitutional rules: It treats children differently based on their biological ancestry, in violation of the Constitution's prohibitions against racial or national-origin-based discrimination; it deprives birth parents of their fundamental right to make choices about the care and custody of their children; it forces citizens into court systems that lack Bill of Rights protections, in violation of due process; it "commandeers" state officials, compelling them to implement federal rules that contradict state policy; it unconstitutionally delegates lawmaking power; and it even violates the principles that govern the personal jurisdiction of courts.[2]

Only two of those issues—ICWA's racially discriminatory provisions and the commandeering question—were before the Supreme Court in *Haaland v. Brackeen*,[3] and only the latter was ultimately decided. The Court declined to address other questions, finding 7–2 that the plaintiffs (both private citizens and state governments) lacked standing. The decision therefore invites future litigation over ICWA's race-based restrictions—restrictions that, as Justice Brett Kavanaugh observed in his concurrence, "raise significant questions under bedrock equal protection principles."[4] Given the Court's choice not to address these significant issues, the *Brackeen* ruling has little immediate effect beyond postponing the day when the injustices ICWA inflicts are confronted. But as a matter of constitutional law, the most interesting aspect of the competing opinions—especially Justice Neil Gorsuch's concurrence and Justice Clarence Thomas's dissent—may be the dispute over a fundamental theoretical question: What is the source and scope of Congress's power *vis-à-vis* tribes, and particularly Congress's allegedly "plenary" power?

---

[2] For thorough discussions of these and other constitutional problems with ICWA, see Timothy Sandefur, *Escaping the ICWA Penalty Box: In Defense of Equal Protection for Indian Children*, 37 CHILD. LEGAL RTS. J. 1 (2017); Timothy Sandefur, *The Unconstitutionality of the Indian Child Welfare Act*, 26 TEX. REV. L. & POL. 55 (2021); Timothy Sandefur, *The Federalism Problems with the Indian Child Welfare Act*, 26 TEX. REV. L. & POL. 429 (2022).

[3] 143 S. Ct. 1609 (2023).

[4] *Id.* at 1661 (Kavanaugh, J., concurring).

I. How ICWA Works

ICWA is not a well-known statute, and although it is relatively brief, it is also extremely unusual compared to other federal laws. For example, it appears to be the only federal statute that is *exclusively* enforced by *state* officers. And it is the only federal Indian law triggered not by tribal membership or residency on tribal lands, but by a person's biological ancestry alone. Given unusual features like these, and the fact that most people, including many experienced family-law attorneys, are unfamiliar with ICWA, a brief background is necessary to appreciate what was at stake in *Brackeen*.

A. "Indian Child"

Before Congress passed ICWA in 1978, state and federal governments often pursued policies aimed at coercively assimilating Native Americans into white society. Among other things, they sought to take Native American children from their parents' custody and place them in boarding schools or with white families, where they were sometimes abused, forced into manual labor, and punished for speaking Native languages or practicing their religions. The injustices inflicted through these policies—policies often rationalized as a way of "helping" Natives—were the principal focus of Justice Gorsuch's concurring opinion in *Brackeen*.[5]

But instead of halting such policies and providing strong legal protections for Indian children—and instead of focusing on children residing on tribal lands—ICWA focused on enhancing the powers of tribal government officials and curtailing the powers of state officials with respect to proceedings that do *not* occur on tribal lands.[6] It did this by dictating how state child welfare departments and state courts may act when dealing with "Indian children." And the problems with ICWA begin with its definition of that term.

ICWA defines an "Indian child" as a minor who is either (1) a tribal member or (2) *"eligible"* for membership and the *biological child* of a tribal member.[7] Different tribes have different eligibility criteria, but all rely exclusively on biological ancestry. (No tribe, for example,

---

[5] *See id.* at 1641–47 (Gorsuch, J., concurring).

[6] ICWA's substantive and procedural requirements do not apply in tribal court, only in state court. 25 C.F.R. § 23.103(b)(1).

[7] 25 U.S.C. § 1903(4) (emphasis added).

conditions membership on fluency in a tribal language or participation in tribal ceremonies.) This means children may be deemed
"Indian" under ICWA even if they are not and never become tribal
members; all that matters is biological eligibility and the existence of
a biological parent who is a member. Indeed, not only are the presence of cultural, political, religious, linguistic, or social ties between
the child and a tribe considered irrelevant, but most state courts
today consider it positively unjust to consider these factors.[8]

This explains why, in 2016, a six-year-old California girl known
as Lexi qualified as an Indian child even though her sole connection to the Choctaw tribe was a centuries-distant ancestor.[9] On the
other hand, a child who is *fully* acculturated to a tribe will *not* qualify
as an Indian child if she lacks the biological prerequisites for tribal
membership—for example, if she is the adopted, rather than the biological, child of a tribal member.[10] Under ICWA, the fictional Linda
Wishkob from Louise Eldrich's novel *The Round House* (a white child
raised by an Ojibwe family, who is fully acculturated to the tribe)
would not qualify, due solely to biological factors. Neither would William Holland Thomas (a white man who became chief of the Eastern
Band of Cherokees in the nineteenth century) or Sam Houston (who
was adopted by the Cherokee as a teenager and served as the tribe's
Ambassador to the United States). This is because no amount of cultural or political affiliation with a tribe will make children "Indian"
under ICWA if they lack the required DNA—and no lack of political

---

[8] Beginning in the 1980s, some courts began employing the so-called existing Indian family doctrine, whereby ICWA was held inapplicable to cases in which a child's
sole connection to a tribe was biological. The doctrine was a "saving construction,"
designed to prevent ICWA from being applied based solely on a child's race. But
it came under severe criticism from Indian law scholars, who characterized it as a
form of racism, on the theory that it empowered state judges to determine whether a
child was "Indian enough." *See, e.g.*, Cheyañna L. Jaffke, *The "Existing Indian Family"
Exception to the Indian Child Welfare Act: The States' Attempt to Slaughter Tribal Interests
in Indian Children*, 66 LA. L. REV. 733, 748 (2006). Consequently, virtually all state
courts have now repudiated the doctrine, and as a result ICWA not only *does* apply
based exclusively on a child's biological ancestry, but *must* apply only on that basis.
There is lingering debate, however, whether the Supreme Court effectively mandated some version of the doctrine in *Adoptive Couple v. Baby Girl*, 570 U.S. 637 (2013),
when it said that ICWA did not apply to a child with whom no tie to an Indian family
had been established.

[9] *See In re* Alexandria P., 204 Cal. Rptr. 3d 617 (Cal. Ct. App. 2016).

[10] *See, e.g.*, *In re* Francisco D., 178 Cal. Rptr. 3d. 388, 396 (Cal. Ct. App. 2014).

or cultural connection will *dis*qualify children who *do* fit the racial profile. In short, ICWA is triggered by what the Supreme Court has elsewhere called "an immutable characteristic determined solely by the accident of birth."[11]

It's worth emphasizing that "Indian child" status under ICWA is *not* synonymous with tribal membership.[12] Tribal membership is a function of tribal law, and tribes are free to set their criteria however they want.[13] By contrast, "Indian child" status is a function of federal and state[14] law, which means the definition must conform to constitutional limitations. ICWA does not, therefore—as some commentators would have it—preserve the power of tribes to determine their own membership. Tribes would have the same sovereign authority to do that even if ICWA did not exist. Instead, ICWA dictates to state governments how they must act with respect to children that federal and state law classify as "Indian," based on the possibility that they could, due to their biological ancestry, become tribal members someday.

B. ICWA's Separate and Less-Protective Rules for Indian Children

ICWA imposes a set of procedural and substantive rules on cases involving Indian children—rules that, shockingly enough, are *less* protective of children than are the rules that apply to their non-Indian peers. In *Brackeen*, the plaintiffs challenged two of these: the "active efforts" rule and the "placement preferences" for adoption and foster care.

1. "Active Efforts"

If a child is being abused by her parents and the state seeks to protect her, the state may take her into protective custody or put her

---

[11] Frontiero v. Richardson, 411 U.S. 677, 686 (1973) (plurality op.).

[12] *See In re* Abbigail A., 375 P.3d 879, 885 (Cal. 2016) (noting this distinction).

[13] Federal regulations do require that tribal membership be based on ancestry. *See* 25 C.F.R. § 83.11(e).

[14] Some states have their own state-law versions of ICWA, which sometimes differ from the federal version. The Minnesota Indian Family Preservation Act (MIFPA), for example, defines "Indian child" based solely on biological eligibility for tribal membership; it does not require that a biological parent be a tribal member. Minn. Stat. § 260.755(8). Consequently, a child is deemed "Indian" under MIFPA based exclusively on ancestry.

in foster care. Under the laws of every state, as well as the federal Adoption and Safe Families Act,[15] the state must first make "reasonable efforts" to restore that child to her family.[16] These "reasonable efforts" typically take the form of making social services available to the parents—sobriety programs, for example, or anger management classes—to help them get back on their feet. This is a sensible precaution for avoiding the unnecessary breakup of families. But, reasonably enough, this is *not* required in cases that involve "aggravated circumstances," such as drug addiction or child molestation.[17] The reason is obvious: It would be irrational to return abused children to homes where the state knows they are only going to be harmed again.

ICWA imposes a different rule for Indian children. It mandates that states make not "reasonable efforts," but *"active* efforts."[18] Although ICWA does not define this term,[19] state courts have interpreted it as requiring more than "reasonable" efforts,[20] and the obligations this standard imposes can be burdensome and vague. For example, the South Carolina Supreme Court declared in one case that it required state child protection officers to "stimulate [a] Father's desire to be a parent," whatever that means.[21] What's more, unlike "reasonable efforts," the "active efforts" requirement is *not* excused by the existence of aggravated circumstances. That means state social workers are legally required to return abused Indian children to parents who have abused them, even where evidence shows they will only be harmed again—a requirement that does not apply to children who are white, black, Asian, Hispanic, etc. The consequences have been—in case after case—the preventable murders of Indian children by parents

---

[15] Pub. L. No. 105-89, §§ 101-501, 111 Stat. 2115, 2116-21.

[16] *Id.* § 101.

[17] 42 U.S.C. § 671(a)(15)(D)(i). State law is the same. *See, e.g., In re* A.L.H., 468 S.W.3d 738, 744–45 (Tex. App.—Houston [14th Dist.] 2015, no pet.).

[18] 25 U.S.C. § 1912(d) (emphasis added).

[19] Federal regulations, however, define "active efforts" as "affirmative, active, thorough, and timely efforts intended primarily to maintain or reunite an Indian child with his or her family," which can include such things as "employing all available and culturally appropriate family preservation strategies." 25 C.F.R. § 23.2.

[20] *See, e.g.,* People ex rel. A.R., 310 P.3d 1007, 1015 (Colo. Ct. App. 2012).

[21] Adoptive Couple v. Baby Girl, 731 S.E.2d 550, 562 (S.C. 2012), *rev'd,* 570 U.S. 637 (2013).

whom the state knew to be unfit, but to whom ICWA required the state to return those children.[22]

Although ICWA was intended to restrict the power of government and private adoption agencies, rather than to apply to interfamily disputes, some courts have interpreted it to apply to the latter as well. This has had the perverse consequence of blocking Native parents from protecting their own children from harm. In *S.S v. Stephanie H.*,[23] for example, a tribal-member father sought to terminate the rights of his ex-wife due to her drug addiction and abandonment of the children. Had they been non-Indian, state law would have applied and the termination would likely have been approved. But because the children were Indian, ICWA's "active efforts" rule applied instead. That meant the father—a tribal member—was prohibited from terminating the mother's rights due to his not having taken steps to "prevent the breakup of the Indian family."[24] In other words, he had not tried to reunite the children with the same mother he was seeking to protect them from. This irrational outcome did not prevent the breakup of the Indian family, which is ICWA's stated purpose.[25] Instead, it blocked an Indian parent from promoting the best interests of his own kids.

This is far from unusual. ICWA frequently blocks Native parents from pursuing their children's best interests. For example, it often obstructs adoption by stepparents when Native parents, wishing to terminate the rights of unfit exes, seek to have their new spouses

---

[22] *See* Timothy Sandefur, *Suffer the Little Children*, REGULATION, 16, 18 Winter 2017/18 (describing the case of Declan Stewart, a 5-year-old Cherokee boy beaten to death by his mother's boyfriend despite the state knowing of the abuse); Angie Koehle, *DCS Claims "Jurisdictional, Legal Issues" in Phoenix Toddler's Death Case*, ABC15.COM, Oct. 16, 2018 https://bit.ly/3E3t3w2 (case of one-year-old Josiah Gishie, killed by mother's neglect despite the state knowing the risk); Nora Mabie, *A Deeper Look into the Indian Child Welfare Act and its Possible Role in Antonio Renova's Death*, GREAT FALLS TRIBUNE, Nov. 25, 2019 https://bit.ly/3KPoqJK (5-year-old beaten to death by parents after he was returned to them under ICWA); Mark Flatten, *Death on a Reservation*, GOLD-WATER INST., June 10, 2015 https://bit.ly/3P5qY96 (describing the cases of Laurynn Whiteshield, who was murdered after being sent to live on a reservation pursuant to ICWA, and Shayla H. and her sisters, who were sexually molested after being returned to a custodial adult pursuant to ICWA).

[23] 388 P.3d 569 (Ariz. Ct. App. 2017).

[24] *Id.* at 572 (quoting 25 U.S.C. § 1912).

[25] *See* 25 U.S.C. § 1901(4).

legally adopt their children.[26] Consider the case of Arizona mother Justine R.[27] Justine is a member of Tohono O'odham nation, but she does not live on the reservation, which is only a short distance from her Tucson home. She sought to terminate the rights of her ex due to his criminal activity, in hopes that her new husband could legally adopt her son. Had her child been white, black, Asian, Hispanic, or of any other ancestry, Arizona law would have applied—with its "reasonable efforts" requirement.[28] And if she had lived on reservation, Tohono O'odham law would have applied—which happens to be identical with Arizona law on this subject, meaning that, again, "reasonable efforts" would have been the rule.[29] But because the child is Indian and lived off-reservation, ICWA applied, with its *active* efforts" requirement. That and other requirements[30] are so burdensome that they barred Justine from terminating her ex's rights.

Even more irrational was the case of *In re Adoption of T.A.W.*,[31] in which a tribal-member mother sought to terminate the parental rights of her non-Native ex-husband, who was in jail and against whom she had obtained a restraining order. She did so because she had remarried—to a tribal member—and wanted her new husband to legally adopt her son. Yet the Washington Supreme Court ruled that because the child was an Indian child, ICWA required her to make "active efforts" to reunite the child with the birth father, even though the birth father was not even of Indian ancestry. ICWA was intended to prevent the breakup of Indian families. Yet here, and in other cases, it prevented the *formation* of an Indian family—for the benefit of a non-Indian.

Outcomes like these not only contradict ICWA's alleged goals, but also violate the fundamental rights of Native American parents. The Supreme Court held in *Troxel v. Granville* that birth parents have a fundamental constitutional right to make decisions about the "care,

---

[26] *See further* Timothy Sandefur, *Family Malpractice*, WASHINGTON EXAMINER, Apr. 13, 2018 https://bit.ly/47DXMgP.

[27] Justine R. v. Quigley, No. CV-17-0298-PR (Ariz. Feb. 13, 2018) (on file with the Goldwater Institute).

[28] ARIZ. REV. STAT. § 8-846(A).

[29] Tohono O'Odham Code tit. 3, ch. 1, art. 5, § 1501; *see also* § 1514(E).

[30] The other requirements include the "beyond a reasonable doubt" and expert witness requirements discussed below in part III.

[31] 383 P.3d 492, 502 (Wash. 2016).

custody, and control of their children."[32] Yet ICWA deprives the parents of Indian children of this right—*not* in order to protect these children, let alone their parents, but to serve the interests of tribes as corporate units, of whom the children are treated as mere constituent parts.[33] *Troxel* held it unconstitutional for the government to empower "third part[ies]" to "overturn [a] decision by a fit custodial parent."[34] But, as the Supreme Court admitted in *Mississippi Band of Choctaw Indians v. Holyfield*, ICWA gives tribal governments rights over Indian children "distinct from but on a parity with the interest of the parents."[35] In short, the active efforts provision deprives Indian children of the protections that state law would otherwise provide, forces state officials to place Indian children in harm's way, and even blocks the parents of Indian children from promoting their best interests.

2. The "Placement Preferences"

ICWA also imposes a series of "placement preferences" on foster care or adoption—rules that specify who may open their homes to Indian children in need. These preferences are based on the racial ancestry of the adults in question.

ICWA specifies that a child in need of a foster home must be placed (1) with family members if possible (which is unobjectionable), but, if that is not possible; (2) with a foster home approved by the child's tribe, and if this is also not possible; (3) with "*an* Indian foster home" or with "an Institution . . . approved by *an* Indian tribe."[36] Note that

---

[32] 530 U.S. 57, 65 (2000) (plurality op.). Although there was no majority opinion in *Troxel*, a majority of the Justices agreed that this is a fundamental right. *See id.* at 66; *id.* at 78–79 (Souter, J., concurring); *id.* at 80 (Thomas, J., concurring).

[33] ICWA's purposes section states that it is intended to "protect[] and preserv[e] . . . Indian tribes and their resources." 25 U.S.C. § 1901(2). The "resources" in question are, of course, children. As Justice Gorsuch put it, ICWA is intended to help preserve "an enduring place . . . in the structure of American life" for "the Tribes" and to preserve "Indian communities"—which is a fundamentally different goal than the protection of Indian children *qua* children. *Brackeen*, 143 S. Ct. at 1661 (Gorsuch, J., concurring). Illogically, Justice Gorsuch's concurrence celebrates the fact that "Indian children are not (these days) units of commerce," *id.*, while simultaneously affirming the constitutionality of a statute predicated on treating these children as "resources" subject to regulation under the Commerce Clause.

[34] 530 U.S. at 67 (plurality op.).

[35] 490 U.S. 30, 52 (1989) (quoting *In re* Adoption of Halloway, 732 P.2d 962, 969–970 (1986)).

[36] 25 U.S.C. § 1915(b) (emphasis added).

this does not say *the child's* tribe—*any* tribe will do. ICWA does not seek to place, for example, Shoshone children in Shoshone homes and Penobscot children in Penobscot homes, but to place "Indian" children in "Indian" homes, and to keep them out of black, white, Asian, Hispanic, etc. households. ICWA imposes similar placement preferences on adoption. An Indian child seeking a permanent, loving, adoptive home must be placed (1) with family where possible, and if not possible; (2) with other members of the child's tribe, and, if that is not possible; (3) with "other *Indian* families," rather than with families of different ethnic backgrounds.[37]

No similar rule applies to children of other races. On the contrary, federal law makes it illegal to delay or deny an adoption on the basis of race.[38] Yet Congress carved out one exception from that guarantee: It does not apply to Indian children. They are the only children in America against whom it is legal—indeed, mandatory—to discriminate based on their biological ancestry.

The consequence of these preferences is, of course, to deprive abused and neglected Indian children of opportunities for finding safe, loving, permanent homes with adults willing to help them. There is a drastic shortage of Indian foster homes—for example, in all of Los Angeles County, with its population of over 10 million people, there is only *one*.[39] Consequently, Indian children are typically placed in what is called "non-ICWA-compliant" foster care with adults of other races; and because this is not ICWA-compliant, tribal governments can then demand that such children be removed on a moment's notice from their foster families and placed elsewhere. This, indeed, is the typical move of tribal governments whenever a non-Indian foster family expresses interest in adopting an Indian child. That accounts for such shocking episodes as the Lexi case, in which a six-year-old child was taken from the foster family with whom she had lived for four years and sent to live with strangers in another state, instead.[40]

The emotional trauma caused by snatching a child away from the only parents she has ever known—with whom she has lived for

---

[37] 25 U.S.C. § 1915(a) (emphasis added).

[38] 42 U.S.C. § 1996b.

[39] *See* Daniel Heimpel, *L.A.'s One-and-Only Native American Foster Mom*, THE IMPRINT, June 14, 2016 https://bit.ly/45h1Wtz.

[40] *See* Charlotte Alter, *Inside the Agonizing Custody Fight over Six-Year-Old Lexi*, TIME, Mar. 27, 2016 https://bit.ly/3E3M69F.

two-thirds of her life—is certainly extreme. Yet federal regulations explicitly prohibit state judges from considering that fact when deciding an Indian child's fate.[41] This, again, is exactly the opposite of the rule for non-Indian children; in their cases, emotional well-being is the court's foremost concern. As one California court put it, a child is not "like an old lamp" that can be moved from place to place at will: "As time passes, the paramount concern becomes the stability of the child, who has a fundamental interest in a safe and permanent home; indeed, there is a compelling state interest in protecting this need."[42] But ICWA overrides that compelling interest with respect to Indian children, depriving them of the stability their welfare demands. What's more, given the emotional strain that ICWA inflicts on adults willing to foster or adopt an Indian child—not to mention the bureaucratic and legal burdens—many families who would otherwise volunteer to help these children choose not to.[43]

3. An "Indian Best Interests" Test?

At this point, it's natural to ask: What about the child's best interests? The best interests of the child standard is traditionally the "lodestar,"[44] the "primary consideration,"[45] and the "foremost concern"[46] in child welfare cases. The best-interests test is a totality-of-the-circumstances evaluation; it's individualized, meaning it requires a judge to assess the *particular* needs of that *specific* child in his or her *individual* situation.[47] This makes the test effectively the

---

[41] 25 C.F.R. § 23.132(e).

[42] Guardianship of Ann S., 41 Cal. Rptr. 3d 709, 727 (Cal. Ct. App. 2006) (quoting Guardianship of Kassandra H., 64 Cal. App. 4th 1228, 1239 (1998)). *See also* Guardianship of Ann S. 45 Cal 4th 1110, 1136 n.19 ("[T]he child's best interest becomes the paramount consideration after an extended period of foster care.").

[43] *See* Elizabeth Stuart, *Native American Foster Children Suffer under a Law Originally Meant to Help Them*, PHOENIX NEW TIMES, Sep. 7, 2016 https://bit.ly/45xsOWp. *See also In re* Bridget R., 49 Cal. Rptr. 2d 507, 529 (Cal. Ct. App. 1996) ("[O]n the sole basis of race, [ICWA] deprives [children]of equal opportunities to be adopted that are available to non-Indian children and exposes them, like the twin girls in this case, to having an existing non-Indian family torn apart through an after the fact assertion of tribal and Indian-parent rights.").

[44] State v. Matthew W. (*In re* Jaydon W.) 909 N.W.2d 385, 395 (Neb. Ct. App. 2018).

[45] TEX. FAM. CODE § 153.002.

[46] *In re* Marriage of Pooler, 136 P.3d 1153, 1155 (Or. Ct. App. 2006).

[47] *See, e.g., In re* Adoption of Kelsey S., 1 Cal. 4th 816, 845–50 (1992) ("best interests" standard focuses on the child's individual circumstances).

opposite of a legal "presumption." In fact, the Supreme Court has said that due process bars states from substituting presumptions for an individualized assessment of the child's best interests. In *Stanley v. Illinois*, it struck down a state law that established a legal presumption that unmarried fathers were unfit to raise children.[48] "Procedure by presumption is always cheaper and easier than individualized determination," it said. "But when, as here, the procedure forecloses the determinative issues of competence and care, when it explicitly disdains present realities in deference to past formalities, it needlessly risks running roughshod over the important interests of both parent and child."[49]

Yet ICWA overrides the best interests rule and imposes a blanket presumption: specifically, that it is virtually always in all Indian children's best interest to be placed with "Indian" households.[50] Indeed, the Bureau of Indian Affairs (BIA) has said that "ICWA establishes the placement preferences as being in the child's best interest"[51]— that is, ICWA creates a single, nationwide standard purporting to dictate what is in every Indian child's best interest per se.

Some courts have viewed this as meaning that there are two different best interests tests: one for children of non-Indian ancestry, and one for Indian children. Under this theory, a child's specific needs are the "paramount"[52] concern if the child is white, black, etc.—but if the child is Indian, that is *not* the paramount concern. Instead, an Indian child's specific needs are only to be "take[n] . . . into account as one of the constellation of factors,"[53] to be compromised with respect to other considerations. Of course, the usual term for a situation in which there are two different legal standards going by the same name—pursuant to which children are treated differently based solely on their ancestry—is "separate but equal."

[48] 405 U.S. 645 (1972).

[49] *Id.* at 656–57.

[50] *See, e.g.*, Dep't of Hum. Servs. v. Three Affiliated Tribes of Fort Berthold Rsrv. (*In re K.R.C.*), 238 P.3d 40, 48 (Or. Ct. App. 2010) (ICWA "establishes a presumption that an adoptive placement in accordance with the preference criteria is in an Indian child's best interests.").

[51] 81 Fed. Reg. at 38826 (2016).

[52] *Guardianship of Ann S.*, 202 P.3d at 1106 n.19.

[53] *In re Alexandria P.*, 204 Cal. Rptr. 3d at 634. Amazingly, Texas courts have even declared the best interests test an "Anglo" principle, inapplicable to "Indians." Yavapai-Apache Tribe v. Mejia, 906 S.W.2d 152, 168 (Tex. App. 1995).

Other state courts have used more moderate terms to character-ize ICWA's Indian-best-interests rule, seeing it not as overriding the traditional best interests inquiry, but as merely creating a rebuttable presumption.[54] But this does not resolve the problem, because unless a court bases its decision on all relevant factors and circumstances— that is, unless it uses the traditional, individualized best interests test—such a presumption is still constitutionally inadequate.[55] And ICWA sharply limits a party's ability to challenge that presumption. A party must show "good cause" to depart from the placement prefer-ences, but ICWA does not define that phrase, and the BIA's regulations sharply limit the considerations that a court may weigh.[56] For exam-ple, good cause may exist when the child has "extraordinary physical, mental, or emotional needs" which cannot be met "in the community where families who meet the placement preferences live," but *ordinary* physical, mental, or emotional needs do not suffice.[57]

It's worth mentioning here that the traditional best interests test *would* include consideration of a child's tribal connections, meaning there is no reason to suppose that applying the standard, individu-alized best-interests test would bar a court from placing an Indian child in an Indian household, where doing so would best serve the child's needs.[58] Because the traditional test is an all-things-considered

---

[54] *See, e.g., Dep't of Hum. Svs.*, 238 P3d at 48; *In re* G.C., 157 Cal. Rptr. 3d 826, 831 (Cal. Ct. App. 2013).

[55] *See, e.g.*, Adoption of Kelsey S., 823 P.2d 1216, 1236 (Cal. 1992) (A court may em-ploy presumptions, but when a party challenges that presumption, "[a] court should consider all factors relevant to [the best interests] determination.").

[56] 25 U.S.C. §§ 1915(a), (b).

[57] *Compare* 25 C.F.R. § 23.132(4) (listing factors) *with id.* § 23.132(e) (specifying that "ordinary bonding or attachment" do *not* count).

[58] Responding to this argument, some scholars and judges have defended ICWA's presumption by contending that the traditional best interests standard is too subjec-tive. *See, e.g., In re* Custody of S.E.G., 521 N.W.2d 357, 363 (Minn. 1994). But the best interests test is no more subjective than any other legal test, and a blanket presump-tion which purports to declare what is in the best interests of all Indians—based on their biological ancestry—is hardly an improvement. Actually, technically speaking, ICWA's placement preferences are not "presumptions"; they're a *prejudice*. A presump-tion is a rebuttable default rule, based on a rational calculation of costs and benefits of likely outcomes. A prejudice, by contrast, is an assumption that people with some logically unrelated trait—such as biological ancestry—must have certain psychologi-cal or social characteristics. ICWA's rule that Indian children should not be raised by adults with of non-Native ancestry falls into the latter category.

evaluation, it probably is in a child's best interests to retain tribal connections where they exist. But rather than apply such an individualized assessment, ICWA replaces the all-things-considered evaluation with what the *Holyfield* Court called "a Federal policy that, where possible, an Indian child should remain in the Indian community."[59] In other words, it displaces the individualized assessment with a stereotype that Indian kids should virtually never be raised by white, black, Asian, Hispanic, etc., adults.

There are many other ways in which ICWA puts abused or neglected Indian children at a legal disadvantage—such as its rules giving tribal courts jurisdiction over their cases absent the "minimum contacts" required for such jurisdiction,[60] or provisions that force their cases into tribal courts where the Bill of Rights does not apply[61]—but there is no room to address them here. Instead, we must turn to the two questions at issue in *Brackeen*: Whether ICWA unconstitutionally commandeers the states, and whether it constitutes race-based lawmaking.

II. The *Brackeen* case

A. The Facts and the Litigation

A.L.M. was born in 2015 to a Navajo mother and a Cherokee father. They were unable to care for him, so when he was ten months old, the state placed him in foster care with Chad and Jennifer Brackeen, a non-Native family in Texas. After A.L.M. had lived with the Brackeens for two years, they and his birth parents decided it would be best for him if the Brackeens legally adopted him. It is worth emphasizing that the adoption here was not involuntary. A.L.M. was not being forcibly removed from his birth parents.[62] Thus, had he been of any other race, adoption would have been quickly resolved as a matter of Texas law, which prioritizes a child's best interests and prohibits discrimination in adoption cases based on race.[63]

---

[59] *Holyfield*, 490 U.S. at 37 (citation omitted).

[60] *See* Timothy Sandefur, *Recent Developments in Indian Child Welfare Act Litigation: Moving Toward Equal Protection?*, 23 TEX. REV. L. & POL. 425, 456–61 (2019).

[61] *See* Timothy Sandefur, *Federalism Problems, supra* note 2, at 448–52.

[62] In *Holyfield*, too, the birth parents volunteered the child for adoption, and the Court held that ICWA allowed the tribe to veto that choice.

[63] *See In re* Adoption of Gomez, 424 S.W.2d 656, 657–658 (Tex. Civ. App.—El Paso 1967) (per curiam).

But because he is an Indian child, ICWA applied, which meant the tribe[64] was allowed to intervene and demand that A.L.M. be placed with tribal members in Utah, instead.[65] A state trial court accordingly ordered him taken from the Brackeens—who, as A.L.M.'s birth father testified, were the only family he had ever known[66]—and sent to live with strangers he had never met, in a state he had never visited. Fortunately, the court stayed that order, and the Brackeens' petition to adopt A.L.M. was ultimately approved. Yet the Brackeens also sought to adopt his half-sister, known as Y.J. Given the risk that ICWA would again be applied and potentially bar the Brackeens from adopting her, they brought a federal lawsuit for injunctive relief.[67]

They were joined in that effort by two other families: the Librettis and the Cliffords. The Librettis sought to adopt Baby O., a Pueblo child whose biological mother volunteered her for adoption by the Librettis. The tribe intervened and moved to block the adoption, but after litigation began, the tribe changed its position and allowed the Librettis to adopt. The Librettis, however, hoped to foster and possibly adopt additional children in need. Given the emotional stress, financial expense, and delay of ICWA-related proceedings, the Librettis sought injunctive relief to prevent the application of ICWA in future cases. The Clifford family wished to adopt a child referred to as P. Although Child P. is of Ojibwe ancestry, she was not eligible for tribal membership, given her blood quantum. Yet once litigation began, the tribe asserted that Child P. was a tribal member "for purposes of ICWA only,"

---

[64] Just before the adoption hearing, attorneys for the Cherokee and Navajo tribes decided in the hallway of the state courthouse to deem A.L.M. a Navajo child. *See* First Amended Complaint, Brackeen v. Zinke, No. 4:17-cv-868-O ¶ 120 (N.D. Tex. filed Dec. 15, 2017). This despite the immense cultural, linguistic, and historical differences between the Cherokee and Navajo tribes, whose homelands are nearly as far apart as Paris and Moscow.

[65] 25 U.S.C. § 1911(c).

[66] *See* Transcript of Aug. 1, 2017 Adoption Hearing (Appellant's Appendix, Tab H), *In re* A.L.M., Nos. 02-17-00298-CV & 02-17-00300-CV (Tex. Ct. App. 2d Judicial Dist.) at 55:20-58:6 ("I would love for him to stay with the foster parents . . . [b]ecause he's been with them ever since he was basically born almost . . . . [They are] the only parents he knows."). Bizarrely, some commentators have asserted that the phrase "the 'only parents' the child had ever known" is a racist rhetorical device for "demoniz[ing] Indian families"—even though this phrase was the testimony of A.L.M.'s Cherokee father. *See* Matthew L.M. Fletcher & Wenona T. Singel, *Lawyering the Indian Child Welfare Act*, 120 MICH. L. REV. 1755, 1757, 1780 (2022).

[67] At the time of this writing, Y.J.'s case was still pending in Texas court.

whatever that means.[68] As a consequence, state courts ordered Child P. removed from the Cliffords' custody and placed with a tribal member, instead—where she remains today.

In their federal lawsuit, the Brackeens, Librettis, and Cliffords argued that ICWA is unconstitutional because, among other things, it constitutes a race-based distinction. They were joined as plaintiffs by the states of Indiana, Louisiana, and Texas, who argued that ICWA also unconstitutionally commandeers state officials and violates a host of other federalism-related rules.[69]

The plaintiffs prevailed in the federal district court, but the Fifth Circuit reversed in a 2–1 decision which upheld ICWA in all respects, over a dissent by Judge Priscilla Owen, who believed ICWA violates the anti-commandeering principle.[70] Then came en banc rehearing, which resulted in a labyrinthine set of overlapping opinions totaling more than 300 pages—a ruling so complicated that the court was forced to provide an "issue-by-issue summary" so lawyers could figure out what had been decided.[71] In the end, the judges were fairly evenly split. A bare majority rejected the argument that ICWA is race-based, but a bare majority also found the law problematic on commandeering grounds.[72]

---

[68] Brackeen v. Zinke, 338 F. Supp. 3d 514, 527 (N.D. Tex. 2018). ICWA does not contemplate such a creature as tribal membership "for purposes of ICWA only." *Cf.* Nielson v. Ketchum, 640 F.3d 1117, 1124 (10th Cir. 2011) ("Congress did not intend the ICWA to authorize this sort of gamesmanship on the part of a tribe—e.g. to authorize a temporary and nonjurisdictional citizenship upon a nonconsenting person in order to invoke ICWA protections.").

[69] Among other things, the plaintiffs argued that ICWA unconstitutionally delegates power to tribal governments, because it permits tribal governments to establish alternatives to the placement preferences, which states are then forced to follow. *See generally* Sandefur, *Federalism Problems, supra* note 2, at 474–84.

[70] Brackeen v. Bernhardt, 937 F.3d 406, 441–42 (5th Cir. 2019), *aff'd in part, rev'd in part en banc sub nom.* Brackeen v. Haaland, 994 F.3d 249 (5th Cir. 2021), *aff'd in part, rev'd in part sub nom.* Haaland v. Brackeen, 143 S. Ct. 1609 (2023).

[71] Brackeen v. Haaland, 994 F.3d 249, 267 (5th Cir. 2021) (en banc), *aff'd in part, rev'd in part sub nom.* Haaland v. Brackeen, 143 S. Ct. 1609 (2023).

[72] The court of appeals was equally divided on whether the "other Indian families" provisions in ICWA's placement preferences satisfy the rational basis test. 994 F.3d at 268 (en banc). This meant the district court's finding that these provisions are unconstitutional remained in place, but without a precedential opinion, and the Supreme Court did not address the question. The court of appeals also found that ICWA does not unconstitutionally delegate lawmaking authority to tribes. For more on that issue, *see* Sandefur, *Federalism Problems, supra* note 2, at 474–84.

The Supreme Court was therefore presented with four separate petitions. Because each side of the case had won some and lost some, all parties sought Supreme Court review—and the oral arguments consumed some four hours. Then, after all that buildup came the anticlimax: the Court issued a modest, 34-page ruling rejecting the state's[73] federalism challenges and finding that nobody had standing to argue that ICWA is unconstitutionally race-based. On the race question, in fact, the majority remained studiously silent. Yet the majority opinion by Justice Amy Coney Barrett, the concurring opinion by Justice Gorsuch, and the dissent by Justice Thomas clashed over a more fundamental issue: the source and nature of Congress's authority to legislate with respect to tribes. Before addressing that, we will examine how the Court resolved the two primary disputes.

III. Commandeering

The anti-commandeering rule says that while Congress may pass laws that states must obey, states cannot be required to implement those laws. States may not *interfere* with federal implementation of federal law, but they can stand back and refuse to participate. As the Supreme Court put it in *Printz v. United States*, "[i]t is no more compatible with [states'] independence and autonomy that their officers be 'dragooned' . . . into administering federal law, than it would be compatible with the independence and autonomy of the United States that its officers be impressed into service for the execution of state laws."[74] There is a significant caveat, however: A federal mandate does not qualify as "dragooning" if it is "even-handed"—that is, if it applies to both private and public parties equally. For example, provisions of the Affordable Care Act that require employers to provide certain kinds of insurance to employees do not violate the anti-commandeering rule when they apply to government employers, since private employers must do the same.[75]

Two categories of commandeering arguments were at issue in *Brackeen*. The first involved a typical commandeering claim: that ICWA forces state executive-branch officials to implement its

---

[73] By the time it reached the Supreme Court, Illinois and Louisiana had dropped out of the case, leaving Texas as the sole state petitioner.

[74] 521 U.S. 898, 928 (1997) (citation omitted).

[75] *See* Ohio v. United States, 849 F.3d 313, 322 (6th Cir. 2017).

substantive mandates. It does this by forcing state child welfare officers to take steps they otherwise would not take—for example, seeking racially matched households to provide foster care for abused Indian children whom the state has taken into custody, or maintaining various special types of records regarding the placement of Indian children, which are not necessary in cases involving non-Indian children.

The second commandeering argument was more unusual. It involved the commandeering of state *judges*. The Supreme Court has never before addressed how, or even whether, the anti-commandeering rule applies to state courts. The Constitution itself requires state judges to implement federal law notwithstanding anything in a state's constitution or laws to the contrary.[76] There is thus an intuitive difficulty with the idea that it is even logically possible for a state judiciary to be unconstitutionally "dragooned." Yet the argument made sense in *Brackeen*, given an unusual feature of ICWA.

Ordinarily, a federal law will create some substantive right or establish a legal cause of action, which state courts must then enforce. This presents no commandeering problem. But ICWA doesn't do that. Instead, it dictates the evidentiary or procedural rules that state judges must follow when they apply *state* law. In other words, whereas federal laws usually create the *what*, ICWA dictates the *how*—forcing state judges to use ICWA's methods when applying *state* law regarding child welfare. That, the plaintiffs argued, is "dragooning."

Consider the rules that govern the termination of parental rights (TPR): If a state seeks to terminate the rights of an abusive parent, it must prove to a state judge that certain facts exist—facts that *state law* says will justify TPR. Those facts must be proven by "clear and convincing evidence." That is the standard in every state, because it was mandated by the Supreme Court in *Santosky v. Kramer*, a 1982 case which said that the "preponderance of the evidence" standard was too lax and that the "beyond a reasonable doubt" standard was too demanding.[77] The former risked making it too easy for the state to take people's children away, while the latter "would erect an unreasonable barrier to state efforts to free permanently

---

[76] *See* U.S. CONST. art VI cl. 2.

[77] 455 U.S. 745, 768–69 (1982).

neglected children for adoption."[78] ICWA, however, imposes that unreasonable barrier; in fact, it goes further. It requires that in a TPR case involving an Indian child, the state court must find the existence of the required facts beyond a reasonable doubt, based on the testimony of expert witnesses.[79] This is an evidentiary burden even more severe than that which applies to criminal law (where expert witness testimony is not required). Given that TPR is a necessary step before adoption, this provision of ICWA literally makes it easier to put a criminal on death row than to find an adoptive home for an Indian child in need. To reiterate, ICWA does not set forth the substantive standards for TPR or create a federal substantive right involving TPR. It dictates to state judges how they must implement the state's *own* TPR statute.[80] This presents a unique commandeering problem.

Yet in *Brackeen*, the Court rejected the argument that ICWA commandeers either the state executive or judicial branches. With respect to the executive branch, the Court concluded that while ICWA does require state executive entities to take certain actions, this isn't commandeering, because private parties must also take those steps. For example, the "active efforts" requirement, which forces state child welfare agencies to return abused Indian children to abusive households, also applies to private parties, as in the *T.A.W.* and *S.S.* cases described above.[81] Thus ICWA is "even-handed."

---

[78] *Id.* at 769.

[79] 25 U.S.C. § 1912(f). The statute specifically requires *qualified* expert witnesses, a term the BIA defines as someone "qualified to testify as to the prevailing social and cultural standards of the Indian child's Tribe." 25 C.F.R. § 23.122(a). This sharply narrows the number of available experts—how many child psychologists, capable of testifying about a child's needs, also happen to be experts on the culture of any particular tribe? Moreover, this regulation inherently biases ICWA proceedings by effectively giving the tribe—which is typically a party to the case—veto power over which experts are allowed to testify. A non-Native would-be adoptive parent seeking TPR might wish to offer testimony from (say) a world-renowned child psychologist who can prove that granting TPR is crucial to the child's well-being—but because the psychologist is not also an expert on the prevailing standards of (say) the Augustine Band of Cahuilla Indians, the psychologist's testimony would simply not count.

[80] Some state courts have said ICWA doesn't impose an evidentiary standard on state law, but merely adds an additional element to federal law. But the latter is just as much commandeering as the former—perhaps more so. *See* Sandefur, *Federalism Problems, supra* note 2, at 459 n.155.

[81] *See Brackeen*, 143 S. Ct. at 1631–33.

There are three problems with that conclusion: First, there's no reason to believe ICWA was intended to apply to interfamily disputes such as *T.A.W.* and *S.S.* at all. On the contrary, ICWA declares that it was intended to apply to "agencies," and it expressly does not apply to divorce proceedings.[82] That and its historical background suggest that state courts have erred in holding, as they did in *T.A.W.*, *S.S.*, and similar cases, that ICWA applies to interfamily disputes. Yet the *Brackeen* majority simply assumed that these decisions were correct.

Second, while ICWA does impose mandates on private parties in other situations—it expressly applies to private adoption agencies, for example—it does so as a condition of their obtaining a state-court judgment. ICWA is not like, say, a statute that requires state governments to provide certain types of insurance to its employees, just as private employers must do—which would be a typical "even-handedness" situation. Rather, ICWA provides that a state judge may not grant a judgment to a party (on a matter of state law) without first finding that the party has taken certain steps (i.e., "active efforts"). Viewed that way, ICWA does not regulate plaintiffs; it regulates state courts. Its unique evidentiary rules therefore straddle the line between executive and judicial commandeering in ways that cause the common-sense notion of "even-handedness" to collapse.

Third, even if it is true that ICWA, correctly interpreted, theoretically applies both to public and private entities, the reality on the ground is that the vast majority of cases involving TPR are those in which a state child protection agency is the moving party. They are the entities that states entrust to protect abused and neglected children, and the historical record shows that they are the entities at which ICWA was principally aimed. The fact that ICWA might incidentally also apply to private parties should not be taken as an excuse to ignore the degree of commandeering at issue. Yet on this point, the *Brackeen* Court struck a highly formalistic note, brushing aside this argument on the grounds that "[t]he record contains no evidence supporting the assertion that States institute the vast majority

[82] 25 U.S.C. § 1903(1).

of involuntary proceedings."[83] If formalism means "screening off . . . [the] factors that a sensitive decisionmaker would otherwise take into account" and blindly following "the force of the language in which rules are written,"[84] then surely this appeal to the text instead of the facts that any reasonable person knows is an extraordinary exercise in formalism.

Even more striking was the short shrift the *Brackeen* majority gave to the judicial commandeering argument. It found that ICWA's provisions dictating how state courts must apply their own state statutes are just an ordinary application of the Constitution's Supremacy Clause. Rejecting the plaintiffs' "distinction between requiring state courts to entertain federal causes of action and requiring them to apply federal law to state causes of action," the majority concluded that when Congress adopts a law, states must comply, "[e]nd of story."[85]

But that is surely not the end of the story. The Supremacy Clause does not give Congress power to override all matters of state law. If it did, the Constitution would be only a single sentence long. It would consist only of the Supremacy Clause, and ours would be a consolidated, national government—which, as the Framers and the Court have repeatedly explained, it is not.[86] Congress could not, for example, forbid state courts from convicting any defendant of robbery under state law absent a confession, or forbid state judges from giving effect to holographic wills unless there are four witnesses.[87] If that is because such matters fall so clearly within the province of state law that no fair reading of congressional authority would allow Congress to dictate to state courts how to implement such state-law principles, then exactly the same is true of

---

[83] *Brackeen,* 143 S. Ct. at 1632.

[84] Frederick Schauer, *Formalism,* 97 YALE L.J. 509, 510 (1988).

[85] *Brackeen,* 143 S. Ct. at 1635.

[86] *See, e.g.,* United States v. Morrison, 529 U.S. 598, 618 n.8 (2000); United States v. Lopez, 514 U.S. 549, 552 (1995).

[87] *See, e.g.,* THE FEDERALIST No. 33 at 199–200 (C. Rossiter, rev. ed. 2003) (Alexander Hamilton) (regarding it as fanciful that Congress could ever "attempt to vary the law of descent [i.e., intestacy] in any State"); Sandefur, *Federalism Problems, supra* note 2, at 461–62.

state-court child welfare proceedings, which are also quintessential matters of state law.[88]

The only way to justify ICWA, therefore, is to appeal to some source of congressional power that supersedes the ordinary rules of federalism. And the *Brackeen* majority tried this move by asserting that Congress has "plenary" power with respect to tribes. That argument fails, for reasons we will see in part V below. Yet there is a more theoretically plausible move the Court could have made—a clause never invoked by any party, but which would have provided a firmer basis for ICWA's mandates on state executive and judicial branches: Section Five of the Fourteenth Amendment.

Section Five gives Congress extraordinarily broad power over states when necessary to remedy perceived violations of constitutional rights. For example, the Court has already held that Congress can use this power to strip states of sovereign immunity.[89] It thus seems likely that Congress could also use this power to mandate variances from state-law evidentiary burdens, even with respect to state law causes of action. Indeed, the Fourteenth Amendment was created specifically

---

[88] The Court cited three examples of federal law dictating the mechanism for applying substantive state law: the Federal Employees' Group Life Insurance Act (FEGLIA), the National Service Life Insurance Act (NSLIA), and the Employee Retirement Income Security Act (ERISA). *See Brackeen*, 143 S. Ct. at 1635. None of these are analogous, however. FEGLIA created a federal insurance program—i.e., it created substantive federal rights—and then dictated how state courts should implement those rights. *See* Hillman v. Maretta, 569 U.S. 483, 486–87 (2013). NSLIA likewise creates substantive federal rights, such as the right to designate the recipients of life insurance policies, which obviously overrode contrary California law in *Wissner v. Wissner*, 338 U.S. 655, 661 (1950). ERISA regulates plan administrators by directing them to take certain actions, notwithstanding state law to the contrary—it does not dictate to state judges what procedural or evidentiary standards to use when applying their own substantive state law. *See* Sandefur, *Federalism Problems, supra* note 2, at 467 (discussing Egelhoff v. Egelhoff *ex rel.* Breiner, 532 U.S. 141 (2001)). None of these statutes bears any resemblance to ICWA, which does *not* create substantive federal rights or a substantive cause of action. Rather, ICWA simply dictates to state judges what evidentiary standards they must use when applying *state law* causes of action or implementing *state law* rights. The Fifth Circuit in *Brackeen* actually offered a better analogy: the Servicemembers Civil Relief Act, which allows members of the military to re-open adverse state-court judgments (involving state law causes of action) rendered in their absence while on duty. *See Brackeen*, 994 F.3d at 318 (opinion of Dennis, J.). But even that example fails, because under that act, state courts can refuse to reopen such cases if (inter alia) the party lacks a meritorious *state-law* defense. *See* Sandefur, *Federalism Problems, supra* note 2, at 463. Thus, that Act respects federalism in ways ICWA does not.

[89] *See, e.g.*, Fitzpatrick v. Bitzer, 427 U.S. 445, 456 (1976).

to enable Congress to protect citizens from the kinds of abuses that, as Justice Gorsuch detailed, inspired ICWA's adoption. Of course, had this issue been raised, the Court would have had to decide whether ICWA's mandates are "congruent and proportional" to the harms Congress sought to redress.[90] Whether or not ICWA could pass that test is debatable, but no such debate occurred. One thing is clear: This approach would be far more constitutionally rational than the ill-conceived "plenary" power theory that the majority employed.

IV. Is ICWA Race-Based?

Before proceeding to the dispute over "plenary" power, however, a word about the blockbuster argument in *Brackeen*: whether ICWA is unconstitutional race-based legislation. The majority chose not to answer this question, adopting a weirdly strict interpretation of the all-too-malleable doctrine of standing. This was disappointing not only as a legal matter—because this application of standing appears opportunistic—but as a practical matter, too, given that the Court has shown so little interest in ICWA. In the 45 years of that Act's existence, the Justices have addressed it in only three cases—about once a generation. It is only too possible that the *Brackeen* decision could doom another generation of Indian children to the deprivations ICWA imposes on them.

A. Standing: The Lack of State Defendants Proves Fatal

Federal courts will not resolve a dispute unless the parties have standing to raise it, meaning the kind of direct stake in the case that makes them the appropriate litigants to present it. Unfortunately, standing can be an amorphous concept, and as Clark Neily has written, it can, "[w]hen misapplied, . . . amount to little more than a 'get out of court free' card for the government."[91] That is what happened in *Brackeen*.

The Court found that the plaintiffs lacked standing to challenge ICWA as race-based because although the Brackeens were then in the midst of state-court adoption proceedings to which ICWA would probably make all the difference, no state officials responsible for implementing ICWA were named as defendants. That, said the Court,

---

[90] *See, e.g.*, Nev. Dep't of Hum. Res. v. Hibbs, 538 U.S. 721, 736–38 (2003).

[91] Clark Neily, District of Columbia v. Heller: *The Second Amendment Is Back, Baby*, 2007–2008 CATO SUP. CT. REV. 127, 138 (2008).

meant "an injunction would not give petitioners legally enforceable protection from the allegedly imminent harm."[92] In other words, the Brackeens needed to have sued Texas state judges in order for any potential judgment to provide relief.

This seems like motivated hair-splitting, however, given that state officials implement ICWA because they are forced to by federal law. The *Brackeen* majority opinion itself says that when Congress mandates something, state judges must comply, "[e]nd of story."[93] Why, then, is that not the end of the story as far as standing is concerned? On the merits, the Court considers it natural to regard state officials as mere instruments in the hands of Congress—but in its standing inquiry, the Court shifts gears and acts as if state officers have sufficient discretion that a plaintiff must enjoin them separately from the federal officials responsible for ICWA's implementation. That seems to be trying to have it both ways.

Further, existing precedent does not require such particularity in choice of defendants. Ordinarily, the question in a standing inquiry is whether the plaintiffs' injuries would be *redressed* by a favorable decision. That redress need not be perfect or total; plaintiffs only need to show that the relief they request "would lessen" their injuries or "significant[ly] increase . . . the likelihood" of their being shielded from future injuries.[94] A ruling that ICWA is unconstitutionally race-based would unquestionably have accomplished that, because state judges would then not apply ICWA's racially discriminatory provisions. That, in turn, would have eliminated the race-based barriers placed on the Brackeens' efforts to adopt, and would have enabled the Clifford family to seek to recover custody of Child P., who was taken from them under ICWA. Yet the *Brackeen* Court effectively said the plaintiffs could not sue the master without also suing the servant. That is certainly not the law.[95]

---

[92] *Brackeen*, 143 S. Ct. at 1639.

[93] *Id.* at 1635.

[94] *See, e.g.*, Utah v. Evans, 536 U.S. 452, 464 (2002); Inclusive Cmtys. Project, Inc. v. Dep't of Treasury, 946 F.3d 649, 655 (5th Cir. 2019).

[95] *See, e.g.*, Graham v. Fed. Emergency Mgmt. Agency, 149 F.3d 997, 1003 (9th Cir. 1998) ("Plaintiffs need not demonstrate that there is a 'guarantee' that their injuries will be redressed by a favorable decision."); Beno v. Shalala, 30 F.3d 1057, 1065 (9th Cir. 1994) ("[T]o have standing, a federal plaintiff must show only that a favorable decision is *likely* to redress his injury, not that a favorable decision *will inevitably* redress his injury.") (emphasis in original); *cf.* Poulin v. Graham, 147 A. 698, 699 (Vt. 1929) (plaintiff in *respondeat superior* need not sue servant to sue master).

B. Race and Rice, Membership and Mancari

The majority declined to address the question of whether ICWA violates rules against race-based legislation,[96] as did—rather surprisingly—the concurring opinion by Justice Gorsuch. But Justices Kavanaugh, Thomas, and Samuel Alito did proceed to address these questions. Kavanaugh, in a brief concurrence, said that while he believed the plaintiffs lacked standing, "the equal protection issue is serious."[97] Thomas, in dissent, observed that a law like ICWA would never be tolerated if it "tried to regulate the child custody proceedings of U.S. citizens who are eligible for Russian, Mexican, Israeli, or Irish citizenship."[98] And Alito's dissent noted that ICWA "advance[s] [tribal government] interests at the expense of vulnerable children and their families," "even when the child is not a member of a tribe and has never been involved in tribal life, and even when a child's biological parents object."[99]

It might seem obvious that a law which deprives children of legal protections based on their biological ancestry qualifies as race-based discrimination.[100] Race-based laws are laws "which single[] out 'identifiable classes of persons . . . solely because of their ancestry or ethnic characteristics.'"[101] Such laws are subject to the virtually insurmountable test of "strict scrutiny." Yet in the 1974 case of *Morton v. Mancari*,[102] the Court said that laws differentiating between Indians and non-Indians are not necessarily race-based. Tribes are political communities, it reasoned, which means tribal membership is "political rather than racial in nature."[103] Consequently, laws triggered by tribal membership are subject only to the more lenient "rational basis" test.

---

[96] The Court notably characterized its holding as "declin[ing] to disturb" the Fifth Circuit, rather than affirming it or upholding ICWA's constitutionality. *Brackeen*, 143 S. Ct. at 1631.

[97] *Id.* at 1661 (Kavanaugh, J., concurring).

[98] *Id.* at 1664 n.1 (Thomas, J., dissenting).

[99] *Id.* at 1688–89 (Alito, J., dissenting).

[100] Or, in the alternative, discrimination based on national origin, which implicates the same strict scrutiny as race-based laws. *See* Sandefur, *Unconstitutionality*, *supra* note 2, at 64–67.

[101] Rice v. Cayetano, 528 U.S. 495, 515, (2000) (citations omitted).

[102] 417 U.S. 535 (1974).

[103] *Id.* at 553 n.24.

Nevertheless, the Court has indicated that *Mancari* does not give Congress carte blanche to differentiate between Indians and non-Indians. In *Rice v. Cayetano*, it said *Mancari* was quite limited—"confined to the authority of the [Bureau of Indian Affairs], an agency described as *'sui generis'*"[104]—and the *Mancari* case itself made a point of emphasizing that the law at issue there was "not directed towards a 'racial' group consisting of 'Indians,'" but at people who had chosen to become or remain members of tribes.[105]

Into which bucket, then, does ICWA fall? Does it treat people differently based on their political affiliations, in which case it is subject to *Mancari*'s rational basis standard? Or does it treat identifiable classes of people differently based on ancestry or ethnicity and therefore trigger strict scrutiny under *Rice*? The answer is plainly the latter. As Ojibwe writer David Treuer puts it, "[c]ulture isn't carried in the blood, and when you measure blood, in a sense you measure racial origins."[106] Blood, however, is all that counts under ICWA. It applies based not on political, cultural, linguistic, or religious connections to a tribe—which, again, are considered irrelevant—but on "a characteristic determined solely by the accident of birth."[107] Its placement preferences even mandate that children be placed with Indian families of different tribes rather than with non-Indians—based, again, on "a Federal policy that, where possible, an Indian child should remain in the Indian community."[108] All of this can only be explained by the fact that ICWA is premised not on tribal identity, but on "Indian" identity. That concept of generic "Indianness," however, is a racial, not a political category. In short, ICWA actually *is* aimed at a racial group consisting of Indians—whom it deprives of legal protections that other Americans enjoy.

Rather than confronting those questions, however, the majority focused its attention on the nature and scope of Congress's power to adopt a statute such as ICWA in the first place. And on this issue, so much depends upon the unhelpfully ambiguous word "plenary."

---

[104] *Rice*, 528 U.S. at 520.

[105] 417 U.S. at 553 n.24.

[106] DAVID TREUER, THE HEARTBEAT OF WOUNDED KNEE: NATIVE AMERICA FROM 1890 TO THE PRESENT 382 (2019).

[107] Jimenez v. Weinberger, 417 U.S. 628, 631 (1974).

[108] *Holyfield*, 490 U.S. at 37 (citation omitted).

V. The "Plenary" Power Theory

A. Does "Plenary" mean "Exclusive" or "Unlimited"?

Where does Congress get authority to adopt a statute like ICWA? Questions of child neglect, adoption, and so forth are quintessentially matters of state law, and Congress has no enumerated power to regulate such things. It is not plausible to interpret the Commerce Clause as authorizing such a statute; child abuse is not a commercial matter, and the Court has repeatedly made clear that Congress cannot use that Clause as an excuse to intrude into the realm of state criminal or domestic law.[109] While Congress may have power over child welfare matters on tribal lands, ICWA does not regulate these; it controls state courts addressing ordinary child welfare matters involving kids who live *off* reservation—cases that, but for ICWA, would fall within state jurisdiction. Obviously, Congress could not adopt a law dictating to states how they may treat child custody cases involving, say, American children whose Jewish ancestry makes them eligible for Israeli citizenship. How, then, can Congress purport to pass such a law governing children eligible for tribal membership?

The answer the Court embraced was the "plenary" power. It acknowledged that the "contours" of this power are "undefined," but it made no effort to consider what those contours might be.[110] And this raises some significant problems, given the ambiguity of the word "plenary." In short, the word has two distinct meanings, and *Brackeen*—like many cases in the realm of Indian law—relies heavily on blurring that distinction.

One definition of "plenary" is *supreme*. In that sense, "plenary" means that Congress may legislate in this area without interference from states. But that cannot be what "plenary" means here, because under the Supremacy Clause, states can never interfere, even implicitly, with *any* legislation Congress constitutionally adopts. If "plenary" is a mere synonym for the Supremacy Clause, then it really tells us nothing, because the Constitution's federalism and Bill of Rights principles still limit what Congress can do, regardless of the Supremacy Clause. After all, the Court has also characterized other

---

[109] *See, e.g., Morrison*, 529 U.S. 598, 613; Jones v. United States, 529 U.S. 848, 857 (2000); *Lopez*, 514 U.S. 549, 567–68.

[110] *See Brackeen*, 143 S. Ct. at 1628 (citations omitted).

federal powers as "plenary" in the sense that states cannot interfere: It has called Congress's power to regulate interstate commerce plenary.[111] It has called the foreign affairs powers plenary.[112] It has described Congress's power over the military,[113] over the residents of Washington, D.C.,[114] over immigration,[115] and over "all persons and things for [purposes of] taxation"[116] as "plenary." Yet nobody would contend that Congress can, in these contexts, disregard federalism principles such as the anti-commandeering rule or Bill of Rights principles such as the prohibition on race-based laws. Thus, *Brackeen* could not have meant the word plenary as a synonym for supreme—if that is what it meant, then the word does nothing to answer the question of whether ICWA's commandeering or race-based provisions are constitutional.

The other definition of "plenary" is *absolute* or *unlimited*.[117] But this definition cannot apply, because Congress does not have limitless power over *anything whatever*. It only has those powers enumerated in the Constitution, or necessary and proper to effectuating such powers, and all these powers are subject to Bill of Rights limitations.[118] Nothing in the Constitution empowers Congress to write a code of federal family law that states must abide by, and a statute that deprives Indian children of due process rights based on their ancestry plainly violates the Bill of Rights. In other words, if "plenary" is used as a synonym for "limitless" or "extra-constitutional," then it clearly cannot apply to Congress.

Nevertheless, the courts have often described Congress's power to legislate with respect to tribes as "plenary" in this second sense, and the Fifth Circuit claimed that this "plenary" power gives the federal government the power to do whatever is "reasonably related to the special government-to-government political relationship between

---

[111] *See* Gonzales v. Raich, 545 U.S. 1, 29 (2005); Gibbons v. Ogden, 22 U.S. (9 Wheat.) 1, 46 (1824).

[112] *See* Bd. Of Trs. Of Univ. of Ill. v. United States, 289 U.S. 48, 56 (1933).

[113] *See* Chappell v. Wallace, 462 U.S. 296, 301 (1983).

[114] *See* El Paso & N.E. Ry. Co. v. Gutierrez, 215 U.S. 87, 94 (1909).

[115] *See* Kleindienst v. Mandel, 408 U.S. 753, 766 (1972).

[116] *See* Smith v. Turner, 48 U.S. (7 How.) 283, 421 (1849).

[117] *See Brackeen*, 143 S. Ct. at 1684–85 (Alito, J., dissenting) (citing dictionaries).

[118] *Lopez*, 514 U.S. at 552; *Raich*, 545 U.S. 1.

the United States and the Indian tribes."[119] That is a truly startling proposition. If true, it would mean that Congress could disregard *all* constitutional and legal protections for individual rights whenever it acts in a way that it believes will foster the "relationship" between federal and tribal governments. During oral argument, Justice Alito underscored the extreme implications of this idea when he asked,

> Could Congress go further than it has gone in ICWA and say that an Indian child may not be adopted by . . . a non-Indian couple under any circumstances . . . ? Could Congress enact a law that alters the substantive law that states apply in areas like contracts or torts or rules of evidence when one of the parties in the case is an Indian?[120]

Indeed, if Congress truly has the power to do anything reasonably related to preserving the existence of tribes as collective entities, it could presumably forbid tribal members from marrying outside of the tribe,[121] or from using birth control,[122] or from surrendering their tribal citizenship,[123] or from advising others to do any of these things.[124]

The *Brackeen* majority paid little attention to such questions. It paid lip service to the principle of enumerated powers and purported to

---

[119] *Brackeen*, 994 F.3d at 334 (en banc).

[120] Transcript of Oral Argument at 107, 109–10, Haaland v. Brackeen, 143 S. Ct. 1609 (2023) (Nos. 21-376, 21-377, 21-378, and 21-380).

[121] *Cf.* Lesley M. Wexler, *Tribal Court Jurisdiction in Dissolution-Based Custody Proceedings*, 2001 U. Chi. Legal F. 613, 646 (2001) ("Marriage outside the tribe . . . currently present[s] the same threat to tribal sovereignty and survival that adoption and foster care once did.").

[122] Some ICWA scholars have even argued that ICWA applies to children *before conception*, based on a future child's genetic makeup. *See* Daune Cardenas, *ICWA in a World with Assisted Reproductive Technology*, Ariz. Att'y, Apr. 2019, at 18, 20 ("[P]arents conceiving children via [assisted reproductive technology] who know or have reason to know the resulting child may be an 'Indian child' as defined in ICWA should comply with the federal mandates under ICWA.").

[123] *Contra* United States *ex. rel.* Standing Bear v. Crook, 25 F. Cas. 695, 699 (C.C.D. Neb. 1879) ("The question of expatriation has . . . always been claimed and admitted by our government, and it is now no longer an open question [that] . . . the individual Indian possesses the clear and God-given right to withdraw from his tribe and forever live away from it.").

[124] The First Amendment does not prohibit laws that bar speech soliciting illegal acts. United States v. Williams, 553 U.S. 285, 298 (2008). So if Congress could make it illegal to quit a tribe, it could also ban speech encouraging others to do so.

acknowledge that "Congress's Indian affairs power 'is not absolute'" and "not unbounded."[125] Yet it gave no hint as to what the boundaries might be. And if Congress can use this plenary power to strip children of legal protections based on their biological ancestry, force American citizens into courts where the Bill of Rights is inapplicable, and dictate to state judges how to interpret state statutes, it's hard to imagine where the boundaries could lie.

What's more, the source of this allegedly plenary power remains obscure. The majority opinion stitched it together out of what Justice Thomas called a "smorgasbord" of constitutional provisions:[126] the Commerce Clause (which entitles Congress to regulate "commerce with foreign nations, and among the several states, and with the Indian tribes"), the Treaty Clause (which entitles the President to "make treaties" with senatorial advice and consent), and something the majority called "preconstitutional powers" that are "inherent in the Constitution's structure."[127] According to the majority, this congeries of constitutional elements overlaps to generate a power not actually specified in the Constitution—one which overrides the limits normally applicable to federal authority.

Certainly none of these clauses by itself would support ICWA. Child welfare matters are not "commerce" any more than violence against women or carrying firearms near a school are "commerce."[128] Nor would the treaty power suffice, because among other things, ICWA is a statute, not a treaty.[129] As for "preconstitutional" or "structural principles," this concept owes its origin to *United States v. Curtiss-Wright Export Corporation*, which concerned foreign affairs.[130] Foreign affairs precedents might be instructive

---

[125] *Brackeen*, 143 S. Ct. at 1629 (citations omitted).

[126] *Id.* at 1662 (Thomas, J., dissenting).

[127] *Id.* at 1628 (majority op.) (citations omitted).

[128] *See* Lopez, 514 U.S. 549; *Morrison*, 529 U.S. 598. *See further* Robert G. Natelson, *The Original Understanding of the Indian Commerce Clause*, 85 DENVER U. L. REV. 201 (2007).

[129] The majority's response to this point was truly odd. It brushed aside this argument by saying it "does not get [the petitioners] very far . . . since Congress did not purport to enact ICWA pursuant to the Treaty Clause power." *Brackeen*, 143 S. Ct. at 1631. But the plaintiffs were not seeking to justify ICWA on the basis of the treaty power; they were arguing that ICWA was *not* constitutional, and that the Treaty Clause would not have authorized it *even if* Congress had relied upon that Clause. Thus, the fact that ICWA was not based on the treaty power can hardly count against the plaintiffs.

[130] 299 U.S. 304, 315–322 (1936).

in understanding Congress's power *vis-à-vis* tribes, but no principle of federal or international law suggests that Congress could use foreign affairs powers to dictate to states how to decide child custody cases involving children and adults who are American citizens. On the contrary, the Court made clear as recently as 2014, in *Bond v. United States*, that Congress may not use a treaty to aggrandize to itself powers that belong to the states.[131] And in *Reid v. Covert*, the Court said that an international treaty was unconstitutional because it subjected American citizens to legal proceedings that lacked Bill of Rights protections.[132]

In any event, among the most basic "structural principles" of the Constitution are the principles that Congress has only "few and defined" powers[133] and that neither Congress nor the states may treat people differently based solely on biological ancestry.[134]

Even stranger is that the "plenary" theory the majority embraced is exactly what caused the abuses which led to ICWA's creation in the first place. As Justice Gorsuch explained in his concurrence, the "plenary" theory owes its origins to the 1886 case of *United States v. Kagama*,[135] a case decided toward the end of the Indian wars, when most of the tribes on the western plains had been militarily defeated and relegated to reservations. The *Kagama* Court characterized indigenous Americans as conquered foreign enemies whose fates were at the federal government's mercy, and over whom it had corresponding charitable obligations. Being the "weak and diminished" "remnants" of "a separate people," *Kagama* said, Indians were now "wards of the [United States]" due to their "weakness and helplessness."[136] As Justice Gorsuch observed, that proposition was interpreted in subsequent years as justify-

---

[131] 572 U.S. 844, 866 (2014).

[132] 354 U.S. 1, 6 (1957). ICWA requires state courts to transfer child welfare proceedings into tribal court. 25 U.S.C. § 1911(b). Bill of Rights protections do not apply in tribal court. *Duro*, 495 U.S. at 693. *See further* Sandefur, *Unconstitutionality, supra* note 2, at 78–79.

[133] THE FEDERALIST No. 45, *supra* note 87, at 289 (James Madison).

[134] Hirabayashi v. United States, 320 U.S. 81, 100 (1943) ("Distinctions between citizens solely because of their ancestry are by their very nature odious to a free people whose institutions are founded upon the doctrine of equality.").

[135] 118 U.S. 375 (1886).

[136] *Id.* at 381, 384.

ing "a 'virtually unlimited [federal] authority to regulate [T]ribes' in every respect."[137] And one of the things this allegedly absolute power was viewed as authorizing was the program of coercive assimilation of Indian children.

For that reason, it was truly bizarre that in *Brackeen*, it was the tribal governments who defended this plenary power theory and the plaintiffs who attacked it. Justice Alito brought out the irony, not to say cynicism, of this fact by asking Deputy Solicitor General Edwin Kneedler during oral argument, "What about the boarding school law? Congress had the power to do that?"—to which Kneedler, defending ICWA, replied affirmatively: "Congress had the power."[138] Justice Gorsuch was right in concluding that "Indian boarding schools and other assimilationist policies" would "[not] have been possible without this Court's plenary-power misadventure."[139] Yet in *Brackeen*, the majority persisted in that misadventure, relying on the plenary theory as the constitutional basis for ICWA—and without seeking to justify the plenary theory beyond the fact that a "long line of cases" supports it.[140] As Justice Thomas wrote in dissent, the plenary power "appears to have been born of loose language and judicial *ipse dixit*," and the *Brackeen* majority chose to continue indulging this ill logic.[141] This brings us to another irony of *Brackeen*: the fact that Justices Gorsuch and Thomas joined in rejecting the "plenary" power, even while reaching opposite conclusions regarding ICWA's constitutionality.

B. The Concurrence of the Dissents

After describing the historical abuses that led to ICWA's enactment and detailing the "incoherence" of the plenary power theory, Gorsuch concluded that ICWA "must stand."[142] Yet he did not address, let alone resolve, whether ICWA is a race-based statute, con-

---

[137] *Brackeen*, 143 S. Ct. at 1658 (Gorsuch, J., concurring) (quoting Michalyn Steele, *Plenary Power, Political Questions, and Sovereignty in Indian Affairs*, 63 UCLA L. REV. 666, 670 (2016)).

[138] Transcript, *supra* note 120, at 108.

[139] *Brackeen*, 143 S. Ct. at 1658–59 (Gorsuch, J., concurring).

[140] *Id.* at 1627 (majority op.).

[141] *Id.* at 1662 (Thomas, J., dissenting).

[142] *Id.* at 1659, 1660 (Gorsuch, J., concurring).

cluding his concurrence instead with an unusual address to the reader: "You must decide for yourself if ICWA passes constitutional muster."[143] Gorsuch's concurrence is therefore clearly not the end of the story.

Instead, Gorsuch focused on the meaning of the Indian Commerce Clause, which he interpreted expansively as encompassing "the management of tribal relations," rather than as limited to commercial transactions and the like.[144] In other words, despite the fact that the word "commerce" appears only once in the Commerce Clause ("Congress shall have power . . . to regulate commerce with foreign nations, and among the several states, and with the Indian tribes"), Gorsuch interpreted that word as having two, perhaps three different meanings, based on the object to which it applies.[145] He justified this counterintuitive—indeed, ungrammatical—move by appeal to the history of federal-tribal relations. In his view, the Indian Commerce Clause authorizes federal control over not just commercial matters, but over anything relating to "how non-Indians . . . engage with Indians."[146]

Justice Thomas reached a different conclusion, concluding that ICWA is unconstitutional, but he shared Gorsuch's view that the plenary power theory is untenable. Rejecting the majority's appeal to penumbras formed by emanations from the treaty, commerce, and other powers, Thomas observed that all the historical examples of federal Indian laws that the majority mustered to demonstrate the existence of a plenary power actually fell "easily" within the "normal understanding of the Constitution's enumerated powers."[147] They did not prove that Congress has a free-floating plenary authority.[148] Indeed, he observed that the majority was "treating [the]

---

[143] *Id.* at 1660.

[144] *Id.*

[145] *Id.* at 1655.

[146] *Id.* at 1661.

[147] *Id.* at 1670 (Thomas, J., dissenting).

[148] Days after *Brackeen* was announced, Justice Thomas concurred in *Arizona v. Navajo Nation*, 2023 WL 4110231 (U.S. June 22, 2023), writing that the concept of the tribal "trust" in Indian law is likewise infected with ambiguity and that it "seems to lack a historical or constitutional basis." *Id.* at *9 (Thomas, J., concurring).

loose 'plenary power' language as talismanic," in order to "transform[] that power into the truly unbounded, absolute power that [it] disclaim[s]."[149]

Thomas therefore agreed with Gorsuch that ICWA must stand or fall on the Commerce Clause—but he concluded that it must fall. The Constitution's authors, he noted, expressly chose *not* to give Congress power to regulate "Indian affairs"—the phrase which occurred in the Articles of Confederation, and which the Constitution replaced with the more limited power to regulate "commerce."[150] And Thomas offered evidence that "[w]hen discussing 'commerce' with Indian tribes, the Founders plainly meant buying and selling goods and transportation for that purpose," not an expansive power over all relations between Native Americans and American citizens.[151] Still, Thomas saw a "saving grace" in the decision: The majority had not decided that ICWA is actually within Congress's authority, but merely postponed that question for a later day.[152] He, too, recognized that *Brackeen* is far from the end of the story.

Justices Kavanaugh and Alito also found ICWA troubling. While Kavanaugh agreed that the plaintiffs lacked standing, he wrote a separate concurrence to "emphasize that . . . the equal protection issue remains undecided" and that the law's race-based differential treatment "raise[s] significant questions under bedrock equal protection principles."[153] Alito, too, concluded in his dissent that ICWA "run[s] roughshod" over constitutional principles "when the State seeks to protect one of its young citizens" who, for biological reasons alone, is statutorily defined as "Indian."[154] Chiding the majority for exploiting the ambiguity of the word "plenary," Alito concluded that nothing in American legal history can justify ICWA's violation of "the fundamental structure of our constitutional order."[155]

---

[149] *Brackeen*, 143 S. Ct. at 1678 (Thomas, J., dissenting).

[150] *Id. See further* Lorianne Updike Toler, *The Missing Indian Affairs Clause*, 88 U. CHI. L. REV. 413 (2021).

[151] *Brackeen*, 143 S. Ct. at 1672 (Thomas, J., dissenting).

[152] *Id.* at 1683.

[153] *Id.* at 1661 (Kavanaugh, J., concurring).

[154] *Id.* at 1687 (Alito, J., dissenting).

[155] *Id.* at 1685.

C. The Ignored Citizenship of Indian Children

Yet in all the debate over history, one crucial—indeed, decisive—historical incident was left unmentioned, one that, if properly appreciated, would render much of that debate irrelevant: the Indian Citizenship Act of 1924.[156]

Virtually all of the historical discussion in the competing *Brackeen* opinions about the meaning of the word "commerce," or the "smorgasbord" of war, treaty, and foreign affairs powers, relied on legal conceptions fashioned at a time when Indians were not American citizens. Consequently, much of this debate implicitly assumed some sort of analogy between Indians and foreign nationals. Yet that analogy has not been tenable for a century.

When the Indian Commerce Clause and the Fourteenth Amendment were ratified, Indians were viewed as aliens, outside the American polity; they were even expressly exempted from constitutional citizenship.[157] It was natural, therefore, that the framers of these and other provisions viewed federal power with respect to Indians as quite extreme. Federal power is at its zenith with respect to foreign nationals. They can be deported, their property rights can be limited, their employment opportunities can be restricted, their entitlement to government benefits can be curtailed—even their freedom of speech can be abridged.[158] But citizenship moved Native Americans out of the class of people against whom federal power has its greatest leverage and placed them in the same category as natural-born citizens. And Congress does not have plenary power over citizens—quite the contrary.[159]

That means legal theories about federal power with respect to Indians that were fashioned before the Indian Citizenship Act can be enormously misleading. *Kagama*, for example, explicitly based its expansive notion of federal authority on the fact that Indians "owe[d] no allegiance to the states."[160] Citizenship changed that: Indeed, it

---

[156] 8 U.S.C. § 1401b.

[157] U.S. Const. amend. XIV.

[158] *See* Mathews v. Diaz, 426 U.S. 67, 80 (1976); *Kleindienst*, 408 U.S. at 769–70; Graham v. Richardson, 403 U.S. 365, 376–78 (1971); Harisiades v. Shaughnessy, 342 U.S. 580, 591–92 (1952).

[159] *See* Saikrishna Prakash, *Against Tribal Fungibility*, 89 Cornell L. Rev. 1069, 1116 (2004) ("[T]he federal government does not have plenary power over all U.S. citizens.")

[160] *See Kagama*, 118 U.S. at 384.

marked a tectonic shift in the nature of the relationship between Native Americans and federal and state governments—because those governments owe duties of protection to citizens, particularly minors, that they do not owe non-citizens.[161] As the Court said in *Duro v. Reina*, "That Indians are citizens does not alter the Federal Government's broad authority to legislate with respect to enrolled Indians as a class, whether to impose burdens or benefits . . . [but] Indians like other citizens are embraced within our Nation's 'great solicitude that its citizens be protected . . . from unwarranted intrusions on their personal liberty.'"[162]

Yet none of the Justices recognized this distinction in *Brackeen*. Justice Gorsuch's concurrence, for example, relied overwhelmingly on the fact that during the founding and for many years afterwards, Indians were members of "a 'distinct community'"[163] who were "simply not part of the state polities."[164] But that's not true today. Now they are citizens entitled to the same legal protections as all other citizens. Gorsuch likewise favorably quoted John Marshall's 1832 reference to Indians as members of "a 'distinct community'" to support the proposition that states can no more legislate with respect to tribes "than they could legislate for one another or a foreign sovereign."[165] But while tribal members were analogous to foreigners in 1832 and stood outside state authority in most respects, today they are dual citizens. They are *within* state jurisdiction in most respects, at least when living off tribal lands. Again, Gorsuch relied on an 1866 decision to assert that "the power to regulate commerce with Indian Tribes . . . extends to the entire 'intercourse between the citizens of the United States and those [T]ribes.'"[166] But in 1866, it was

---

[161] *See, e.g., In re* E.G., 549 N.E.2d 322, 327 (Ill. 1989) ("[T]he State has a *parens patriae* power to protect those incompetent to protect themselves. '[I]t is well-settled that the State as parens patriae has a special duty to protect minors . . . .'") (quoting *In re* Hamilton, 657 S.W.2d 425, 429 (Tenn. App. 1983)).

[162] 495 U.S. 676, 692 (1990) (quoting Oliphant v. Suquamish Indian Tribe, 435 U.S. 191, 210 (1978)).

[163] *Brackeen*, 143 S. Ct. at 1649 (Gorsuch, J., concurring) (quoting Worcester v. Georgia, 31 U.S. (6 Pet.) 515, 561 (1832)).

[164] *Id.* at 1648 (quoting Robert N. Clinton, *The Dormant Indian Commerce Clause*, 27 CONN. L. REV. 1055, 1150 (1995)).

[165] *Id.* at 1652.

[166] *Id.* at 1655–56 (quoting United States v. Holliday, 70 U.S. (3 Wall.) 407, 417 (1866)).

natural for the Court to use a locution like "between the citizens of the United States and [Indians]," a phrase that is tautologous today, since Indians are citizens of the United States.

The point is that pre-citizenship precedents interpreted federal authority with respect to Native Americans based on the assumption that they were foreigners, subject simultaneously to the strongest form of government power and the weakest degree of government responsibility. That assumption is no longer applicable, and the ancient maxim *cessante rationae, cessat ipsa lex*— when the reason for a legal principle changes, the principle itself changes[167]—indicates that the lessons of those precedents can no longer govern. Surely, if it is wrong to "disdain[] present realities in deference to past formalities,"[168] then constitutional theories based on circumstances that later changed so fundamentally can no longer be blindly followed. The Indian Citizenship Act means Native Americans do not stand outside the American polity, and that means pre-1924 understandings of federal power with respect to them cannot be uncritically followed in modern times.

Ignoring the significance of citizenship resulted in *Brackeen*'s final irony. Gorsuch remarked that "when this Court elides text and original meaning in favor of broad pronouncements about the Constitution's purposes," the result can "bake[] in the prejudices of the day"[169]—and he then proceeded to do precisely that. By anchoring his theory of the Indian Commerce Clause on precedents that assumed (or said outright) that Indians were owed none of the fiduciary duties owed to citizens, he baked into his interpretation of federal authority the prejudices of a long-ago era when Indians were "a separate people" whose rights Congress could override at will.[170]

---

[167] *See generally* Frederick G. McKean, Jr., *A Useful Maxim*, 4 N.C. L. Rev. 118 (1926).

[168] *Stanley*, 405 U.S. at 657.

[169] *Brackeen*, 143 S. Ct. at 1658 (Gorsuch, J., concurring). *But see* United States v. Vaello Madero, 142 S. Ct. 1539, 1557 n.4 (2022) (Gorsuch, J., concurring) ("In the last few years, some have attempted a revisionist account of the *Insular Cases* . . . [according to which] this Court's decision to withhold full constitutional protection from 'unincorporated' Territories (now) serves the beneficial end of safeguarding traditional cultures . . . . [This] merely drape[s] the worst of their logic in new garb . . . . Our government may not deny constitutionally protected individual rights out of (purportedly) benign neglect any more than it may out of animus.").

[170] *Kagama*, 118 U.S. at 381.

VI. Striding Toward Freedom?

Notwithstanding the Court's assertion, *Brackeen* is certainly not the end of the story. On the contrary, its refusal to address ICWA's race-based differential treatment must leave all sides of the issue unsatisfied. The Justices merely postponed the debate everyone cares about—and put litigators in child custody cases on notice that they must raise constitutional challenges to ICWA's application in *every* appropriate proceeding, to preserve the issue for appeal. Eventually, courts will have to confront this question.

Unfortunately, time is not something Indian children can afford. They are the most at-risk demographic in the United States, facing greater threats of neglect,[171] violence,[172] gang activity,[173] drug and alcohol addiction,[174] and suicide[175] than any other group of children. They suffer higher rates of abuse than kids of any other race[176] and are overrepresented in foster care; although they make up only one percent of the national population, they account for two percent of children in foster care.[177] They also tend to spend far longer in foster care than children of other races,[178] meaning they are more likely to "age out" instead of finding permanent, loving

---

[171] *See, e.g.*, Tara Culp-Ressler, *The Shocking Rates of Violence and Abuse Facing Native American Kids*, THINKPROGRESS, Nov. 18, 2014, https://bit.ly/47THhNU.

[172] *See, e.g.*, Attorney General's Advisory Committee on American Indian/Alaska Native Children Exposed to Violence: Ending Violence so Children Can Thrive (U.S. Dep't of Justice, 2014), https://wapo.st/3E57ZoO.

[173] *See, e.g.*, Aline Major et al., *Youth Gangs in Indian Country*, OJJDP JUV. JUST. BULL., Mar. 2004, https://bit.ly/3Z0ZPYB.

[174] Bettina Friese et al., *Drinking among Native American and White Youths: The Role of Perceived Neighborhood and School Environment*, 14 J. ETHNICITY IN SUBSTANCE ABUSE 287 (2015).

[175] Suicide Prevention Resource Center, Suicide Among American Indians/Alaska Natives, https://bit.ly/3KRVgdf.

[176] U.S. Dep't of Health & Hum. Servs., Child Maltreatment 2019 at 21, https://bit.ly/3YIFHu3.

[177] U.S. Dep't of Health & Hum. Servs., The AFCARS Report (June 23, 2020) at 2, https://bit.ly/3QJc0XM.

[178] Richard P. Barth et al., *Adoption of American Indian Children: Implications for Implementing the Indian Child Welfare and Adoption and Safe Families Acts*, 24 CHILD. & YOUTH SERVS. R. 139, 142 (2002).

adoptive homes.[179] The good news is that there are many people of all races who stand ready and willing to help these children. The bad news is that ICWA says they're not allowed to—because their skin is the wrong color.

The first step toward fixing this problem is to erase that color line—to recognize that every child has a right to have his or her *individual* interests take precedence over racial or political considerations. Indian children cannot be regarded as outsiders, relegated to a system that deprives them of legal protections and bars their parents from promoting their best interests. But even when the day comes that Indian children are given the equal protection of the laws, that will not be the end of the story. It will be just the start of the hard labor of fixing what this country has so badly damaged. "The Indian story does not, of course, end with an intellectual accommodation with the past or even a moral coming to terms," writes historian Fergus Bordewich. "Indeed, the story does not end at all . . . . There will be no end to history, but an end may be put to the invention of distorting myth. With that may come a recognition that Indians are not, at last, poignant vestiges of a lost age, but men and women of our own time, struggling to solve [modern] problems with the tools of our shared civilization."[180]

---

[179] Tribal governments typically blame these disparities on racism by child welfare agencies. *See, e.g.*, National Indian Child Welfare Association, *Setting the Record Straight: The Indian Child Welfare Act Fact Sheet* (Sept. 2015), https://bit.ly/3OOfzZY (blaming "widespread non-compliance" by state governments). But the more plausible explanation is that Native children disproportionately suffer from poverty, isolation, lack of access to services, and other risk factors. As one expert observes, ICWA "does little to alter the conditions that Congress held responsible for the unwarranted breakup of Indian families . . . . [Its] emphasis is on removal and placement, not prevention." Russel Lawrence Barsh, *The Indian Child Welfare Act of 1978: A Critical Analysis*, 31 HASTINGS L.J. 1287, 1334 (1980).

[180] FERGUS M. BORDEWICH, KILLING THE WHITE MAN'S INDIAN: REINVENTING NATIVE AMERICANS AT THE END OF THE TWENTIETH CENTURY 343 (1996).

Biden v. Nebraska: The New State Standing and the (Old) Purposive Major Questions Doctrine

*Jed Handelsman Shugerman**

The last decision standing at the end of the October 2022 term was *Biden v. Nebraska*.[1] By a vote of 6–3, the Supreme Court invalidated the Biden administration's student-debt waiver as an executive overreach of the emergency powers delegated by Congress in the HEROES Act of 2003.[2] Chief Justice John Roberts's majority opinion was just the second time that a Supreme Court majority opinion used the phrase "major questions case" or "major questions doctrine," following his use in *West Virginia v. EPA* one year earlier.[3]

The climactic set of opinions in the case fit its end-of-term timing. A case about emergency powers produced a tone of emergency about the Court's legitimacy, a blistering exchange between Chief Justice Roberts and Justice Elena Kagan about tensions that had built up over the Term. It also included a concurrence by Justice Amy Coney Barrett attempting an end-of-term big-picture methodological review, which also seemed concerned with the Court's legitimacy. The substance on the major questions doctrine received the most attention, but it also had hidden significance with an implicit

* Professor of Law and Joseph Lipsitt Scholar, Boston University School of Law. Thanks to Jonathan Adler, Beau Baumann, Blake Emerson, Nestor Davidson, David Driesen, Liza Goitein, and Richard Re for engaging in dialogue about the major questions doctrine; to my Administrative Law students and Presidency seminar students who helped me sharpen these arguments with incisive questions; to Brian H. Pandya and Duane Morris LLP for shepherding my amicus, with wise feedback that is reflected in this article; and to Thomas Berry for outstanding editing; and full faith and credit to Danya Handelsman.

[1] 143 S. Ct. 2355 (2023).

[2] Higher Education Relief Opportunities for Students Act of 2003 (HEROES Act). 117 Stat. 904.

[3] 142 S. Ct. 2587, 2605, 2610 (2022).

new rule on procedure and standing. Furthermore, it is an appropriate end-of-term decision because it was shaped by, and makes sense of, some earlier cases this term.

In other words, one way to interpret *Biden v. Nebraska* is to understand what is *not* in it. Some of the clarifications of what the Court was really doing are found in unpersuasive counterarguments in other opinions, even different cases from the October 2022 term. Another clarification was a question posed by a Justice in oral argument, but no Justices were willing to answer that question in writing.

First, Chief Justice Roberts's majority opinion does not explain how Missouri would have standing under the traditional test (where is the concrete and particularized injury?). In a different case decided just a week earlier, *United States v. Texas*, Justice Neil Gorsuch concurred (joined by Justice Barrett) and made a special point of rejecting "the special solicitude of states" for standing.[4] That "special solicitude" seems to be the best explanation for letting Missouri stand in for the insulated corporation that it created. Thus, *Biden v. Nebraska* should be reconciled as a new state-standing precedent, despite (or because of) its avoiding this explanation.

Second, Chief Justice Roberts did not explain the interpretive basis for the new major questions doctrine (MQD), but he implied that it is purposive. Justice Barrett wrote a solo concurrence arguing that the MQD is based on neither purposivism nor a substantive canon (the constitutional avoidance of a nondelegation problem), but rather is simply textualism. Her opinion is so counter-persuasive that it confirms that the major questions doctrine is still an exception in favor of purposivism, as well as an exception to *Chevron* deference. The view of MQD as a substantive canon (previously espoused by Justice Gorsuch) is still an alternative explanation that remains more descriptively accurate than Barrett's pseudo-textualism, but none of the Justices wrote to say so.

Third, in oral argument, Justice Brett Kavanaugh cited an amicus brief (in fact, mine)[5] and asked, "A professor says this is a case study in abuse of executive emergency powers. . . . And I want to get your assessment . . . of how we should think about our role in assertion

---

[4] 143 S. Ct. 1964, 1977 (2023) (Gorsuch, J., concurring).

[5] *See* Jed Handelsman Shugerman, *Major Questions and an Emergency Question Doctrine*, (Fordham Law Legal Studies Research Paper No. 4345019, 2023), https://tinyurl.com/53td7sdp.

of presidential emergency power given the Court's history."[6] Indeed, as this article will recount, the Biden administration's reliance on COVID-19 was a pretext to exploit an emergency provision in the statute it relied upon, the post-9/11 HEROES Act of 2003, to achieve its longer-term policy goal of student-debt relief. The Biden administration arguably had a better legal basis in the Higher Education Act of 1965, but that statute required the far longer and less predictable administrative process of negotiated regulation. The Biden administration seemed to prioritize the political calendar, wishing to finalize the policy in time for the November 2022 midterm election.

The Biden debt-waiver political backstory is just one of many examples of the ongoing bipartisan abuse of emergency executive powers, but no one addressed Justice Kavanaugh's question—not the parties and not even the Justices themselves in their final opinions. This article focuses on how the Supreme Court may have solved one problem but created another. A solution is beyond the scope of this genre, but I will tease that a solution connects the second and third themes of interpretation and emergencies: methods of statutory interpretation to address the tricky problem of delegating power for real but unspecified future emergencies.

Part I is a slightly different summary of the case than what one might read in a standard article: It tells the story of the Biden student-debt relief as a story about the use of COVID-19 as a pretext and about the abuse of emergency powers. Part II jumps to the unsatisfactory majority opinion on standing and Justice Kagan's valid questions. Part II then discusses Justice Gorsuch's rejection of "state" standing a week earlier—an out-of-place proxy battle about what was likely the best explanation behind closed doors for Missouri's standing, despite no concrete injury. Part III suggests that the Chief Justice's approach to the major questions doctrine was more purposive than anything else, and it also suggests that Justice Barrett's argument for textualism against purposivism and substantive canons was so unpersuasive that it backfired. As a solo concurrence with such marginal and muddled arguments, it confirmed that Roberts's purposive approach is the definitive doctrine. Part IV returns to the unresolved problem of emergencies and the ongoing bipartisan abuse of emergency powers and sketches a solution to the Roberts Court's overcorrection.

---

[6] Transcript of Oral Argument at 60–61, Biden v. Nebraska, 143 S. Ct. 2355 (2023) (No. 22-505).

A commentary on *Biden v. Nebraska* would default if it failed to account the Justices' concluding sharp exchanges, and no one had the legal capital to suggest the other side was morally bankrupt.

I. A COVID-19 Emergency Pretext and a Standing Dodge

The student-debt case was not the first or second time that the Supreme Court has reviewed emergency executive action responding to the COVID-19 pandemic. In the Vaccine-or-Test Mandate cases, the government cited the COVID-19 emergency to bypass regular process.[7] In this student-debt case, the government again invoked emergency powers to bypass administrative process. Although the Higher Education Act of 1965 provided a textual basis for issuing waivers, it also required a longer process for rescinding regulations from the Obama administration and a year of notice-and-comment process in order to issue new regulations.[8] Instead of relying on the statute with the better fit and a longer process, the government invoked an emergency to use the misfit statute and put the action on an emergency track.

A key question for whether agency action was properly delegated or was *ultra vires*: How close is the nexus between the emergency and the action allegedly taken pursuant to the emergency? If the nexus is close to the claimed ends in the statute, then it is more likely that the action was congressionally authorized. If the nexus is strained—and if the policy is broader in scope than the emergency—then the agency has gone beyond the congressional delegation from that statute.

A second key question here, as posed by the emergency questions doctrine that I wish to develop, is whether other parts of the statute and its purposes give legally intelligible context and contours to an otherwise open-ended emergency clause. The HEROES Act of 2003 helpfully contains a "findings" section to provide some limiting principles and constraints. The Act allows the Secretary of Education to make major changes to policy if "a national emergency" caused student borrowers to be "placed in a worse position financially."[9]

---

[7] *See, e.g.*, NFIB v. DOL, OSHA, 142 S. Ct. 661, 663 (2022) (an emergency exception to "ordinary notice-and-comment procedures"); *cf.* Alabama Ass'n of Realtors v. HHS, 141 S. Ct. 2485, 2487 (2021).

[8] *See* 20 U.S.C. § 1082(a).

[9] 20 U.S.C. § 1098bb(a)(2)(A).

The HEROES Act provided its own textual basis for its context and purposes with a consistent section on "findings." The list of six findings is entirely focused on military contexts, with multiple references to "active service."[10] Even if one can logically extend the purposes from a military context to a pandemic, this context suggests that the emergency powers would have to be analogous from "active service" to the active pandemic. This would require a more direct causal impact on the individuals receiving relief, with the emergency having a concrete impact on their education or economic circumstances.

The Office of Legal Counsel's (OLC) and the Department of Education's own lawyers agreed with the bottom line that a causal nexus was necessary, but the Department of Education promulgated a program that did not even follow its own lawyers' interpretation. Both the OLC and the Department of Education issued memoranda in August validating the legality of the proposed policy, and both memos conceded that the program would have to be tailored to the COVID emergency in order to fit the statute. The OLC memo concludes, "Thus, to invoke the HEROES Act in the context of COVID-19, the Secretary would need to determine that the COVID-19 pandemic *was a but-for cause of the financial harm to be addressed by the waiver or modification.*"[11]

The Department of Education memo suggests the same limitation: The HEROES Act emergency authority is not "boundless" but is rather "limited *inter alia* . . . to certain categories of eligible individuals or institutions . . . and to a defined set of purposes."[12] The memo acknowledges a causation requirement: "The Secretary's determinations regarding the amount of relief, and the categories of borrowers for whom relief is necessary, should be informed by evidence regarding the financial harms that borrowers have experienced, or will likely experience, *because of* the COVID-19 pandemic."[13]

---

[10] *See* 20 U.S.C. § 1098aa(b)(1)-(6) (listing four references to "active service" or "active duty," as well as reference to members of the military "put[ting] their lives on hold").

[11] OLC memorandum, "Use of the HEROES Act of 2003 to Cancel the Principal Amounts of Student Loans," at 21 (Aug. 23, 2022) (emphasis added), https://tinyurl.com/ypva98jy.

[12] Lisa Brown, General Counsel, Department of Education, "The Secretary's Legal Authority for Debt Cancellation," at 2–3 (Aug. 23, 2022) (citations omitted), https://tinyurl.com/yrev38y9.

[13] *Id.* (emphasis added)

The Department of Education noted that the authority under the statute "can be exercised categorically to address the situation at hand; it does not need to be exercised 'on a case-by-case basis.'"[14] The program "may provide relief on a categorical basis as necessary to address the financial harms of the pandemic."[15]

However, when the program was announced, there was no hint that the categories created were related to COVID. Eligibility for the program was based on a means-tested income threshold, but a category based solely on income does not indicate whether COVID itself had a negative impact on the class of claimants' financial position. These problems of causation were immediately apparent, and there was ample time to tailor the program to COVID causation or to switch to a statute that matched the breadth and purpose of this program.[16]

The regulatory process here is a case study for how the executive branch abuses emergency powers: The government lawyers seized onto the word "emergency" in the statute and interpreted it as a broad delegation, without examining the rest of the statutory text or putting it in context. Notably, neither the OLC nor the Department of Education engaged with recent precedents on COVID emergencies or major questions. They assumed that the word "emergency" was an open-ended delegation. The OLC memo failed to cite any of the recent major question doctrine cases: not *FDA v. Brown & Williamson Tobacco Corp.*;[17] not *King v. Burwell*;[18] not even the COVID cases *Alabama Ass'n of Realtors v. HHS*[19] (the eviction moratorium) and *NFIB v. DOL, OSHA*[20] (the vaccine-or-test mandate). Instead, the OLC assumed that invoking the word "emergency" and narrow textual arguments would be sufficient. In a 25-page memo, less than one page focused on the HEROES Act's purpose and legislative history.

---

[14] *Id.* at 3 (quoting 20 U.S.C. § 1098bb(b)(3)).

[15] *Id.*

[16] *See* Elizabeth Goitein, *Biden used 'emergency powers' to forgive student debt? That's a slippery slope*, WASH. POST (Sept. 1, 2022), https://tinyurl.com/bd55xy5u; Jed Shugerman, *Biden's Student-Debt Rescue Plan is a Legal Mess*, THE ATLANTIC (Sept. 4, 2022), https://tinyurl.com/mra4wh7z.

[17] 529 U.S. 120 (2000).

[18] 576 U.S. 473 (2015).

[19] 141 S. Ct. 2485 (2021).

[20] 142 S. Ct. 661 (2022).

The OLC did not acknowledge the Act's findings section, which indicates a narrower purpose related to active emergencies and direct impacts. The obvious context of the 2003 law was the September 11 terrorist attacks and the subsequent wars in Afghanistan and Iraq. That is consistent with the preamble of statutory findings, which emphasizes military "active duty," "active" emergencies, and active direct impacts on claimants. And as noted above, the textual or common-sense linguistic canons *ejusdem generis* and *noscitur a sociis* provide guidance for interpreting the associated list "war or other military operation or national emergency."[21] Even if "emergency" generalizes beyond the military contexts, this list is consistent with the finding's emphasis on "active duty," and "active service,"—i.e., an active emergency.

Of course, COVID was a national emergency from March 2020 into 2021. However, it was already doubtful by August 2022, when the program was announced, that COVID was still a national emergency comparable to post-9/11 and the military action that followed. The HEROES Act's findings section repeatedly refers to "active duty" and "active service," which provides a context and purpose for the term "active emergencies." The late stages of the COVID emergency—after many rounds of vaccines, the stabilization of the economy, and a return to social normalcy—did not fit the context and purpose of "active" emergencies.

During this period of normalcy, the government also could not excuse its overbroad policy on the urgency of the emergency. No exigent circumstances forced the government to skip the statutory requirements of establishing causality. Yet the final debt-relief program required no basic indicia of causation or even correlation with the COVID emergency. The one-time income threshold established by the program did not indicate whether a borrower was "in a worse position financially" because of the emergency. Surely many middle-class Americans with student loans are worse off, but many are not. Some sectors of the economy improved during COVID, and some improved *because of* COVID (e.g., many fared well in industries like pharmaceuticals, remote communications technology, information technology, and food and grocery delivery). It would have been feasible to create categories along these lines or, even simpler, to ask for a single pre-COVID tax return to compare with the already-required mid-COVID tax return.

---

[21] *See* 20 U.S.C. § 1098aa(b)(1)-(6) (listing four references to "active service" or "active duty," as well as reference to members of the military "put[ting] their lives on hold").

Thus, the program's overbreadth and its reliance on categories unrelated to COVID indicated that COVID was only a pretext. The Biden administration could have tailored the program to COVID causation in accordance with the HEROES Act's statutory provision. Or, if the administration wanted a policy broader than just relief from the effects of COVID, it could have relied on a broader structural non-emergency statutory provision in the Higher Education Act of 1965. But it did neither.

At a late stage, the Department of Education added a new rationale: When debt payment requirements are restarted after long moratoria, many debtors default or go bankrupt.[22] Again, the total waiver is a much broader means for that stated ends. A gradual phase-in of payments would have been a better fit than a total waiver. Again, the Biden administration's shifting to new reasons indicates a precommitment to a broad policy and then a search for a *post hoc* emergency rationale.

This timeline of public statements is further evidence of pretext and further corroborates the need for a new approach to emergency powers:

> August 25, 2022: Soon after the administration announced it would start the administrative process for a waiver program, President Joe Biden gave a speech emphasizing that the waiver would serve non-emergency long-term purposes. Biden mentioned the COVID emergency just once.[23]
>
> September 19, 2022: Biden stated on *60 Minutes*: "The pandemic is over."[24]
>
> October 12, 2022: The Department of Education finalized and published the program, less than a month before Election Day.[25]
>
> January 31, 2023: One day after the administration announced that it would extend the emergency declarations to May 15 and end them thereafter, President Biden answered a press question about

---

[22] *Nebraska*, 143 S. Ct. at 2393 & n.2 (Kagan, J., dissenting).

[23] The White House, "Remarks by President Biden Announcing Student Loan Debt Relief Plan" (Aug. 25, 2022), https://tinyurl.com/ym4eb744.

[24] *Biden says Covid-19 pandemic is "over" in U.S.*, CBS NEWS (Sept. 19, 2022), https://tinyurl.com/3m34zzad.

[25] *See* 87 Fed. Reg. 61512, 61514.

the reason for this timing: "We've extended it to May the 15th to make sure we get everything done. That's all."[26]

This is backwards: The existence of an emergency should be the reason for an emergency policy. A desire to achieve policy goals should not be the reason for deciding whether or not there is an emergency. Again, if the emergency is over, there is no good excuse for ignoring the HEROES Act's requirement to show that recipients of relief suffered harm *caused* by the emergency.

On the one hand, COVID-19 was clearly an emergency, and there is good reason to think that COVID-19 played a role in the Biden campaign's March 2020 endorsement of student-debt cancellation. Many other candidates for the 2020 Democratic nomination had campaigned on this proposal well before the pandemic began.[27] However, it appears from public records that then-candidate Biden did not endorse student-debt cancellation until March 13, 2020. That was several days after five states had declared a state of emergency, two days after the World Health Organization declared COVID-19 a pandemic, and the same day President Donald Trump issued the Proclamation on Declaring a National Emergency. Biden expanded on this proposal in late March and early April 2020.

On the other hand, there is a pattern of emergency pretexts and overbreadth, used for both circumventing process and stretching substance.

The public record of contradictions and pretexts in the student-debt case is even more stark. From the official announcement in August 2022 through the finalization of the program, the Biden administration never hinted that it was considering eligibility questions that would establish a causal link between COVID and a borrower's "financial position." There is no evidence that this basic statutory requirement was discussed but set aside for pragmatic reasons. There is no sign that the Department of Education took seriously its own lawyers' memo or the OLC opinion that the HEROES Act required COVID causation.

[26] The White House, "Remarks by President Biden Before Marine One Departure" (Jan. 31, 2023), https://tinyurl.com/2ppw38mx.

[27] *See, e.g.*, Press Release, Elizabeth Warren, Senator, "Senator Warren, House Majority Whip Clyburn Introduce Legislation to Cancel Student Loan Debt for Millions of Americans" (July 23, 2019), perma.cc/L9D4-ASRY; Annie Nova, *Where the 2020 Democratic Candidates Stand on Student Debt*, CNBC (Sept. 21, 2019), perma.cc/AF47-JRNY.

The administration's advocates have often invoked the phrase, "Never let a crisis go to waste." This quotation has been misattributed to historical figures on the left and the right, but the administration's surrogates have used it often in the context of COVID.[28] The phrase has been used repeatedly in other COVID contexts. A crisis can sharpen, clarify, highlight, and exacerbate a pre-existing social problem, and it can mobilize support for a solution. But sometimes the crisis is merely a pretext for achieving a pre-existing policy goal, after the crisis has shifted power to a new administration. When it is the latter, the pretext is an administrative law problem.

No matter which party is in power, the political logic of leveraging a crisis to implement a longstanding policy agenda makes sense. But the *legal* logic of administrative law requires that the executive must give the real reasons for taking an action, and the policy must fit those real reasons. If the crisis is the real reason, the policy must be tailored to fit the crisis. That is where the Biden administration fell short.

II. Standing: The New "Special Solicitude for States"

Eight states sued to challenge the administration's debt-cancellation plan, but the district court concluded that none of the eight had standing. On appeal, the Eighth Circuit then concluded that Missouri would likely have standing through the Missouri Higher Education Loan Authority (MOHELA), a public corporation created by the state of Missouri to hold and service student loans.[29] And the Supreme Court agreed with the Eighth Circuit. In the majority opinion written by Chief Justice Roberts, the Court first acknowledged:

> Under Article III of the Constitution, a plaintiff needs a "personal stake" in the case. That is, the plaintiff must have suffered an injury in fact—a concrete and imminent harm to a legally protected interest, like property or money—that is fairly traceable to the challenged conduct and likely to be redressed by the lawsuit.[30]

[28] *See* Rahm Emanuel, *Let's make sure this crisis doesn't go to waste*, WASH. POST (March 25, 2020), https://tinyurl.com/yc2f793k.

[29] *Nebraska v. Biden*, 52 F.4th 1044, 1047 (8th Cir. 2022).

[30] *Nebraska*, 143 S. Ct. at 2365 (citing TransUnion LLC v. Ramirez, 141 S. Ct. 2190 (2021); Lujan v. Defenders of Wildlife, 504 U. S. 555, 560–561 (1992)).

It is important to note that because of the expedited nature of this "lightning docket" case and because the district court did not find standing, the factual record about MOHELA's losses and its relationship to Missouri remains unclear. However, it seems clear that MOHELA would have suffered an injury in fact if the plan had gone into effect, estimated at about $44 million per year in lost fees that it otherwise would have received without the debt waivers.[31] Chief Justice Roberts next made a key logical move, reasoning that MOHELA's losses could be treated as losses to Missouri: "[W]e conclude that the Secretary's plan harms MOHELA and thereby directly injures Missouri—conferring standing on that State."[32] This sentence appears to sum up the Court's analysis: If the plan harms MOHELA, it thereby injures Missouri.

The problem is that Missouri incorporated and designed MOHELA to be completely financially independent. In dissent, Justice Kagan reviewed the precedents on standing:

> A court may address the legality of a government action only if the person challenging it has standing—which requires that the person have suffered a "concrete and particularized injury." It is not enough for the plaintiff to assert a "generalized grievance[]" about government policy. And critically here, the plaintiff cannot rest its claim on a third party's rights and interests. The plaintiff needs its own stake—a "personal stake"—in the outcome of the litigation. If the plaintiff has no such stake, a court must stop in its tracks. To decide the case is to exceed the permissible boundaries of the judicial role.[33]

Turning to the facts of this case, she observed,

> But not even Missouri, and not even the majority, claims that MOHELA's revenue loss gets passed through to the State. . . . MOHELA is financially independent from Missouri—as corporations typically are, the better to insulate their creators from financial loss. So MOHELA's revenue decline—the injury in fact claimed to justify this suit—is not

---

[31] *See id.* at 2366

[32] *Id.* at 2365.

[33] *Id.* at 2386 (Kagan, J., dissenting) (citations omitted).

in fact Missouri's. The State's treasury will not be out one penny because of the Secretary's plan. The revenue loss allegedly grounding this case is MOHELA's alone.[34]

Kagan showed that, as a matter of Missouri state statutes and corporate design, "MOHELA's assets, including the fees gained from that contract, are not 'part of the revenue of the [S]tate' and cannot be 'used for the payment of debt incurred by the [S]tate.' On the other side of the ledger, MOHELA's debts are MOHELA's alone; Missouri cannot be liable for them."[35] She cited a Missouri Supreme Court case holding that another state corporation with the same design was "'not the [S]tate,' and that its activities are not state activities."[36] Kagan asked rhetorically:

> [This] leads to an obvious question: Where's MOHELA? The answer is: As far from this suit as it can manage. . . . MOHELA was "not involved with the decision of the Missouri Attorney General's Office" to file this suit. And MOHELA did not cooperate with the Attorney General's efforts. When the AG wanted documents relating to MOHELA's loan-servicing contract, to aid him in putting forward the State's standing theory, he had to file formal "sunshine law" demands on the entity. MOHELA had no interest in assisting voluntarily.[37]

And that's not all, for Kagan did not even mention some other problematic details: From the beginning of this case, it was widely understood that Missouri's relation to MOHELA was the key to standing. But only *Nebraska's* solicitor general James Campbell represented the plaintiffs at oral argument, leading to some predictably awkward exchanges along the lines of "Where's MOHELA?" It was convenient that Missouri officials did not have to answer. It is unclear why Missouri Solicitor General Josh Divine was unavailable.[38]

---

[34] *Id.* at 2386–87.

[35] *Id.* at 2387 (citations omitted).

[36] *Id.* (citing Menorah Medical Ctr. v. Health and Ed. Facilities Auth., 584 S.W.2d 73, 78 (Mo. 1979)).

[37] *Id.*

[38] I noted at the time that Missouri's Solicitor General appeared to be well qualified to argue the case. *See* Jed Shugerman (@jedshug), TWITTER (Mar. 9, 2023, 11:20 AM), https://tinyurl.com/47yfjzvw.

Missouri state officials dodged these questions, and Chief Justice Roberts also avoided answering Justice Kagan's questions. He recounted a long list of effects that would spill over from MOHELA to Missouri's citizens, but those effects were hard to distinguish from the generalized, widespread, and diffuse kinds of harms that the Court has held insufficient to establish Article III standing. Roberts offered a long passage that seemed to deliberately avoid describing the harms as "concrete" or "imminent," even though, in the preceding pages on standing law, Roberts had pulled out those words as the standing requirements from precedents like *Lujan*.[39]

Note that Roberts's analysis did not discuss the likelihood, nor immediacy, nor concreteness of the harm to Missouri. The theme of his standing analysis was that the state's status as a public entity with special public interests and performing public functions permits the state to serve as a stand-in for possible widespread harms to the state's citizens. It is most appropriate to let Roberts speak for himself (and for the specialness of states):

> The plan's harm to MOHELA is also a harm to Missouri. MOHELA is a "public instrumentality" of the State. Missouri established the Authority to perform the "essential public function" of helping Missourians access student loans needed to pay for college . . . see *Todd v. Curators of University of Missouri*, 347 Mo. 460, 464, 147 S. W. 2d 1063, 1064 (1941) ("Our constitution recognizes *higher education as a governmental function*."). To fulfill this public purpose, the Authority is empowered by the State to invest in or finance student loans . . . Its profits help fund education in Missouri: MOHELA has provided $230 million for development projects at Missouri colleges and universities and almost $300 million in grants and scholarships for Missouri students.[40]

Let's pause and observe that there is still no sign of any harm yet, concrete or not. These sentences are all descriptions of the lofty public services that MOHELA provides.

Roberts next moved on to the close governing relationship between the state of Missouri and MOHELA, but this special relationship still provided no evidence of likely harm:

---

[39] *Nebraska*, 143 S. Ct. at 2366 (citing *Lujan*, 504 U.S. at 560–561).
[40] *Id.* (emphasis added).

> The Authority is subject to the State's supervision and control. Its board consists of two state officials and five members appointed by the Governor and approved by the Senate. The Governor can remove any board member for cause. MOHELA must provide annual financial reports to the Missouri Department of Education, detailing its income, expenditures, and assets. The Authority is therefore "directly answerable" to the State. The State "set[s] the terms of its existence," and only the State "can abolish [MOHELA] and set the terms of its dissolution." By law and function, MOHELA is an instrumentality of Missouri: It was created by the State to further a public purpose, is governed by state officials and state appointees, reports to the State, and may be dissolved by the State.[41]

Roberts was much more interested in describing MOHELA as an extension of the state of Missouri than in describing any harm. When Roberts eventually got to the point about Missouri's injuries, it was a speculative leap:

> The Secretary's plan will cut MOHELA's revenues, impairing its efforts to aid Missouri college students. This acknowledged harm to MOHELA in the performance of its public function is necessarily a direct injury to Missouri itself.[42]

The first problem with this argument is that Roberts's harm analysis was more or less the same as what a Missouri citizen and taxpayer would argue: "MOHELA's losses may have some effect on my access to education funding." A thousand Missouri citizens could sue, or dozens of Missouri non-profits could sue, all claiming standing based on their potential lost opportunity caused by MOHELA's marginal losses of funds—and they would all lose. These standing claims are classic examples of the "generalized grievances" and "attenuated" harms that Supreme Court precedents reject as beyond Article III "cases and controversies."[43] The most plausible way to understand how Roberts was able to distinguish Missouri's general and attenuated harms from those of a

---

[41] *Id.* (internal citations omitted).

[42] *Id.*

[43] *See, e.g.*, Lexmark Int'l, Inc. v. Static Control Components, Inc., 572 U.S. 118, 127 n.3 (2014); Allen v. Wright, 468 U.S. 737, 750, 752 (1984).

thousand hypothetical Missourian individual plaintiffs is that the state of Missouri serves to collect their private harms into a recognized public entity with special constitutional status. Yet in several ways, Missouri's harms are more attenuated and more abstract than a thousand private Missouri citizens: Those citizens are more concretely and directly injured by losing access to education funding, whereas Missouri's losses amount to budgetary items that can be moved around on state ledgers.

Another problem with Roberts's standing argument is that the record lacks any indication that Missouri citizens would lose educational opportunities if MOHELA lost revenue. MOHELA is a heavily regulated non-profit established by the state. As long as MOHELA has sufficient assets, it would seem to be able to continue to execute its role in the public interest. It is unclear whether or how losses to MOHELA would get passed down to Missourians. If the state of Missouri lost tax revenue, it is certainly imaginable that Missourians might lose some resources. But the record is far from clear how and when Missourians would be concretely hurt.

This unaddressed question is a problem under the Court's standing doctrine. As the Court recently held in *Spokeo, Inc. v. Robins*, an injury must "actually exist" or there must be a "risk of real harm" for the injury to be "concrete" enough to establish standing.[44] True, a harm can be "widely shared" yet still concrete enough to be a sufficient injury in fact.[45] Although some past precedents required that the concrete harm must be "real, immediate, and direct,"[46] those qualifications do not seem to have been as salient. A more repeated and salient rule is that the Court has required "sufficient likelihood" of a "real and immediate" injury, and even a "certainly impending" real harm, one that is not mere conjecture or speculation.[47] But standing in this case *was* based on merely speculative and conjectured harms.

[44] 136 S. Ct. 1540, 1548–49 (2016).

[45] *See* Massachusetts v. EPA, 549 U.S. 497, 517, 522 (2007).

[46] *See* Davis v. FEC, 554 U.S. 724, 734 (2008).

[47] *See* City of Los Angeles v. Lyons, 461 U.S. 95, 111 (1983); Rizzo v. Goode, 423 U.S. 362, 372 (1976); O'Shea v. Littleton, 414 U.S. 488, 494 (1974); Clapper v. Amnesty Int'l USA, 568 U.S. 398, 410–11 (2013) (holding that, in order to demonstrate Article III standing, a plaintiff seeking injunctive relief must prove that the future injury, which is the basis for the relief sought, must be "certainly impending"; a showing of a "reasonable likelihood" of future injury is insufficient).

It was unclear from the evidence before the courts whether a cut in MOHELA's revenue would concretely harm Missouri's present and future college students—or the state of Missouri. Possible? Imaginable? Of course—but not established as likely from this lightning docket and thin and hasty record. Missouri's statehood was doing the work in this analysis, not the specific facts nor the concreteness of any harm.

Roberts and Kagan also engaged in a debate over the meaning of a 1953 case, *Arkansas v. Texas*,[48] which concerned the state of Arkansas's capacity to stand in for a state university. Roberts ultimately came to the same point: "But we concluded that Arkansas was in fact seeking to protect its *own* interests because the University was 'an official state instrumentality.' . . . Because the Authority is part of Missouri, the State does not seek to 'rely on injuries suffered by others.' . . . It aims to remedy its own."[49] Again, statehood is doing the work. In Roberts's account of both cases, the special relationship between a state as public-interest-entity and its instrumentality serving the public interest creates a special standing rule.

If we were reading about these diffuse, general, indirect impacts on a *private* plaintiff caused by a policy's effect on a corporation, the private plaintiff's claim for standing would be dismissed as a paradigmatic "generalized" widespread harm. It would be rejected as a claim akin to taxpayer standing, which is insufficient to get into federal court. Or suppose a corporation had spun off an entirely independent new corporation with a separate corporate board, but the two boards shared many of the same members. And suppose the new corporation affected the original corporation in close but indirect ways. If the original corporation attempted to sue on the basis of injuries to the spin-off, the courts would dismiss the original corporation's claim to stand in for the spin-off's injuries. But here, Missouri has standing on behalf of its independent spin-off because of its collective institutional capacity to stand in for the people of Missouri—a more significant status than its capacity to stand in for MOHELA.

---

[48] 346 U.S. 368 (1953).

[49] *Nebraska*, 143 S. Ct. at 2367 (quoting Justice Kagan's dissent in *Nebraska*) (emphasis in original).

If Missouri's special status as a state was the real reason that the Court lowered the threshold for a concrete "certainly impending" or "sufficiently likely" harm to Missouri itself, then why didn't Roberts just say so and cite a precedent like *Massachusetts v. EPA*[50] for the "special solicitude" of states? One possible answer is that Roberts had vigorously dissented in that case 16 years earlier.

Another answer is that there was no majority for such an explanation, as we know from *United States v. Texas*,[51] decided exactly one week before *Biden v. Nebraska*. In that case, Texas and Louisiana had sued to challenge the Biden administration policy pausing deportations in cases without a threat to "national security, public safety, and border security." The Fifth Circuit had ruled in favor of the states, finding that they had standing and blocking the Biden administration policy. The Supreme Court reversed the Fifth Circuit 8–1, finding that the states did not have standing. Justice Kavanaugh, joined by Chief Justice Roberts and Justices Sonia Sotomayor, Kagan, and Ketanji Brown Jackson, wrote the majority opinion, which focused on the established limits on challenges to prosecutorial discretion. Justice Samuel Alito dissented, writing that he would have found the states had standing based on what he called "the obvious parallel" of *Massachusetts v. EPA*.[52] Alito cited its reasoning about states' "'quasi-sovereign interes[t]' in avoiding the loss of territory" and quoted its rule of "special solicitude" for states' standing.[53] Alito also cited other decisions with similar reasoning, and concluded:

> I understand that what we have called "'drive-by jurisdictional rulings'" are not precedents, see *Arbaugh v. Y & H Corp.*, 546 U. S. 500, 511 (2006), but the Court should not use a practice of selective silence to accept or reject prominently presented standing arguments on inconsistent grounds.[54]

---

[50] 549 U.S. 497, 520 (2007).

[51] 143 S. Ct. 1964 (2023).

[52] *Id.* at 1996 (Alito, J., dissenting) (observing that *Massachusetts v. EPA* "has been called 'the most important environmental law case ever decided by the Court'") (quoting Richard Lazarus, The Rule of Five: Making Climate History at the Supreme Court 1 (2020)).

[53] *Id.* at 1996–97 (citing *Massachusetts*, 549 U.S. at 520).

[54] *Id.* at 1998.

This sentence is telling, and perhaps a "tell" (in the poker sense) of behind-the-scenes deliberation. Was Alito commenting on the "selective silence" and "inconsistent grounds" about state standing not only in *United States v. Texas*, but also in the then-forthcoming *Biden v. Nebraska* opinion? Should *Biden v. Nebraska* also be considered a "drive-by jurisdictional ruling" of selective convenience?

Justice Gorsuch concurred in *United States v. Texas*, joined by Justices Clarence Thomas and Barrett, in part to respond to Justice Alito and contest his standing arguments. The math becomes clear: one Justice went on record in *United States v. Texas* endorsing "special solicitude" for state standing, and three Justices went on record against it—covering four of the six Justices in the *Biden v. Nebraska* majority. Roberts and Kavanaugh would exercise their right to remain silent in both majorities. And Gorsuch, like Alito, called out the *Texas* majority's silence regarding "special solicitude." Like Alito, Gorsuch was not explicitly talking about Missouri's standing in the student-debt case (since *Nebraska* had then not yet been issued). But reading between the lines, Gorsuch's derisive references to silence seem loud enough.

In his *United States v. Texas* concurrence, Gorsuch wrote that the same standing rules apply "whether the plaintiff is a private person or a State. After all, standing doctrine derives from Article III, and nothing in that provision suggests a State may have standing when a similarly situated private party does not."[55] For that proposition, Gorsuch cited Chief Justice Roberts's dissent in *Massachusetts v. EPA*.[56] Gorsuch continued, taking aim more at Justice Kavanaugh (and perhaps Chief Justice Roberts) than at Justice Alito's dissent:

> Before *Massachusetts v. EPA*, the notion that States enjoy relaxed standing rules "ha[d] no basis in our jurisprudence." [549 U.S.] at 536 (ROBERTS, C. J., dissenting). Nor has "special solicitude" played a meaningful role in this Court's decisions in the years since. *Even so, it's hard not to wonder why the Court says nothing about "special solicitude" in this case. And it's hard not to think, too, that lower courts should just leave that idea on the shelf in future ones.*[57]

---

[55] *Id.* at 1976 (Gorsuch, J., concurring).

[56] *Id.* (citing *Massachusetts*, 549 U. S. at 536–38 (Roberts, C.J., dissenting)).

[57] *Id.* (emphasis added).

Indeed: "It's hard not to wonder why the Court says nothing about 'special solicitude'" in either *United States v. Texas* or *Biden v. Nebraska,* issued a week apart. Was Gorsuch reading the student-debt draft opinions as he wrote this concurrence in June 2023, noting the double silence on "special solicitude" across both cases? Had there been memos or drafts in which "special solicitude" for state standing had been discussed in either (or both)? Had Gorsuch written a response and a potential concurrence in *Biden v. Nebraska* arguing against state standing, only to see those arguments dropped? This is conjecture and speculation (standing reference intended), but it would explain both Alito's and Gorsuch's unusually sharp focus on the silence in the *Texas* majority opinion, when the same silence is unmistakable in *two* different majority opinions.

One role of legal commentators is to make sense of judicial opinions and elucidate the rules that emerge from common law case-by-case decision making. Those rules often have gaps—gaps that are sometimes inevitable due to the case-by-case nature of adjudication, sometimes the product of negotiation on a multi-member court, and sometimes deliberate gaps left open as a kind of compromise. It seems the Roberts Court was more interested in getting to the substance of the legality of the student debt waiver and developing the major questions doctrine, and less interested in developing standing doctrine. The majority's silence on state standing seems deliberate, but that avoidance should not obscure the underlying reasoning that makes sense of the result.

The best way to understand the majority opinion's standing reasoning is that it did, in fact, lower its Article III standards to grant Missouri standing, recognizing an even less concrete, more attenuated, and more indirect harm to the state of Missouri than it would have recognized for a parallel claim by thousands of Missouri citizen-plaintiffs, who would have lost. And that lower standard is a "special solicitude for states" in our federal system.

B. In Defense of "Special" State Standing

The "special solicitude" of state standing is the way to understand what the majority was actually doing. It is not just a better fit descriptively, but also has normative virtues.[58] An amicus brief from

---

[58] *Massachusetts,* 549 U.S. at 520.

Professors Samuel Bray and William Baude supporting the Biden administration raised concerns about "extravagant theories" of state standing.[59] However, this case was no extravagant extension of the "special solicitude" doctrine. In fact, allowing states slightly more latitude in establishing standing to raise constitutional questions and to challenge the abuse of executive power strikes an appropriate balance through federalism: States can seek access to justice and enforce the rule of law on behalf of their constituents, without the problems that would come from opening up the courts to many more attenuated and unmanageable cases. Given the concerns about the abuses of federal executive power, it is important to affirm that states do indeed have "special solicitude" in our federal system.

Let's go back to first principles and *Marbury v. Madison*: "The very essence of civil liberty certainly consists in the right of every individual to claim the protection of the laws, whenever he receives an injury. One of the first duties of government is to afford that protection. . . . [I]t is a general and indisputable rule, that where there is a legal right, there is also a legal remedy by suit or action at law, whenever that right is invaded."[60] Constitutional rights and the protections of the laws become a dead letter if standing law raises artificially high parchment barriers to the courts. If the executive branch can shield itself from legal challenges by arguing for high thresholds for standing after reverse-engineering and gerrymandering its policies to make sure no one has standing, the executive would be above the law. Here, the Biden administration attempted to simultaneously circumvent both administrative law and standing law. Granting the states special solicitude to challenge the administration's policy ensured that the debt-cancellation plan's legality would not be insulated from judicial review.

III. The *Biden v. Nebraska* MQD as Old Purposivism

What is the interpretive basis for the major questions doctrine? Where does it come from? *Biden v. Nebraska* helped answer these questions, in part through the majority opinion's silence and in part through its implied reasoning.

---

[59] Brief for Samuel L. Bray and William Baude as Amici Curiae in Support of Petitioners at 9–15, Biden v. Nebraska, 143 S. Ct. 2355 (2023) (No. 22-506).

[60] *Marbury v. Madison*, 5 U.S. (1 Cranch) 137, 163 (1803).

There has been a recent debate among scholars as to whether the major questions doctrine that has developed over the past two decades is simply an exception to *Chevron* deference, or whether it also triggers a shift in methods of statutory interpretation. Does the major questions doctrine trigger a shift from textualism to purposivism? Many legal scholars have argued that it does, and have usually been more critical of this shift or its inconsistency.[61] In fact, in her *West Virginia v. EPA* dissent, Justice Kagan suggested that earlier MQD cases were purposive: "[I]n the relevant cases, the Court . . . has asked, in a common-sensical (or call it purposive) vein, about what Congress would have made of the agency's view—otherwise said, whether Congress would naturally have delegated authority over some important question to the agency, given its expertise and experience."[62]

Kagan is still skeptical of this convenient selectivity of methods and its vulnerability to cherry-picking. Nevertheless, she is right about the common sense of purposivism, especially for major questions, as I argued in my amicus brief.[63] When the questions are major,

[61] *See* Shugerman, *supra* note 5, at 3, 6 (discussing *Brown & Williamson* and *King v. Burwell* as "MQD 1.0"); *see also* Jonathan H. Adler & Michael F. Cannon, King v. Burwell *and the Triumph of Selective Contextualism*, 2014–2015 CATO SUP. CT. REV. 35 (2015); David Driesen, *Does the Separation of Powers Justify the Major Questions Doctrine?*, 2024 U. ILL. L. REV. (forthcoming 2024) (manuscript at 6–12), https://tinyurl.com/mr3kjpb6 (placing the MQD in the Holy Trinity "spirit" method of statutory interpretation); Edward Rubin, *A Major Answer to the Major Questions Doctrine*, JOTWELL (Jan. 25, 2023) (reviewing David M. Driesen, *Does the Separation of Powers Justify the Major Questions Doctrine?* (2022), and highlighting Driesen's reading of an antitextual "spirit" method), https://tinyurl.com/yvx4dysp; Nathan Richardson, *Keeping Big Cases from Making Bad Law: The Resurgent "Major Questions" Doctrine*, 49 CONN. L. REV. 355, 406 (2016); Jacob Loshin & Aaron Nielson, *Hiding Nondelegation in Mouseholes*, 62 ADMIN. L. REV. 19, 45–46 (2010); *cf.* Richard M. Re (@RichardMRe), TWITTER (Mar. 3, 2023, 8:30 AM), https://tinyurl.com/ybbu2t2f (Richard Re on a more general assumed purpose, like a substantive canon—"Example: 'We presume that Congress intends to make major policy decisions itself, not leave those decisions to agencies.'") (quoting U.S. Telecom Ass'n v. FCC, 855 F. 3d 381, 419 (D.C. Cir. 2017) (Kavanaugh, J., dissenting from denial of rehearing en banc)).

[62] West Virginia v. EPA, 142 S. Ct. 2634 (Kagan, J., dissenting). *See also* Lisa Schultz Bressman, *The Jurisprudence of "Degree and Difference": Justice Breyer and Judicial Deference*, 132 YALE L.J. FORUM 729, 748 (2022); Kevin Tobia, *We're Not All Textualists Now*, 78 N.Y.U. ANN. SURV. AM. L. 243, 258–59 & n.73 (2023).

[63] *See* the draft article formatted version of the brief, Shugerman, *supra* note 5, at 1, 3, 6.

with "vast" significance and robust national salience: (1) There is less reason to engage in judicial interpretive triage via *Chevron*, unlike the thousands of mid-to-low-level cases where deference and simpler textualism is more appropriate than spending the judicial time and effort to dig into purposes; and (2) judges are more similarly situated, relative to agency experts, to know or discern the broader major public purposes of a statute, unlike in mid-to-low-level cases raising esoteric and technical textual issues. Others argue that the major questions doctrine is primarily a substantive canon of constitutional avoidance, invoked to avoid potential nondelegation problems. In the recent past, Gorsuch has been most vocal in offering this justification.[64]

The best way to understand the early MQD cases was as an exception to textualism, in favor of purposivism. The Roberts Court inherited one major-questions-doctrine precedent, *FDA v. Brown & Williamson*, a case about whether tobacco was a "drug" and whether cigarettes were "devices." As a matter of 1930s dictionary definitions and basic textualism, the answer would have been yes—with or without *Chevron* deference. But as a matter of purpose and political common sense, the 1930s Congress would not have imagined that it was effectively banning tobacco (or anything like tobacco) when it passed the law in question.[65] The Supreme Court was avoiding the result dictated by *Chevron* deference plus textualism, so it created a special exception to both. In questions of "vast 'economic and political significance,'"[66] the Court had less reason to defer, and it preferred to rule on such questions with a mix of common sense and purposivism, rather than a thin textualism.

King v. Burwell was similar. Neither *Burwell* nor *Brown & Williamson* established anything like a "clear statement" rule, and in fact, their emphasis on purposivism was very much unlike the textualism of "clear statement" rules. The Affordable Care Act (ACA) had the

---

[64] *See NFIB*, 142 S. Ct. at 669 (Gorsuch, J., concurring) ("Whichever the doctrine [MQD or nondelegation], the point is the same. Both serve to prevent 'government by bureaucracy supplanting government by the people.'"); *West Virginia*, 577 U.S at 2619 (Gorsuch, J., concurring).

[65] If tobacco were classified as a "drug," the FDA would have to find it was "safe and effective" to allow it to be sold, and tobacco's side effects clearly outweigh its benefits.

[66] *See* Util. Air Regul. Grp. v. EPA, 573 U.S. 302, 324 (2014) (coining this phrase).

opposite of a clear statement as to whether "state exchanges" could include "federal exchanges" (the question at issue in the case). And yet the Court in *Burwell* found its way to concluding that "state exchanges" could indeed include "federal exchanges" by emphasizing purpose over text. The Court introduced its analysis with roughly four pages about the broader purposes of the ACA statute, its complicated market-oriented mechanisms, and its interrelated policy goals.[67] *Burwell* eventually made some textual moves in the tradition of the "whole act" canon, but those ancillary moves distinctly followed the purposive framing that opened and drove the decision.[68]

Thus, after *Brown & Williamson* and *King v. Burwell*—and continuing with the Eviction Moratorium[69] and the Vaccine Mandate decisions[70]—the original major questions doctrine was (1) an exception to *Chevron* deference; and (2) an apparent exception to the rule that text is normally emphasized over purpose. In *West Virginia v. EPA* in 2022, Roberts continued those two rules, and also added a clear-and-specific statement rule more clearly and specifically than before,[71] which was more suggestive of the nondelegation doctrine problem and constitutional avoidance.

In *Biden v. Nebraska*, Chief Justice Roberts implicitly endorsed the purposivism approach to major questions. Justice Barrett wrote a concurrence to justify and explain the MQD as regular textualism. Her concurrence was mostly intended to reject Justice Gorsuch's substantive canon approach, but also seemingly to reject Chief Justice Roberts's purposivism. The fact that Justice Barrett wrote on her own—and wrote so unpersuasively in ways that backfired—suggests that Roberts's implied purposive approach is more likely the majority's governing rule. Gorsuch's nondelegation substantive

---

[67] *Burwell*, 576 U.S. at 479–83.

[68] *See* Adler & Cannon, *supra* note 61, at 35. Roberts has hinted at purposive sympathies before in *City of Arlington* and in *West Virginia v. EPA*. *See* Jonathan H. Adler, *West Virginia v. EPA: Some Answers about Major Questions*, 2021–2022 Cato Sup. Ct. Rev. 37, 58–59, 64.

[69] Ala. Ass'n of Realtors v. Dep't of Health & Human Serv., 141 S. Ct. 2485 (2021) (focusing on the mismatch between the broad moratorium and the more limited purposes of the statute).

[70] NFIB v. DOL, OSHA, 142 S. Ct. 661 (2022) (focusing on the mismatch between the OSHA broader policy to increase national vaccination rates and the statute's purposes to focus on workplace safety).

[71] *See* Adler, *supra* note 68, at 64.

canon seems to be a stronger alternative framework than Barrett's isolated pseudo-textualism, but Gorsuch's decision not to write a concurrence in *Nebraska* suggests some degree of acquiescence to Roberts's purposivism, at least for now.

Gorsuch has frequently adopted Justice Scalia's old aphorism that courts should be skeptical of finding "elephants in mouseholes."[72] That phrase primarily reflects a purposive approach (Congress's purpose was small, and the agency is trying to pull off something big and out of step with that purpose) more than it hints at a non-delegation problem. Indeed, the phrase implies that it is *permissible* for Congress to enact elephant-sized holes, so long as it does so in clear statutory delegation. Chief Justice Roberts does not wield that metaphor very often, but in *Biden v. Nebraska*, he offered a similar metaphor about matching sizes. Roberts referred to the clause of the HEROES Act that the Biden administration relied upon as "a wafer-thin reed on which to rest such sweeping power."[73] Roberts then engaged in a back-and-forth about "congressional purpose,"[74] contrasting the dissenters' interpretation of purpose with his own arguments about purpose. Notably, he did not criticize purposivism as in any sense less legitimate relative to textualism. Instead, he took the "congressional purpose" argument as legitimate and worth as much analysis as any other point about statutory interpretation. Of course, there is the usual question about the separation of powers:

> The question here is not whether something should be done; it is who has the authority to do it. Our recent decision in *West Virginia v. EPA* involved similar concerns over the exercise of administrative power. . . . Under the Government's reading of the HEROES Act, the Secretary would enjoy virtually unlimited power to rewrite the Education Act. . . . The dissent is correct that this is a case about one branch of government arrogating to itself power belonging to another. But it is the Executive seizing the power of the Legislature . . . .[75]

These are arguments not against congressional power, but against executive power exceeding congressional delegations. And Roberts

[72] *See* Whitman v. Am. Trucking Ass'ns, 531 U.S. 457, 468 (2001).

[73] *Nebraska*, 143 S. Ct. at 2371.

[74] *Id.* at 2372.

[75] *Id.* at 2372–73.

engaged in a debate about the valid scope of those delegations in distinctly purposive terms, focusing on congressional intent rather than text:

> The dissent asks us to "[i]magine asking the enacting Congress: Can the Secretary use his powers to give borrowers more relief when an emergency has inflicted greater harm?" The dissent "can't believe" the answer would be no. But imagine instead asking the enacting Congress a more pertinent question: "Can the Secretary use his powers to abolish $430 billion in student loans, completely canceling loan balances for 20 million borrowers, as a pandemic winds down to its end?" We can't believe the answer would be yes. Congress did not unanimously pass the HEROES Act with such power in mind.[76]

Roberts summed it up again using purposive terms about congressional intent, not text: "All this leads us to conclude that '[t]he basic and consequential tradeoffs' inherent in a mass debt cancellation program 'are ones that Congress *would likely have intended* for itself.'"[77]

Many commentators have already criticized Justice Barrett's unpersuasive and confusing concurrence, which argued that the MQD is simply textualism with appropriate "context."[78] In particular, her textual argument suggested a series of assumptions about what Congress should do, a normative interpretation. But textualism asks judges to follow what Congress actually wrote as text—a descriptive-and-not-normative approach to statutory interpretation. One of the defining features of textualism is that it asks judges to set aside their normative views and policy preferences. In his seminal 1997 lectures, Scalia argued that textualism was a guard against "judicial lawmaking," against "look[ing] over the heads of the crowd and pick[ing] out your friends" to get to the result "desired by the Court," rather than the one enacted by the legislature.[79] Scalia questioned

---

[76] *Id.* at 2374

[77] *Id.* at 2375 (emphasis added).

[78] *See* Kevin Tobia, Daniel Walters, & Brian G. Slocum, *Major Questions, Common Sense?*, 97 So. Cal. L. Rev. (forthcoming 2023), https://tinyurl.com/42t342vb; *see also* Adrian Vermeule, *Text and "Context,"* Yale J. on Reg.: Notice & Comment (July 13, 2023), https://tinyurl.com/4yxpk83f.

[79] Antonin Scalia, A Matter of Interpretation 21–22, 36 (1997).

such "dice-loading rules,"[80] and Barrett even cited this passage in her own opinion, which was even more critical of what she calls "strong-form" rules[81]—yet the next section of her concurrence then loads the dice with a series of "strong-form" normative claims about what Congress should do (or less generously, her own preferences about what Congress should do). Even Barrett's opening misfires and backfires:

> So what work is the major questions doctrine doing in these cases? I will give you the long answer, but here is the short one: The doctrine serves as an interpretive tool reflecting "common sense as to the manner in which Congress is likely to delegate a policy decision of such economic and political magnitude to an administrative agency." (citing *FDA v. Brown & Williamson Tobacco Corp.*, 529 U.S. 120, 133 (2000)).[82]

Her "short answer" quoting *FDA v. Brown & Williamson* is a strange start for a textualist, for reasons discussed above. To reiterate: As a matter of text, general dictionaries, and technical usage, tobacco plainly is a "drug" and cigarettes plainly are "devices." Instead of relying on the four-cornered text or on general statute-writing norms, the *Brown & Williamson* Court turned to circa 1930s America and its background socio-political realities of tobacco usage. Specifically, it looked to legislative history and purposes on the subject of drug regulation. And after favorably citing *Brown & Williamson*, Barrett's concurrence gets even more muddled. She asks the reader to "imagine that a grocer instructs a clerk to 'go to the orchard and buy apples for the store,'" suggesting that "a reasonable clerk would know that there are limits" to this authority based on context.[83] This statutory interpretation set piece clearly leads to context-as-purposive interpretation, not textual context.[84] As a text, grocers generally might mean their employees to go buy dozens or hundreds, even thou-

---

[80] *Id.* at 27–29.

[81] *Nebraska*, 143 S. Ct. at 2377 (Barrett, J., concurring) ("But a strong-form canon 'load[s] the dice for or against a particular result' in order to serve a value that the judiciary has chosen to specially protect.") (citing ANTONIN SCALIA, A MATTER OF INTERPRETATION 27 (1997); Amy Coney Barrett, *Substantive Canons and Faithful Agency*, 90 B. U. L. REV. 109, 124, 168–169 (2010)).

[82] *Nebraska*, 143 S. Ct. at 2378 (Barrett, J., concurring).

[83] *Id.* at 2378–79.

[84] *Id.*

sands of apples. The "context" would not be in the text or discernable from "genre" text—grocers-speak does not clarify whether it might be a dozen or a thousand. The employee would know from specific purpose and background details about the store—in other words, purposivism and legislative history.

The babysitter set piece also goes off the textualist rails. Barrett paints a picture: A parent tells a babysitter "Make sure the kids have fun."[85] What "fun" is appropriate? She cites no text or "genre" or general parenting norm. The context is specific to the family and the timing—the parents, their kids, their values, the specifics of a daytime babysitting schedule, a nighttime schedule, whether the kids have to be up early for school or some other event the next day. Again, her examples demand purposivism and legislative history, beyond the text and the context of the genre. Unwittingly, Barrett stumbled into some good explanations for the necessity of purposivism and the inevitable limits of textualism.

Perhaps the biggest problem with Barrett's argument is her conflation of the normative and descriptive in the last half of her concurrence.[86] Textualism is supposed to be descriptive: What did Congress actually enact in writing, what did Congress vote on, and what did that text mean? And purposivism is also supposed to be descriptive: What did Congress intend, what mischief did it aim to solve,[87] and what solution did it enact? But Barrett did not engage in a descriptive analysis of Congress; she instead put forward a normative prescription, driven by a sympathy for nondelegation. Nondelegation theories ask what Congress *should* be doing, as a matter of Article I design and the original public meaning of "legislative Powers" in the Constitution. Defenders of nondelegation argue that this design requires Congress to decide major questions and not delegate them.

Barrett may indeed be right as a matter of constitutional law. My study of the word "vesting" lends some historical weight to her intuitions: the Constitution's Legislative Vesting Clause uses the word "all" ("All legislative Powers . . . shall be vested in a Congress."),[88]

---

[85] *Id.* at 2379–80

[86] *Id.* at 2380–84.

[87] *See* Beau Baumann, *The Mischief Rule vs. the Major Questions Doctrine*, ADMINWAN-NABE (Oct. 5, 2022), https://tinyurl.com/yc7vk6xm (reviewing Samuel L. Bray, *The Mischief Rule*, 109 Geo. L.J. 967 (2021), in the context of the major questions doctrine).

[88] U.S. CONST. art. I, § 1.

whereas the Executive Vesting Clause does not ("The executive Power shall be vested in a President . . . .").[89] Justices Thomas and Gorsuch have emphasized the word "all" as part of their nondelegation arguments, and the historical usage of "vesting" supports their intuition.[90] My study of the usage of "vest" in the historical databases suggests that there was a difference between "vested," "fully vested" ("vesting all"), and "partially vested" and the like.[91] This study of "vesting" usage between 1776 and 1789 is no slam dunk, but reasonable people can point to it for a more restrictive nondelegation doctrine—as a *normative* constitutional argument about what Congress may and may not do.

That normative argument matters precisely because of what Congress actually does: punt with excessively ambiguous delegations. As a historical and empirical matter, Barrett is wrong that Congress "normally 'intends to make major policy decisions itself, not leave those decisions to agencies.'"[92] Her analysis tracks Ilan Wurman's proposal of a "linguistic canon" of presumed clarity for any major policy, which is also more normative than prescriptive.[93] Legisla-

---

[89] U.S. Const. art. II, § 1, cl. 1.

[90] *See* Jed Handelsman Shugerman, *Vesting*, 74 Stan. L. Rev. 1479, 1556 (2022) (citing Gorsuch and Thomas).

[91] *See id.*

[92] *Nebraska*, 143 S. Ct. at 2380 (Barrett, J., concurring) (quoting U.S. Telecom Ass'n v. Fed. Commc'ns Comm'n, 855 F. 3d 381, 419 (D.C. Cir. 2017) (Kavanaugh, J., dissenting from denial of reh'g en banc).

[93] Ilan Wurman, *Importance and Interpretive Questions*, Va. L. Rev. (forthcoming 2023), https://tinyurl.com/47tash4s. Wurman posits: "[O]rdinarily, lawmakers and private parties tend to speak clearly, and interpreters tend to expect clarity, when those lawmakers or parties authorize others to make important decisions on their behalf." *Id.* at 7. Unfortunately, the empirical basis for this claim is unclear. Wurman first claims, "There is no empirical evidence to suggest that Congress legislates on important matters through ambiguity, however; the only available study suggests the opposite." *Id.* at 37. The Civil Rights Act was famously ambiguous on "discrimination." Many open-ended emergency clauses have also been collected by the Brennan Center. *See A Guide to Emergency Powers and Their Use: The 148 statutory powers that may become available to the president upon declaration of a national emergency*, Brennan Ctr. for Just. (last updated Feb. 8, 2023), https://tinyurl.com/ynnx8x8r. And see below for more "opposite" historical examples. To his credit, Wurman later concedes recent work showing the opposite. Wurman, *supra*, at 40 (citing Nathan Richardson, *Antideference: Covid, Climate, and the Rise of the Major Questions Canon*, 108 U. Va. L. Rev. Online 174, 201 (2022); and Victoria F. Nourse & Jane S. Schacter, *The Politics of Legislative Drafting: A Congressional Case Study*, 77 NYU L. Rev. 575, 594–97 (2002)).

tures often deliberately speak unclearly, sometimes out of necessity to delegate power to address unclear future problems like emergencies (more below), and sometimes out of political reality, sometimes out of the reality of limited time and limited consensus.

Historians and political scientists who study major legislation have explained that Congress often likes to punt.[94] For example, the classic studies of the Interstate Commerce Act of 1887, which created the Interstate Commerce Commission (ICC), reflect Congress's political interest in punting tough detailed questions to agencies. Political scientists like Morris Fiorina saw Congress so clearly punting a major thorny question that they coded Congress's move as "SR": "Shifting Responsibility."[95] My study offered a slightly different take on the Interstate Commerce Act: Yes, Congress punted (as in, it ambiguously delegated) major substance to the ICC, but the Senate insisted on a commission of members appointed to six-year terms that it could control more than life-tenured Article III judges, which would have had more power in the House's bill.[96] There are too many examples of Congress punting to other branches to list here. There is a growing literature on "strategic ambiguity," borrowing from the world of diplomacy and national security, where parties derive an advantage from being unclear in order to deter, to retain flexibility, to have plausible deniability, etc.[97] Private parties bargaining contracts derive similar advantages, especially given limited time and resources to spell out all details. Of course, Congress would behave the same way, too. It seems there is an equally plausible descriptive linguistic

[94] Kevin Tobia, Daniel Walters, & Brian G. Slocum, *Major Questions, Common Sense?*, 97 So. CAL. L. REV. (forthcoming 2023).

[95] Morris P. Fiorina, *Legislative Choice of Regulatory Forms: Legal Process or Administrative Process?*, 39 PUB. CHOICE 33, 46–49 (1982); Morris P. Fiorina, *Legislator Uncertainty, Legislative Control, and the Delegation of Legislative Power*, 2 J. L. ECON. & ORG. 33, 46–47 (1986); Thomas W. Gilligan, William J. Marshall & Barry R. Weingast, *Regulation and the Theory of Legislative Choice: The Interstate Commerce Act of 1887*, 32 J. L. & ECON. 35, 47–48 (1989) (linking Fiorina's "SR" observation to the historical literature on the development of the administrative state and independent agencies).

[96] Jed Handelsman Shugerman, *The Dependent Origins of Independent Agencies: The Interstate Commerce Commission, the Repeal of the Tenure of Office Act, and the Rise of Modern Campaign Finance*, 31 J.L. & POL. 139, 146 (2016).

[97] Roderick Hills, *Strategic Ambiguity and Article VII: Why the Framers Decided Not to Decide*, 1 AM. J. CONST. HIST. 379 (2023); Jed H. Shugerman, *The Indecisions of 1789: Inconstant Originalism and Strategic Ambiguity*, 171 U. PA. L. REV. 753 (2023).

canon that parties engage in ambiguity balanced with clarity, and observers expect parties to engage in ambiguity. Whether one thinks such punting is good, bad, or a necessary evil, as a descriptive historical matter, Congress is often unclear, and it seems fair to say that the public often expects a lack of clarity, for better or for worse.

The bottom line is that Barrett's lone concurrence was so unpersuasive a challenge to Roberts's purposivism and to Gorsuch's substantive canon-ism that it clarified that those two approaches are (at least descriptively) the number 1 and number 2 explanations for what the Roberts Court is doing. Barrett merely clarified that her approach is isolated and appropriately marginal.

IV. The Emergency Problem

In oral argument, Justice Kavanaugh asked a question that started with a reference to my amicus brief:

> JUSTICE KAVANAUGH: Last question. Broadening it out and thinking about, you mentioned emergencies, the history of this Court with respect to executive assertions of emergencies. Some of the biggest mistakes in the Court's history were deferring to assertions of executive emergency power. Some of the finest moments in the Court's history were pushing back against presidential assertions of emergency power. And that's continued not just in the Korean War but post-9/11 in some of the cases there. So, given that history, there's a concern, I suppose, that I feel at least about how to handle an emergency assertion. You know, some of the amicus briefs, one of them from a professor says this is a case study in abuse of executive emergency powers. I'm not saying I agree with that. I'm just saying that's the assertion. And I want to get your assessment – this is a big-picture question, so I'll give you a little time – of how we should think about our role in assertion of presidential emergency power given the Court's history.[98]

Unfortunately, the Solicitor General did not address the question directly, and in the end, none of the Justices discussed it. And we are left in between two bad outcomes when it comes to emergencies. The United States Code is full of statutes delegating emergency powers

---

[98] Transcript, *supra* note 6, at 60–61.

in deliberately ambiguous and open-ended terms.[99] Such is the nature of planning for emergencies, the proverbial known unknowns and the unknown unknowns. On the one hand, the HEROES Act of 2003 and the Biden administration's student-debt waiver was one of far too many examples of Presidents and bureaucrats exploiting those open-ended statutory texts as pretexts for their policy goals:[100] "Never let a crisis go to waste."[101] To its credit, the Roberts Court set limits on that problem in *Biden v. Nebraska*. But did it go too far? In the next emergencies, will the Supreme Court keep expanding the major questions doctrine and strike down any measure that Congress did not explicitly and clearly specify? For better or for worse, most significant emergency policies would be invalidated by the rules in *West Virginia v. EPA* and *Biden v. Nebraska*. But there is an alternative, which was the point of my amicus brief and which will be explored in a future essay: An *emergency* questions doctrine, following the original MQD combination of no-*Chevron* plus purposivism, would seem manageable and would allow flexibility.[102] Unfortunately, the Roberts Court's silence on this emergency problem—on top of its deliberate silence on state standing and its merely implicit embrace of purposivism—leaves too many open questions and too much confusion. If the Court's activism in questions of "vast political and economic significance" is leading to so many major questions about legitimacy, consistency, and predictability, maybe the emergency is the Roberts Court itself.

Conclusion: Sound and Fury, Signifying . . .

It would be a major oversight to comment on *Biden v. Nebraska* without noting the Justices taking bank shots at each other, and without noting the debts owed to early precedents. Kagan began,

---

[99] See the many open-ended emergency clauses collected by the Brennan Center, *supra* note 93.

[100] Jonathan Adler has also called these cases the problem of "regulatory pretext." Adler, *supra* note 68, at 64 ("If, however, the agency decides to address A for the purpose of B—and Congress has not authorized B—this raises the prospect of what we might call "regulatory pretext.").

[101] *See supra* Part I.

[102] Jed Handelsman Shugerman, *Major Questions and an Emergency Question Doctrine: The Biden Student Debt Case Study*, (Fordham Law Legal Studies Research Paper No. 4345019, 2023), https://tinyurl.com/53td7sdp.

"In every respect, the Court today exceeds its proper, limited role in our Nation's governance." On standing: this Court "violates the Constitution" and "blows through a constitutional guardrail intended to keep courts acting like courts." Kagan concludes, "[N]o proper party is before the Court. A court acting like a court would have said as much and stopped. [Roberts] ends by applying the Court's made-up major-questions doctrine . . . ."[103] One can understand her frustration with Roberts's own standing dodges, but she was silent about the Biden administration's own standing dodges. Given the implicit background of *Massachusetts v. EPA*, a majority opinion formed from a broad ideological coalition of Justices John Paul Stevens, Anthony Kennedy, David Souter, Ruth Bader Ginsburg, and Stephen Breyer, it was hyperbole to say that the Roberts Court "violates the Constitution" or Article III, even if Roberts would not invoke the precedent. As for the substance, yes, *West Virginia v. EPA* and *Biden v. Nebraska* went further than earlier MQD cases. But given the long line of major questions cases over a quarter century—and cutting in different ideological directions—it is also hyperbole to suggest that the doctrine is "made-up," relative to *Chevron* or the various flavors of "arbitrary and capricious" interpretations over the years. And given Kagan's appropriate votes against Trumpian overreach and/or pretexts in *Trump v. Hawaii, New York v. Department of Commerce*, and *Regents v. DHS*, and even with the plaintiffs' own standing or procedural stretches in each of those cases, it is disappointing that she had sharp words for Roberts about "constitutional guardrails" but only deference to the Biden administration. The abuse of emergency powers as a pretext for a broader political or policy agenda is a bipartisan problem. Kagan rejected the Trump administration's arbitrary and capricious *ad hoc* pretexts, but she defended the Biden administration's.

Meanwhile, Roberts did not cloak himself in glory or grace in his overreaction. "It has become a disturbing feature of some recent opinions to criticize the decisions with which they disagree as going beyond the proper role of the judiciary. . . . It is important that the public not be misled either. Any such misperception would be harmful to this institution and our country."[104] Talk about judicial overreach. If Roberts deliberately avoided explaining how he could rec-

---

[103] *Nebraska*, 143 S. Ct. at 2385, 2388, 2400 (Kagan, J., dissenting).
[104] *Id.* at 2375–76 (majority op).

oncile standing with past precedents without invoking special state standing, and if he avoided explaining whether the major questions doctrine is textualism, purposivism, or a substantive canon, then the public can be forgiven if they feel misled by such a laconic opinion, another standing dodge. Congress is not the only multi-member body that turns to "strategic ambiguity." Building consensus is hard, and ambiguity and strategic silence can bridge many gaps inside and outside of law. Nevertheless, as a judge, Chief Justice Roberts had a rule-of-law duty to give consistent reasons, and he did not have much of a leg or a moral high ground to stand on. Nor did Justice Barrett in her confusing concurrence, and nor did Justices Gorsuch and Alito, who had vigorously taken opposing sides on state standing in *Texas* a week earlier, but then retreated to uncharacteristic silence in *Biden v. Nebraska*, just when the question was even more salient and dispositive.

In the end, the Roberts Court majority reached the right result, but it does not seem apt to say "Right result, wrong reasons." More like, "Right result, but for what reasons?" And one could also ask if the 2022–2023 term ended "full of sound and fury, signifying what exactly?"

Sackett v. EPA II: Ascertaining the Scope of Wetlands Jurisdiction under the Clean Water Act

*Damien M. Schiff**

Introduction

Sackett v. EPA proves that when ordinary American citizens team up with public interest litigators to protect property rights from the lawless commands of an abusive federal agency, extraordinary things can happen. Represented by attorneys from Pacific Legal Foundation, Mike and Chantell Sackett began their lawsuit against the Environmental Protection Agency (EPA) in April 2008. The 15 years since then have witnessed two Supreme Court rulings that have resulted in fundamental changes, for the better, in how federal environmental law operates. The first high court ruling, in 2012, expanded the circumstances in which a person injured by administrative action may sue to challenge that action.[1] The second, from this past Term, resolved an enduring and vexing controversy over the geographic reach of the Clean Water Act (CWA).

I have already written in this *Review* about the first decision.[2] Here, I focus on the second, beginning with the Sacketts' initial efforts—stymied by EPA—to build their dream family home near the shores of Priest Lake, Idaho. I then move to a background discussion of the nearly half-century-long legal dispute about the Clean Water Act's scope that culminated in the Court's ruling in *Sackett* this past Term. I next explain the substance of the *Sackett* majority and concurring

---

* Senior attorney, Pacific Legal Foundation; counsel of record in *Sackett v. EPA*, 143 S. Ct. 1322 (2023).

[1] *See* Sackett v. EPA (*Sackett I*), 566 U.S. 120 (2012).

[2] *See* Damien M. Schiff, Sackett v. EPA: *Compliance Orders and the Right of Judicial Review*, 2011–2012 Cato Sup. Ct. Rev. 113, 114–15 (2012).

opinions. And I then conclude with a critical analysis of those opinions, as well as a few thoughts about *Sackett* as a microcosm of the past and future of the Court's environmental and administrative law jurisprudence.

The mise en scène

In 2004, the Sacketts purchased a vacant lot in a largely built-out residential subdivision near Priest Lake, Idaho. At its north end, the lot is bounded by Kalispell Bay Road, a 30-foot-wide paved county road. Immediately on the north side of that road runs a manmade ditch that drains a large complex of wetlands known as the Kalispell Fen (which is situated north of the road and the subdivision). The roadside ditch travels west about a half-mile, where it terminates at Kalispell Creek, which then connects about a third of a mile south with Priest Lake itself. Immediately to the south of the Sacketts' lot is a graveled drive known as Old Schneider Road, and immediately to the south of that road is a row of developed houses that front Priest Lake itself. There is no standing water on the Sacketts' lot, nor is there any surface-water connection between the Sacketts' lot and the ditch north of Kalispell Bay Road, or the lot and Priest Lake.

In the spring of 2007, the Sacketts began construction of their family home by removing the lot's topsoil and trucking in gravel and other material more suitable for a building pad. Just a few days after the work had begun, officials from EPA and the Army Corps of Engineers entered the property and informed the Sacketts' work crew that the lot likely contained wetlands subject to regulation under the Clean Water Act. These officials recommended that all work cease until the Sacketts' compliance with the Act could be established.

A Statutory Prelude

Enacted in 1972, the Clean Water Act[3] is the preeminent federal water-quality statute. Its passage marked a significant change in Congress's approach to federal regulation, embodying "a 'total restructuring' and 'complete rewriting' of the existing water pollution legislation."[4] Under the prior federal approach, pollutant

---

[3] 33 U.S.C. §§ 1251–1389.

[4] City of Milwaukee v. Illinois, 451 U.S. 304, 317 (1981) (quoting remarks from the legislative history).

discharges were in practice only prohibited when they led to nuisances or water quality standard violations. The Clean Water Act, by contrast, established a system that not only enhanced enforcement and penalties but also regulated (and sometimes prohibited) certain discharges at their source, regardless of any resulting nuisance or standard exceedance.[5]

Briefly stated, the Act forbids the unpermitted discharge of "pollutants" from "point sources" to "navigable waters."[6] It defines "navigable waters" as "the waters of the United States, including the territorial seas."[7] Although the statute defines "territorial seas," it does not define "the waters of the United States" (commonly abbreviated "WOTUS"). Nonexempt discharges to "navigable waters" require a permit from either EPA (called a National Pollutant Discharge Elimination System, or NPDES, permit) or, if the discharge involves "dredged or fill material," from the Corps (commonly called a Section 404 permit).[8] In practice, the Clean Water Act's permitting regime is "arduous, expensive, and long."[9] "In deciding whether to grant or deny a permit, [the agencies] exercise[] the discretion of an enlightened despot, relying on such factors as 'economics,' 'aesthetics,' 'recreation,' and 'in general, the needs and welfare of the people.'"[10] Even when obtained, a permit can result in significant changes to the proposed project and dramatically limit the use of the property.[11] As for enforcement, the Act is a "potent

---

[5] *See* EPA v. Cal. *ex rel.* State Water Res. Control Bd., 426 U.S. 200, 202–05 (1976).

[6] 33 U.S.C. §§ 1311(a), 1362(12).

[7] *Id.* § 1362(7).

[8] *See id.* §§ 1342(a), 1344(a). The Act authorizes EPA to transfer NPDES and Section 404 permitting authority to the states. *See id.* §§ 1342(b), 1344(g)–(h).

[9] *See* U.S. Army Corps of Eng'rs v. Hawkes Co., Inc., 578 U.S. 590, 594–95, 601 (2016) (a Section 404 permit typically takes more than two years and $250,000 in consulting costs to secure).

[10] Rapanos v. United States, 547 U.S. 715, 721 (2006) (quoting 33 C.F.R. § 320.4(a) (2004)) (plurality op.).

[11] *See* Daniel R. Mandelker, *Practicable Alternatives for Wetlands Development Under the Clean Water Act*, 48 ENVTL. L. REP. NEWS & ANALYSIS 10894, 10913 (2018) ("The [Clean Water Act's] practicable alternatives requirement functions . . . as a conditioned permit that requires project modifications to reduce a development's effect on wetlands resources.").

weapon," imposing "'crushing' consequences 'even for inadvertent violations.'"[12] Indeed, discharging pollutants without a required permit, or violating permit conditions, risks cease-and-desist orders, compliance orders, tens of thousands of dollars per day in administrative and civil penalties, injunctions, and even criminal prosecution for mere "negligent" violations of the statute.[13]

For purposes of this article, however, the most important point to bear in mind about the Act's framework is that everything hinges on the meaning of "navigable waters"—if whatever you're doing does *not* result in pollutants being added to "navigable waters," then your activity is not regulated by the Act.

A Ponderous WOTUS Opus

The significant costs and liabilities that the Clean Water Act can impose underscore the importance of clearly demarcating the Act's scope. Unfortunately, the "reach of the Clean Water Act is notoriously unclear,"[14] and attempting to define it has proved to be "a contentious and difficult task"[15] which "has sparked decades of agency action and litigation."[16] This is especially true with respect to non-navigable wetlands such as those that EPA alleged to exist on the Sacketts' lot.

Shortly after the Clean Water Act was passed, EPA and the Corps adopted regulations defining "navigable waters."[17] EPA's interpretation was quite broad,[18] whereas the Corps's was notably more limited. Guided by the Supreme Court's longstanding construction of the phrase "navigable waters of the United States" as it was employed in predecessor statutes, the Corps construed the Act principally to reach interstate waters that are navigable in fact or readily

---

[12] Sackett v. EPA (*Sackett II*), 143 S. Ct. 1322, 1330 (2023) (quoting *Hawkes*, 578 U.S. at 602 (Kennedy, J., concurring)).

[13] *See id.* at 1330–31. *See also* 33 U.S.C. § 1319(a)–(g).

[14] *Sackett I*, 566 U.S. at 132 (Alito, J., concurring).

[15] Nat'l Ass'n of Mfrs. v. Dep't of Defense, 138 S. Ct. 617, 624 (2018).

[16] *Sackett II*, 143 S. Ct. at 1332.

[17] 38 Fed. Reg. 13,528, 13,529 (May 22, 1973); 39 Fed. Reg. 12,115, 12,119 (Apr. 3, 1974).

[18] *See* 40 C.F.R. § 125.1(p)(2), (4), (6) (1974) (claiming authority over all "[t]ributaries" of navigable waters, as well as all "lakes, rivers, and streams" used by "interstate travelers" or used in interstate "industrial" commerce).

susceptible of being rendered so.[19] In 1975, a federal district court rejected this interpretation as too narrow.[20] The Corps did not appeal the ruling.[21] Instead, following EPA's example, the Corps promulgated much broader regulations.[22]

The Corps's revised regulations were meant to extend the scope of "navigable waters" to the outer limits of Congress's power to regulate interstate commerce.[23] Thus, federal permitting authority was asserted not just over *inter*state waters, but also *intra*state waters with various relationships to interstate or foreign commerce. Authority also extended to all tributaries of such waters and all "wetlands"[24] that are "adjacent" to—i.e., bordering, contiguous with, or neighboring—any regulated water.[25] In the ensuing years, EPA and the Corps also claimed authority over isolated waters used by migratory birds, pursuant to the so-called "Migratory Bird Rule,"[26] as well as "ephemeral streams" and "drainage ditches" with an ordinary high water mark.[27] These were the regulations still on the books when the Sacketts were told to stop building their home.

* * *

During this initial period of agency rulemaking and revision, the Supreme Court began to weigh in on the WOTUS question. Its first such decision was *United States v. Riverside Bayview Homes*.[28] There, the Court considered whether EPA and the Corps had reasonably

---

[19] *See Rapanos*, 547 U.S. at 723 (citing The Daniel Ball, 77 U.S. (10 Wall.) 557, 563 (1871), and 39 Fed. Reg. 12,115, 12,119 (Apr. 3, 1974)).

[20] Nat. Res. Def. Council, Inc. v. Callaway, 392 F. Supp. 685, 686 (D.D.C. 1975).

[21] The Corps wanted to appeal, but the Justice Department declined to do so. Summary & Comments, *Comprehensive Wetlands Protection: One Step Closer to Full Implementation of §404 of the FWPCA*, 5 ENVTL. L. REP. 10099, 10101 (1975). During the district court litigation, the Corps was particularly disappointed with the Justice Department's failure to raise various arguments, such as "the difference between dredged and fill material and other pollutants." *Id.* at 10102.

[22] *See Rapanos*, 547 U.S. at 724.

[23] *Id.* (citing 42 Fed. Reg. 37,122, 37,144 n.2 (July 19, 1977)).

[24] These were defined as "those areas that are inundated or saturated [so as to support] a prevalence of vegetation typically adapted for life in saturated soil conditions." 33 C.F.R. § 323.2(c) (1978).

[25] 33 C.F.R. § 323.2(a)(2)–(5), (d) (1978).

[26] *Rapanos*, 547 U.S. at 725 (citing 51 Fed. Reg. 41,206, 41,217 (Nov. 13, 1986)).

[27] *Id.* (citing 65 Fed. Reg. 12,818, 12,823 (Mar. 9, 2000)).

[28] 474 U.S. 121 (1985).

interpreted the Act to regulate wetlands that were immediately adjacent to a navigable-in-fact water.[29] The Court began its statutory analysis by citing its then-recent decision in *Chevron, U.S.A., Inc. v. Natural Resources Defense Council, Inc.*[30] for the proposition that the Court must defer to an agency's reasonable interpretation of ambiguous text within a statute that the agency is charged with administering.[31] Looking to the text of the Clean Water Act, the Court conceded that, on "a purely linguistic level, it may appear unreasonable to classify 'lands,' wet or otherwise, as 'waters.'"[32] But weighing in favor of EPA and the Corps's view was Congress's aim, as the Court understood it, to regulate at least some waters besides those that are navigable-in-fact,[33] as well as the agencies' scientific judgment that wetlands play an important role in protecting water quality.[34] In light of this legislative intent and administrative expertise, the Court concluded that the agencies had reasonably resolved the line-drawing ambiguity raised by the Act's regulation of "waters" by including within such aquatic features those wetlands that are "inseparably bound up with the 'waters' of the United States."[35]

Second, in *Solid Waste Agency of Northern Cook County (SWANCC) v. Army Corps of Engineers*,[36] the Court considered whether EPA and the Corps may regulate "nonnavigable, isolated, intrastate waters" based on how the use of such waters could affect interstate commerce, pursuant to the Migratory Bird Rule.[37] The Court began its analysis by analyzing *Riverside Bayview*, determining that it was the "significant nexus" of geographic closeness between wetlands and the adjacent waters with which they were "inseparably bound up" that led the *Riverside Bayview* Court to affirm the agencies' authority over such wetlands.[38] This kind of shoreline connection is, in contrast, necessarily absent with respect to features like the abandoned

[29] *See id.* at 124.
[30] 467 U.S. 837 (1984).
[31] *Riverside Bayview*, 474 U.S. at 131.
[32] *Id.* at 132.
[33] *See id.* at 133, 138–39.
[34] *Id.* at 133–34
[35] *Id.* at 134.
[36] 531 U.S. 159 (2001).
[37] *Id.* at 162, 165–66.
[38] *Id.* at 167 (quoting *Riverside Bayview*, 474 U.S. at 134).

and ponded gravel pits at issue in *SWANCC*, which were *"not* adjacent to open water."[39] In light of that important distinction, the Court
in *SWANCC* concluded that the Act cannot be stretched to the latter.
As the Court underscored, the agencies "put forward no persuasive
evidence that the Corps mistook Congress' intent in 1974"[40]—namely,
that the Act was merely an exercise of Congress's commerce power
over navigation, and that the statute's use of the "term 'navigable'
has at least the import of showing us what Congress had in mind as
its authority for enacting the [Clean Water Act]: its traditional jurisdiction over waters that were or had been navigable in fact or which
could reasonably be so made."[41] Buttressing that conclusion was the
Court's observation that acceptance of the agencies' reading of the
Act to reach isolated waters such as the gravel pits at issue would,
by trenching upon "the States' traditional and primary power over
land and water use," raise "significant constitutional and federalism
questions."[42] Yet, far from wanting to implicate such issues, "Congress chose to 'recognize, preserve, and protect the primary responsibilities and rights of States . . . to plan the development and use . . .
of land and water resources.'"[43]

A few years later, the Court in *Rapanos v. United States*[44] addressed
the middle question left after *Riverside Bayview* and *SWANCC*—
whether the Act allows for the regulation of wetlands adjacent to
non-navigable ditches and other waters that ultimately flow into
traditional navigable waters.[45] Five members of the Court held the
agencies' regulations asserting control over such waters to be invalid
insofar as they purported to regulate all tributaries of traditionally
navigable waters and all wetlands adjacent to such tributaries.[46] But
no opinion explaining why the Act cannot be so construed garnered
a majority of the Court.

Writing for himself and three other members of the Court, Justice
Antonin Scalia began his analysis by noting that, however the

[39] *Id.* at 168 (emphasis in original).

[40] *Id.*

[41] *Id.* at 172.

[42] *Id.* at 174.

[43] *Id.* (quoting 33 U.S.C. § 1251(b)).

[44] 547 U.S. 715 (2006).

[45] *See Rapanos,* 547 U.S. at 729–30 (plurality op.).

[46] *Id.* at 728 (plurality op.); *id.* at 759 (Kennedy, J., concurring in the judgment).

qualifiers "navigable" and "of the United States" may limit the Act's scope, that scope surely can extend no further than "waters."[47] Justice Scalia then proceeded to explain, based on (1) an ordinary meaning analysis of the statutory text, (2) the Court's rulings in *Riverside Bayview* and *SWANCC*, and (3) Congress's desire to preserve traditional state authority over land and water, that "waters" include "only those relatively permanent, standing or continuously flowing bodies of water 'forming geographic features' that are described in ordinary parlance as 'streams[,] . . . oceans, rivers, [and] lakes.'"[48] "Wetlands" would not normally fall under such a definition.[49] But as Justice Scalia pointed out, there is a difference between considering a wetland on its own to be a "water" and concluding that inevitably some wetlands may be regulated as "waters," given the "inherent ambiguity in drawing the boundaries of any 'waters.'"[50] Indeed, it was that line-drawing ambiguity which convinced the Court in *Riverside Bayview* to allow for the regulation of "all abutting wetlands as waters."[51] Thus, *"only* those wetlands with a continuous surface connection to bodies that are 'waters of the United States' in their own right, so that there is no clear demarcation between 'waters' and wetlands, are 'adjacent to' such waters and covered by the Act."[52] Put another way, the surface water connection must be so substantial that the wetland and abutting water are rendered *"indistinguishable."*[53]

Although Justice Anthony Kennedy provided the fifth vote to support the Court's judgment rejecting the agencies' expansive regulation, he disagreed with the plurality's rationale for that rejection.[54] Instead of a boundary-drawing-problem test for determining when a wetland may be deemed a "water," Justice Kennedy proposed a "significant nexus" standard, which he purported to derive from *SWANCC*. According to this rule, a wetland may be regulated if it, either alone or in combination with other "similarly situated"

---

[47] *Id.* at 731 (plurality op.).

[48] *Id.* at 739 (quoting Webster's New International Dictionary 2882 (2d ed. 1954)).

[49] *See Riverside Bayview*, 474 U.S. at 132.

[50] *Rapanos*, 547 U.S. at 740 (plurality op.).

[51] *Id.* at 742.

[52] *Id.* (emphasis in original).

[53] *Id.* at 755 (emphasis in original).

[54] *Id.* at 759 (Kennedy, J., concurring in the judgment).

wetlands in the "region," significantly affects the physical, chemical, and biological integrity of "waters more readily understood as 'navigable.'"[55]

Scene Shift: EPA Commences Enforcement, and the Sacketts Go to Court

Less than a year after *Rapanos*, the Sacketts began construction of their family home. But they were stopped days later by EPA and Corps officials who, as noted above, informed the Sacketts' crew that construction should cease because a federal permit was likely required. Following the agencies' initial site visit, EPA sent the Sacketts a "Request for Information" concerning their building project.[56] In their written response, the Sacketts explained that they had all local building permits in hand, that their site was bordered by developed properties and roads, and that nothing in their deed of title or other paperwork suggested that their lot contained wetlands. A couple of months later, EPA followed up with a voicemail, informing the Sacketts that the agency needed to do "additional research" and inquiring as to whether the Sacketts would comply with its "request" that they remove the fill from their property.[57] Answering by letter, the Sacketts requested "a response from the EPA in writing as to a rational reason why the property . . . needs to be reclaimed," while noting that the agency had still not provided "any official notification in writing of any violation."

That notification was delivered in November 2007, in the form of an administrative compliance order.[58] This EPA directive asserted that the Sacketts' lot contained "navigable waters" subject to the Clean Water Act. Specifically, EPA found that the property contained "wetlands" as defined by regulation, and that these alleged wetlands were among "the waters of the United States" because of their alleged relationship to Priest Lake. Thus, EPA's order determined

[55] *Id.* at 780.

[56] *Cf.* 33 U.S.C. § 1318(a)(A) (authorizing EPA to demand from any owner or operator of a "point source" "such . . . information as [EPA] may reasonably require").

[57] In a prior telephone conversation, EPA personnel had informed Chantell Sackett that the Sacketts "would not have gotten a permit to build there" and thus that the agencies would "ask [them] to restore [the] site [and] build elsewhere."

[58] *Cf.* 33 U.S.C. § 1319(a)(3) (authorizing EPA to issue such orders, "on the basis of any information available," for a variety of alleged violations).

that the Sacketts had violated the Act by trying to build their home without first having obtained a Clean Water Act permit. The Sacketts were therefore ordered to refrain from further construction and to immediately begin to "restore" their property. Failure to comply would subject them to tens of thousands of dollars per day in administrative and civil penalties.[59]

Believing that their lot did not contain "navigable waters" subject to federal authority, the Sacketts requested from EPA an administrative hearing on the agency's order, to no avail. The Sacketts therefore proceeded, in April 2008, to file an action under the judicial review provisions of the Administrative Procedure Act (APA).[60] They contended that EPA's compliance order was arbitrary and capricious because the Clean Water Act did not grant EPA authority to regulate their property. EPA moved to dismiss the suit, arguing that the compliance order was not judicially reviewable. The district court granted EPA's motion and the Ninth Circuit affirmed, but the Supreme Court granted certiorari and reversed, holding that the order constituted "final agency action" subject to judicial review under the APA.[61]

On remand to the district court, the parties cross-moved for summary judgment, with the district court ultimately ruling in EPA's favor on the basis of the agency's invocation of the "significant nexus" test. The Sacketts appealed again, and again were rebuffed by the Ninth Circuit, which affirmed the district court's judgment that EPA has authority over the wetlands alleged to exist on the Sacketts' property.[62] The court began its merits analysis with a review of circuit case law applying the *Marks* framework[63] for interpreting fractured decisions like *Rapanos*, and it concluded that, under *Marks*, the significant nexus test set forth in Justice Kennedy's concurrence should govern.[64] The court then affirmed

---

[59] *See* Schiff, *supra* n.2, at 114–15.

[60] 5 U.S.C. §§ 701–06.

[61] *Sackett I*, 566 U.S. at 131.

[62] Before reaching the merits, the Ninth Circuit confirmed that the Sacketts' appeal remained live despite EPA's voluntary, non-binding withdrawal of the compliance order during the appeal, because the Sacketts' "central legal challenge" to EPA's jurisdiction remained "unresolved." Sackett v. EPA, 8 F.4th 1075, 1084–86 (9th Cir. 2021) *rev'd*, 143 S. Ct. 1322 (2023).

[63] *See* Marks v. United States, 430 U.S. 188 (1977).

[64] *Id.* at 1087–91.

EPA's determination that the agency has jurisdiction over the Sacketts' lot because (1) the property contains, within the meaning of the agencies' regulations, "wetlands" that are "adjacent" to a "tributary" of Priest Lake (namely, the roadside ditch); and (2) the site's purported two-thirds-of-an-acre wetland, in combination with the few dozen acres of wetlands on the other side of Kalispell Bay Road, bears a significant nexus to Priest Lake.[65]

Sackett v. EPA II: A "Watershed"[66] Decision

In the forecourts: seeking cert a second time

The Sacketts sought cert, phrasing their question presented in terms of a competition between *Rapanos* opinions: Should the *Rapanos* plurality's standard govern wetlands jurisdiction, or should the Kennedy significant nexus test, adopted by EPA and the Corps and most lower courts,[67] prevail? The Court granted cert in January 2022, but in doing so it rephrased the question presented to delete any reference to or dependence on *Rapanos* and instead simply asked whether the Ninth Circuit had articulated the correct test for wetlands jurisdiction. As we shall see, that change in the question presented may have been due in part to concerns among some Justices that no opinion from *Rapanos* had the right answer.

The decision—first reading

Although the case was argued on the first day of the October 2022 Term, the Court did not issue its decision until late May 2023. Justice Samuel Alito wrote a majority opinion for the Court, fully joined by Chief Justice John Roberts and Justices Clarence Thomas, Neil Gorsuch, and Amy Coney Barrett. Justices Thomas, Elena Kagan, and Brett Kavanaugh each wrote a concurrence, although the latter

---

[65] *Id.* at 1092–93.

[66] I have precedent for what might otherwise be a cringe-worthy pun! *See SWANCC*, 531 U.S. at 175 (Stevens, J., dissenting) ("It is fair to characterize the Clean Water Act as 'watershed' legislation.").

[67] Whether one of the *Rapanos* opinions was controlling was a most vexing issue for the lower courts. *See generally* M. Reed Hopper, *Running Down the Controlling Opinion in* Rapanos v. United States, 21 U. Denv. Water L. Rev. 47 (2017). But in the Supreme Court, neither the Sacketts nor EPA argued that any *Rapanos* opinion was controlling under *Marks*, and the Supreme Court concluded, in a brief analysis, that none was. *See Sackett II*, 143 S. Ct. at 1329 n.3.

two opinions (to which Justices Sonia Sotomayor and Ketanji Brown Jackson joined) concurred in the judgment only.

Before proceeding to the various opinions in *Sackett II*, I think it important to note, given the many press accounts of the decision describing the ruling as divided along ideological lines,[68] that there were no dissenting opinions and that the Court was unanimous in two critical respects: None of the Justices agreed with EPA's position that the significant nexus test should control wetlands jurisdiction, and none of the Justices believed that the Sacketts' property should be regulated under the Clean Water Act.[69] This unanimity should be highlighted given the politicization of WOTUS and given that EPA and its amici considered adoption of the significant nexus test to be essential to protecting the nation's waters.

Split decision no more:

Justice Alito's majority opinion adopts the Rapanos *plurality*

The short answer to the question "What is the holding of *Sackett II*?" is—the *Rapanos* plurality.[70] The analysis that Justice Alito provided to reach that result is divided into two main parts. First, like the *Rapanos* plurality, he explained what qualifies as a regulable "water." Then, again tracking the *Rapanos* plurality, he explained when a wetland may be considered a regulable "water."[71]

As to the first step, Justice Alito quoted the *Rapanos* plurality's test that "the CWA's use of 'waters' encompasses only those relatively permanent, standing or continuously flowing bodies of water forming geographical features that are described in ordinary parlance as streams, oceans, rivers, and lakes."[72] In adopting the *Rapanos* plurality standard for "waters," Justice Alito's opinion offered a number of reasons in support of that standard: the statute's use of the plural term "waters," which commonly denotes discrete bodies of water; the fact

---

[68] *See, e.g.,* Ian Millhiser, *A new Supreme Court opinion is terrible news if you care about clean water,* Vox (May 25, 2023), https://tinyurl.com/4c5sjjms; Oliver Milman, *US supreme court shrinks clean water protections in ruling siding with Idaho couple,* THE GUARDIAN (May 25, 2023), https://tinyurl.com/yc3d4xyr.

[69] *See Sackett II,* 143 S. Ct. at 1344; *id.* at 1369 (Kavanaugh, J., concurring).

[70] *Id.* at 1341 (majority op.).

[71] Thus, by limiting the analysis to what qualifies as a "water," the majority opinion (like the *Rapanos* plurality) did not address when a water is "of the United States." *See Sackett II,* 143 S. Ct. at 1344 (Thomas, J., concurring).

[72] *Id.* at 1336 (majority op.) (cleaned up).

that the operative definitional term is "navigable waters," which typically are features like rivers, lakes, and oceans; how the term "waters" is used in other sections of the statute, and in other federal statutes, in a way that clearly indicates bodies of open water; and how the Court itself in prior opinions has used the term.[73]

In rejecting EPA's argument that the term "waters" includes any feature marked by the mere presence of water, Justice Alito explained that such a standard would, absurdly enough, include even puddles, which few would describe as "waters." Moreover, it would be inconsistent with *SWANCC*, which held that "isolated waters" are not regulable. And it would make otiose *Riverside Bayview*'s effort to justify regulation of presumptively non-water wetlands through its extensive discussion of the challenge in delineating the outer reaches of waters. Finally, such a broad standard would conflict with Congress's aim to preserve the states' "primary" authority over land and water resources.[74]

Having established the standard for a regulable "water," Justice Alito proceeded to explain when a wetland can be considered part of a regulable water. He started off his analysis with the same premise as *Riverside Bayview*—namely, in ordinary parlance one would not consider a wetland to be a water.[75] But, just as in *Riverside Bayview*, so too Justice Alito acknowledged that the Clean Water Act must regulate at least some wetlands, because of Congress's 1977 addition of the statute's Section 404(g). That provision authorizes EPA to transfer Section 404(a) permitting authority (which otherwise rests with the Corps) to the states, but that transfer authority is limited by a carve-out in a parenthetical. Specifically, Section 404(g)(1) provides that EPA may transfer permitting authority for:

> the discharge of dredged or fill material into the navigable waters (other than those waters which are presently used, or are susceptible to use in their natural condition or by reasonable improvement as a means to transport interstate or foreign commerce shoreward to their ordinary high water mark, including all waters which are subject to the ebb and flow of the tide shoreward to their mean high water mark, or mean higher high water mark on the west coast, *including wetlands adjacent thereto*).[76]

[73] *Id.* at 1336–38.

[74] *Id.* at 1338.

[75] *Id.*

[76] 33 U.S.C. § 1344(g)(1) (emphasis added).

The "other than" parenthetical indicates, per Justice Alito, that at least some wetlands are considered regulable "navigable waters." But which ones? The answer to that question cannot be resolved wholly by Section 404(g)(1), because "it is not the operative provision that defines the Act's reach."[77] Rather, one must harmonize Section 404(g)(1) with Section 502(7), which defines the term at issue, *viz.*, "navigable waters," as "the waters of the United States." Such harmonization is achieved by focusing upon Section 404(g)(1)'s use of "including." That, per Justice Alito, signals that "adjacent" wetlands are regulable only if they are "includ[ed]" among "the waters of the United States," i.e., if they "qualify as 'waters of the United States' in their own right."[78] In other words, "they must be indistinguishably part of a body of water that itself constitutes 'waters' under the CWA," which is to say, as the *Rapanos* plurality observed, that they maintain a continuous surface connection to a bona fide "water" such that it is difficult to determine where the water ends and the wetland begins.[79]

Justice Alito then proceeded to expand upon his earlier point that, as *Riverside Bayview* itself observed, Section 404(g)(1) cannot be determinative of the scope of the Act. To be sure, "adjacent" can in many contexts mean something less than "immediately abutting," but "construing statutory language is not merely an exercise in ascertaining the outer limits of a word's definitional possibilities, and here, only one meaning produces a substantive effect that is compatible with the rest of the law."[80] Moreover, in a nod to the major questions doctrine,[81] Justice Alito observed that because Congress does not typically hide

---

[77] *Sackett II*, 143 S. Ct. at 1339.

[78] *Id.*

[79] *Id.* at 1341.

[80] *Id.* at 1339–40 (cleaned up).

[81] *See generally* West Virginia v. EPA, 142 S. Ct. 2587, 2609 (2022) ("Extraordinary grants of regulatory authority are rarely accomplished through modest words, vague terms, or subtle devices. Nor does Congress typically use oblique or elliptical language to empower an agency to make a radical or fundamental change to a statutory scheme. . . . [¶] Thus, in certain extraordinary cases, both separation of powers principles and a practical understanding of legislative intent make us reluctant to read into ambiguous statutory text the delegation claimed to be lurking there. To convince us otherwise, something more than a merely plausible textual basis for the agency action is necessary. The agency instead must point to clear congressional authorization for the power it claims.") (cleaned up).

"elephants in mouseholes," "it would be odd indeed if Congress had tucked an important expansion to the reach of the CWA into convoluted language in a relatively obscure provision concerning state permitting programs."[82] To read Section 404(g)(1) as so doing would effectively amend Section 502(7) such that "navigable waters" would comprise "the waters of the United States *and their adjacent wetlands.*" Yet, as Justice Alito underscored, that would be inconsistent with Section 404(g)(1) itself, which merely states that navigable waters "includ[e] wetlands adjacent thereto," as opposed to "adjacent" wetlands constituting a separate, regulable category of hydrogeographic features. Thus, the better reading of Section 404(g)(1) is that certain types of adjacent wetlands are regulable but only because they are *already* part of the "waters of the United States," since they are indistinguishably associated with "waters" as typically understood.[83]

Following this close textual analysis, Justice Alito proceeded to a discussion of various clear-statement canons[84] to demonstrate how EPA's interpretation of the statute cannot be sustained. Recall that EPA's primary counterargument to the *Rapanos* plurality standard was that the significant nexus test, as originally articulated in Justice Kennedy's concurring opinion in *Rapanos*, is the best interpretation of the Act's wetlands coverage.[85] Justice Alito concluded that, besides conflicting with the Act's text and structure, the significant nexus test failed to satisfy the "federalism" and "fair notice" canons.

As to the former, Justice Alito recited the Court's tradition of requiring a clear statement from Congress whenever the latter "wishes to significantly alter the balance between federal and state power and the power of the Government over private property."[86] Such a clear statement requirement is particularly apt with respect to the Clean Water Act, as the statute expressly declares Congress's aim to preserve the states' traditional authority over land and water

---

[82] *Sackett II*, 143 S. Ct. at 1340.

[83] *Id.*

[84] *See generally* Biden v. Nebraska, 143 S. Ct. 2355, 2376–77 (2023) (Barrett, J., concurring) ("There are many such canons on the books, including constitutional avoidance, the clear-statement federalism rules, and the presumption against retroactivity. Such rules effectively impose a 'clarity tax' on Congress by demanding that it speak unequivocally if it wants to accomplish certain ends.") (cleaned up).

[85] *See Sackett II*, 143 S. Ct. at 1341.

[86] *Id.*

resources.[87] EPA's reading of the statute would directly undercut that aim: The amount of acreage the agency would claim authority to regulate would be "truly staggering."[88] Yet far from containing any clear statement supporting EPA, the Clean Water Act "never mentions the 'significant nexus' test, so the EPA has no statutory basis to impose it."[89]

As to the "fair notice" canon, Justice Alito explained that due process requires Congress to define penal statutes—such as the Clean Water Act[90]—"with sufficient definiteness that ordinary people can understand what conduct is prohibited" and "in a manner that does not encourage arbitrary and discriminatory enforcement."[91] But the significant nexus test offers no such guidance; to the contrary, the "freewheeling inquiry" that it invites "provides little notice to landowners of their obligations under the CWA."[92] That lack of notice, combined with the statute's imposition of significant penalties for "otherwise . . . ordinary activities," means that Congress must be quite clear that it intends such a rule. The significant nexus test "falls far short of that standard."[93]

Justice Alito then concluded his opinion by quickly dispatching with EPA's main rearguard argument—namely, that through Section 404(g)(1) Congress ratified the broad understanding of the scope of the Clean Water Act as expressed in the Corps's 1975 and 1977 regulations construing "the waters of the United States." In rejecting EPA's ratification argument, Justice Alito emphasized the textual analysis that underpins the majority's adoption of the *Rapanos* plurality standard—Congress has never amended the "operative" definitional text of "the waters of the United States," which is effectively what EPA would be asking the Court to do by accepting the agency's ratification argument. Further, EPA's ratification argument had already been rejected in substance by *SWANCC* and *Riverside Bayview*, the former in holding that isolated waters are not regulable

---

[87] *See* 33 U.S.C. § 1251(b).

[88] *Sackett II*, 143 S. Ct. at 1342.

[89] *Id.*

[90] *See* 33 U.S.C. § 1319(c).

[91] *Sackett II*, 143 S. Ct. at 1342 (quoting McDonnell v. United States, 579 U.S. 550, 576 (2016)).

[92] *Id.*

[93] *Sackett II*, 143 S. Ct. at 1342–43.

even though the Corps's 1970s regulations would have covered them, and the latter in holding that Section 404(g)(1) does not place a "definitive" interpretation on the Act's scope, instead indicating at most that wetlands are not necessarily excluded from regulation. Finally, Justice Alito explained that EPA had failed to produce the "overwhelming evidence" needed to make a ratification argument; at best, the evidence was mixed.[94]

A step further:

Justice Thomas's concurrence

Justice Thomas, joined by Justice Gorsuch, issued a lengthy concurrence in which he fully agreed with the majority's adoption of the *Rapanos* plurality standard for when hydrogeographic features may be deemed regulable "waters" as well as for when wetlands can be treated as "waters."[95] His concurrence instead addressed when a water can be considered "of the United States." Justice Thomas proceeded through an exhaustive review of the history of federal water quality regulation under the Commerce Clause, for which he sadly recounted there "would be little need . . . if the agencies had not effectively flouted our decision in *SWANCC*, which restored navigability as the touchstone of federal jurisdiction under the CWA."[96] Based on that discussion, he concluded that when Congress enacted the Clean Water Act, it intended to regulate consistent with a traditional understanding of its power over the interstate channels of commerce, as a corollary of its power "[t]o regulate [c]ommerce . . . among the several States."[97] That traditional understanding is reflected in Congress's choice of the phrase "waters of the United States," which, according to Justice Thomas, means waters that are capable of serving as units of an interstate channel of commerce.[98]

---

[94] *Id.* at 1343. Justice Alito also made short work of EPA's policy argument that the significant nexus test is necessary to ensure that water quality remains good throughout the nation. *See id.* ("But the CWA does not define the EPA's jurisdiction based on ecological importance, and we cannot redraw the Act's allocation of authority.").

[95] *Id.* at 1344 (Thomas, J., concurring).

[96] *Id.* at 1355.

[97] U.S. Const. art. I, § 8, cl. 3.

[98] *See Sackett II*, 143 S. Ct. at 1352–56 (Thomas, J., concurring).

In practice, Justice Thomas's understanding of "waters of the United States" would mean that only those waters that are navigable in fact could be regulated under the Clean Water Act. But he readily acknowledged that, even under a less demanding standard, the Sacketts' dispute should be an easy one to resolve: "Here, no elaborate analysis is required to know that the Sacketts' *land* is not a *water*, much less a water of the United States."[99] Justice Thomas concluded his concurrence by lamenting how the Court's Commerce Clause jurisprudence "has significantly departed from the original meaning of the Constitution," and "[p]erhaps nowhere is this deviation more evident than in federal environmental law, much of which is uniquely dependent upon an expansive interpretation of the Commerce Clause."[100] But he also emphasized that, "while not all environmental statutes are so textually limited, Congress chose to tether federal jurisdiction under the CWA to its traditional authority over navigable waters," a decision that "EPA and the Corps must respect."[101]

A sardonic déjà vu:

Justice Kagan's concurrence

Justice Kagan wrote a short and somewhat acerbic concurrence, joined by Justices Sotomayor and Jackson.[102] She concurred in the judgment, but she did not agree with the majority's test, which in her view is insufficiently protective of the environment.[103] For Justice Kagan, the correct test for wetlands jurisdiction under the

[99] *Id.* at 1357–58 (emphasis in original).

[100] *Id.* at 1358.

[101] *Id.* at 1358–59.

[102] That it was somewhat contentious may be reflected in the fact that Justice Kavanaugh did not join it. One also wonders whether it was among those opinions in the mind of the Chief Justice when he wrote his majority opinion in the student-loan cases. *See Nebraska*, 143 S. Ct. at 2375 ("It has become a disturbing feature of some recent opinions to criticize the decisions with which they disagree as going beyond the proper role of the judiciary.").

[103] *Sackett II*, 143 S. Ct. at 1359 (Kagan, J., concurring in the judgment). Kagan made the de rigueur reference to the burning Cuyahoga, and she encouraged readers, if they've "lately swum in a lake, happily drunk a glass of water straight from the tap, or sat down to a good fish dinner," to thank the Act for it. *Id.* at 1360 Interestingly, in the four decisions of the Supreme Court construing "waters of the United States," the Cuyahoga is cited only in dissenting opinions, perhaps demonstrating rhetorical backfiring.

Clean Water Act is established by Section 404(g)(1): A wetland is regulated whenever it is "adjacent" to a covered water, adjacency being understood according to its ordinary meaning. Thus, a wetland can be regulated "not only when it is touching, but also when it is nearby" a covered water.[104] In settling upon a narrower standard, the majority opinion improperly put "a thumb on the scale for property owners—no matter that the Act (i.e., the one Congress enacted) is all about stopping property owners from polluting."[105]

Justice Kagan was particularly critical of the majority's use of clear-statement canons "not to resolve ambiguity or clarify vagueness, but instead to 'correct' breadth."[106] In this perceived misuse of such canons, Justice Kagan saw a parallel between the supposed analytical inadequacies of the majority opinion in *Sackett II* and those of the majority opinion in *West Virginia v. EPA* the previous Term.[107] In her view, *Sackett II* is of a piece with *West Virginia*, in that both employed "special canons 'magically appearing as get-out-of-text-free cards' to stop the EPA from taking the measures Congress told it to."[108] And the error in both cases led to the same result: "the Court's appointment of itself as the national decision-maker on environmental policy."[109]

A "bank shot" textualism?

Justice Kavanaugh's concurrence

Justice Kavanaugh also concurred, joined by Justices Kagan, Sotomayor, and Jackson. But unlike Justice Kagan's, Justice Kavanaugh's concurrence expressly stated his agreement with the majority's rejection of the significant nexus test and with the majority's conclusion that the Sacketts' property should not be regulated.[110] There, however, the agreement with the majority ended. In Justice Kavanaugh's view, the correct test comes from

---

[104] *Id.* at 1359.

[105] *Id.* at 1361.

[106] *Id.*

[107] 142 S. Ct. 2587 (2022).

[108] *Sackett II*, 143 S. Ct. at 1361 (Kagan, J., concurring in the judgment) (quoting *West Virginia*, 142 S. Ct. at 2641 (Kagan, J., dissenting)).

[109] *Id.* at 1361–62.

[110] *Id.* at 1362 (Kavanaugh, J., concurring in the judgment).

Section 404(g)(1)[111]—this despite his expression of misgiving at oral argument that expanding Section 502(7) to reach adjacent wetlands by means of Section 404(g)(1) would be "kind of a bank shot way to do it."[112]

According to Section 404(g)(1) as understood by Justice Kavanaugh, a wetland can be "adjacent" not just if it adjoins a water but also if it "is separated from a covered water only by a man-made dike or barrier, natural river berm, beach dune, or the like."[113] Congress is not unfamiliar with the distinction: Justice Kavanaugh pointed out several instances in the statute where certain features are described as "adjoining."[114] Buttressing this textual analysis is the fact that every administration since President Jimmy Carter's has interpreted the Act to reach at least some non-abutting wetlands.[115] Another supporting consideration for Justice Kavanaugh was Congress's decision in 1977 to add Section 404(g)(1) in response to the controversies of the early 1970s over the scope of the original Act. Congress's adoption of the parenthetical containing the phrase "wetlands adjacent thereto" signaled Congress's approval of the agencies' view that some wetlands can be regulated, and this represented an implied expansion of Section 502(7)'s definition of "the waters of the United States."[116] Justice Kavanaugh concluded his opinion by adverting to how the majority's rule may harm the environment by inhibiting flood protection or allowing, for example, the Chesapeake Bay to be polluted through destruction of its non-adjoining wetlands. And in Justice Kavanaugh's view, it may also make things worse for the regulated public through the "regulatory uncertainty" created by perceived ambiguities in the surface-connection test.[117]

---

[111] *Id.*

[112] Transcript of Oral Argument at 79, Sackett v. EPA (*Sackett II*), 143 S. Ct. 1322 (2023) (No. 21-454).

[113] *Sackett II*, 143 S. Ct. at 1363–64 (Kavanaugh, J., concurring in the judgment).

[114] *Id.* at 1364.

[115] *Id.* at 1365.

[116] *Id.* at 1367–68.

[117] *Id.* at 1368–69.

"We Weren't All Textualists Then,"[118] But We Sure Are Now

In this final section of the article, I assess the majority opinion in light of the Kagan/Kavanaugh criticism,[119] framing the analysis with respect to four considerations: textualism, deference to executive interpretation, theories of congressional ratification of agency interpretation, and clear statement canons.

Whose textualism?

Let's begin with the most important contrast, for this is truly a case of dueling textualisms. Notably, both Justice Alito and Justice Kavanaugh professed to adopt tests for wetlands jurisdiction that are compelled by the statutory text. But for Justice Alito, the defect in Justice Kavanaugh's test is that it pays no attention to Section 502(7): "Textualist arguments that ignore the operative text cannot be taken seriously."[120] This is the decisive point in favor of Justice Alito's opinion. Although other parts of the statute may inform the meaning of "navigable waters" as used in Section 502(7),[121] nevertheless, how that term is *defined* in the statute should be privileged over possibly contrary or broader inferences drawn from non-definitional parts of the statute.[122] That is precisely what Justice Kavanaugh's opinion

---

[118] Transcript, *supra note* 112, at 52 (capitalization altered).

[119] Notably, Justice Alito's majority opinion contained only one brief paragraph responding, very broadly, to the Kagan and Kavanaugh concurrences. *See Sackett II*, 143 S. Ct. at 1344. Perhaps that light touch was a result of Justice Kagan's protestations earlier in the Term about excessive attention being given in majority opinions to dissents. *See* Andy Warhol Found. for the Visual Arts, Inc. v. Goldsmith, 143 S. Ct. 1258, 1293 (2023) (Kagan, J., dissenting) ("One preliminary note before beginning in earnest. As readers are by now aware, the majority opinion is trained on this dissent in a way majority opinions seldom are. Maybe that makes the majority opinion self-refuting? After all, a dissent with 'no theory' and '[n]o reason' is not one usually thought to merit pages of commentary and fistfuls of comeback footnotes.").

[120] *Sackett II*, 143 S. Ct. at 1344.

[121] *See* Mont v. United States, 139 S. Ct. 1826, 1833–34 (2019) (observing that "the whole-text canon requires consideration of the entire text, in view of its structure and logical relation of its many parts") (cleaned up).

[122] *See* Van Buren v. United States, 141 S. Ct. 1648, 1657 (2021) ("When a statute includes an explicit definition of a term, we must follow that definition, even if it varies from a term's ordinary meaning.") (cleaned up).

fails to do. It instead makes determinative the tangential and parenthetical use of the phrase "wetlands adjacent thereto" in a provision of a statute that does not define "navigable waters" but rather uses that term to delimit EPA's permit-transfer authority. Put another way, Justice Alito's opinion is superior because it respects the age-old canons of construction that a court must read the statute as a whole, that it must read terms in context, and that it must try to harmonize all parts of a statute.[123] The only response Justice Kavanaugh had on this point was to declare that Section 404(g)(1) *is* the operative text: "In 1977, when Congress allocated permitting authority, Congress expressly included 'adjacent' wetlands within the 'waters of the United States.'"[124] This, however, is not really an acknowledgment of Section 502(7)'s privileged status as operative text but is instead an argument for Section 502(7)'s implied amendment by Section 404(g)(1). Once properly characterized as such, Justice Kavanaugh's defense falls apart, given the absence of the "clear and manifest" evidence that the Court typically requires to credit a statutory amendment by implication.[125]

Admittedly, there exists a tension in the statute. Going all the way back to *Riverside Bayview*, the Court has acknowledged that, in ordinary parlance, a wetland is not a water. At the same time, Section 404(g)(1) is very strong evidence that Congress believed that at least some types of wetlands that are "adjacent" to covered waters are themselves regulated.[126] But it is Justice Alito's opinion, not Justice Kavanaugh's, that appropriately balances and resolves this tension. Justice Alito's opinion does so by affirming that, yes, some wetlands can be regulated, but only those wetlands that plausibly can be considered "waters" in their own right, i.e., those falling on the "adjoining" end of the "adjacent" spectrum. In contrast, Justice Kavanaugh's textualist argument ignores Section 502(7) to artificially ease the statutory

---

[123] *See* FDA v. Brown & Williamson Tobacco Corp., 529 U.S. 120, 133 (2000) ("A court must therefore interpret the statute as a symmetrical and coherent regulatory scheme and fit, if possible, all parts into an harmonious whole.") (cleaned up).

[124] *Sackett II*, 143 S. Ct. at 1367 (Kavanaugh, J., concurring in the judgment).

[125] *See id.* at 1340 (majority op.) (quoting Nat'l Ass'n of Home Builders v. Defs. of Wildlife, 551 U.S. 644, 662–664 & n.8 (2007)).

[126] Here is another defect in Justice Kavanaugh's analysis: The "plain" meaning of Section 404(g)(1) is *not* that *all* adjacent wetlands are regulated, but rather only those wetlands adjacent to certain types of traditional navigable waters.

tension and ends up violating the first principle of textualism—that one must take the text as one finds it and not add text to support one's interpretation.[127]

Deference-lite?

Perhaps the strongest point Justice Kavanaugh mustered in favor of his "adjacent" wetlands test is longstanding agency interpretation. Since the 1970s, across eight presidential administrations (as Justice Kavanaugh emphasized repeatedly), EPA and the Corps have consistently interpreted the statute to regulate not just wetlands that immediately abut or adjoin a regulated water, but also wetlands that are to varying degrees farther away from a regulated water.[128] But the force of Justice Kavanaugh's longstanding agency interpretation point is very much undercut by his inability to cast it in cognizable legal form. That is to say, Justice Kavanaugh never cited *Chevron*[129] or *Skidmore*.[130] So one is left to ask, what is the relevance of the fact that the agencies have interpreted the statute consistently over the course of several decades? Justice Alito did not respond directly to Justice Kavanaugh's longstanding agency interpretation point, but it is fair to assume that the majority's adoption of the *Rapanos* plurality standard included that opinion's rejection of the same deference argument: "a curious appeal to entrenched executive error," amounting to "a novel principle of administrative law—a sort of [then] 30-year adverse possession that insulates disregard of statutory text from judicial review."[131]

The reason Justice Kavanaugh failed to employ any legally cognizable theory of deference is likely that, for him (as for Justice Alito and Justice Scalia), the interpretive question is one of plain meaning,

---

[127] *See generally* Bostock v. Clayton County, Ga., 140 S. Ct. 1731, 1738 (2020) ("After all, only the words on the page constitute the law adopted by Congress and approved by the President. If judges could add to, remodel, update, or detract from old statutory terms inspired only by extratextual sources and our own imaginations, we would risk amending statutes outside the legislative process reserved for the people's representatives.").

[128] *See Sackett II*, 143 S. Ct. at 1365 (Kavanaugh, J., concurring in the judgment).

[129] *See* Chevron, U.S.A., Inc. v. Nat. Res. Def. Council, 467 U.S. 837, 842–44 (1984).

[130] *See* Skidmore v. Swift & Co., 323 U.S. 134, 140 (1944).

[131] Rapanos v. United States, 547 U.S. 715, 752 (2006) (plurality op.).

for which theories of deference generally are irrelevant.[132] But even if Justice Kavanaugh had made an express argument based upon a recognized theory of deference, it would still have foundered because the reasons for *why* the agencies have consistently interpreted the statute to reach more than just adjoining wetlands over the years are remarkably inconsistent. In the 1970s, EPA and the Corps thought that they could regulate essentially all wetlands.[133] By the 1990s and 2000s, the agencies had adopted a somewhat less broad version of what could be regulated but nevertheless believed that they could regulate the majority of the wetlands in the country.[134] By the time of the Trump administration, EPA and the Corps had retreated to a narrower understanding of their wetlands jurisdiction.[135] But with the advent of the Biden administration, the agencies reverted to a much more capacious view of wetlands jurisdiction.[136] This history of regulatory ping-pong, marked by vastly different rationales for why the statute should be construed to go as far or not as far as it might—variously, a broad understanding of the Commerce Clause,[137] a "hydrological connection" theory of statutory jurisdiction,[138] the significant nexus test,[139] and a modified version of the *Rapanos* plurality's continuous surface connection test[140]—is not an ideal context in which to conclude that the agencies have some considered advantage over the judicial branch in interpreting the statute. That they all would have included some non-adjoining wetlands within "the waters of the United States" seems more a function of regulatory happenstance than any special insight into congressional intent.

---

[132] Justice Kavanaugh attempted to finesse this conceptual mismatch by conceding that longstanding agency practice merely "reinforces the ordinary meaning of adjacency." *Sackett II*, 143 S. Ct. at 1364 (Kavanaugh, J., concurring in the judgment).

[133] See 33 C.F.R. § 323.2(a)(2)–(5), (d) (1978).

[134] See *Rapanos*, 547 U.S. at 724 (plurality op.).

[135] See 33 C.F.R. § 328.3(c)(1) (2021).

[136] *Id.* § 328.3(a)(4), (c)(2) (2023).

[137] See *id.* § 323.2(a)(5) & n.2 (1978).

[138] See *Rapanos*, 547 U.S. at 729–30 (plurality op.).

[139] See *Sackett II*, 143 S. Ct. at 1341.

[140] 33 C.F.R. § 328.3(c)(1) (2021).

Section 404(g)(1):

Is it a ratification, an implied amendment, or merely an interpretive signal?

Justice Kavanaugh's main defense to Justice Alito's charge of unserious textualist analysis is Section 404(g)(1). For Justice Kavanaugh, that provision encapsulates Congress's resolution of the controversy that immediately followed enactment of the Clean Water Act. Aware that the Corps had interpreted the original version of the Act to reach "adjacent" wetlands, Congress effectively ratified (although Justice Kavanaugh does not use this term) the Corps's interpretation through Section 404(g)(1)'s reference to "wetlands adjacent thereto."[141] In contrast, for Justice Alito and the majority, that reference merely confirms that some wetlands are regulated; it does not operate to impliedly amend the Act's definitional provisions.

Before addressing the merits of this argument, it is important to note that Justice Kavanaugh's ratification theory for Section 404(g)(1) is somewhat less ambitious than that advanced by EPA, in that Justice Kavanaugh does not contend that Section 404(g)(1) ratified every "jot and tittle" of the Corps's 1977 regulations.[142] Rather, Justice Kavanaugh's view is simply that Congress recognized in Section 404(g)(1) that wetlands "adjacent" to other covered waters are regulated.

But although Justice Kavanaugh's ratification argument is somewhat more modest than EPA's, it nevertheless fails to convince for many of the same reasons. The most significant defect in Justice Kavanaugh's ratification argument is that, like EPA's version, it is being employed in a posture that ill fits the theory of congressional intent which underlies ratification. Recall that the Corps's interpretation of wetlands jurisdiction was (and is) advanced as an interpretation of what Justice Alito called the "operative" provision of the statute—namely, Section 502(7)'s definition of "navigable waters" as "the waters of the United States." That fact forces Justice Kavanaugh to accept that Congress in 1977 chose to adopt the Corps's interpretation of the 1972 Act's Section 502(7) *not* by amending Section 502(7)'s operative text—again, the object of the Corps's

---

141 *Sackett II*, 143 S. Ct. at 1366–67 (Kavanaugh, J., concurring).
142 *Cf. Rapanos*, 547 U.S. at 751 (plurality op.).

purportedly ratified regulation—but rather by adding a parenthetical reference to wetlands in a new statutory section dealing with
permitting authority. I am aware of no other case where the Court
has affirmed such tangential ratification. The oddity of the asym-
metry in the ratification argument founded on Section 404(g)(1) is
well captured by Justice Thomas's concurrence: "To infer Congress'
intent to upend over a century of settled understanding and effect an
unprecedented transfer of authority over land and water to the Federal Government, based on nothing more than a negative inference
from a parenthetical in a subsection that preserves state authority, is
counterintuitive to say the least."[143]

Clear statement canons:

Vindicating congressional intent or judicially overriding it?

As I have already noted in describing the majority ruling, Justice
Alito's opinion relies on three different clear statement canons: the
federalism canon, a "fair notice" canon, and a version of the major
questions doctrine. His employment of these canons receives sharp
criticism from Justice Kagan.[144] But before addressing who has the
better argument on canons, I think it important to emphasize that a

---

[143] *Sackett II*, 143 S. Ct. at 1355 (Thomas, J., concurring). Although not cited in any
of the *Sackett II* opinions, a piece of legislative history from the 1977 amendments
casts doubt on both Justice Kavanaugh's and EPA's ratification arguments. During the
House floor debate on the 1977 conference report, Rep. Robert Bauman (R-MD) noted
that "there has been some controversy as to exactly how this new legislation will be
applied," adding that it was his understanding that "the Federal Government will
retain through the Corps of Engineers jurisdiction over navigable waters." 123 CONG.
REC. 38924, 38972 (1977). He then went on to inquire of the conference report manag-
ers: "[B]ut what does 'adjacent wetlands' mean? How far will that go? I represent
counties where when the tide comes up, a third of those countries [sic] could suddenly
be adjacent wetlands. I would hope that the States would be able to have delegated to
them control over such areas." In response, Rep. Donald Clausen (R-CA) (who man-
aged the conference report for the minority, *see id.* at 38952) stated: "I would interpret
the word 'adjacent' to mean immediately contiguous to the waterway." *Id.* at 38972.

[144] *Sackett II*, 143 S. Ct. at 1360 (Kagan, J., concurring in the judgment) ("So the
majority proceeds to its back-up plan. It relies as well on a judicially manufactured
clear-statement rule."). Justice Kavanaugh did not appear to question the propriety of
the majority's clear statement canons, just their relevance to the dispute at hand. *See id.*
at 1367 (Kavanaugh, J., concurring in the judgment) ("In any event, the decisive point
here is that the term 'adjacent' in this statute is unambiguously broader than the term
'adjoining.' On that critical interpretive question, there is no ambiguity.").

good deal of the criticism from the Kagan/Kavanaugh concurrences about how the majority uses the canons is unfair. It is unfair because the principal target of the majority opinion's use of the canons is *not* the "adjacent" wetlands standard advocated by Justice Kagan and Justice Kavanaugh, but rather EPA's significant nexus test.[145] And that is the very test that all of the Justices, including Kagan and Kavanaugh, rejected.

And as against EPA's interpretation, Justice Alito's employment of the canons of construction is beyond reproach. Let's begin with the federalism canon. That canon of construction is not only well established,[146] but also written into the statute's prefatory "declaration of goals and policy."[147] And contrary to Justice Kavanaugh's contention that the federal government "has long regulated the waters of the United States, including adjacent wetlands,"[148] the Clean Water Act's codification of the federalism canon is a direct refutation of Justice Kavanaugh's expansive reading of the regulatory and statutory history. But one need look no further than Justice Thomas's concurrence to see that, traditionally, Congress had chosen to regulate only those waters that serve as channels of interstate commerce. In short, there is no longstanding tradition of Congress seeking to regulate as far afield as the significant nexus test would regulate, or for that matter as far as Justice Kavanaugh's "adjacent" wetlands test would reach.[149]

With respect to the majority's use of what I have termed the "fair notice" canon, it is again nothing unusual for the Court to expect Congress to speak clearly when it seeks to impose significant penalties for ordinary conduct.[150] That is simply a particular application of the well-established canon of constitutional avoidance: The Court will be reluctant to adopt an administrative construction of a statute that raises significant constitutional questions.[151] For her part, Justice Kagan contended that the majority improperly put a "thumb on the

---

[145] *Sackett II*, 143 S. Ct. at 1341–43.

[146] *See* Solid Waste Ag. of N. Cook County v. U.S. Army Corps of Eng'rs (*SWANCC*), 531 U.S. 159, 172–74 (2001).

[147] 33 U.S.C. § 1251(b).

[148] *Sackett II*, 143 S. Ct. at 1367 (Kavanaugh, J., concurring in the judgment).

[149] *See id.* at 1345–54 (Thomas, J., concurring).

[150] *Id.* at 1342 (majority op.).

[151] *See, e.g., SWANCC*, 531 U.S. at 174.

scale" for property owners "to cabin the anti-pollution actions Congress thought appropriate."[152] It is true that the Sacketts are property owners and that Justice Alito's majority opinion is principally concerned with the impact that EPA's significant nexus test has on landowners. Nevertheless, these points do not mean that the majority adopted a biased interpretation of the statute meant to favor, contrary to congressional intent, private property owners over the environment. Rather, the majority simply focused on one prominent segment of the *regulated* public. It just so happens that, with respect to the Clean Water Act, the regulated public typically are landowners.[153] The majority opinion simply requires Congress to treat the regulated public in environmental matters with the same concern for fair notice and due process that we would expect Congress to evince with respect to any other issue.

Finally, what one might call a proto-version of the major questions doctrine appears briefly in Justice Alito's majority opinion—specifically, when Justice Alito rejected EPA's ratification argument based upon Section 404(g)(1). One reason he gave for that rejection is that Congress does not "hide elephants in mouseholes," i.e., "alter the fundamental details of a regulatory scheme in vague terms or ancillary provisions."[154] That of course is precisely what EPA's ratification argument, coupled with its significant nexus test, would have accomplished. Justice Kagan and Justice Kavanaugh did not respond to this elephants-in-mouseholes point directly, but rather impliedly argued that it is inapposite because Section 502(7) is not a mousehole, Section 404(g)(1) effectively amended Section 502(7), and Congress clearly intended to enact an elephant. Or, as Justice Kagan put it, "make no mistake: Congress wrote the statute it meant to. The Clean Water Act was a landmark piece of environmental legislation, designed to address a problem of 'crisis proportions.'[155] But here as with the other canons, the criticism from the concurrences is largely misplaced. Justice Alito did not say that the *concurrences'* standard would result in elephants in mouseholes, but rather that *EPA's* standard of significant nexus would do so. As for

---

[152] *Sackett II*, 143 S. Ct. at 1361 (Kagan, J., concurring in the judgment).

[153] *Id.* at 1335–36 (majority op.).

[154] *Id.* at 1340.

[155] *Id.* at 1359 (Kagan, J., concurring in the judgment).

the concurrences, the only thing Justice Alito had to say was, as noted above, on a high level of textualist methodology, uninflected by any clear-statement canon.

Parting Thoughts

In many respects, the saga of the WOTUS wars, from *Riverside Bayview* in 1985 to *Sackett II* in 2023, represents a microcosm of the significant changes in the Supreme Court's jurisprudence during that same period with respect to statutory interpretation generally.

Take deference. *Riverside Bayview* in 1985 was one of the Court's first important post-*Chevron* decisions. *SWANCC* in 2001 represented something of a retreat from *Chevron*, but not much: The Court avoided its command by basing the decision in the statute's plain meaning and clear statement canons, although *Chevron* figured prominently in the dissent.[156] By *Rapanos* in 2006, *Chevron*'s influence had waned further, receiving only passing attention in the plurality and Kennedy concurrences, though still relied on in the dissent.[157] Yet by *Sackett* in 2023, *Chevron* failed to merit a citation in any of the opinions. And as for deference generally, there are only two mentions: a glancing and unadorned reference in Justice Alito's majority opinion to EPA's request that the Court "defer to its understanding of the CWA's jurisdictional reach, as set out in its most recent rule defining 'the waters of the United States,'"[158] and Justice Kavanaugh's recitation of the supposed consistent agency interpretation supporting his "adjacent" wetlands standard.

The same with legislative history. *Riverside Bayview* is chock-full of citations to committee reports, floor debates, and failed bills. Even *SWANCC* had some of that, especially with respect to Section 404(g)(1). But with *Rapanos*, legislative history was largely relegated to the dissent. And in *Sackett II*, it is nowhere to be found, which is particularly remarkable given the concurrences' heavy reliance on Section 404(g)(1)'s supposed ratification of the Corps's earlier regulations.

---

[156] *Compare SWANCC*, 531 U.S. at 172–74 with *id*. at 191 (Stevens, J., dissenting).

[157] *See* Rapanos v. United States, 547 U.S. 715, 739 (2006) (majority op.); *id*. at 766 (Kennedy, J., concurring in the judgment); *id*. at 789, 793 (Stevens, J., dissenting).

[158] *Sackett II*, 143 S. Ct. at 1341.

And the same with textualism. *Riverside Bayview* admits that the plain meaning of Section 502(7) doesn't include wetlands, but it relies on a congeries of statutory purpose, legislative history, and expert agency judgment to read the statute to regulate wetlands. By *SWANCC*, text was triumphant, but *Rapanos* perhaps signaled a retreat, with the strongly anti-textual significant nexus test prevailing in the lower courts. And yet again, with *Sackett II*, everybody is a textualist: Justice Alito's main argument is his close textual exegesis of "waters," and he rejected EPA's test principally because the agency "has no statutory basis to impose it."[159] As for the concurrences, their main criticism of the majority's continuous surface connection test is a textualist one.[160] Indeed, at points Justice Kagan sounded like Justice Scalia redivivus: "So the majority shelves the usual rules of interpretation—reading the text, determining what the words used there mean, and applying that ordinary understanding even if it conflicts with judges' policy preferences."[161]

In summary, I believe that the Court's second *Sackett* decision will be an important one for environmental law for three reasons.

First, it signals the end of the days of reflexive agency deference, of what one might call the "green canon,"[162] of the judiciary placing a thumb on the scale for the environment. Not only is the majority opinion lacking any reference to or reliance on the water-quality purposes or goals of the Act, but those concerns are largely absent from Justice Kavanaugh's and Justice Kagan's concurrences as well. Their analyses are based principally upon the text of the statute, and although they do note the importance of wetland protection for water quality, what drives their arguments is not the effort to vindicate that purpose as such but rather their conclusion that Congress has clearly spoken through Section

---

[159] *Id.* at 1342.

[160] *See id.* at 1359 (Kagan, J., concurring in the judgment).

[161] *Id.* at 1360.

[162] The locus classicus for such a green canon would undoubtedly be *TVA v. Hill*, 437 U.S. 153, 174 (1978) ("Concededly, this view of the Act will produce results requiring the sacrifice of the anticipated benefits of the project and of many millions of dollars in public funds. But examination of the language, history, and structure of the legislation under review here indicates beyond doubt that Congress intended endangered species to be afforded the highest of priorities.") (footnote omitted).

404(g)(1). Whether one agrees with that conclusion or not, nevertheless we have come quite a ways from the days of *Riverside Bayview*, where most of the Court's opinion was consumed with the discussion of how the expert administrative agencies had determined that regulation of wetlands was essential to vindicating Congress's water quality goals in the Clean Water Act. And we have certainly come a long way from Justice John Paul Stevens's full-throated *Chevron*-based defense, in dissent in *Rapanos*, of EPA and the Corps's view of the statute.

Second, the *Sackett II* decision confirms that, indeed, we are all textualists now. Not a single vote was given for EPA's significant nexus test, which, after all, was devised by Justice Kennedy not that long ago. *Sackett II* highlights how, on this Court nowadays, one must have a text-based argument to have even a chance of winning.

And Third, the Court's development of a "fair notice" clear-statement canon promises to have significant effects in cases dealing with other environmental statutes. One can easily imagine instances where federal environmental law regulates everyday activities, and in many such statutes Congress has chosen to significantly punish violations.[163] To maintain that toxic combination will require Congress to speak clearly. *Sackett II* thus effectively precludes any federal agency from successfully invoking a vague textual interpretation if the statute is one which severely penalizes ordinary conduct.

* * *

And one final observation. The immense improvements to administrative and environmental law that the Sackett litigation has achieved for property owners in this country could not have been secured without the Sacketts themselves. The courage and perseverance reflected in their 15-year-plus fight against the abusive administrative state are to be commended. They have set the gold-standard for public interest litigants. May they soon enjoy the home they have for so long hoped to build.

---

[163] *See*, for example, the Endangered Species Act, 16 U.S.C. §§ 1531–44, which imposes significant civil and even criminal penalties on the "tak[ing]" of protected species, *see id.* § 1540(a)–(b), an action that is defined very broadly, *see id.* § 1532(19).

The *Moore* the Merrier: How *Moore v. Harper*'s Complete Repudiation of the Independent State Legislature Theory Is Happy News for the Court, the Country, and Commentators

Vikram David Amar*

Moore v Harper[1] was remarkably easy and uneasy at once. The case was extraordinarily easy because the core question presented, the validity of the so-called "Independent State Legislature" theory (ISL),[2] could reasonably admit of only one answer; the claim at the heart of ISL—that the word "legislature" in Article I's Elections Clause[3] (and presumably in Article II's Electors Clause[4] as well) refers to a "particular" entity within each state (an entity I shall call here the "ordinary elected legislature"), such that each state's ordinary elected

---

* Distinguished Professor of Law, UC Davis School of Law; Professor of Law and former Dean, University of Illinois, Urbana-Champaign, College of Law.

[1] 143 S. Ct. 2065, 2081 (2023).

[2] For background on ISL, *see generally* Vikram David Amar, *The People Made Me Do It: Can the People of the States Instruct and Coerce Their State Legislatures in the Article V Constitutional Amendment Process?*, 41 Wm. & Mary L. Rev. 1037 (2000) (demonstrating how ISL makes no constitutional sense, in an essay that appears to be the first law review article or judicial opinion to use the phrase "independent legislature" or "independent state legislature," and that was published before even the Bush-versus-Gore election); Vikram David Amar & Akhil Reed Amar, *Eradicating Bush-League Arguments Root and Branch: The Article II Independent-State-Legislature Notion and Related Rubbish*, 2021 Sup. Ct. Rev. 1 (2022) (thoroughly debunking ISL in both Articles II and I) (hereinafter *Eradicating*); Brief of *Amici Curiae* Professors Akhil Reed Amar, Vikram David Amar and Steven Gow Calabresi in Moore v. Harper, 143 S. Ct. 2065 (2023) (No. 21-1271) (same) (hereinafter *Amici Brief*).

[3] The Clause provides in relevant part that the "Times, Places and Manner of holding Elections for Senators and Representatives, shall be prescribed in each State by the Legislature thereof. . . ." U.S. Const. art. I, § 4, cl. 1.

[4] U.S. Const. art. II, § 1, cl. 2.

legislature is entitled by the federal Constitution to regulate federal elections all by itself—is thoroughly foreclosed by federal constitutional text and founding ideology,[5] the overwhelming weight of public-meaning originalist evidence,[6] and clear unbroken U.S. Supreme Court precedent spanning over a century.[7] The notion that each state's ordinary elected legislature is free from (or "independent" of) interference by any *other* institution, organ, or actor within state government, including the state constitution that created that ordinary elected legislature, the Governor, a state court enforcing state constitutional limitations, or the state's electorate itself, is as constitutionally wrong as wrong can be. Yet *Moore* was disturbingly uneasy because of the stakes involved,[8] because at least five members of the current Court had seemed to embrace (albeit sometimes provisionally) untenable ISL notions over the past decade,[9] and because,

---

[5] *See Moore*, 143 S. Ct. at 2083 (noting that the Court had already observed that founding-era dictionaries define "legislature" capaciously); *id.* at 2082 (pointing out that in *Wesberry v. Sanders*, 376 U.S. 1 (1964), the Court had read "Congress" in the Elections Clause to include the President); Vikram David Amar, *(Yet) Another Reason ISL Theory is Wrong About the Meaning of the Term State "Legislature": The Constitution's References to the Federal Counterpart — "Congress"*, JUSTIA.COM (June 30, 2022), https://bit.ly/3s2iymR (pointing out that in several places where the Constitution empowers "Congress"—even without the "by law" modifier—"Congress" does not refer specifically to a particular institution, i.e., the House combined with the Senate, but instead means the entire federal lawmaking system, which includes the President); *Amici Brief, supra* note 2, at 17–18 (same); *Moore*, 143 S. Ct. at 2084 (pointing out that in *McPherson v. Blacker*, 146 U.S. 1 (1892), the Court equated a state's "legislative power" with the "State" itself).

[6] *See Moore*, 143 S. Ct. at 2079–81, 2086–88; *Eradicating, supra* note 2, at 19–30; *Amici Brief, supra* note 2, at 7–22.

[7] *See Moore*, 143 S. Ct. at 2081–86; *Eradicating, supra* note 2, at 30–36; *Amici Brief, supra* note 2, at 28–29.

[8] If embraced, ISL would permit ordinary elected legislatures (provided they comply with federal statutory timelines) to displace state voters or state courts in the selection of presidential electors under Article II, notwithstanding state constitutional requirements regarding the roles of voters and state courts. *See Eradicating, supra* note 2, at n.117 & accompanying text.

[9] *See* Ariz. State Legis. v. Ariz. Indep. Redistricting Comm'n (AIRC), 576 U.S. 787, 824 (2015) (Roberts, C.J., dissenting, joined by Thomas & Alito, JJ.—as well as Scalia, J.); Democratic Nat'l Comm. v. Wisc. State Legis., 141 S. Ct. 28, 34 n.1 (2020) (mem.) (Kavanaugh, J., concurring in denial of application to vacate stay); Republican Party v. Degraffenried, 141 S. Ct. 732, 732–33 (2021) (mem.) (Thomas, J., dissenting from the denial of certiorari); *id.* at 738 (Alito, J., joined by Gorsuch, J., dissenting from the denial of certiorari); *Moore*, 143 S. Ct. at 2100 (Thomas, J., joined by Gorsuch, J., dissenting).

although the 6–2[10] *Moore* Court forcefully repudiated the crux of ISL once and for all, not everyone seems to fully and deeply understand the ruling. Seemingly based on a failure to fully appreciate how the various parts of the Court's opinion *necessarily* fit together (against the background of judicial federalism first principles), some in the academy[11] and elsewhere mistakenly suggest that ISL notions might continue to make significant mischief.

More specifically, the pessimists point to the fact that even as the *Moore* majority gave the lie to ISL—and made clear the Court has no tolerance for the ISLers' claim that the "Elections Clause insulates state legislatures from review by state courts for compliance with state law"[12]—the Court in the last part of its opinion observed that state-court rulings relating to federal elections, even state-court rulings rendered under *state* constitutions, technically raise federal questions that are subject to federal-court review to ensure compliance with federal constitutional provisions. Accordingly, the Court said, state courts "do not have free rein" in this realm and could be subject to federal judicial oversight if they exceed "ordinary judicial review."[13] While the Court's (to my mind banal) mention of reserved federal judicial power may cause some lawsuits to be filed, this last part of the *Moore* opinion must be understood in conjunction with *Moore*'s earlier and thorough rejection of ISL's premise that the federal Constitution protects ordinary elected legislature entities in particular. Properly understood, this last part of the *Moore* opinion and the federal judicial review it necessarily contemplates should not lead to significant problematic intermeddling going forward. Indeed, one goal of this article is to set the worriers straight and ease their minds.

---

[10] Justice Samuel Alito didn't register a view on the merits, although he joined the part of the dissent arguing that the case was moot. I do not address the mootness question in this short article, except to say I believe (and argued) that the Court had power to reach the merits. *See* Vikram David Amar & Jason Mazzone, *The Court Should Maintain Optionality in Resolving the So-Called "Independent State Legislature" (ISL) Theory by Granting Cert. in* Huffman v. Neiman *Right Away as the Justices Chew on Whether* Moore v. Harper *is Moot,* JUSTIA.COM (May 1, 2023), https://bit.ly/3OWbTXj.

[11] *See, e.g.,* Richard H. Pildes, *The Supreme Court Rejected a Dangerous Elections Theory. But It's Not All Good News.,* N.Y. TIMES (June 28, 2023), https://bit.ly/3OzS9Yq; Richard L. Hasen, *There's a Time Bomb in Progressives' Big Supreme Court Voting Case Win,* SLATE.COM (June 27, 2023), https://bit.ly/45amDHx.

[12] *Moore,* 143 S. Ct. at 2078.

[13] *Id.* at 2088–89.

But another goal is to celebrate a ruling that favored principle over politics at a time when many people accuse the Justices of being political hacks and many commentators predicted the conservative wing of the Court would go along with Republican-backed ISL notions. As discussed below, this case has many winners, including a large number of academics who rose to the occasion when ISL made a (re)appearance in 2020, and who should now feel at least somewhat better about the Court and the country. So before we look down the road to where the Justices will go after *Moore*, let us first dwell on how much *Moore* itself reflects important (and for many cynical critics unexpected) movement by many key members of the Court.

Moore on the Merits

Perhaps no member of the Court personifies the evolving and now perfectly clear high-Court rejection of ISL more than Chief Justice John Roberts. After all, he wrote the lead dissent in *Arizona Legislature v. Arizona Independent Redistricting Commission (AIRC)*,[14] a 2015 case in which an ISL claim was unsuccessfully brought to challenge an Arizona direct-democracy initiative that relocated districting power from the ordinary elected legislature to a newly created independent districting commission. In *AIRC*, Roberts suggested (without meaningful analysis) that there was a difference between a state's (permissible) decision to *supplement* the work of the ordinary elected legislature in federal-election regulation and the state's (impermissible) decision to *supplant* the work of the ordinary elected legislature altogether via the creation of an alternative regulatory body.[15] By the time of *Rucho v. Common Cause*,[16] four years later, Roberts appeared to have quietly abandoned this untenable distinction.[17] In *Rucho* he wrote an opinion for the Court that effectively blessed voter-created independent districting commissions, but he pointedly declined to cite or rely on *AIRC* as support. In *Moore*, by contrast, Roberts's opinion for the Court affirmatively and fully embraced *AIRC*'s result and

---

[14] 576 U.S. 787 (2015).

[15] *See id.* at 841 (Roberts, C.J., dissenting).

[16] 139 S. Ct. 2484 (2019).

[17] *See* Vikram David Amar, *Response to Baude/McConnell on ISL*, JUSTIA.COM (Oct. 17, 2022), https://bit.ly/3Yy5iFZ (demonstrating the distinction makes no sense in this context—in part because the Elections Clause uses the word "prescribe"—and is unworkable in any event).

reasoning. He acknowledged that, as a logical matter, *AIRC* followed from ("reinforced")[18] the reasoning in *Smiley v. Holm*[19] nearly a century earlier, a case which upheld against ISL challenge the use of a Governor's veto in congressional districting legislation. Crucially, Roberts made clear that the reasoning (underlying both *Smiley* and *AIRC*) "commands our continued respect."[20]

En route to his (and the Court's) full embrace of *AIRC*,[21] Roberts necessarily rejected not only the untenable supplement/supplant distinction that he had cryptically invoked in his *AIRC* dissent, but also the nebulous "procedure/substance" distinction that ISLers have been pressing. According to this inscrutable notion, while procedures that ordinary elected legislatures use in regulating federal elections can be dictated by the state, the substantive policy decisions such elected legislatures make cannot. As Roberts wrote in *Moore* refuting this distinction, "the [petitioners and the dissent fail to] . . . offer a defensible line between procedure and substance in this context."[22]

In light of Roberts's repudiation of these two attempts to define and protect any particular state lawmaking entity in this realm, it is no surprise that his recapitulation of the basic principle embodied in *AIRC* was clear and broad: "[A]lthough the Elections Clause expressly refers to the state 'Legislature,' it does not preclude a State from vesting congressional redistricting authority in a body other than the elected group of officials who ordinarily exercise lawmaking power."[23] In other words—and this is the nub of the matter—"Legislature" in this context means not a specific entity (the ordinary elected legislature) but whatever lawmaking system a state has selected to make rules for

---

[18] *Moore*, 143 S. Ct. at 2082.

[19] 285 U.S. 355 (1932).

[20] *Moore*, 143 S. Ct. at 2083.

[21] The majority opinion did not hedge on *AIRC* in any way, nor did it remotely intimate that *Moore*'s result would have been the same even if *AIRC* had come out the other way or were overruled. Instead, the *Moore* majority described *AIRC* as having "reinforced [but not extended or extrapolated] the teachings" of *Hildebrant* (a predecessor case) and *Smiley*, and having "embraced the core principle espoused in *Hildebrant* and *Smiley*" that redistricting must be done in accordance with each state's "prescriptions" for lawmaking. *Id*. And near the end of its analysis, *Moore* featured *AIRC* as one of the cases that had "rejected the contention that the Elections Clause vests state legislatures with exclusive and independent authority when setting the rules governing federal elections" and that the dissent simply could not account for. *Id*. at 2082–83.

[22] *Id*. at 2086.

[23] *Id*. at 2083.

federal elections. Under *AIRC,* he observed, states "'retain autonomy to establish their own governmental processes.'"[24]

Chief Justice Roberts has thus fully come around on *AIRC* and its embrace of the idea that "legislature" means "lawmaking system" rather than "particular entity." This conversion meant that he also necessarily, if gently, had to move away from what his predecessor, Chief Justice William Rehnquist (for whom Roberts himself clerked), had written in a concurring opinion in *Bush v. Gore*[25] in 2000. Rehnquist had asserted that the Elections Clause is one of "a few exceptional cases in which the Constitution imposes a duty or confers a power on a *particular*" entity within a state's government, insulating that entity from judicial review under the state constitution.[26] In other words, Rehnquist had read "legislature" to mean a particular entity, not a lawmaking system, something that *Smiley, AIRC,* and now John Roberts and the Court have emphatically rejected. Unsurprisingly, Roberts consciously declined to adopt the standard for federal-court review of state courts in this realm that Rehnquist had offered, a choice by Roberts that makes sense given his refutation of the premise on which Rehnquist's ISL-based standard of review rested. The current Chief Justice deserves kudos for *Moore*'s outcome, and for *Moore*'s thorough explanation of why the ISL dog, as one might say in North Carolina (where *Moore* arose), simply won't hunt.

Justice Brett Kavanaugh joined *Moore*'s majority opinion in full, and thus he too walked away from some pro-ISL things he had written in the runup to the 2020 election.[27] In a 2020 opinion, Kavanaugh seemed, albeit provisionally, to read "legislature" (at least in Article II) in the same way that Chief Justice Rehnquist had read it two decades earlier, to mean a particular entity (the ordinary elected legislature) whose "clearly expressed intent . . . must prevail," such that "a state

[24] *Id.* In this vein, his description of what the Court ruled in *AIRC* included the following sweeping quote: "Nothing in [the Elections] Clause instructs, nor has this Court ever held, that a state legislature may prescribe regulations on the time, place and manner of holding federal elections in defiance of provisions of the State's constitution." *Id.* (quoting *AIRC,* 576 U.S. at 817–18) (brackets in original). Thus, under *AIRC* and *Moore,* it is the state constitution, and not the will of the ordinary elected legislature, that matters.

[25] 531 U.S. 98, 111 (2000) (Rehnquist, C.J., joined by Scalia & Thomas, JJ., concurring).

[26] *Id.* at 112 (emphasis added).

[27] Indeed, Kavanaugh's writing in 2020 (which he did not follow through on in *Moore*) was the first post-2000 writing by a Justice that invoked *Bush v. Gore* to embrace ISL. *See Eradicating, supra* note 2, at 37.

court may not depart from the state election code," notwithstanding what the state's constitution may provide.[28] But *Moore* makes clear that the ordinary legislature's intent, no matter how forcefully expressed, cannot override the state constitution. Kavanaugh's joining of the majority opinion in *Moore* thus necessarily signals a reversal of course on his embrace of Rehnquist's belief that the word "legislature" in this setting denotes and protects a particular entity. Although Kavanaugh also wrote a concurrence in *Moore* (discussed in more detail below), his embrace of Roberts's opinion is a cause for celebration (even as his vote was not necessary to reach five).

Justice Amy Coney Barrett joined the majority opinion in full as well, even though she (like Roberts and Kavanaugh) had played a litigation role in *Bush v. Gore* on the Republican Party side. This serves as a good reminder that one's views as a jurist can be quite distinct from the positions one took as an advocate.

Justices Ketanji Brown Jackson, Sonia Sotomayor, and Elena Kagan were all excellent at oral argument in the case (especially Justice Jackson) and joined the majority opinion in full (and may have done even more behind the scenes). Three cheers for them!

Justice Samuel Alito viewed the case to be moot and registered no views on the merits, declining to double down on troubling pro-ISL things he had previously written. As for the latter, good for him.[29]

Justices Clarence Thomas and Neil Gorsuch did not embrace the majority's views.[30] Both Justices Thomas and Gorsuch had written strongly pro-ISL opinions long before the flood of recent scholarship and amicus briefs. Candidly, if one begins by seeing the duck, it is often hard to see the rabbit. But even these two Justices were forced to address (and ultimately chose to embrace) *Smiley*, its predecessor *Ohio ex. rel. Davis v. Hildebrant*,[31] and *AIRC*. Given that Justice Thomas dissented in *AIRC* and now seems to appreciate (or at least accept) it, this seems to be genuine progress.

[28] Democratic Nat'l Comm. v. Wisc. State Legis., 141 S. Ct. 28, 34 n.1 (2020) (Kavanaugh, J., concurring in denial of application to vacate stay) (quoting *Bush v. Gore*, 531 U.S. at 120 (Rehnquist, J., concurring)).

[29] *Cf.* Ritter v. Migliori, 142 S. Ct. 1824 (2022) (mem.) (Alito, J., dissenting from the denial of an application for a stay) (explicitly acknowledging, in an election dispute, that further briefing could change his views from what they were in the context of a request for emergency relief).

[30] *See Moore*, 143 S. Ct. at 2100 (Thomas, J., joined by Gorsuch, J., dissenting).

[31] 241 U.S. 565 (1916).

The Thomas-Gorsuch dissent is also careful in its tone and its bottom line. For example, the dissent nowhere clearly states that these two Justices, had they found the case still live, would have reversed the North Carolina Supreme Court's exercise of judicial review under the state constitution on the merits. Moreover, while these two Justices wrote they did not think the majority's "merits reasoning [was] persuasive,"[32] they found the majority's views on the merits to be of "far less consequence" than the majority's rejection of mootness.[33] And, importantly, the dissent seemed to concede that an ordinary elected legislature *can be* divested of federal-election regulation power so long as the state's constitution vests lawmaking power in another body as well. This position, which is consistent with these two Justices' embrace (or at least acceptance) of *AIRC*, essentially repudiates ISL's core claim that "legislature" means ordinary elected legislature and can mean nothing else.[34]

---

[32] *Moore*, 143 S. Ct. at 2100 (Thomas, J., joined by Gorsuch, J., dissenting).

[33] *Id. But see Degraffenried*, 141 S. Ct. at 737 (mem.) (Thomas, J., dissenting from the denial of certiorari) (arguing that the ISL question falls within the "capable of repetition yet evading review" exception to mootness).

[34] Justice Thomas seemed to suggest that for a state to take advantage of the flexibility it enjoys in this realm, the state constitutional text must itself vest "legislative" power in bodies other than the ordinary elected legislature. *Moore*, 143 S. Ct. at 2101 n.8. It is on this basis that he distinguished the Arizona situation in *AIRC* (where the Arizona constitution textually conferred legislative power in the people via the initiative process) from the North Carolina situation (where Thomas apparently believed that the state constitution did not reserve all sovereign power to the people, even though it actually did). This proffered distinction is specious insofar as it wasn't the *people* in Arizona who were themselves promulgating federal election rules in 2015, but the Independent Commission doing so (*see, e.g., Moore*, 143 S. Ct. at 2083, stating that *AIRC* held that the "redistricting [itself] is a legislative function"), and there is nothing in the Arizona Constitution conferring "legislative" power on the Commission. Moreover, in *Smiley*, the "legislative" power in Minnesota's constitution was textually vested in Minnesota's House and Senate and not the Governor, and yet Justice Thomas seemed to accept the legitimacy of the gubernatorial involvement at issue there. To the extent Thomas might counter by observing that the Governor is included in the lawmaking process elsewhere in the Minnesota constitution so too are the courts in every state; everyone agrees that, as a general matter, state courts in each state are given the power of judicial review by the state constitution to determine which statutory enactments are consistent with the state constitution and thus valid "laws." On top of all this, where does Justice Thomas's apparent insistence on clear state constitutional text come from? The question of who has been given legislative authority under a state constitution is itself a state-law question, one as to which Justice Thomas is no expert. None of his reasoning here hangs together, and Justice Thomas's failure to engage any of the direct originalist material relied on by the majority (and provided by the briefs) is more than a bit disappointing.

Is There Any *Moore* of ISL Still to Be Dealt With?

So much for how we got here. Where do things go from here? As noted earlier, the *Moore* Court said that while "ordinary" judicial review by state courts poses no federal constitutional problems, state courts do not enjoy "free rein" insofar as federal courts "have an obligation to ensure that state court interpretations of [state] law do not evade federal law" or "stifle the 'vindication . . . [of] federal . . . rights'" or "circumvent federal constitutional provisions" or "intrude upon the role specifically reserved to state legislatures."[35] What are we to make of the reservation of federal judicial power to oversee state courts in this realm?

First, rejection of state-court "free rein" in such a context is nothing new. Everyone already appreciated that state-court rulings applicable to federal elections can technically raise federal questions because of the federal-election context involved.[36] And state courts never enjoy "free rein" to interpret state law in ways that run afoul of a federal right someone claims to enjoy.[37]

Second, the federal judicial oversight of state courts that *Moore* adverts to is limited to instances in which the state courts are exercising "judicial review" under their state constitutions. As noted earlier—and this is a significant point—the majority opinion expressly recognizes that a state can vest federal-election regulatory power in entities other than the ordinary elected legislature. (Once more, "legislature" here means "state lawmaking system"; it does not refer to any particular organ of state government.) If a state were to confer *lawmaking* (rather than judicial) power on its courts in this area, nothing in *Moore* would prevent such a delegation. *Moore*'s admonition that state-court judicial review must be "ordinary" is limited to instances in which the state court has been given power to enforce the limits in the state constitution, but has not been given any lawmaking power in the federal-election realm. (And whether

---

[35] *Moore*, 143. S. Ct. at 2088–90.

[36] For example, there was unanimity among the Justices in the Bush-versus-Gore election episode that the Florida court rulings affecting the presidential election technically implicated federal questions under Article II that were within the subject-matter jurisdiction of the federal courts.

[37] After conducting several Westlaw searches, I could find not a single case in which the Court had ever used the term "free rein" in the context of latitude enjoyed by state courts, much less in any case technically presenting a federal question.

there has been such a delegation would itself be a question under state law.)

Third, and of critical importance, any constraints on state-court interpretation of state law in this realm are themselves limited to the objective of enforcing *federal* "rights," "law," and "constitutional provisions." These are the terms the Court uses, seemingly interchangeably. Preventing such federal rights and provisions from being flouted is the *only basis* for federal-court review that the *Moore* Court suggests. That is, state-court interpretations of state law pose no substantial questions appropriate for federal courts to review except to the extent that such interpretations run afoul of identifiable values reflected in federal constitutional or statutory provisions.[38] Thus, after *Moore*, the question is whether there are identifiable federal values housed uniquely in the Elections Clause that a state-court interpretation of state law might violate. The answer, given the repudiation of ISL in the bulk of *Moore*, turns out to be a rather clear: "no."[39]

The answer is "no" because there is only one federal "right" that ISLers (or others) have argued federal courts must protect to vindicate the distinctive federal interests embodied in the Elections Clause, namely, the "right" of the ordinary elected legislature to have its statutorily expressed will implemented, free from interference or oversight by other state actors. But that is precisely the "right" that was rejected, on the merits, in *Moore*. Going forward, all federal judges must heed *Moore*'s holding that the "federal rights" to be enforced under the Elections Clause have nothing to do with Article I, section 4's use of the word "legislature." *Moore* fundamentally rejects the notion that "Legislature" in Article I refers to any entity in particular. That is why those commentators who have characterized the latter part of *Moore* (reserving federal judicial oversight) as embracing a mild version of ISL are simply wrong. The residual federal-court review of state courts in this realm has nothing to do with respecting the work-product of ordinary state legislatures *per se*, much less ordinary state legislatures that are in any way "independent" from or protected vis-à-vis their state constitutions, which

[38] This is unlike the situation in which a state court asserts "adequate and independent state-law grounds" to block the raising of an unrelated federal right. In the Elections Clause context, the state-court decision would itself have to violate Article I.

[39] Other provisions, of course, might provide norms for federal courts to enforce. *See Eradicating, supra* note 2, at 43–50.

is the sum and substance of the ISL theory. The post-*Moore* review by federal courts, whatever it properly should be, would exist whether or not the misbegotten set of notions that together form ISL had ever occurred to or been advocated by anyone.

To wit, *Moore* makes three foundational principles clear: (1) state Governors can continue to exercise veto power (for any reason they like) in the congressional-election-regulation setting; (2) independent, unelected redistricting commissions can be created and can draw congressional district lines based on commissioners' views of the best election-regulation policies; and (3) the people of each state can enact explicit language into their constitutions (which state courts can then enforce), reflecting detailed and comprehensive policy judgments about the substance and procedure of congressional-election regulation. From these principles it follows ineluctably that the ordinary elected set of legislators—the body that ISL says is specially empowered and insulated to prescribe federal-election regulations—doesn't have a federally protected prerogative to "prescribe" anything at all.

Thus, after *Moore*, there is no Article I (or Article II) federal right or federal policy that confers special powers or protections upon ordinary elected state legislatures vis-à-vis other institutions of state government. Relatedly, there is no substantive federal value, in either Article I or Article II, demanding emphatically literal (or narrow) adherence to the text of state enactments. *There simply is no general federal interest in implementing any particular intra-state separation-of-powers regime or any specific textual methodology for construing state laws in this domain.*[40]

So the only "federal right" embodied directly in the Elections Clause is the right to have state courts *comply with state law.* Put differently, the "role specifically reserved to [ordinary elected] state legislatures" in Article I (to use the words from the end of *Moore*'s opinion that may have caused some people to think there is anything

---

[40] Of course, other provisions of the Constitution, unlike Articles I and II, use specific language that reflects specific and documented historical concerns with some state governmental institutions vis-à-vis others. For example, section 2 of the Seventeenth Amendment, in a single sentence, pointedly differentiates between the legislatures and executive authorities of states, and it confers appointment powers only on the latter. See Vikram David Amar, *Are Statutes Constraining Gubernatorial Power to Make Temporary Appointments to the United States Senate Constitutional under the Seventeenth Amendment?*, 35 HASTINGS CONST. L. Q. 727 (2008).

left of ISL) is precisely—no more than and no less than—whatever role state law has decided to confer. As Justice Potter Stewart put the point in an analogous context in *Oregon v. Mitchell*, "[t]he Constitution thus adopts as the federal standard the standard which each State has chosen."[41] Post-*Moore*, there is no separate federal interest in protecting the work-product of ordinary elected legislatures or anybody or anything else; the power of ordinary elected legislatures is protected under the Elections Clause only *because and to the extent that* state law chooses to protect it. And it is emphatically the province of the state courts to decide what the scope of state-law protections of the ordinary elected legislature is.

It's one thing to review state courts when a federal provision (constitutional or statutory) tells states they must regulate the filling of congressional vacancies in particular ways (i.e., the Fifteenth Amendment's command against discrimination on the basis of race) or through the use of particular actors (i.e., the Seventeenth Amendment's admonition that Governors rather than potentially gerrymandered legislative bodies appoint temporary Senators).[42] In these situations, a federal court can compare the state court's actions against the specifics of the federal substantive or procedural commands. But the matter is entirely different when there is no particular federal command other than the command that a state undertake regulation in whatever ways and through whichever actors the *state* in fact has chosen. That is the situation in the aftermath of *Moore*. Once again, recall the words of the *Moore* majority recapitulating and affirming *AIRC*: a state may "vest[] congressional redistricting authority in a body other than the elected group of officials who ordinarily exercise lawmaking power" because "[s]tates . . . . 'retain autonomy to establish their own governmental processes.'"[43] Accordingly, the Elections Clause is understood (properly, today) as if the word "state," instead of "legislature," had been used.[44]

---

[41] 400 U.S. 112, 288 (1970) (Stewart, J., joined by Burger, CJ., & Blackmun, J., concurring in part and dissenting in part).

[42] *See supra* note 40.

[43] *Moore*, 143 S. Ct. at 2083.

[44] To say that "legislature" and "state" in the Elections Clause are modernly interchangeable is not to say that the use of "legislature" at the founding didn't have certain clarifying advantages. *See Eradicating, supra* note 2, at 25–26; *Amici Brief, supra* note 2, at 19–20.

From now on, Election Clause challenges can't involve claims that state courts are ignoring a particular federally selected norm or directive (ISLers lost on the assertion of such a norm exalting the work of ordinary elected legislatures, a norm state courts necessarily and permissibly override when engaging in judicial review). Instead, Elections Clause challenges are limited to claims that state courts are misapplying or misunderstanding state law. And state law, of course, is the bailiwick of state, not federal, judges. That is Federal Courts 101. Given that: (1) there is no federal value to be enforced beyond the idea that each state should follow whatever state law the state has chosen to adopt; and (2) the bedrock starting point is that state courts are authoritative interpreters of state law, then there is very, very little left for federal courts to do. Regardless of whether the *Moore* majority fully appreciated (or preferred to downplay[45]) how much its repudiation of ISL's core minimizes the resulting role for federal courts, the ballgame was essentially over once the Court rejected the essence of ISL on the merits.

Indeed, if the U.S. Supreme Court were to assume a large role in making sure state courts rightly interpret state constitutions (pause for a minute to consider how weird that concept sounds from a federalism standpoint), such an outcome would flout more than a century of clear teachings by the Court. In *Green v. Lessee of Neal*,[46] the Court emphatically held that state courts are the master interpreters of state law. A century later, the Court in *Erie R.R. v. Tompkins*[47] reaffirmed this principle in observing that whether state law comes from statutes or judicial rulings is no concern of the federal government. And even more broadly still, in a seminal ruling from the founding era, *Calder v. Bull*,[48] the Court made clear its understanding that states have broad power under the Tenth Amendment (subject, of

[45] It is possible (perhaps even likely) that the Court in the last part of its opinion chose some language (e.g., that state courts cannot "arrogate" power that does not belong to them) in the hope of dissuading state courts from being too adventurous in this realm. Indeed, such language probably explains why some academics understandably have expressed concern about the future. But even if the Court would *prefer* state courts to be strait-laced in this realm, the rejection of the "independence" of ordinary elected legislatures, combined with background federalism principles, prevents the federal judiciary from meddling significantly even when state courts innovate.

[46] 31 U.S. (6 Pet.) 293, 297 (1832).

[47] 304 U.S. 64, 78 (1938).

[48] 3 U.S. (3 Dall.) 386, 387–88 (1798).

course, to republican government principles) to blend legislative and judicial roles.

Conferral of a large role on federal courts in this arena would also ignore the structural ways in which state supreme court judges (who are often elected by statewide, ungerrymandered electorates and thus accountable to them) are very different from appointed and life-tenured federal judges, who are rightly much more confined in their lawmaking powers.

To be sure, state courts can get state law wrong, but we normally think they are empowered to decide what state law is. And constitutionally speaking, there is no distinctive basis for distrust in this realm. Remember, ISL purports to be based on the "deliberate" use of the word "legislature" in Article I, section 4. But nowhere does Article I, section 4 mention state courts or state judges, much less single out these actors (any more than Governors or independent commissions or the state electorates) for any special (negative) treatment.[49] If state courts are to be distrusted here, the distrust would apply even if Article I, section 4 had directly used the word "state" rather than "legislature." Similarly, if state courts were to warrant distrust in this realm, then they would have to be distrusted as to state-law interpretations anytime anyone alleged a federal violation more generally. After all, interpretation of state law by state courts could conceivably implicate alleged federal rights in virtually any domain—tort law, family law, criminal law, etc.—and yet in all those settings federal courts rightly take a hands-off approach, absent a particular reason to think state courts are being manipulative.

All of this explains why the writers of all the opinions in *Moore* effectively recognize (albeit using different language to convey the point) that instances in which state courts exercise judicial review in a way that is not "ordinary" will necessarily be quite rare. Justice Thomas's dissent, in particular, points out that federal-court review will have to be "forgiving" now that state courts need not defer to the wishes of the ordinary legislature (insofar as all judicial review involves at least the potential override of those wishes). This is

---

[49] Indeed, as the briefing and majority opinion in *Moore* make clear, state-court judicial review to enforce provisions of state constitutions was well known and well accepted even before the creation of the U.S. Constitution. There is no meaningful suggestion in the historical record that either Article I or Article II represented an exception to this background state-court power.

especially true given that all constitutions (federal and state) mark, as a textual matter "only . . . [the] great outlines" of that which is allowed and prohibited.[50] For this reason, an argument that many ISLers have often made—that state courts cannot invoke "vague" state constitutional provisions in the federal-election regulation arena—will (rightly) go nowhere. (Imagine if the U.S. Supreme Court could not undertake "ordinary" judicial review simply because the constitutional provision in question were worded in grand or vague terms.)

Justice Thomas also (rightly) intimates that methods of appropriate constitutional interpretation (including the weight given to *stare decisis*) permissibly vary by state, making federal-court review necessarily more deferential.[51] Justice Kavanaugh's concurring opinion highlighted deference as well, and it provisionally embraced Chief Justice Rehnquist's suggestion that a state court would have to "impermissibly distort[]"[52] state law before a federal court could intervene. The "impermissibly distort" standard connotes a requirement of intentional deception about the meaning of state law rather than a mere good-faith (if heated) disagreement over inevitably controversial and indeterminate state-law questions. Chief Justice Roberts, for his part, invoked similar verbs—"evade," "circumvent," and "sidestep"[53]—that suggest a requirement of intentional and conscious manipulation by state courts before a substantial federal question would be presented.

A day after *Moore* issued and in a different majority opinion (*Biden v. Nebraska*), Roberts again drove home the key point that judicial interpretations (directly applying or informed by constitutional values)

[50] *Moore*, 143 S. Ct. at 2015–06 (Thomas, J., joined by Gorsuch J., dissenting).

[51] *See id.* at 2105. Given the range of substantive and methodological diversity that characterizes state constitutions and their proper interpretation, we should remember that what might seem at first blush to the Supreme Court to be state-court overreaching might actually be proper under that state's legal and interpretive traditions. There is no general federal common law of state constitutional interpretation (or state statutory interpretation or state common-law interpretation). A proper test here cannot be whether a state supreme court is suitably "textualist," as some members of the U.S. Supreme Court might seek to define textualism. A given state legislature, the state people who elect that state legislature, and the spirit of that state's overarching state constitution might well prefer a state-law jurisprudence that is more purposive, or structural and holistic, or precedent-based, or representation-reinforcing, or democracy-promoting, or canon-driven, than relentlessly textual.

[52] *Id.* at 2090 (Kavanaugh, J., concurring).

[53] *Id.* at 2088.

can be contentious and controversial without coming close to exceeding the judicial function. In words that seem tailor-made to guide the post-*Moore* "ordinary judicial review" inquiry, he wrote:

> It has become a disturbing feature of some recent opinions to criticize the decisions with which they disagree as going beyond the proper role of the judiciary. . . . We have employed the traditional tools of judicial decisionmaking . . . [in reaching the decision we reach today, and while] [r]easonable minds may disagree with our analysis—in fact, at least three do—[w]e do not mistake this plainly heartfelt disagreement for disparagement. It is important that the public not be misled either. Any such misperception would be harmful to this institution and our country."[54]

The same observations about damage to institutions and the country apply, perhaps even more forcefully, with respect to federal judicial intervention in state-court interpretation of state law. For these reasons, a federal court will have to tread very carefully before overturning a state-court ruling interpreting state law on the ground that the state court exceeded its judicial role within the meaning of state law.

These points also help show why the examples of federal judicial oversight *Moore* mentions—examples which are sensible on their own terms—in reality demonstrate that second-guessing under the Elections Clause would be exceptional and problematic. *Moore* invokes three cases in two constitutional settings in which the Supreme Court declined to reflexively accept state courts' interpretations of state law. Crucially, in both of those settings—involving the Takings Clause and Contracts Clause, respectively—state law interpretation is logically antecedent to the protection of a separate federal right. Indeed, each setting concerns a dependent downstream federal right that exists against the state itself. The Takings Clause and the Contracts Clause both protect federal interests (in property and contract rights, respectively) beyond what a state chooses to protect. By contrast, post-*Moore*, the Elections Clause protects only those interests that a state has itself chosen to protect.

When there exists a separate federal right (albeit a right dependent on state-law definitions), state courts obviously cannot be fully trusted to apply state law consistent with the vindication of such a

---

[54] Biden v. Nebraska, 143 S. Ct. 2355, 2375–76 (2023).

federal entitlement. This is especially so where the federal right in question runs against the state itself such that all state entities—including state courts—might be tempted to warp state law to protect the state fisc.[55] It is thus not remotely surprising that in the two cases *Moore* cites in the takings context, *Phillips v. Washington Legal Foundation*[56] and *Webb's Fabulous Pharmacies Inc. v. Beckwith*,[57] the Supreme Court was wary of accepting at face value state-court definitions of property that might defeat the claims asserted by the federal claimants. What is perhaps most noteworthy in these two cases is that the Court explicitly confined its willingness to (somewhat independently) examine the contours of state law to circumstances where the right in question was against the state and involved the state fisc such that all state institutions, including state courts, had an incentive to distort state law. For example, the Court's observation in *Phillips* that "a State may not sidestep the Takings Clause by disavowing traditional property interests long recognized under state law" was overtly limited to "confiscatory regulations (as opposed to those regulating the use of property)."[58]

Similar features explain the case the *Moore* Court cited in the Contracts Clause setting, *Indiana ex. rel. Anderson v. Brand*.[59] In that dispute, public school teachers claimed that the state had reneged on a long-term contract that they had with the state itself. It was in that context that the Court observed:

> The Supreme Court [of Indiana] has decided, however, that it is the state's policy not to bind school corporations by contract for more than one year. On such a question, one primarily of state law, we accord respectful consideration and great weight to the views of the state's highest court, but, in order that the constitutional mandate may not become a dead letter, we are bound to decide for ourselves whether a contract was made, what are its terms and conditions, and whether the State has, by later legislation, impaired *its [own] obligation.*[60]

[55] For more on this point, *see Eradicating, supra* note 2, at n.111 & accompanying text.

[56] 524 U.S. 156 (1998).

[57] 449 U.S. 155 (1980).

[58] *Phillips*, 524 U.S. at 167 (parenthetical in original).

[59] 303 U.S. 95 (1938).

[60] *Id.* at 100 (emphasis added). In the final case cited by *Moore*, General Motors v. Romein, 503 U.S. 181, 186 (1992), the Court fully followed the state-law interpretation of the state courts.

Unlike the Takings and Contracts Clause cases cited by Chief Justice Roberts, the Elections Clause—post-*Moore*—does not involve any federal right that is separate from state-law entitlements and that state courts might have an incentive to evade, circumvent, or sidestep. Simply put, the Elections Clause does not embody any federal decision to protect any particular entity or particular substantive interest within state decisionmaking. Once again, the authority of an ordinary elected state legislature (or any other organ of state government) is protected by the Elections Clause only to the extent that state law has chosen to protect it: "The Constitution thus adopts as the federal standard the standard which each State has chosen."[61] If federal courts were to be skeptical of state-court determinations of state law in the Elections Clause arena, there would be literally no reason for federal courts not to be skeptical of all state-court interpretations of state law. And if that happened all of federalism would become a dead letter.

Of course, state (and federal) court judges might have political biases. But potential judicial bias is present and relevant in any setting—think of environmental or employment regulation or tax policy (areas where partisan disagreements are pronounced). Yet we don't, as a general matter, say that the possibility of bias forecloses courts from performing their general dispute-resolution and norm-declaration roles throughout our legal system. We expect that state judges in congressional-election or presidential-election disputes can reasonably engage in the same kinds of judicial processes and consider the same kinds of interpretive factors that have historically guided them to resolve election contests and other important state statutory and constitutional questions. As long as state courts can reasonably be said to be doing so, federal courts will necessarily defer to state-court understandings of state statutory and constitutional law meanings.

With these principles clearly in mind, one can see that the better constitutional analogy to post-*Moore* federal-court review under the Elections Clause is not review under the Takings Clause or the Contracts Clause, but instead review under a clause much closer to (the Election Clause's) home—Article I, section 2. This provision, which governs *who* is eligible to vote in federal elections as distinguished from the Election Clause's treatment of *how* federal elections shall

---

61 *Mitchell*, 400 U.S. at 288 (Stewart, J., concurring in part and dissenting in part).

be run, provides in relevant part: "the [voters] in each State [for the House of Representatives] shall have the Qualifications requisite for [voters] of the most numerous [legislative branch in state elections]."[62] Pursuant to this provision, voter eligibility for congressional elections incorporates whatever voter-eligibility standards exist in state law for state elections. The Constitution does not mandate any particular set of qualifications, but instead delegates decisions over eligibility to the state governments themselves. In the same way, the Elections Clause (as understood in *Moore*) does not mandate within each state who shall regulate federal elections or what those regulations must look like, but instead directs states themselves to make such decisions.[63] In the setting of Article I, section 2, it would quite unusual indeed for the Supreme Court to second-guess a state high court's interpretation of state-election eligibility laws, even though the (resulting) question of federal voting eligibility would, technically, raise a federal question susceptible of review in federal courts.

Another good analogy is the creation of federal crimes in federal enclaves located within state boundaries. The so-called Assimilated Crimes Act (ACA)[64] provides that federal criminal law incorporates the state criminal law of the state surrounding the federal enclave.[65]

Under the ACA, the federal system (albeit this time Congress rather than the Constitution itself) has similarly chosen to delegate federal regulation to the states. When applying this statute, federal courts recognize that although the question whether a crime has been committed under the ACA is appropriate for the federal courts to resolve, federal judges should (tightly) follow the state-law interpretations of state courts. As the Fourth Circuit explained in one case, for example:

> The Assimilative Crimes Act [ACA] by its own terms incorporates into federal law only the criminal law of the jurisdiction within which the federal enclave exists.

---

[62] U.S. CONST. art I, § 2, cl. 1. The same essential language is also used for Senate elections in the Seventeenth Amendment.

[63] Cf. *Moore*, 143 S. Ct. at 2084 (quoting *McPherson*, 146 U.S. at 25, for the notion that "State" and "legislative power" are essentially interchangeable in the federal election context).

[64] 18 U.S.C. § 13.

[65] *See, e.g.,* United States v. Eure, 952 F.2d 397 (4th Cir. 1991) (per curiam).

> The Supreme Court of Virginia has held [state law to mean X].
> *We, of course, must accept this authoritative interpretation of Virginia law.*[66]

To be sure, both Article I, section 2 and the ACA do not merely confer federal-election-regulation powers and duties upon the states, but also require that the states themselves utilize the same regulations that will apply federally. And there is safety in generality.[67] The Elections Clause, by contrast, does not require that a state regulate federal and state elections identically.[68] As I have written before,[69] where a state chooses to regulate federal elections differently than state elections (either in the lawmaking system used for federal-election regulation or in the regulations themselves), a federal court might be justified in ensuring that the state has a valid, non-invidious reason for such differentiation. But in the overwhelming majority of real-world situations, state-court rulings in the election-law realm apply to both state and federal elections, and in all such cases it makes no sense for federal courts to apply rigorous review of state-court decisions.

In discussing federal judicial oversight, the instinct to try to formulate clear standards of deference is understandable (and many of the Justices in *Moore* seemed interested in doing that.) But specifying a standard of review in abstract terms may be less helpful to understanding the actual oversight federal courts are expected to perform in the real world than is specifying the consequences that would inevitably ensue in a given case if the applicable level of deference were overcome to justify federal-court intervention. This brings us to a very useful point that builds on the preceding discussion. Just as "safety in generality" calls for a very high level of deference, if that deference is overcome by evidence of state

---

[66] United States v. Rowe, 599 F.2d 1319, 1320 (4th Cir. 1979) (per curiam) (emphasis added). Even those circuits that say state cases are not binding appear to use "binding" only "in the traditional sense of a higher court's caselaw controlling decisions of a lower court. *See* United States v. Smith, 965 F. Supp. 756, 761 (E.D. Va. 1997). "Obviously, because state courts do not review federal-court decisions, state substantive criminal caselaw is not binding in this traditional sense." *Id.* Moreover, even circuits that purport not to be bound by state-court rulings virtually always end up applying and following the relevant state-court decisions.

[67] *Cf.* Railway Express Agency, Inc. v. New York, 336 U.S. 106, 112 (1949) (Jackson, J., concurring) (explaining that broader application of a law is a safeguard against unreasonable or unfair legislation).

[68] *See AIRC*, 576 U.S. at 819 n.25.

[69] *See Eradicating, supra* note 2, at 46.

judicial wrongdoing and infidelity to state law sufficient to violate the Elections Clause, then such evidence would for similar reasons also always (I can't think of a plausible real-world hypothetical in which it wouldn't) call for preventing state courts from applying their misbegotten interpretation to *state elections* too. (For example, if a federal court were to reject state-court determinations of voter eligibility in the context of Article I, section 2 in a federal election, that rejection would inevitably have to apply to state-election voter eligibility as well.)

In other words, if the Supreme Court believes that state courts have misbehaved by flouting state law in violation of the Elections Clause, then the federal court would have to be prepared to ensure that state elections are free from the same egregious state-court action. Lawlessness so severe as to violate the Elections Clause would also seem inevitably to run afoul of many federal constitutional provisions when applied to state elections. A state-court ruling sufficiently corrupt, aberrant or irrational to warrant federal-court oversight under the Elections Clause would also fail, for use in state elections, to survive even rational basis review under the Equal Protection Clause (which requires a rational fit to a *permissible* government purpose), much less the heightened scrutiny that is implicated on account of the fundamental "right to vote" in any election, state or federal.[70] And state-court rulings concerning state separation-of-powers or state-law individual rights that are so far-fetched and unforeseeable as to not count as good-faith interpretations of state law would also violate the due process, fair notice, and rule-of-law concerns embodied in the Fourteenth Amendment (and, I would argue, also in the Guarantee Clause and elsewhere in the Constitution).[71] Put conversely, if a state

---

[70] *See, e.g.*, Harper v. Va. Bd. of Elections, 383 U.S. 663, 670 (1966).

[71] *See, e.g.*, Roe v. Alabama, 68 F.3d 404 (11th Cir. 1995) (affirming finding of a likely due process violation when state-court ruling that ignored clearly stated absentee-ballot-signature requirements seemingly came from nowhere, disregarded past practice, and upset settled expectations of voters, would-be voters, and political campaigns). Thus, while a state-court ruling that so mangles state law as to be truly unfaithful to it certainly can implicate a federal interest, such an interest, though perhaps implicit in the Elections Clause, would not be uniquely grounded in Article I. If a federal court is inclined to find that a state court genuinely disregarded, rather than interpreted, state law with regard to the lawmaking system the state has chosen for federal-election regulation or with regard to the federal-election regulations themselves, then the high bar that would have been met would be akin to the one applied in due process settings, and such a conclusion by a federal court would doom application of the state-court ruling in state elections as well as federal contests, provided that the state was regulating state and federal elections in the same ways, thus illustrating that the constitutional flaw is not distinctively limited to Article I.

judicial interpretation is rational enough to pass federal constitutional review for purposes of state elections, it would be hard if not impossible to conceive of a basis for saying the state courts misinterpreted state law for purposes of the Elections Clause.[72]

At the end of the day, the "federal law," "federal constitutional rights," and "federal constitutional provisions" whose enforcement requires (according to *Moore*) federal-court review in this arena will have to involve one or both of two kinds of federal law. First are particular federal statutes and federal constitutional provisions relating to elections (such as the Voting Rights Act and the Fifteenth, Nineteenth, and Twenty-Sixth Amendments) that reflect particular concerns (often relating to equality). And second are more generally applicable due process/rule-of-law/republican-government "states must not flout state law on which voters rely in election settings" principles (that are not specific to, but that can be said to be implicated by, the Elections Clause) that prevent state courts, acting as courts, from truly making things up out of nowhere in ways that upset the settled expectations of voters. But, and here's the key point, all of these federal provisions and values operate to constrain state courts when those courts issue rulings affecting *state*, and not just *federal*, elections. So a federal court should (whenever states are treating federal and state elections similarly) not be prepared to characterize a state court's invocation of judicial review in a federal election setting as other than "ordinary" unless the federal court is prepared to do so for purposes of state elections as well. And that sets a high bar indeed.[73]

---

[72] To be sure, Article I, section 4 governs *federal* elections, such that the federal system has a stake in the game. But remember that Article I's drafters and ratifiers explicitly, consciously and publicly chose to confer power on state governments to administer congressional elections (opting for a presumptively decentralized, rather than an inherently federalized, election system), and specifically identified Congress (along with the President)—*not the Supreme Court*—as the federal entity empowered to regulate congressional elections, or refuse to seat ostensibly elected members of Congress, when states are doing bad things. As far as I can tell there is no originalist evidence to suggest federal courts play a key role here. And the same goes for Article II and presidential elections, even more so given the lack of explicit congressional power to regulate selection of presidential electors.

[73] "Ordinary judicial review," it should also be noted, is not limited to state-court rulings that invalidate statutory enactments in the name of the state constitution. Ordinary judicial review in state court also includes interpretations of state statutes, via avoidance techniques and the like, in the light of, or against the backdrop of, the state constitution. Federal courts do likewise all the time.

Moore Winners

The winners in *Moore* include, but are not limited to, the respondents. Perhaps the biggest winner is American democracy itself. Within the realm of congressional elections alone, an opposite result in *Moore* would have, as a necessary logical matter, called *AIRC* into doubt and made solving the partisan gerrymandering problem much harder. An opposite result in *Moore* would have had even more dangerous implications for presidential elections. To be sure, I have previously explained why ISL is much less plausible for Article II than for Article I in any event, and indeed why ISL's embrace in Article I would actually have made its embrace in Article II by fair-minded jurists even *less* defensible.[74] But the reality is that had *Moore* come out the other way, many folks would have argued that ordinary elected legislatures enjoy unfettered power over presidential elections, even to the point of having the authority (provided it were exercised in a manner consistent with federal statutory timelines) to oust the state peoples and the state courts from their traditional roles (roles often embodied in state constitutions) in selecting presidential electors. In the context of the 2024 presidential election and the modern partisan makeup of elected state legislatures,[75] that would have been catastrophic.

A win for petitioners would also have been devastating for the Court (and for its leader, John Roberts). ISL was and is an embarrassingly weak theory, especially judged by the originalist yardstick to which the Court has recently committed itself. Had the Court embraced ISL after what the Justices said in *Dobbs* and *Bruen* about the importance of history and original understandings, very, very few honest analysts would have been able to take the Court seriously. And the drive on Capitol Hill to impose radical reforms on the Court would have (rightly) picked up a great deal of steam, notwithstanding any efforts Chief Justice Roberts might make to forestall intrusion by Congress and the president.

---

[74] *See Eradicating, supra* note 2, at n.90 & accompanying text; *Amici Brief, supra* note 2, at 30–31.

[75] *See* Vikram David Amar, *Musings on Last Week's New York High Court Ruling Invalidating Partisan Gerrymandering, With Special Attention to the So-Called Independent-State-Legislature Theory,* Justia.com (May 6, 2022), https://bit.ly/445eym0.

That points up another winner—originalism. If one asks how Chief Justice Robert's (6–2 merits) opinion in *Moore* differs from Justice Ruth Bader Ginsburg's narrow 5–4 majority opinion in *AIRC*—which also rejected ISL—the most significant answer is that *Moore* contains a whole section on originalism, on the history right before and right after the Constitution's adoption concerning the alleged "independence" of ordinary elected legislatures. That, more than anything else, might explain the apparent change of heart by so many Justices. Notably, not a *single* brief by the parties or the amici in the *AIRC* litigation mentioned (much less analyzed) *any* of the originalist evidence featured in *Moore*. For those Supreme Court advocates who don't yet understand, *Moore* is another signal that where originalist evidence is relevant, litigants who disregard it or (like the petitioners in *Moore*) fail to plausibly account for it, do so at their peril.

That brings me to the final winner—legal and history[76] scholars. Whether or not their briefs and articles were cited in the Justices' opinions, scholars who participated as amici and who published essays in the years leading up to *Moore* were clearly influential in resolving this case. The respondents' briefs made effective use of scholarship, and examination of the structure and content of the majority opinion suggests that the ideas and evidence scholars contributed had significant impact. Indeed, scholars provided something none of the parties actually did—a full-throated explanation of how ludicrous ISL is, and how one can't embrace ISL and at the same time accept *Smiley* and *AIRC*.

The respondents were understandably reluctant to insult many of the Justices who had worked on *Bush v. Gore* and who had expressed at least provisional support for ISL. The respondents thus tried to offer the Court an approach that would have recognized constitutionally mandated "primacy"[77] with respect to the actions of the ordinary elected legislature (and that would have essentially allowed the Court to undo *AIRC*, since, as the petitioners forcefully ob-

---

[76] Some of the best and perhaps most influential amicus briefs relating to founding history came from law professors as well as professional historians. This is particularly heartening given the questions that have been raised about how a Court lacking in professional history training can properly do originalism. *See, e.g.*, N.Y. State Rifle & Pistol Ass'n v. Bruen, 142 S. Ct. 2111, 2130 n.6 (2022).

[77] *See* Non-State Respondent's Brief at 24, Moore v. Harper, 143 S. Ct. 2065 (2023) No. 21-1271).

served, fully displacing an elected legislature is hardly consistent with respecting its "primacy"). This approach was certainly much less dangerous than an even more robust ISL, but it was not fully coherent either. "Legislature" refers either to a "particular" entity (as ISL says) or to a "lawmaking system chosen by the state," as history, theory, and analogy to the meaning of "Congress" in the Constitution[78] all establish.[79] If the former holds, *AIRC* (and *Smiley* too) cannot survive. If the latter holds, then there is nothing to the idea of a federally mandated "primacy" of ordinary elected legislatures or any other organ of state government.

Happily, the Court opted for the latter, rejecting facile distinctions such as process/substance and supplement/supplant. The Court's straightforward repudiation of ISL is reflected in *Moore's* restatement of the heart of *AIRC*: The "Elections Clause['s] express[] . . . refer[ence] to the 'Legislature,' . . . does not preclude a State from vesting congressional redistricting authority in a body other than the elected group of officials who ordinarily exercise lawmaking power," because "[s]tates . . . 'retain autonomy to establish their own governmental processes.'"[80] This position was urged by members of the scholarly community[81] much more forcefully than the parties, and it was the position that prevailed. Crucially, the Court's embrace of this position on the merits is, as explained above, what makes further mischief by federal courts very unlikely. This should undoubtedly provide a shot in the arm for conscientious scholars who are needed now more than ever to help the skilled Supreme Court bar and the Justices themselves.

---

[78] *See* Amar, *supra* note 5.

[79] As Yogi Berra reportedly said: "When you come to a fork in the road, take it." Although ridiculed, the adage does rightly suggest that, at least sometimes, you simply have to make a choice.

[80] *Moore*, 143 S. Ct. at 2083 (quoting *AIRC*, 576 U.S. at 816).

[81] *See, e.g., Amici Brief, supra* note 2. The Court's opinion aligned with most of the basic points we urged in our brief. It bears noting, in this regard, that dozens of well-known and highly regarded academics wrote, submitted, or joined amicus briefs critiquing ISL, while only one person who is famous (if not always for good reasons) and who has been recently associated with an academic institution weighed in to support the petitioners: John Eastman.

Intellectual Property in OT 2022: Two Baby Steps in the Right Direction

Gregory Dolin, M.D.[*]

Introduction

One of the key conundrums of intellectual property is its ability to simultaneously "promote the Progress of Science and useful Arts"[1] and inhibit such progress.[2] The ability to acquire patents, copyrights, trademarks, and other types of intellectual property serves as a potential reward for creating new knowledge and thus serves as an engine driving innovation.[3] However, once the relevant intellectual property right is granted, the non-owners who may seek to move the knowledge further still must now pay the rights-holder for using the work. Thus, a movie director must pay a license fee to an author of a book if the director wants to turn that book into a movie, and someone wishing to sell the McRib must pay McDonald's for the right to use that name. Of course, if the book author refuses to sell the rights to the movie producer, then the movie will not be made. And to the extent McDonald's doesn't wish to license its name to a particular sandwich shop, consumers will have fewer locales where they can purchase the McRib. As the Seventh Circuit observed "[o]nce a work has been written and published, any rule requiring people to compensate the author slows progress in literature and art, making

[*] Associate Professor of Law, University of Baltimore School of Law; Georgetown University Law Center, J.D.; State University of New York at Stony Brook School of Medicine, M.D.; The George Washington University, M.A.; Johns Hopkins University, B.A.

[1] U.S. Const. art I, § 8, cl. 8.

[2] *See, e.g.,* Dmitry Karshtedt, *Photocopies, Patents, and Knowledge Transfer: "The Uneasy Case" of Justice Breyer's Patentable Subject Matter Jurisprudence,* 69 Vand. L. Rev. 1739, 1750 (2016).

[3] *See, e.g.,* Gregory Dolin, *Do Patent Challenges Reduce Consumer Welfare?,* 84 U. Chi. L. Rev. Online 256, 259–60 (2017).

useful expressions 'too expensive,' forcing authors to re-invent the wheel, and so on."[4]

It is this tension between the costs and benefits of intellectual property rights where most disputes arise and where courts and Congress have attempted to craft an appropriate balancing test or, as Judge Learned Hand observed early in the 20th century, pick a correct level of generality at which to evaluate competing claims of rights.[5]

Overlaying the general tension are First Amendment concerns.[6] A reader of a book has a First Amendment right to comment on the book's content, critique its approach, and the like. Someone wishing to praise or criticize the taste of the McRib needs to use the word "McRib" to do so, even if it is a registered trademark of the McDonald's corporation. But direct commentary on a prior work of art, such as "worst book I ever read," or "best sandwich ever," is not the only type of commentary that people engage in and that the law is attuned to. For example, people often parody famous works of art or existing trademarks. Someone making a movie or writing a book or painting a scene may include McDonald's famed Golden Arches in the depicted scenes, or may have one of the characters hold a copyrighted photo. If every movie director had to compensate every single trademark holder whose restaurant, car, or baseball cap appeared in one of the shots, it would be nearly impossible to make any movie—certainly impossible to make one that is shot on the streets of a real city. At the same time, letting newcomers use prior copyrighted works and marks, in any context and with only small alterations, would undermine the very purpose of the congressionally created intellectual property regimes.[7]

In two cases heard in the October Term 2023, the Supreme Court faced essentially the same question—what does it take for the later work to count as a "commentary," or "parody" on the original work and thus escape liability for trespassing on the property rights of the

---

[4] Nash v. CBS, Inc., 899 F.2d 1537, 1540 (7th Cir. 1990).

[5] *See* Nichols v. Universal Pictures Corp., 45 F.2d 119, 121 (2d Cir. 1930).

[6] *See* Harper & Row Publishers, Inc. v. Nation Enterprises, 471 U.S. 539, 584 n.7 (1985).

[7] *See, e.g.,* Graver Tank & Mfg. Co. v. Linde Air Prod. Co., 339 U.S. 605, 607 (1950) ("[T]o permit imitation of a patented invention which does not copy every literal detail would be to convert the protection of the patent grant into a hollow and useless thing.").

original work's creator? The issues in these two cases were remarkably similar, although one case concerned the construction of the Copyright Act, while the other touched on the Lanham Act (which governs federal trademark law). Particularly interesting is that although the cases reached a consistent outcome, Justice Elena Kagan authored the unanimous opinion in one case but filed a rather biting dissent in another. The overall message from the Court, however, is clear—one remains free to comment on, critique, parody, or transform prior works, without worry that one will be held liable for infringement. However, one is not free to free ride on the efforts of others in order to promote one's own art or business without properly compensating the original creators. It is this focus on "free riding" that, at least in the OT 2023 Term, got the Court to understand and say that "intellectual property" is indeed *property*.

I. Jack Daniel's v. VIP Products

Jack Daniel's turned out to be perhaps the less controversial of the two cases and resulted in a unanimous opinion by Justice Kagan.[8]

At issue in the case was a chewable toy produced by respondent VIP Products and called "Bad Spaniels."[9] The toy itself is shaped like a miniature bottle of Jack Daniel's Old No. 7 whiskey with its familiar square shape (which is trademarked).[10] The writing on the toy is in the same font as, and utilizes the same filigree as, the original whiskey bottle.[11] There are, of course, differences. Instead of using the words "Jack Daniel's," the chewable toy sports a "Bad Spaniels" logo. And instead of the words "Old No. 7 Brand Tennessee Whiskey," the toy makes an attempt at some (admittedly sophomoric) humor, sporting "The Old No. 2 on Your Tennessee Carpet" writing.[12]

Jack Daniel's, however, either did not see or did not appreciate the humor. Instead, it sued VIP Products, alleging that VIP infringed its marks by leading consumers to think that Jack Daniel's had created,

---

[8] Justice Sonia Sotomayor filed a concurring opinion that was joined by Justice Samuel Alito. Justice Neil Gorsuch also filed a concurring opinion joined by Justices Clarence Thomas and Amy Coney Barrett. Nevertheless, all justices joined in Justice Kagan's opinion.

[9] Jack Daniel's Properties, Inc. v. VIP Prod. LLC, 599 U.S. 140, 149 (2023).

[10] *Id.*

[11] *Id.*

[12] *Id.*

or was otherwise responsible for, the dog toy. Additionally, Jack Daniel's argued that VIP had diluted its marks by associating the famed whiskey with dog excrement.[13]

The law of trademark infringement (although often taught as a semester-long stand-alone course in U.S. law schools) can be rather simply stated—a person is liable for infringing another's mark if a "reasonably prudent consumer" is likely to be confused as to the source of the goods in question.[14] In other words, if a consumer upon seeing Mark A is likely to believe (even if erroneously) that goods bearing such a mark really come from a company owning Mark B, then Mark A infringes Mark B. For example, a reasonable consumer may be misled into thinking that "MacDonald's" or "McDonald" is really the same company as the original McDonald's, and therefore the former two marks would infringe the original McDonald's trademark.

The law also provides an additional layer of protection for so-called "famous" trademarks. A "famous" mark is one that "is widely recognized by the general consuming public."[15] So McDonald's, Nike, Budweiser, and Mercedes are all famous marks, whereas your local (and hypothetical) "Matryoshka Russian Restaurant" isn't. A famous mark is protected not only against copycats who seek to utilize confusingly similar marks, but also from "dilution," either by "blurring," or as more relevant here, "tarnishment."[16] A mark is diluted by tarnishment whenever it is used by the accused infringer in a way "that harms the reputation of the famous mark."[17] Usually, courts "find tarnishment only in cases where a distinctive mark is depicted in an obviously degrading context, often involving a sexual activity, obscenity, or illegal activity."[18]

At the same time, the Lanham Act permits "fair use" of trademarks by people other than trademark holders.[19] However, one key

---

[13] *Id.* at 144.

[14] *See* Dreamwerks Prod. Grp., Inc. v. SKG Studio, 142 F.3d 1127, 1129 (9th Cir. 1998); 15 U.S.C. §1114(1)(A).

[15] 15 U.S.C. § 1125(c)(2)(A).

[16] *Id.* § 1125(c)(1).

[17] *Id.* § 1125(c)(2)(C).

[18] Kellogg Co. v. Exxon Mobil Corp., 192 F. Supp. 2d 790, 809–10 (W.D. Tenn. 2001).

[19] 15 U.S.C. § 1115(b)(4).

consideration is that in order to avail oneself of the "fair use" defense, the accused infringer must be using the protected mark "otherwise than as a mark."[20] For example, if CNN wanted to have a story about the trends in sales of Nike shoes, it could put up a Nike logo on the screen as an illustration to the story without risking a lawsuit for infringement. It can do so because in the just-described context, CNN is not using the Nike logo *as a trademark*, i.e., as an indicator of the source of its own goods.

As always, though, hard cases arise on the margins of these two categories. One such case was a 1989 decision by the Second Circuit in *Rogers v. Grimaldi*.[21] In that case, Ginger Rogers sued defendants over the use of her name in Federico Fellini's movie *Ginger and Fred*, which defendants produced and distributed. Rogers's main contention was that defendants, *inter alia*, "violated section 43(a) of the Lanham Act . . . by creating the false impression that the film was about her or that she sponsored, endorsed, or was otherwise involved in the film,"[22] or in plain language engaged in acts that would cause a reasonable consumer to mistakenly believe that Ginger Rogers herself was the "commercial source" of the movie.[23] The Second Circuit rejected the claim, writing that the Lanham "Act should be construed to apply to artistic works only where the public interest in avoiding consumer confusion outweighs the public interest in free expression."[24] The real question, reasoned the court, was whether artistic works use the mark or celebrity's name in a "misleading" fashion, not whether they use them at all. Thus, "some titles—such as 'Nimmer on Copyright' and 'Jane Fonda's Workout Book'—explicitly state the author of the work or at least the name of the person the publisher is entitled to associate with the preparation of the work."[25] And if such titles were not *actually* authored or authorized by Nimmer or Jane Fonda, respectively, then the use of those names would be misleading.[26] On the other hand, an artistic

---

[20] *Id.*

[21] 875 F.2d 994 (2d Cir. 1989).

[22] *Id.* at 997.

[23] *Id.*

[24] *Id.* at 999.

[25] *Id.*

[26] *See id.*

work *about* Nimmer, or Jane Fonda, or Ginger Rogers, or McDonald's Corporation does not mislead the consumer to such an extent as to justify limiting traditional First Amendment protections.

It is for this reason that *even if* a reasonable consumer were to think that Andy Warhol's paintings of soup cans (a topic to which we shall return in the subsequent part) were actually authorized by Campbell's, thus causing some confusion, the paintings are protected by the First Amendment and do not violate the strictures of the Lanham Act. As there is no other way to depict Campbell's soup cans other than by drawing, well, Campbell's soup cans, the artist's freedom cannot be restricted. But what should be evident is that in this situation, the First Amendment defense easily fits with the statutory fair use defense—Warhol was not using Campbell's *as a trademark*, for he was not trying to get consumers to think that when buying those silk screens (or reproductions) they were buying a Campbell's product. To the contrary, he wanted consumers to think that they were buying a *Warhol*. The soup cans served no identification function other than in their style of execution, which pointed not to the soup-maker, but to the artist.

Of course, not all usage of trademarks in art is laudatory or even neutral. Consider the movie *Super Size Me*.[27] It's a documentary showing the movie director eating only McDonald's food for 30 days—to an entirely expected ill-effect on his own health. Needless to say, the movie used McDonald's trademarks (everything from the name of the chain, to "Big Mac," to the very title of the movie, as "Super Size" is a registered trademark). Yet, the movie makers did not have to worry about an allegation of trademark dilution because the use of the trademark was in service of commentary on the mark and/or the owner of the mark. Like Warhol's soup cans, the makers of *Super Size Me* were not using the trademark to entice consumers to buy their wares, but to entice consumers to critically consider the wares sold by McDonald's. To say it in other way, the movie would likely have been just as successful if instead of investigating the effect of McDonald's fast food, it chose to investigate Burger King's or Arby's offerings.

A pattern thus emerges from these cases—the First Amendment and the fair use doctrine protect the use of trademarks by others

[27] SUPER SIZE ME (The Con 2004).

when they talk *about* the protected marks, but are of no help when they *use* the protected marks as their own marketing tool.

All of this brings us back to Bad Spaniels' chew toy. VIP Products (the maker of the toy) argued for about 13 pages of its brief that it should incur no liability because Bad Spaniels is a "parody" of the Jack Daniel's mark and is "a work of artistic expression and noncommercial speech."[28] In VIP's view, the matter should never have gone to trial, and the courts should have never inquired whether there is a "likelihood of confusion" or "tarnishment," because these questions were preempted by the First Amendment defense. In essence, VIP argued that *even if* there is a likelihood of confusion, in view of the fact that the chew toy is an obvious parody, no liability can attach. (It is a rather odd argument though, because if the parody is *obvious*, it is highly *unlikely* that any consumer would be confused.) The upshot of VIP's argument was that under *Rogers*, the First Amendment protects not merely commentary on an existing mark, but more broadly protects uses of another mark in "artistic works," except in very narrow categories, *viz.*, when "the challenged use of a mark 'has no artistic relevance to the underlying work' or [when] it 'explicitly misleads as to the source or the content of the work.'"[29] Under that approach, *Rogers* would become a threshold that any trademark owner would have to cross prior to presenting its likelihood-of-confusion evidence, rather than a mere subset of the fair use doctrine, where the burden is on the defendant to show that the protected mark was used "otherwise than as a mark."[30]

The Ninth Circuit endorsed this view, holding that "because Bad Spaniels 'communicates a humorous message,' it is automatically entitled to *Rogers'* protection."[31]

The Supreme Court disagreed. While it declined to endorse or abrogate *Rogers* wholesale, it was explicit that that case has no application "when an alleged infringer uses a trademark in the way the Lanham Act most cares about: as a designation of source for the

---

[28] Brief of Respondent at 12, Jack Daniel's Properties, Inc. v. VIP Prod. LLC, 599 U.S. 140, 149 (2023) (No. 22-148), 2023 WL 2189058.

[29] *Jack Daniel's,* 599 U.S. at 151 (quoting *Rogers,* 875 F.2d at 999).

[30] 15 U.S.C. § 1115(b)(4).

[31] *Jack Daniel's,* 599 U.S. at 158 (quoting VIP Prod. LLC v. Jack Daniel's Properties, Inc., 953 F.3d 1170, 1175 (9th Cir. 2020)).

infringer's own goods."[32] As the Court explained (without necessarily endorsing the logic of lower-court cases), *Rogers* only makes sense in cases where "a trademark is used not to designate a work's source, but solely to perform some other expressive function."[33] Looking back on examples above, *Super Size Me* used McDonald's trademarks not as a source identifier, but as a way to express the movie's views (whether correct or not) about the unhealthiness of McDonald's food. The true test, according to the Court, is whether the accused infringer used a registered trademark as a source identifier of its own goods, irrespective of whether in so doing he also communicated some expressive message. That is so because trademarks often communicate a message above and beyond a source identifier.[34] Applying this test, the Court easily concluded that VIP was using Jack Daniel's trademarks to identify its own products (i.e., the dog chew toys shaped like Jack Daniel's bottles with writings in similar fonts to that employed by the whiskey manufacturer would be readily recognizable by consumers in a variety of settings), and therefore (assuming that Jack Daniel's could actually prove that likelihood of confusion exists) infringing those marks.[35] For the same reason, in three short paragraphs, the Court concluded that VIP's toys, despite being "humorous," are not immune from tarnishment liability.[36]

The main theme of *Jack Daniel's*—that not every expressive use of another's property is "fair" and therefore free from liability—extended, albeit it in a much more muddled way, to *Andy Warhol Foundation for the Visual Arts, Inc. v. Goldsmith*, to which I next turn.

II. Andy Warhol Foundation for the Visual Arts, Inc. v. Goldsmith

Whereas *Jack Daniel's* was a unanimous and almost breezy opinion of 20 pages (followed by three pages of concurring opinions), *Warhol* divided the Court, and the opinions by the warring factions spanned 80 pages and were disdainful of each other, if not outright venomous.

---

[32] *Id.* at 153.

[33] *Id.* at 154.

[34] *Id.* at 157–58.

[35] *Id.* at 160–61.

[36] *Id.* at 161–62.

As in *Jack Daniel's*, the issue before the Court was whether an alleged infringer, who concededly used another's copyrighted work, was entitled to a "fair use" defense.[37] And although the Copyright Act, like the Lanham Act, provides for such a defense, the case presented a clash between two competing provisions of the Copyright Act.

On one hand, the Copyright Act grants authors not merely rights to their original works, but also a right to create derivate works.[38] This means that an author of a book has an exclusive right to make (or license others to make) a movie out of that book.[39] Creating an unauthorized derivate work subjects the creator to infringement liability, no matter how creative, aesthetically pleasing, or imaginative the derivate work may be.[40] For example, *Game of Thrones*[41] was (at least in the early seasons) a spectacular and imaginative retelling of George R.R. Martin's epic *Song of Fire and Ice*. And even though *Game of Thrones* put its own spin on Martin's story (and indeed, in the later seasons created its own story, as Martin still hasn't finished the last two books of the series), the makers of HBO's hit series would have ended up in serious legal trouble if they had proceeded without seeking Martin's license.

At the same time, the Copyright Act protects fair use of preexisting and otherwise protected works. Under the statute, fair use is a viable defense when the copyrighted work is used "for purposes such as criticism, comment, news reporting, teaching . . ., scholarship, or research."[42] However that the work fits into any one of these (or similar) categories is by itself insufficient. Instead, a court must weigh four factors in determining whether

---

[37] Andy Warhol Found. for the Visual Arts, Inc. v. Goldsmith (*Warhol III*), 143 S. Ct. 1258, 1266 (2023).

[38] 17 U.S.C. § 106(2).

[39] *Warhol III*, 143 S. Ct. at 1275.

[40] *See* Bucklew v. Hawkins, Ash, Baptie & Co., LLP., 329 F.3d 923, 930 (7th Cir. 2003) ("[I]t is a copyright infringement to make or sell a derivative work without a license from the owner of the copyright on the work from which the derivative work is derived.").

[41] *Game of Thrones* (HBO, 2011–2019).

[42] 17 U.S.C. § 107.

the use is indeed "fair." These factors, none of which is determinative, and all of which have to be weighed in every case are:

(1) the purpose and character of the use, including whether such use is of a commercial nature or is for nonprofit educational purposes;

(2) the nature of the copyrighted work;

(3) the amount and substantiality of the portion used in relation to the copyrighted work as a whole; and

(4) the effect of the use upon the potential market for or value of the copyrighted work.[43]

In evaluating the first factor, courts look at the allegedly infringing work to see if it "transformed" the underlying protected work, i.e., whether the contribution of the alleged infringer made the underlying work into some new type of work, suitable for new audiences and new uses, or conveying new messages.[44] At this stage, the tension between the two provisions becomes fairly self-evident. On one hand, "transformation" of a work into a new type of artistic expression is not enough, because every derivate work "transforms" the underlying one into something new, and authors of the original works retain exclusive rights to the creation of derivate ones. On the other hand, "transformation" is a key consideration in determining whether the new work used the old one "fairly." It is to this conundrum that the Court addressed itself in *Warhol*, and it is this tension that caused disagreement between the majority and the dissent.

At issue in *Warhol* was the use of a black-and-white photograph depicting the late artist Prince and its transformation into a silk screen painting.[45] The photograph was taken by a famous photographer, Lynn Goldsmith, and was previously licensed to Vanity Fair magazine for a "one time" only use in an article about Prince.[46] Vanity Fair, in turn, hired Andy Warhol to make a silk screen on the basis of the photograph (which was permissible under the terms of the license) and then published the reproduction of the silk print as

---

[43] *Id.*

[44] *See* Campbell v. Acuff-Rose Music, Inc., 510 U.S. 569, 579 (1994).

[45] *Warhol III*, 143 S. Ct. at 1266–71.

[46] *Id.* at 1267.

part of the article.[47] However, Warhol was so taken with Goldsmith's photograph that he used it not only to create the silk screen that was reproduced in the Vanity Fair article, but 13 other silk screen paintings and two pencil drawings.[48] Andy Warhol[49] licensed the use of his paintings to others "for commercial and editorial uses."[50] After Prince died, Warhol licensed one of his images known as the "Orange Prince" to Condé Nast for its use in a magazine retrospective on Prince.[51] Goldsmith (and a variety of other artists) also licensed some of her other photos to other magazines which were running articles on Prince.[52] When Goldsmith saw Condé Nast's cover, she recognized her photograph and notified Warhol of her belief that the cover infringed her copyright.[53] Warhol then filed a declaratory judgment action in the Southern District of New York seeking a judgment of non-infringement or, in the alternative, fair use.[54]

Warhol prevailed at trial, with the district court holding that Warhol's use of Goldsmith's photograph was "transformative" because Warhol's paintings "have a different character, give Goldsmith's photograph a new expression, and employ new aesthetics with creative and communicative results distinct from Goldsmith's."[55] According to the district court, Warhol's paintings "can reasonably be perceived to have transformed Prince from a vulnerable, uncomfortable person to an iconic, larger-than-life figure," such that "each Prince Series work is immediately recognizable as a 'Warhol' rather than as a photograph of Prince."[56] The district court also concluded that the remaining factors favored Warhol and not Goldsmith.

---

[47] *Id.*

[48] *Id.* at 1268.

[49] Technically speaking, it was the Andy Warhol Foundation that licensed the works, as Warhol himself died in 1987. However, for ease of reference, I will refer to both Andy Warhol and the Foundation as "Warhol" and treat them as a single entity.

[50] *Warhol III*, 143 S. Ct. at 1268–69.

[51] *Id.* at 1269.

[52] *Id.*

[53] *Id.* at 1270–71.

[54] *Id.* at 1271.

[55] Andy Warhol Foundation for the Visual Arts, Inc. v. Goldsmith (*Warhol I*), 382 F. Supp. 3d 312, 325–26 (S.D.N.Y. 2019) (quoting Cariou v. Prince, 714 F.3d 694, 708 (2d Cir. 2013)) (alterations omitted), rev'd, 11 F.4th 26 (2d Cir. 2021), aff'd, 143 S. Ct. 1258 (2023).

[56] *Id.*

The Second Circuit reversed, concluding that all four factors actually favored Goldsmith. While the appeals court recognized that Warhol had added his own take on the original photograph, it held that a "secondary work that adds a new aesthetic or new expression to its source material is [not] necessarily transformative."[57] In the Second Circuit's view, "transformative purpose and character must, at a bare minimum, comprise something more than the imposition of another artist's style on the primary work."[58] At the Supreme Court, the dispute was narrowed to the argument over the "transformativeness" of Warhol's work, with Warhol declining to appeal the Second Circuit's findings against him on the remaining factors.[59]

With the dispute thus narrowed, the Supreme Court attempted to define what is sufficient artistic "transformation" to satisfy the fair use analysis. Admittedly, it is not a question susceptible to easy answers. In a colloquial sense, of course Andy Warhol "transformed" Goldsmith's image. There is little question that Warhol's painting elicits a different reaction from a viewer than does the original photograph. One does not need to buy into the district court's assertion (which anyways is better suited for an art critic than a judge) that the original photograph depicted Prince as "a vulnerable, uncomfortable person," whereas the Warhol image depicts him as "an iconic, larger-than-life figure."[60] Whether that's true or not, it is certainly true that the painting (like Warhol's soup cans) "is immediately recognizable as a 'Warhol.'"[61]

But as a matter of copyright law, the retort is "so what?" For example, the movie *No Country for Old Men*[62] may be "instantly recognizable" as a "Coen Brothers," but it does not follow that the movie's adaptation of the original *No Country for Old Men* novel[63] is, ipso facto, "fair use." If that were so, as the Court majority correctly observed, it would give famous, recognizable artists license to steal from lesser-known ones.

[57] Andy Warhol Found. for Visual Arts, Inc. v. Goldsmith (*Warhol II*), 11 F.4th 26, 38–39 (2d Cir. 2021), *aff'd*, 143 S. Ct. 1258 (2023).

[58] *Id.* at 42.

[59] *Warhol III*, 143 S. Ct. at 1272–73.

[60] *Warhol I*, 382 F. Supp. 3d at 326.

[61] *Id.*

[62] NO COUNTRY FOR OLD MEN (Paramount Vantage 2007).

[63] CORMAC MCCARTHY, NO COUNTRY FOR OLD MEN (2005).

By putting their own stamp on prior work, the famous artists could completely eviscerate the lesser-known artists' exclusive right to create derivative works. Conversely, just because *A Serious Man*[64] is a modern-day retelling of the story of Job, it doesn't follow that the Coen brothers would have been found to have infringed that story had it been subject to copyright. If it were otherwise, it would mean that the first artist to express an idea in some sort of permanent medium would be able to lock up all variations of that idea for decades to come, all to the detriment of the "Progress of Science."[65] The question is, as it so often is in law, where to draw the line.

Unfortunately, neither the majority nor the dissent were particularly helpful in line-drawing, each (poorly) mixing and matching several copyright doctrines in an attempt to prove their point. That said, the majority ultimately had the better argument. Writing for the Court, Justice Sonia Sotomayor spent a fair amount of time focusing on the fact that the *purpose* of Warhol's print was much the same as the purpose of Goldsmith's photograph—to illustrate magazine stories about Prince.[66] And therefore, according to the majority, the new work (Warhol's painting) is not "transformative" of the old work (Goldsmith photograph). There are several problems with this analysis, as Justice Kagan rightly pointed out in her dissent.

First, the mere fact that both Goldsmith's photograph and Warhol's painting were sought by and used in various magazines does not mean that they have the same purpose or are essentially interchangeable. It may well be that different types of illustration are suitable to different articles, each having a different focus or tone. Of course, the fact that both works of art illustrate Prince means that they will both be used in stories about Prince and not stories about, say, David Bowie or Madonna. But that does not necessarily mean that because they are so used, they have the same "purpose and character of the use." The problem with the Court's analysis is that it (at least potentially) uses too high a level of generality. Consider one of the Court's earlier cases, *Campbell v. Acuff-Rose Music, Inc.*[67] In *Campbell*,

---

[64] A Serious Man (StudioCanal 2009).

[65] U.S. Const. art. I, § 8 cl. 8.

[66] *See Warhol III*, 143 S. Ct. at 1273 ("As portraits of Prince used to depict Prince in magazine stories about Prince, the original photograph and AWF's copying use of it share substantially the same purpose.").

[67] 510 U.S. 569 (1994).

2 Live Crew—an American hip-hop group—parodied the song "Oh, Pretty Woman" originally written by Roy Orbison and William Dees and in which Acuff-Rose held a copyright.[68] The parody borrowed both lyrics and chords from the original, and as a result, 2 Live Crew was promptly sued for copyright infringement.[69] On a high level of generality, both the original version of "Pretty Woman" and the parody had the same "purpose and character." Both songs sought to provide listeners with musical sounds and words that spoke of sexual longing and desire. Under that view, the first factor of the fair use analysis would favor the original creator. But at a different level of generality, another outcome presents itself. As then-Justice David Souter wrote for a unanimous Court, "2 Live Crew juxtaposes the romantic musings of a man whose fantasy comes true, with degrading taunts, a bawdy demand for sex, and a sigh of relief from paternal responsibility."[70] In this sense, the two songs couldn't have a more different "purpose and character." So how does Justice Sotomayor explain the choice of the level of generality in *Warhol III*? She doesn't, and that leaves this reader not very convinced by the argument.

There is a second problem with the assertion that the first fair use factor favors Goldsmith simply because both the silk screen painting and the original photograph are competitors in the market for illustrations to magazine articles. Congress has listed four factors for the Court to consider, and the fourth factor requires accounting for "the effect of the use upon the potential market for or value of the copyrighted work."[71] This factor focuses on whether the allegedly infringing work serves "as a market replacement" for a copyrighted work.[72] The Court's analysis seems to conflate the two inquiries, because once one concludes that both the earlier and later work have the purpose of operating in the same market, it necessarily follows that the effect of such use would be detrimental to the copyright owner's interests. Justice Kagan's dissent is correct that the majority

---

[68] *Id.* at 572.

[69] *Id.* at 573.

[70] *Id.* at 583.

[71] 17 U.S.C. § 107(4).

[72] *See Campbell*, 510 U.S. at 591.

is essentially "double[] count[ing]" the economic impact of the new work against the alleged infringer.[73]

None of this is to say that Justice Kagan is correct in her dissent. Justice Kagan's opinion is long on invective and baseless worries regarding the future of artistic expression, but short on rooting itself in copyright law. The dissent made two main objections to the majority's conclusion. First, it argued that the painting is a genuine work of art, instantly recognizable as a "Warhol," and that it presents Prince in a different light than the original photograph.[74] (In doing so, Justice Kagan also accused the majority of being philistines, who just "don't understand" art.)[75] The true artistic nature of the painting, according to the dissent, serves as a clear sign that Warhol's work is indeed transformational.[76] Second, Justice Kagan argued that under the majority's view, all sorts of works of art (had the Copyright Act been in effect at the time of their creation) would not have been produced, thus impoverishing the world.[77] Neither of the arguments is particularly convincing.

For starters, no one actually disputes that Warhol's paintings are works of art. (That is not to say that everyone does or has to love this particular artistic expression, but without question it is artistic). But as I have already discussed, the mere fact that a movie is a work of art does not mean that it is not (absent a proper license) infringing.[78] Or consider a musical performance. A good artist often puts his own creativity and skill to work in interpreting a musical composition. That is why it matters who conducts an orchestra—conductors don't just wave their arms until the music stops; they are interpreting the composition. But it doesn't follow that because conductors put their own gloss on pre-existing works, they are free to use such works without compensating the original creator. One can therefore concede that Warhol changed, perhaps even in quite significant ways, Goldsmith's photograph, without concluding that he should avoid

---

[73] *Warhol III*, 143 S. Ct. at 1303 (Kagan, J., dissenting).

[74] *Id.* at 1300 (noting Warhol's "dazzling creativity.").

[75] *Id.* at 1300–01.

[76] *Id.* at 1300.

[77] *Id.* at 1306–11.

[78] *See supra* note 38 and accompanying text.

paying licensing fees for using that photograph as a starting point for his creation.

Justice Kagan's second argument fared no better. She argued that had the majority's rule applied in Renaissance Italy or 19th century France (a fanciful proposition in and of itself), humanity would not have been blessed with Titian's *Venus of Urbino*, which is similar to his teacher Giorgione's *Sleeping Venus* painted about quarter century earlier, or Manet's *Olympia*, which was inspired by the former two paintings. But that argument doesn't hold. As any observer can tell by looking at the three paintings (which the dissent helpfully embeds in the opinion), they illustrate the same subject, but they are not copies or mere variations on one another, any more than Romeo and Juliet is a "mere variation" on Tristan and Isolde.

What Justice Kagan ignores is a long-standing distinction in copyright law, the distinction between an *idea*, which is not protectable, and an *expression* of the idea, which is.[79] The idea of a reclining nude is open to anyone. Velasquez's *Rokeby Venus* or Goya's *La Maja Desnuda* both illustrate a reclining nude female, as do dozens of other classical works. But even if all these works were subject to the 21st-century American copyright law, none of them would necessarily infringe on any preceding work, because they are all different *expressions* of the same *idea*. But the same is not true about Warhol's painting. Warhol was not simply painting Prince. If he were, then any similarity with a pre-existing photograph would be inevitable, expected, and non-infringing. Instead, Warhol was painting a *photograph of Prince*, and because that photograph enjoys its own copyright protection, Warhol had to get a license to use it.

Thus the question (unlike in the copyright context with Campbell's soup cans) is not whether consumers of art would recognize the painting as a "Warhol," but whether in creating the painting Warhol used (and was not merely "inspired by") a work copyrighted by another. In the trademark context, the inquiry is consumer-focused, because the goal is to help consumers identify the source of goods.[80]

---

[79] *See* Google LLC v. Oracle Am., Inc., 141 S. Ct. 1183, 1196 (2021) ("[C]opyrights protect 'expression' but not the 'ideas' that lie behind it.").

[80] *See, e.g.,* Au-Tomotive Gold, Inc. v. Volkswagen of Am., Inc., 457 F.3d 1062, 1067 (9th Cir. 2006).

But in the copyright context the inquiry is focused on the artist and artwork itself, because the goal is to encourage the creation of *new* (rather than imitation or derivative) art by providing artists with exclusive rights.[81]

Fortunately, a better and easier way to resolve this case exists. Unfortunately, neither the majority nor dissent took that route, although Justice Neil Gorsuch, in a concurring opinion joined by Justice Ketanji Brown Jackson, sketched out a better argument.[82] The key to resolving this case and making it fit with *Jack Daniel's*, which was decided a few weeks prior, is to look at the preamble of Section 107 of the Copyright Act.[83] That clause limits "fair use" to uses "for purposes such as criticism, comment, news reporting, teaching . . . scholarship, or research."[84] Although not an exhaustive list, it does limit the use of underlying work to circumstances where such use is *necessary* to create subsequent work. For example, one can hardly write a competent critical review of a book without either quoting from it or discussing its plot and structure. One *needs* to use these copyrighted aspects of the book in order to create a subsequent work. Similarly, in writing a scholarly dissertation one often needs to quote and summarize prior sources. And one needs to use preexisting works if one wishes to conduct research into them. For instance, if one wishes to see whether a romantic comedy and a horror movie produce same or different brain activity in those viewing the films, one needs to actually show those films to the subjects of the experiment. What all of these examples have in common is that "fair use" involves commenting on, critiquing, or researching the *underlying work*, rather than the *subject of that work*.

Think back to the First Amendment issue in trademark law discussed in the preceding part. One retains the right to criticize particular marks or mark-holders, and in so doing may be privileged to use protected marks. But one may not imitate the marks for the purposes of creating one's own product. And so too here. If the new

---

[81] *See* W. Michael Schuster, *Public Choice Theory, the Constitution, and Public Understanding of the Copyright System*, 51 U.C. Davis L. Rev. 2247, 2274 n.173 (2018).

[82] *See Warhol III*, 143 S. Ct. at 1288–91 (Gorsuch, J., concurring).

[83] 17 U.S.C. § 107

[84] *Id.*

work is providing a new take on the underlying work, it is protected. If it merely uses an underlying work to provide a new take on the outside world, it is infringing.

Applying this framework can make sense of both *Campbell* and *Warhol III*. In *Campbell*, 2 Live Crew had a new take on the original "Pretty Woman" song. The new version of the song imitated the original "in such a way as to make [it] appear ridiculous."[85] The new song was "a comment on the naivete of the original of an earlier day, as a rejection of its sentiment that ignores the ugliness of street life and the debasement that it signifies."[86] In contrast (even accepting the dissent's claim "that Warhol transformed Prince from a 'vulnerable, uncomfortable person to an iconic, larger-than-life figure'"[87]), Andy Warhol was commenting on Prince's role in the world, not on Goldsmith's photograph. Warhol was not making a comment on how the photograph did or did not capture the true essence of Prince. Instead, he was simply using and manipulating the photograph to showcase his own version of reality.

But if Warhol has to pay for the use of Goldsmith's photograph, then what of Justice Kagan's claim that such a requirement would stunt the creation of new artworks which may resemble those that came before? How will any artist be able to paint Prince again? The answer to that question isn't hard. Indeed, the Court gave it 120 years ago. In *Bleistein v. Donaldson Lithographing Co.*,[88] the Court was faced with a very similar question. There, the alleged infringers copied several chromolithographs of posters advertising a circus.[89] The Court, while holding this action to be infringement, cautioned that defendants would remain free to make their own drawing of circus groups, even if these drawings ended up looking very similar to the original work. But they could not simply copy the original works. As Justice Oliver Wendell Holmes put it, "The opposite proposition would mean that a portrait by

[85] *Campbell*, 510 U.S. at 580.

[86] *Id.* at 583.

[87] *Warhol III*, 143 S. Ct. at 1301 (Kagan, J., dissenting) (quoting *Warhol I*, 382 F. Supp. 3d at 326).

[88] 188 U.S. 239 (1903).

[89] *Id.* at 248.

Velasquez or Whistler was common property because others might try their hand on the same face. Others are free to copy the original. They are not free to copy the copy."[90] This means that everyone is free to paint a portrait of Prince (or for that matter, a reclining Venus), because in doing so, they would be copying the original. But no one is free to copy the photograph of Prince without a license, because that would be copying not nature, but "the personal reaction of an individual [photographer] upon nature."[91] And it is that personal reaction that is meant to be protected by the Copyright Act. This doctrine, along with the idea/expression dichotomy discussed above, ought to be enough to alleviate Justice Kagan's concerns about any detrimental effect that the majority opinion may have on the art world.

So recast, *Warhol III* perfectly complements *Jack Daniel's*. The First Amendment concerns in both cases are real, but they are best dealt with by allowing broad commentary on, criticism of, teaching of, parodying of, and research in preexisting intellectual property items, without sapping those items of their value as property. This view would also align with patent law, where the definition of infringement explicitly excludes testing and research in, for example, pharmaceutical arts to ensure that your product is comparable to someone else's patented product.

Additionally, this view does not require one to decide whether Warhol's Orange Prince or Campbell's soup cans are really "art." It leaves that question to critics and consumers. Instead, judges would do what they are qualified to do—ask whether the alleged infringer is primarily making commentary on the underlying work (even if such commentary enjoys commercial success) or primarily using the underlying work for the alleged infringer's own commercial purposes (even if such uses also add something new to the underlying work). The former category of uses is protected by the First Amendment and the fair use doctrine, whereas the latter is not and constitutes infringing activity.

---

[90] *Id.* at 249–50.
[91] *Id.* at 250.

Conclusion

What is heartening about the Supreme Court's opinions in *Jack Daniel's* and *Warhol III* is that they, though without explicitly saying so, treat trademarks and copyright as *property*, which can only be trespassed upon in very limited circumstances.

One can make sense of both decisions by considering the First Amendment's limitation on the rights of real property and then analogizing those limits to the intellectual property regimes. On one hand, ownership of real property obviously does not insulate its owner from protests or criticisms about his use of that property. But usually, such criticisms and protests must take place somewhere other than the private property being protested. Of course a protest has an expressive component, whether conducted on the private property in question or elsewhere. But the mere fact that someone is engaged in an expressive activity is not a blanket abrogation of the property owner's right to exclude. Similarly, a fan can pay homage to someone else's style and set up his living room in the same fashion as that of the person he admires. But what he cannot do is to simply move into the living room that is the subject of his admiration.

By anchoring intellectual property in *property*, the legal rules become more clear, stable, predictable, and consistent across the various regimes. There are of course differences between trademarks, patents, copyrights, trade secrets, personal property, and real property. Though these differences need to be taken into account when devising rules of decisions, they are not so vast as to obscure the basic proposition that all of these things are indeed property.

This Term's alignment of rights in trademarks and copyright with traditional rights in real property is a welcome baby step (indeed, two steps) forward for the Court, which in recent years has refused to put other intellectual property rights on par with real property. One can only hope that the Court will soon explicitly tie the intellectual property rights to the law of real property. One also hopes that while doing so, the Court will take a third step in the right direction by again treating patent rights on par with real property. Whether or not these steps are on the horizon, we can celebrate the Court's OT 2022 decisions which protect owners of intellectual property, while leaving plenty of room for others to create, comment, critique, teach, and research.

Looking Ahead: October Term 2023

*Wen Fa**

"The sequel is never as good as the original."[1] Sequels follow block-busters, and the same excitement that prompts the sequel can make it fail to live up to the hype. There are many examples. *Jaws* was once the highest grossing movie of all time. But plaudits for the original gave way to condemnation for the sequel—*Jaws: The Revenge*. Critics derided the latter as a dud—in all parts "[i]llogical, tension-free, and filled with cut-rate special effects."[2] *The Karate Kid* followed a similar trajectory. Famed movie critic Roger Ebert dubbed the original "one of the nice surprises of 1984—an exciting, sweet-tempered, heart-warming story with one of the most interesting friendships in a long time."[3] But that movie was followed by a series of others: *The Karate Kid Part II*, *The Karate Kid Part III*, and *The Next Karate Kid*—each faring worse than the last. The original *Zoolander* received mostly positive reviews and inspired a generation of poses ranging from Blue Steel to Ferrari to Le Tigre.[4] But the antagonist Jacobim Mugatu appears to have had the last laugh as critics lambasted *Zoolander 2* for "its scattershot rehash of a script."[5]

* Wen Fa is the director of legal affairs at Beacon Center of Tennessee, a nonprofit dedicated to eliminating government barriers to opportunity and empowering Tennesseans to pursue the American dream. Beacon's legal department has represented Tennesseans and other Americans free-of-charge in numerous cases involving property rights and economic liberty. The views expressed in this article are solely those of the author, and do not reflect the views of the Beacon Center of Tennessee or its clients.

[1] Chris Compendio, *When a Sequel Is Better than the Original: The 7 Categories of Movie Sequels*, FILM INQUIRY (Jun. 15, 2017), https://tinyurl.com/2zbw448j.

[2] Alex Vo, *The 57 Worst Sequels of All Time*, ROTTEN TOMATOES, https://tinyurl.com/ynvfz5a8 (last visited Aug. 15, 2023).

[3] Roger Ebert, *The Karate Kid*, ROGEREBERT.COM (Jan. 1, 1984), https://tinyurl.com/3a4htdjr.

[4] The *very* subtle differences between the poses—which only the expert eye can discern—is beyond the scope of this article.

[5] *Zoolander No. 2.*, ROTTEN TOMATOES, https://tinyurl.com/5b3f8z3n (last visited Aug. 15, 2023).

Every once in a while, however, audiences will enjoy a sequel even more than the original. Well-known examples include *The Godfather Part II, Star Wars: Episode V - The Empire Strikes Back,* and *The Dark Knight*—all considered by discerning moviegoers and critics as sequels that outmatched the movies they followed.

The last Supreme Court term was a blockbuster. The Court decided cases involving racial preferences in university admissions, the scope of the Clean Water Act, the authority of the executive branch to "cancel" student loans under the HEROES Act, child placement under the Indian Child Welfare Act, and the interplay between the First Amendment and public accommodation laws. Many other cases last term would have garnered more interest if only they had been issued in a different term.

The previous term will be a tough act to follow. Court watchers often quip that just as "the sequel is never as good as the original," a Supreme Court term full of big cases often precedes a term filled with quieter ones. Following that pattern, one might predict that the October 2023 Term will be a tranquil one, lacking in the type of landmark cases that shaped the term before it. But that prediction could prove wrong. With several big cases involving the administrative state, the Second Amendment, the taxing power, trademarks, and social media already on the calendar, and several other important cases on the horizon, the upcoming term might just be the sequel that matches—if not exceeds—the original.

I. The Administrative State

Federal agencies exercise outsized control over American life. The FCC regulates what Americans can see on television or hear on the radio. The FDA dictates what Americans can get from their pharmacist to treat their illness. The EPA can stop a home improvement project in its tracks. Any American who has filed taxes (hopefully) did so in accordance with the rules established by the IRS, and anyone who has flown in the United States in the last two decades has had to interact with agents from the TSA.[6] The

---

[6] For those who don't deal in shorthand, the agencies are the Federal Communications Commission (formed in 1934), the Food and Drug Administration (1906), the Environmental Protection Agency (1970), the Internal Revenue Service (1862), and the Transportation Security Administration (2001).

hundreds of agencies that make up the administrative state are the chimeras of the constitutional system. Although technically residents of the executive branch, federal agencies exercise the executive power to enforce laws, the legislative power to promulgate rules and regulations, and even the judicial power to adjudicate civil actions.

For decades, the judiciary has given agencies free rein to regulate. Courts have countenanced broad delegations of power from Congress to federal agencies and deferred to the latter's interpretation of the law. In recent years, however, courts have appeared increasingly willing to place limits on the authority of the administrative state. The big case last term involved the Department of Education's move to cancel up to $20,000 in student loans per borrower. The Court rebuffed the Department's claim that it had authority to implement the cancellation under the HEROES Act—a 2003 law that allows the Secretary of Education to "waive or modify" any statutory or regulatory provision related to a student aid program "as the Secretary deems necessary in connection with a war or other military operation or national emergency."[7] This Term, the Supreme Court will hear three separate cases involving agency deference, agency enforcement, and agency funding. That could make this Term the most consequential one yet for the administrative state.

A. Agency Deference

In *Loper Bright Enterprises v. Raimondo*, the Supreme Court will consider overruling its roughly 40-year-old precedent in *Chevron v. Natural Resources Defense Council*,[8] "the most talked about, most written about, most cited administrative law decision of the Supreme Court. Ever."[9] In *Chevron*, the Court departed from Chief Justice John Marshall's axiom that it's emphatically the duty of the judiciary to say what the law is.[10] *Chevron* instructs courts to defer to agency interpretations of statutory language that the court considers ambiguous.

---

[7] *See* Biden v. Nebraska, 143 S. Ct. 2355 (2023).

[8] 467 U.S. 837 (1984).

[9] Ronald A. Cass, Chevron—*Complicated, Start to Finish*, 23 FEDERALIST SOC'Y REV. 265 (2022).

[10] Marbury v. Madison, 5 U.S. (1 Cranch) 137, 177 (1803).

Chevron has launched waves of detractors. They contend that *Chevron* is incompatible with the Constitution's structure and unlawfully delegates the judicial power to interpret laws to federal agencies. Another critique is that *Chevron* contravenes basic principles of due process. It has been long said that a man cannot be the judge in his own case, but *Chevron* requires courts to defer to agency interpretations even where the same agency is a litigant in the case. Still more, the Supreme Court has never provided an answer to a threshold question: How much ambiguity is enough to take a question of statutory interpretation out of the hands of a court and vest it in the domain of a federal agency? A law review article from 2017 surveyed over 1,000 cases and found that appellate courts found ambiguity in the statutory language roughly 70 percent of the time.[11] Yet one prominent federal court of appeals judge remarked that same year that he had never found statutory language ambiguous enough to defer to the agency in interpreting it.[12]

Loper Bright presents the Court with the opportunity to overrule *Chevron.* The plaintiffs in *Loper Bright* are commercial fishers who participate in the Atlantic herring fishery. Federal law permits the federal government to require fishing boats to carry observers who monitor compliance with fishery management plans. What federal law does not specify, however, is who must pay for the observers. Faced with budget shortfalls, the National Marine Fisheries Service (NMFS) implemented a rule to require fishers to fund monitors, who perform the same basic functions as observers. That imposes a heavy financial burden on fishers trying to earn a living: The Service itself estimates that the requirement imposes costs of over $700 per day and reduces profits by roughly 20 percent.

The fishers contend that the Magnuson-Stevens Act, a 1976 law that requires fishers to carry observers, did not authorize the agency to require fishers to pay for them. A divided D.C. Circuit panel concluded that the language of the Magnuson-Stevens Act was not "wholly unambiguous" as to whether the NMFS may require fisher-funded monitors.[13] It then proceeded to step two of the *Chevron*

[11] Kent Barnett & Christopher J. Walker, Chevron *in the Circuit Courts*, 116 MICH. L. REV. 1, 33–34 (2017).

[12] Raymond M. Kethledge, *Ambiguities and Agency Cases: Reflections After (Almost) Ten Years on the Bench*, 70 VAND. L. REV. EN BANC 315, 323 (2017).

[13] Loper Bright Enters. v. Raimondo, 45 F.4th 359, 366 (D.C. Cir. 2022).

analysis and upheld the NMFS rule after concluding that the agency's interpretation of the Act was "reasonable."[14]

The decision will have enormous practical consequences. Hundreds of agencies promulgate countless rules that affect individuals across the United States every year. Those Americans sometimes challenge agency rules on the grounds that Congress never provided the statutory authorization for those rules in the first place. How a court decides particular cases can determine whether individuals may keep their hard-earned profits, whether they may build on their own property, or even whether they may remain outside of prison walls.[15] A court applying *Chevron*, however, places a thumb on the scales in favor of the agency. If the court concludes that a statute is ambiguous (or as in *Loper Bright*, not "wholly unambiguous"), it must shirk its duty to say what the law is in favor of any reasonable interpretation offered by the agency—which is typically one of the parties in the case.

B. Agency Enforcement

Loper Bright would be the biggest administrative law case by a mile in most other terms, but not this one. In *SEC v. Jarkesy*, the Supreme Court will review a groundbreaking Fifth Circuit decision that invalidated several aspects of the U.S. Securities and Exchange Commission's (SEC's) powers on several different grounds.

Years ago, George Jarkesy established two hedge funds, which brought in over 100 investors and held roughly $24 million in assets. The SEC initiated an action within the agency, alleging that Jarkesy committed fraud by misrepresenting information about the funds and overvaluing the funds' assets. The SEC's administrative law judge (ALJ) conducted an evidentiary hearing and held in favor of . . . the SEC. The ALJ required Jarkesy and his investment advisor to pay $300,000 in civil penalties and nearly $700,000 in disgorgement. The ALJ also prohibited Jarkesy from associating with brokers, dealers, and advisors.

Jarkesy raised multiple constitutional claims, first with the SEC and then on appeal to the Fifth Circuit. The SEC rejected all of them.

[14] *Id.* at 369.

[15] *See* Babbitt v. Sweet Home Chapter of Cmtys. for a Great Or., 515 U.S. 687, 703–04 & n.18 (1995).

A divided Fifth Circuit panel, however, agreed with Jarkesy on each of the claims that it considered.[16] The court first held that the SEC proceedings violated Jarkesy's Seventh Amendment rights by depriving him of a jury trial. That question turns on whether the rights at issue are historically considered "public rights," which an agency may adjudicate without affording the individual a jury trial. The court reasoned that the fraud claims at issue were quintessentially about the redress of private harms, and thus the SEC violated Jarkesy's Seventh Amendment rights by assigning that type of action to a proceeding devoid of a jury.[17]

The Fifth Circuit then held that the facts gave rise to nondelegation issues because Congress provided the SEC unbridled discretion to determine whether to prosecute individuals in federal district court or through in-house proceedings.[18] Finally, the Court held that the removal restrictions for the SEC's administrative law judges were unconstitutional.[19] As the head of the executive branch, the President must retain sufficient control over ALJs, who perform substantial executive functions. Yet two layers of removal protections impede the President's control over ALJs: ALJs may be removed by SEC commissioners only for good cause established by the Merit Systems Protections Board and SEC commissioners may only be removed by the President for good cause.

Any one of these issues would make *Jarkesy* an important case, but the Supreme Court will consider all three. The Court's decision will also have massive practical ramifications in the financial sector. In Fiscal Year 2022, the SEC initiated over 200 enforcement actions, heard more than 200 civil actions, and imposed over four billion dollars in civil penalties on individuals.[20] The decision will therefore dictate the rights of individuals, like Jarkesy, who find themselves in the crosshairs of SEC enforcement actions. Beyond that, many other federal agencies adjudicate enforcement actions in-house, with such actions adjudicated by ALJs who enjoy some form of tenure protection.

---

[16] Jarkesy v. Sec. & Exch. Comm'n, 34 F.4th 446 (5th Cir. 2022).

[17] *Id.* at 457.

[18] *Id.* at 462–63.

[19] *Id.* at 465.

[20] *See* SEC, Addendum to Division of Enforcement Press Release, Fiscal Year 2022, at 1–2 (Nov. 15, 2022).

The different issues that the Court is considering in this case underscore the conceptual tensions that arise from the unique features of administrative agencies, which don't fit neatly within any single branch of government and instead exercise the powers of all of them. Congress presumably provided removal protections to administrative law judges to mimic, on a smaller scale, the type of tenure protections afforded to federal judges. The issue, however, is that administrative law judges are not members of the federal judiciary, but instead officers of agencies that operate within the executive branch. That fact raises significant due process concerns: In important cases involving hundreds of thousands of dollars in penalties, an agency can serve as the judge in its own case.

C. Agency Funding

In *Consumer Financial Protection Bureau (CFPB) v. Community Financial Services Association of America,* the Supreme Court will consider the legality of the funding mechanism for the CFPB. The CFPB enforces a host of laws whose subjects range from credit cards to student loans. The Bureau garners money through a peculiar funding process. Most agencies receive their funds through the appropriations process—by which Congress directly allocates funds to the agency via statute year after year. But the CFPB draws funds directly from the Federal Reserve—without any congressional action at all. Coincidentally (or maybe not), when a Member of Congress demanded to know which CFPB official authorized an expenditure of 200 million dollars in taxpayer money to refurbish its lobby with a two-story waterfall, the Bureau's then-director responded "why does that matter to you?"[21]

The Supreme Court will review the Bureau's funding mechanism in a challenge to the CFPB's Payday Lending Rule. That Rule prohibits lenders from collecting repayment via preauthorized account access after two consecutive withdraw attempts have failed due to insufficient funds. In the Bureau's view, this practice is "unfair" and "abusive."[22] The Fifth Circuit held that the way in which the CFPB

---

[21] GOPFinancialServices, *Why Does That Matter to You?*, YouTube (Mar. 17, 2015), https://tinyurl.com/5fs79j2m.

[22] *See Cmty. Fin. Servs. Ass'n of Am. v. Consumer Fin. Prot. Bureau,* 51 F.4th 616, 624 (5th Cir. 2022).

receives its funds violated the Appropriations Clause.[23] One problem is that the CFPB receives its funds from the Federal Reserve and not Congress. To make matters worse, the Federal Reserve itself receives funds not from the normal appropriations process but through bank assessments. Just as strange, the CFPB keeps its money not with the Treasury, but in its own account in the Federal Reserve. Such funds are committed to the control of the CFPB's Director, and unspent funds in one year can be rolled over to the next.

If the Supreme Court agrees that the anomalous CFPB funding structure violates the Appropriations Clause, it must confront a thornier question: remedy. If the Court decides that the CFPB's funding structure is unconstitutional, will the Court invalidate the Payday Lending Rule? The CFPB contends that even if it loses on the constitutional question, the Court should keep the Rule in effect and only prevent the Bureau from using unconstitutionally appropriated funds to enforce the Rule in the future. The Fifth Circuit, however, reasoned that because the CFPB promulgated the Payday Lending Rule with illicit gains, an Appropriations Clause violation necessitates vacating the Payday Lending Rule entirely. The remedy the Supreme Court chooses will shape the practical significance of the case. If the Court agrees with the CFPB, Congress may well choose to fix the funding problem and keep the Payday Lending Rule humming along. But if the Court affirms the Fifth Circuit's remedial analysis, the decision could effectively invalidate numerous other rules promulgated by the CFPB, if not all of them.

II. The Second Amendment

In *United States v. Rahimi*, the Court will consider a Second Amendment challenge to a federal law that prohibits persons subject to domestic violence restraining orders from possessing firearms. At different times, the Fifth Circuit has issued rulings for both of the opposing parties in the case. It had originally ruled for the government in upholding the federal law, but after the Supreme Court's decision in *New York State Pistol and Rifle Association v. Bruen*,[24] the Fifth Circuit withdrew its earlier opinion and considered the case anew.

---

[23] *Id.* at 642.

[24] 142 S. Ct. 2111 (2022).

Bruen was enough for the Fifth Circuit to come to a different conclusion. Drawing on the historical analysis that the Supreme Court performed in *Bruen*, the Fifth Circuit concluded that the federal law violated the Second Amendment because there was no historical analogue to the federal firearm prohibition at issue.[25] In the last two decades, there have been several big Supreme Court cases involving the Second Amendment, which had been largely absent at the Court before 2008. But each of those cases, significant as they were, left open obvious questions for future courts to resolve. *Bruen* was no different, and *Rahimi* presents the Court with a significant opportunity to clarify *Bruen's* reach.[26]

III. The Taxing Power

In *Moore v. United States*, the Justices will confront a Sixteenth Amendment question, a subject that rarely makes its way to the Court's docket. The Sixteenth Amendment allows Congress to impose taxes on "income" without apportionment among the several states (apportionment is required for "direct" federal taxes that are not "income"). The word "income" has traditionally meant income realized by the taxpayer. In other words, shareholders might be taxed if the company provides distributed profits to shareholders in the form of dividends, but not if the company reinvests its profits.

In 2017, Congress enacted a one-time Mandatory Repatriation Tax (MRT). That tax was assessed to shareholders who owned over ten percent of the shares of certain American-owned foreign companies. Before 2017, shareholders in this position only paid taxes when the companies distributed earnings. The MRT, however, treated a company's retained earnings (which are not distributed to shareholders) as income and assessed taxes at rates of either eight or 15.5 percent, depending on how the company held the assets.

---

[25] United States v. Rahimi, 61 F.4th 443, 461 (5th Cir. 2023).

[26] Astute readers of *Rahimi* might find that the statute at issue, 18 U.S.C. § 922(g)(8), has a familiar ring. That's because the Gun Free School Zones Act at issue in *United States v. Lopez*, 514 U.S. 549 (1995), was codified at 18 U.S.C. § 922(q). After *Lopez*, Congress added a jurisdictional hook, and the statute now provides that it "shall be unlawful for any individual knowingly to possess a firearm that has moved in or that otherwise affects interstate or foreign commerce at a place that the individual knows, or has reasonable cause to believe, is a school zone." 18 U.S.C. § 922(q)(2)(A).

Over a decade ago, Charles and Kathleen Moore invested in a foreign start-up founded by Charles Moore's friend and former co-worker. The company, which was founded to empower rural farmers in underserved communities in India, sought to import, manufacture, and distribute farming equipment. The business was very profitable. Therefore, although the Moores never received a dividend, they were assessed over $10,000 in taxes under the MRT. The Ninth Circuit rejected the Moores' Sixteenth Amendment challenge, concluding that nothing in the Amendment prohibits the government from taxing shareholders on a pro-rata basis.[27]

Proposals to tax the unrealized income of individuals have already advanced through the House and Senate in recent years, and a Supreme Court decision blessing Congress's authority to impose such taxes might give Congress all the encouragement that it needs to do so.

IV. The First Amendment

The previous term was a big one for the First Amendment. The Court decided *Counterman v. Colorado*,[28] which clarified the interplay between true threats and the First Amendment, and *303 Creative LLC v. Elenis*,[29] which concluded that the First Amendment prohibits Colorado from compelling website designers to create websites expressing messages with which the designers disagree.

This term will feature some notable First Amendment cases of its own. The first concerns an issue near and dear to virtually every millennial's and Gen Z-er's heart: social media blocking. In a pair of cases, the Court will consider whether public officials violate the First Amendment when they block their constituents on social media. The issue is a murky one because "state action" is a prerequisite to any First Amendment claim. But many public officials have personal accounts that they use to communicate issues of public concern. A classic example of this came up a few years ago when then-President Donald Trump blocked individuals on X, the website then known as Twitter. Before the Supreme Court could hear the case, Donald Trump lost his reelection bid and the case became moot.

---

[27] Moore v. United States, 36 F.4th 930, 936 (9th Cir. 2022).

[28] 143 S. Ct. 2106 (2023).

[29] 143 S. Ct. 2298 (2023).

For better or worse, the government officials in the two social media cases to be considered by the Court next term are not as well known. *O'Connor-Ratcliff v. Garnier* involves two school board members in California and *Lindke v. Freed* involves a city manager in Michigan. With social media becoming an increasingly prevalent tool by which government officials communicate important information, the cases could be significant for the ability of individuals (and sometimes even "trolls") to participate in public discourse.

The Court will also hear a trademark case arising out of the Patent and Trademark Office's rejection of a "Trump Too Small" trademark. The Supreme Court has previously invalidated federal trademark laws prohibiting the registration of trademarks that "disparaged" persons or were "immoral or scandalous," finding that both prohibitions infringed First Amendment rights. In *Vidal v. Elster*, the Court will decide whether there are similar First Amendment problems with a federal trademark law that bars trademarks containing names identifying particular living individuals without their written consent. As in the other two cases involving laws on trademark registration and the First Amendment, the government lost in the Federal Circuit but then was successful in getting the Supreme Court to grant review. On the one hand, that may not bode well for the government, since it handily lost the two previous cases. On the other hand, the previous cases involved laws that expressly disfavored certain viewpoints, and it's not obvious that the law in this case does the same.

V. Tester Standing

In *Acheson Hotels LLC v. Laufer*, the Court will decide whether testers have standing to sue for violations of the Americans with Disability Act (ADA). The ADA requires hotels to post adequate information about room accessibility. Deborah Laufer is an ADA "tester"—someone who scours hotel websites for violations of this requirement but has no plans to stay at the hotels that she sues. There is a split of authority among the federal courts of appeals on whether someone in Laufer's position has standing to sue under the ADA, and the Supreme Court's conclusion might hinge on how it defines the injury. If the injury is access to information for its own sake, then we should expect the Court to affirm Laufer's standing to sue. But if the Court concludes that Congress imposed the informational requirements at issue only as a means for future hotel residents to ensure that they can book an accessible room, then the smart money is on a ruling in favor of the hotel.

There's another twist. In late July, Laufer voluntarily dismissed her lawsuit in district court and asked the Supreme Court to take it off its docket. Acheson Hotels also contends that the case is moot, but only because it has now provided all the information that is required under the ADA. Acheson Hotels has accused Laufer of strategic maneuvering and asked the Supreme Court to proceed with arguments. The Supreme Court announced that it will do just that, but it called on the parties to be prepared to answer questions on mootness.

VI. Discrimination

The Supreme Court's current docket doesn't yet carry any case quite like *Students for Fair Admissions v. Harvard*,[30] but it does nonetheless feature two cases involving allegations of discrimination. The Court will hear yet another redistricting case in *Alexander v. South Carolina State Conference of the NAACP*. The three-judge panel agreed with the challengers that South Carolina's congressional map had been racially gerrymandered. The defendants—a group of government officials and election commissioners—reply that the district lines were prompted not by racial considerations, but political ones.

In *Muldrow v. City of St. Louis*, the Court will consider a question that it reframed: Does Title VII prohibit discrimination in transfer decisions absent a separate court determination that the transfer decision caused a significant disadvantage? Intuitively, the answer might be yes, but the Eighth Circuit ruled against Sergeant Jatonya Muldrow, who alleges that she was transferred because the St. Louis Police Department wanted to hire a man for her role. The Eighth Circuit reasoned that Title VII prohibits "adverse employment decisions," and absent a showing of material change in the terms of her employment, Muldrow could not make out a successful Title VII claim. If the Court affirms that rationale, it might leave unchecked transfer decision prompted by considerations of race and sex. That might give government employers who are fixated on racial or gender proportionality another tool to reach their desired outcome even after the *Students for Fair Admissions* cases.

---

[30] 143 S. Ct. 2141 (2023).

VII. Forfeiture

In *Culley v. Marshall,* the Supreme Court is presented with the question of whether civil asset forfeiture without a prompt post-deprivation hearing violates due process. The question is an important one as civil forfeiture—a process by which government takes an individual's property even though the individual has not been convicted of a crime—has expanded over the previous years. Lengthy delays can be particularly problematic for individuals going through the civil-forfeiture gantlet. Such individuals have had property or cash embargoed under government control for months or even years. The importance of this issue is underscored by the ideologically diverse group of organizations that have filed friend-of-the-court briefs in this case. The groups include the Pacific Legal Foundation (my former employer), the Institute for Justice, the American Civil Liberties Union, the Legal Aid Society, the Constitutional Accountability Center, the National Federation of Independent Business Small Business Center, and others.

VIII. On the Horizon

At this time last year, the petitions in several major cases of the Term, from student loan forgiveness to home equity theft, had not yet been granted by the Court. Following that pattern, we should expect the Court to take a few more blockbusters in the next few months. Here are some likely contenders:

A. Property Rights

In *Sheetz v. County of El Dorado,* the Court will have the opportunity to clarify the law on unconstitutional exactions. The Supreme Court previously held in a pair of cases—*Nollan v. California Coastal Commission*[31] and *Dolan v. City of Tigard*[32]—that the government can't indirectly work takings by forcing property owners to surrender their property in exchange for permits. Permit conditions must bear a substantial nexus and be roughly proportional to the permit itself. Those cases involved exactions by agency officers, and a handful of subsequent cases have drawn a distinction between that type of

[31] 483 U.S. 825 (1987).
[32] 512 U.S. 374 (1994).

"adjudicative exaction" and "legislative exactions." The Court will decide whether the latter are exempt from the unconstitutional conditions analysis merely because the exactions were authorized by legislation.

In *Devillier v. Texas*, a group of property owners allege that Texas worked a taking by flooding their land. But the issue presented to the Supreme Court isn't whether Texas violated the Takings Clause; it's whether the state would have to pay just compensation even assuming that the flooding *did* work a taking. That's an open question because there is unresolved tension between two constitutional principles: sovereign immunity, which provides that states are typically immune from claims for money damages, and the Fifth Amendment, which requires states to provide just compensation when they take private property.

In *Community Housing Improvement Program v. City of New York*, a group of plaintiffs contend that New York's rent-control law constitutes a per se taking under the Fifth Amendment. The law at issue covers roughly a million apartment units in New York City and prohibits landlords from taking back possession of their units after the renter's lease expires. The plaintiffs rely heavily on the Court's recent decision in *Cedar Point Nursery v. Hassid*,[33] which held that a California regulation requiring agricultural growers to allow union organizers onto the growers' farms was a per se taking because it destroyed the growers' right to exclude. The plaintiffs in the New York case contend that New York's law similarly deprives them of their right to exclude and should therefore also be treated as a per se taking.

B. Search and Seizure

Verdun v. City of San Diego involves one way that the government enforces those dreaded time limits on parking where no parking meter is in sight. Since the 1970s, San Diego has resorted to "tire chalking" to catch miscreants who don't bother to move their cars. Tire chalking is the low-tech strategy of marking the tires of every car in a time-limited parking area with chalk. The enforcer returns after whatever time limit is in effect (say, two hours later) and places tickets on any remaining chalked cars. The Sixth Circuit previously

[33] 141 S. Ct. 2063 (2021).

held that tire chalking is a search under the Fourth Amendment and does not fall within the "administrative search" exception, for which no warrant is required. The Ninth Circuit in *Verdun* thought the Sixth Circuit got it upside down. The administrative search exception to the warrant requirement has been used to justify warrantless searches of junkyards, massage parlors, and daycare centers. The Ninth Circuit held that tire chalking falls comfortably within that exception, putting it on firm constitutional footing. It remains to be seen whether the Supreme Court will agree.

C. Free Speech

Mazo v. Way involves a First Amendment challenge to an election law that prohibits candidates from using certain slogans. New Jersey allows candidates in primary elections to place slogans of up to six words next to their names on the ballot. Yet candidates cannot reference any individual or corporation in their slogans absent written consent from that individual or corporation. One of the challengers wanted to use the slogan "Bernie Sanders Betrayed the NJ Revolution," but she couldn't do so because she failed to obtain written approval from Bernie Sanders himself.

In *Tingley v. Ferguson*, a licensed marriage and family counselor is asking the Court to review a Washington State law that prohibits conversion therapy for minors. The counselor contends that the Washington law poses both free speech and free exercise problems. If the Court were to take this case, its decision would be significant nationwide. Twenty states and over 100 municipalities have similar laws.

The Supreme Court has called for the views of the Solicitor General in *NetChoice, LLC v. Paxton* and *NetChoice, LLC v. Moody* and might take up those cases this term.[34] The cases involve First Amendment challenges to state laws that regulate social media companies. The Texas law at issue in *Netchoice, LLC v. Paxton* bars large social media platforms from blocking, removing, or demonetizing content based on the social media users' views. The Florida law at issue in *Netchoice,*

---

[34] In mid-August, the Solicitor General filed a brief asking the Court to take both cases, but she indicated the United States' view that not all of the issues presented warrant review. Brief for the United States as Amicus Curiae, Moody v. NetChoice, LLC; NetChoice, LLC v. Moody; NetChoice, LLC v. Paxton, Nos. 22-277, 22-393 and 22-555 (U.S. Sup. Ct. filed Aug. 14, 2023).

LLC v. Moody prohibits social media companies from deplatforming candidates, hiding posts by or about a candidate, or deplatforming "journalistic enterprises."

D. Jurisdiction

In *Federal Bureau of Investigation v. Fikre*, the government is (to no one's surprise) attempting to kick another case out on jurisdictional grounds. Yonas Fikre challenges his placement on the FBI's No Fly List. The government contends that Fikre's challenge is moot because the FBI took Fikre off the list and provided a declaration that Fikre will not be placed on the list in the future based on currently available information. The case may present the Court with an opportunity to clarify the scope of the voluntary cessation doctrine—a mootness exception that guards against government gamesmanship to get rid of a case on mootness grounds only to revert to its old ways once the coast is clear.

E. Equality Under the Law

Coalition for TJ v. Fairfax County School Board involves changes to the admissions policy at one of the most prestigious high schools in the country: The Thomas Jefferson High School for Science and Technology (known to some as "TJ"). Before 2020, TJ admitted students on the basis of a series of standardized tests given to all applicants. But in 2020, board members voiced concerns about the racial composition of TJ, and altered the admissions criteria in hopes of changing the school's racial demographics. The new policy requires TJ to admit a certain percentage of students from each middle school, and led to a dramatic decrease in Asian American students, who the Board presumably considered "overrepresented" at TJ in previous years. The case tees up an important question on the heels of the *Students for Fair Admissions* decision: What does the Equal Protection Clause say about efforts to racially balance schools through facially neutral proxies for race?

Conclusion

Last term will be a tough act to follow. But with several big cases already on the calendar and perhaps many more waiting in the wings, the upcoming term might just be even bigger. It might just be another blockbuster.

Contributors

Akhil Reed Amar is Sterling Professor of Law and Political Science at Yale University, where he teaches constitutional law in both Yale College and Yale Law School. After graduating from Yale College and Yale Law School, Amar clerked for Judge (later Justice) Stephen Breyer. Amar joined the Yale faculty in 1985 at the age of 26. He is Yale's only living professor to have won the University's unofficial triple crown—the Sterling Chair for scholarship, the DeVane Medal for teaching, and the Lamar Award for alumni service. Amar's work has won awards from both the American Bar Association and the Federalist Society, and he has been cited by Supreme Court justices across the spectrum in more than four dozen cases—tops among non-emeritus scholars. He regularly testifies before Congress at the invitation of both parties; and in surveys of judicial citations and/or scholarly citations, he typically ranks among America's five most-cited mid-career legal scholars. He is a member of the American Academy of Arts and Sciences and has written widely for popular publications, including *The New York Times*, *The Washington Post*, *The Wall Street Journal*, *Time*, and *The Atlantic*. He was an informal consultant to the popular TV show The West Wing and his scholarship has been showcased on many broadcasts, including *The Colbert Report*, *Tucker Carlson Tonight*, *Morning Joe*, *AC360*, *11th Hour with Brian Williams*, *Fox News @ Night with Shannon Bream*, *Fareed Zakaria GPS*, *Erin Burnett Outfront*, and *Constitution USA with Peter Sagal*. He is the author of more than a hundred law review articles and several books, most notably *The Bill of Rights* (1998—winner of the Yale University Press Governors' Award), *America's Constitution* (2005—winner of the ABA's Silver Gavel Award), *America's Unwritten Constitution* (2012—named one of the year's 100 best nonfiction books by *The Washington Post*), and *The Constitution Today* (2016—named one of the year's top ten nonfiction books by *Time magazine*). His latest and most ambitious book, *The Words That Made Us: America's Constitutional Conversation, 1760-1840*, came out in May 2021. He has recently launched a weekly podcast, *Amarica's Constitution*.

Vikram Amar is a distinguished professor of law at UC Davis School of Law. Prior to that, he was dean at the University of Illinois College of Law. He has produced several books and over 60 articles in leading law reviews. He has authored and co-authored a number of books on constitutional law, including *Constitutional Law: Cases and Materials* (Foundation Press, 15th ed. 2017), *Treatise on Constitutional Law* (West Publishing Co., 6th ed. 2021), *Federal Practice and Procedure Treatise* (West Publishing Co. 2006), and *American Civil Procedure* (Kluwer, 2008). He writes a biweekly column on constitutional matters for Justia.com and a monthly column on legal education for abovethelaw. com, is a frequent commentator on local and national radio and TV, and has penned dozens of op-ed pieces for major newspapers and magazines. Amar is an elected member of the American Law Institute and has served as a consultant for, among others, the National Association of Attorneys General, the United States Department of Justice, the California Attorney General's Office, the ACLU of Southern California, and the Center for Civic Education. For one year he chaired the Civil Procedure Section of the Association of American Law Schools. Amar earned his bachelor's degree from UC Berkeley and his juris doctor from Yale Law School, where he was an articles editor for the *Yale Law Journal*. He then clerked for Judge William A. Norris of the United States Court of Appeals for the Ninth Circuit and for Justice Harry A. Blackmun of the United States Supreme Court before joining Gibson, Dunn & Crutcher, where he handled a variety of complex civil and white-collar criminal matters. It appears that dean Amar was the first person of South Asian heritage to clerk at the U.S. Supreme Court, and was the first American-born person of Indian descent to serve as a dean of a major American law school.

Eric Franklin Amarante is an associate professor of law at the University of Tennessee College of Law. Amarante joined the UT College of Law in 2017 after teaching at the University of Nevada Las Vegas William S. Boyd School of Law for four years. At UNLV, Amarante taught contracts and small business law, and directed the Small Business and Nonprofit Legal Clinic. Prior to his stint at UNLV, Amarante was the inaugural Whiting Fellow at the University of Denver Sturm College of Law. Amarante received his J.D. from Cornell Law School and his B.A. from the University of Texas. After law school, he joined Sullivan & Cromwell's corporate group in Palo Alto, where his practice primarily focused on mergers and acquisitions, corporate finance, and securities offerings. After several years at Sullivan, he moved to Seattle to join the business transaction group of Davis Wright Tremaine. There he worked on a wide range of projects, from documenting multi-billion dollar joint ventures to counseling entrepreneurs on legal issues facing early-stage companies.

David E. Bernstein is a professor of law and executive director of the Liberty & Law Center at George Mason University Antonin Scalia Law School. A prolific author, Professor Bernstein often challenges the conventional wisdom with prodigious research and sharp, original analysis. He is the author of five books, and coauthor of two more. Professor Bernstein's book *Rehabilitating Lochner* was praised across the political spectrum as "intellectual history in its highest form," a "fresh perspective and a cogent analysis," "delightful and informative," "sharp and iconoclastic," and "a terrific work of historical revisionism." Columnist George Will praised Bernstein's most recent book, *Classified, The Untold Story of Racial Classification in America*, as "perhaps the most consequential American book of 2022." Professor Bernstein has also written dozens of articles and essays published in major law reviews, including *the California Law Review, the Columbia Law Review, the Michigan Law Review*, and *the Yale Law Journal*. An article he coauthored, *Defending Daubert: It's Time to Amend Federal Rule of Evidence 702*, directly inspired a pending amendment to Rule 702. Professor Bernstein blogs at *the Instapundit.com, the Times of Israel*, and *the Volokh Conspiracy*. He is a graduate of *the Yale Law School*, where he was senior editor of *the Yale Law Journal* and a John M. Olin Fellow in Law, Economics, and Public Policy.

Thomas A. Berry is a research fellow in the Cato Institute's Robert A. Levy Center for Constitutional Studies and editor-in-chief of the *Cato Supreme Court Review*. Before joining Cato, he was an attorney at Pacific Legal Foundation and clerked for Judge E. Grady Jolly of the U.S. Court of Appeals for the Fifth Circuit. Berry's areas of interests include the separation of powers, executive branch appointments, and First Amendment freedom of speech. Berry's academic work has appeared in *the NYU Journal of Law and Liberty, the Washington and Lee Law Review Online*, and *the Federalist Society Review*, with shorter pieces in *the Yale Journal on Regulation's Notice & Comment blog, Lawfare*, and *Law & Liberty*. His popular writing has appeared in many outlets including *The Wall Street Journal*, *USA Today*, *CNN.com*, the *National Law Journal*, *the National Review Online*, *Reason.com*, and *The Hill*. Berry has testified before a subcommittee of the U.S. Senate on the Appointments Clause, and his work on the Vacancies Act has been cited by the U.S. District Court for the District of Columbia. Berry holds a JD from Stanford Law School, where he was a senior editor on *the Stanford Law and Policy Review* and a Bradley Student Fellow in the Stanford Constitutional Law Center.

Anastasia P. Boden is the director of the Robert A. Levy Center for Constitutional Studies. Before joining the Cato Institute, Boden was a civil rights attorney at the Pacific Legal Foundation, where she led the organization's equality and opportunity program. She also co-created the podcast *Dissed*, which tells the stories behind infamous Supreme Court dissents. In her decade before joining Cato, Boden represented entrepreneurs in challenges to onerous occupational licensing laws, anti-competitive titling restrictions, and Certificate of Need (CON) programs. She developed nearly a dozen cases challenging CON laws across the country, leading to legislative reform in Montana, Pennsylvania, and West Virginia. Among her other wins are a case invalidating busking restrictions in Houston, several appellate decisions opening up the courthouse doors to civil rights plaintiffs, and legislative repeal of Virginia's happy hour advertising restrictions. Her writings on law and liberty have been featured in *the Washington Post*, *the Wall Street Journal*, *the Los Angeles Times*, *the Chicago Tribune*, *Forbes*, and more, and she has appeared on *Headline News*, *Reason TV*, *Newsmax*, and *John Stossel*. Boden earned her BA with dean's honors from the University of California, Santa Barbara, and her JD from Georgetown University Law Center, where she was research assistant to professor Randy E. Barnett—the intellectual "godfather" of the constitutional challenge to Obamacare.

Clay Calvert is professor emeritus at the University of Florida where until 2023 he held a joint appointment as professor of law at the Fredric G. Levin College of Law and as Brechner Eminent Scholar in Mass Communication in the College of Journalism and Communications. In 2021, Calvert won the University of Florida's Teacher/Scholar of the Year Award. In 2022, Calvert won the SEC Faculty

Achievement Award for the University of Florida. Calvert has authored or co-authored more than 150 law journal articles on freedom of expression-related topics. He is lead author of the undergraduate media law textbook, *Mass Media Law*, 22nd Edition (McGraw Hill 2023), and is the author of *Voyeur Nation: Media, Privacy, and Peering in Modern Culture* (Westview Press 2000). Calvert received his J.D. with Order of the Coif status from the University of the Pacific's McGeorge School of Law. He later earned a Ph.D. in Communication from Stanford University, where he also completed his undergraduate work in Communication, earning a B.A. with Distinction. Calvert is a member of both the State Bar of California and the Bar of the Supreme Court of the United States.

Brannon P. Denning is a Starnes Professor of Law at Samford University's Cumberland School of Law. Denning writes in the area of constitutional law; specifically he has written on the Commerce Clause and the dormant commerce clause; judicial and executive branch appointments; the constitutional amendment process; foreign affairs and the Constitution; and the Second Amendment. He has authored and co-authored a number of books on constitutional law, including *Bittker on the Regulation of Interstate Commerce and Foreign Commerce* (2022), *Guns and the Law: Cases, Materials, and Explanation* (2016), *American Constitutional Law: Powers and Liberties* (2023), *The Glannon Guide to Constitutional Law* (2014), *The Glannon Guide to Constitutional Law: Powers and Liberties* (2019), and *Developing Professional Skills: Constitutional Law* (2014). In 2023, the University Press of Kansas will publish *The Advantage of Being Armed: The Second Amendment in American Culture, Politics, and Law* which he co-authored with George Washington University law professor and legal historian Robert J. Cottrol. Denning's other writings have been published in *Foreign Affairs, Constitutional Commentary, the Northwestern University Law Review, the William and Mary Law Review, the Minnesota Law Review, the American Journal of International Law, the Wisconsin Law Review, the Tulane Law Review,* and *Law and Contemporary Problems* among other journals and periodicals. He was the recipient of the 2008 Harvey S. Jackson Excellence in Teaching Award for upper-level classes and of the Lightfoot, Franklin & White award for Faculty Scholarship, which he won in 2012, 2016, 2019, and 2021. In 2021, he was named in a *University of Chicago Law Review* article as one of the 20 most-cited young legal scholars in the country.

Gregory Dolin is an associate professor of Law at the University of Baltimore School of Law. Professor Dolin's scholarship centers on patent law with a specific focus on how the patent regime affects innovation, especially in bio-pharmaceutical areas. His work in these areas includes a number of scholarly articles, presentations, amicus briefs, and congressional testimony. Dolin is also an associate director of the Center for the Law of Intellectual Property and Technology. From January 2020 to January 2022, Professor Dolin served as a resident Associate Justice of the Supreme Court of the Republic of Palau. He was appointed to that Court by the President of the Republic and sworn into office on January 7, 2020. In this role, Justice Dolin (together with other members of the Court) heard appeals in civil, criminal, administrative, and constitutional law matters. Dolin sits on the board of directors and serves as an appellate counsel for the Jewish Coalition for Religious Liberty, an organization dedicated to preserving the ability of individuals to freely practice their religion without undue government interference. In this capacity, he has authored and co-authored numerous briefs before the U.S. Supreme Court and various Courts of Appeals. He is also a member of the Federalist Society's Administrative Law & Regulation Practice Group Executive Committee, a Scholar at the Antonin Scalia Law School Center for Intellectual Property × Innovation Policy, and an adjunct scholar at the Cato Institute's Robert A. Levy Center for Constitutional Studies. He has previously served as a member of the Maryland State Advisory Committee to the U.S. Commission on Civil Rights. From 2017 to 2020, following appointment by Governor Larry Hogan, Dolin served on the Clifton T. Perkins Center Advisory Board. Prior to joining the University of Baltimore School of Law, Professor Dolin held visiting appointments in other law schools. He also served as a law clerk to the Hon. Pauline Newman, of the U.S. Court of Appeals for the Federal Circuit and the late Hon. H. Emory Widener Jr., of the U.S. Court of Appeals for the Fourth Circuit. He continues to render service to the Fourth Circuit by representing indigent appellants.

Wen Fa is the Director of Legal Affairs at the Beacon Center of Tennessee. Wen leads Beacon's legal department in its efforts to protect the constitutional rights of property owners, entrepreneurs, and other Americans in courts across the United States. Having immigrated to

America from Beijing, Wen believes that property rights, economic liberty, and equality under the law are essential to a free society and strives to advance those principles through his work. Before joining Beacon, Wen was a senior attorney with Pacific Legal Foundation, where he litigated numerous cases involving equality under the law, free speech, economic liberty, and property rights. Wen litigated two Supreme Court cases: *Minnesota Voters Alliance v. Mansky,* which vindicated the free speech rights of voters, and *Cedar Point Nursery v. Hassid,* which secured the property rights of agricultural businesses. Wen has also secured important victories for farmers standing up against a racially discriminatory federal farm loan forgiveness program and small business owners who fought back against racial preferences in small business grants. In addition to litigation, Wen promotes liberty through speeches, debates, and op-eds. Wen testified before Congress in 2021 and has published numerous op-eds in newspapers such as the *Wall Street Journal, The Hill,* and *San Francisco Chronicle.* He has spoken about his work in podcasts, on television, and in speeches to students at Georgetown, Duke, and law schools around the country.

Wen graduated with a bachelor's degree in finance from the University of Texas-Dallas, a master's degree in political theory from the London School of Economics, where he studied under libertarian scholar Chandran Kukathas, and a law degree from the University of Michigan.

Christopher Green is the Jamie L. Whitten Chair in Law and Government at the University of Mississippi School of Law, where he has taught since 2006. He has a JD from Yale, a PhD in philosophy from Notre Dame, and has been cited by Justice Stevens in *McDonald v. Chicago,* by Justice Thomas in *United States v. Vaello-Madero,* and by Justice Gorsuch in *Haaland v. Brackeen.* Green is the author of *Equal Citizenship, Civil Rights, and the Constitution: The Original Sense of the Privileges or Immunities Clause* (Routledge 2015), and the co-author with Scott Gaylord and Lee Strang of the six-volume *Federal Constitutional Law* textbook series, serving as the chief author of the volumes on the Fourteenth Amendment and on executive power. Green's publications cover all aspects of Fourteenth Amendment history, including the legitimacy of Reconstruction, the Privileges or Immunities Clause as a requirement of equal civil rights, the Equal

Protection Clause as an entitlement to protection from violence, and the Due Process Clause as a guarantee for the rule of law. His articles on constitutional theory have given particular attention to distinctions from philosophy such as the sense-reference distinction, stakes-sensitive epistemology, the semantic conception of truth, indexicals, and the ethics of oath-taking. He has been a visiting professor at the University of San Diego and the James Madison Program at Princeton University and is an Affiliated Scholar at the Center for the Study of Constitutional Originalism. Green practiced appellate litigation at Phelps Dunbar in Jackson, Mississippi, after clerking for Judge Rhesa H. Barskdale of the U.S. Court of Appeals for the Fifth Circuit.

Margaret A. Little is senior litigation counsel at the New Civil Liberties Alliance. She has experience as a trial and appellate litigator in complex, high-stakes regulatory, mass-tort, class-action, products liability, securities, commercial and civil rights litigation representing individuals and high-profile litigants including Fortune 50 companies, financial institutions, public companies, and universities in state and federal courts, including the United States Supreme Court. Little is a graduate of Yale College and Yale Law School, where she was awarded the Potter Stewart Prize. She was a law clerk to the Hon. Ralph K. Winter on the U.S. Court of Appeals for the Second Circuit. Prior to starting her own trial and appellate law firm in 1997, where she was appellate consulting counsel to the New Haven firefighters in *Ricci v. DeStefano*, a landmark 2009 United States Supreme Court decision, Little was a partner at Tyler, Cooper & Alcorn in New Haven, Connecticut. From 2004 to early 2018, she directed, part-time, the Federalist Society Pro Bono Center. Little has participated in many national conferences and symposia addressing issues of current importance in constitutional law—specifically state and federal constitutional questions regarding the separation of powers and the first amendment—and regularly speaks, blogs and publishes on the topic of the unconstitutional exercise of governmental power. In May of 2017, she presented her paper, *Pirates at the Parchment Gates*, to a conference of state and federal judges at the Law and Economics Center at the Antonin Scalia Law School. Her work has been published by law reviews, legal publications, *the Federalist Society, the Wall Street Journal, Law and Liberty* and *the Manhattan Institute.*

Timothy Sandefur is the Vice President for Legal Affairs at the Goldwater Institute's Scharf-Norton Center for Constitutional Litigation and holds the Duncan Chair in Constitutional Government. He litigates to promote economic liberty, private property rights, free speech, and other crucial values in states across the country. Sandefur is the author of eight books—*Freedom's Furies* (2022), *Some Notes on the Silence* (2022), *The Ascent of Jacob Bronowski* (2019), *Frederick Douglass: Self-Made Man* (2018), *Cornerstone of Liberty: Property Rights in 21st Century America* (2nd ed., coauthored with Christina Sandefur, 2016), *The Permission Society* (2016), *The Conscience of the Constitution* (2014), and *The Right to Earn a Living: Economic Freedom and the Law* (2010)—as well as scores of scholarly articles on subjects ranging from Indian law and antitrust to copyright law, the constitutional issues involved in the Civil War, and the political philosophy of Shakespeare, ancient Greek drama, and *Star Trek*. A frequent guest on radio and television, he is well known to radio audiences as "Tim the Lawyer" on *The Armstrong & Getty Show*, and his writings have appeared in *Reason*, *The National Review*, *The Weekly Standard*, *The Wall Street Journal*, and *The Objective Standard*, where he is a contributing editor. He has taught classes at Pepperdine University, McGeorge School of Law, George Mason University's Antonin Scalia Law School.

Damien Schiff is a senior attorney at Pacific Legal Foundation. He leads its environmental practice group, a unique initiative that draws broadly from PLF's expertise and success in property rights and separation of powers litigation. Over the years, Damien has represented hundreds of landowners and property rights advocates to defend their liberties against heavy-handed and unwarranted environmental and land-use regulation. His litigation experience includes *Sackett v. U.S. Environmental Protection Agency*, a groundbreaking decision in which the U.S. Supreme Court upheld the right of landowners to challenge Clean Water Act compliance orders issued by EPA, and *Contoski v. Norton*, PLF's successful effort to force the federal government to make good on its promise to delist the bald eagle from the Endangered Species Act. Besides litigation, Damien has written academic articles on a variety of subjects, including the Endangered Species Act, the Clean Water Act, greenhouse gas torts, the duty to rescue, and international water law. He has appeared on a variety of television and radio programs and has been quoted in

The New York Times, The Wall Street Journal, Harper's Magazine, and *The Economist,* among other publications. He obtained his law degree magna cum laude from the University of San Diego School of Law, and his undergraduate degree magna cum laude from Georgetown University. While at USD, he was a research assistant for Professor Bernard Siegan, a leading constitutional theorist and advocate for property rights and economic liberty. Immediately prior to joining PLF, Damien clerked for Judge (and former PLF attorney) Victor Wolski of the United States Court of Federal Claims.

Jed Handelsman Shugerman is a professor of law at Boston University School of Law. He received his B.A., J.D., and Ph.D. from Yale. His book, *The People's Courts* (Harvard 2012), traces the rise of judicial elections, judicial review, and the influence of money and parties in American courts. It is based on his dissertation that won the 2009 ASLH's Cromwell Prize. He is co-author of amicus briefs on the history of presidential power, the Emoluments Clauses, the Appointments Clause, the First Amendment rights of elected judges, and the due process problems of elected judges in death penalty cases. He is currently working on two books on the history of executive power and prosecution in America. The first is tentatively titled *A Faithful President: The Founders v. the Unitary Executive,* questioning the textual and historical evidence for the theory of unchecked and unbalanced presidential power. This book draws on his articles "Vesting" (*Stanford Law Review* forthcoming Spring 2022), "Removal of Context" (*Yale Journal of Law & the Humanities* 2022), a co-authored "Faithful Execution and Article II" (*Harvard Law Review* 2019 with Fordham colleagues Andrew Kent and Ethan Leib), "The Indecisions of 1789" (forthcoming *Penn. Law Review* Fall 2022), and "The Creation of the Department of Justice," (*Stanford Law Review* 2014). The second book project is *The Rise of the Prosecutor Politicians: Race, War, and Mass Incarceration,* focusing on California Governor Earl Warren, his presidential running mate Thomas Dewey, the Kennedys, World War II and the Cold War, the war on crime, the growth of prosecutorial power, and its emergence as a stepping stone to electoral power for ambitious politicians in the mid-twentieth century. He writes about law, history, politics, and sometimes sports on Shugerblog.com.